THE MERGING OF KNOWLEDGE

People in Poverty and Academics Thinking Together

Fourth World—University Research Group

FOURTH WORLD PUBLICATIONS

Alliance
of independent publishers
for another globalization

University Press of America,® Inc.
Lanham · Boulder · New York · Toronto · Plymouth, UK

Copyright © 2007 by
University Press of America,® Inc.
4501 Forbes Boulevard
Suite 200
Lanham, Maryland 20706
UPA Acquisitions Department (301) 459-3366

Estover Road
Plymouth PL6 7PY
United Kingdom

Library of Congress Control Number: 2007930454
ISBN-13: 978-0-7618-3751-0 (paperback : alk. paper)
ISBN-10: 0-7618-3751-5 (paperback : alk. paper)

CONTENTS

LIST OF CONTRIBUTORS

Agents-Authors

Denise Bernia, Fourth World activist, La Louvière (Belgium)

Marie-Hélène Boureau, Fourth World volunteer corps member, Marseille (France)

Léon Cassiers, Emeritus Professor of Medicine, UCL (Belgium)

Didier Clerbois, Fourth World activist, Brussels (Belgium)

Marc Couillard, Fourth World activist, Brussels (Belgium)

Françoise Digneffe, Professor of Criminology, UCL (Belgium)

Jacques Fierens, Professor of Law, Namur (Belgium)

Pierre Fontaine, Emeritus Professor of Psychology, UCL (Belgium)

Hector Guichart, Fourth World activist, Brussels (Belgium)

Carl Havelange, Researcher in History, Liege (Belgium)

Marie Jahrling, Fourth World activist, Noisy-le-Grand (France)

Daniel Lebreton, Fourth World activist, Rennes (France)

Danielle Lebrun, Fourth World activist, Dinan (France)

Martine Le Corre, Fourth World activist, Caen (France)

Jean Marie Lefevre, Fourth World activist, Cherbourg (France)

Odette Leroy, Fourth World activist, Caen (France)

Pierre Maclouf, Professor of Sociology, Paris I (France)

Joëlle Meurant, Fourth World activist, La Louvière (Belgium)

Luigi Mosca, Researcher in Physics, Saclay Research Center (France)

Georges Mus, Fourth World activist, Charleroi (Belgium)

Ides Nicaise, Researcher in Economics, Leuven (Belgium)

Marie-Jeanne Notermans, Fourth World volunteer corps member, Heerlen (Netherlands)

Patrice Nouvel, Fourth World volunteer corps member, Lyon (France)

Jacques Ogier, Fourth World volunteer corps member, Paris (France)

Gaston Pineau, Professor of Education, Tours (France)

Christian Scribot, Fourth World activist, Lille (France)

Paul Taylor, Professor of Education, Tours (France)

Françoise Vedrenne, Fourth World volunteer corps member, Lille (France)

Jean Maurice Verdier, Professor of Law, Paris X (France)

Pierre Yves Verkindt, Professor of Law, Lille II (France)

Paulette Vienne, Fourth World activist, Lille (France)

and from March 1996–April 1997: Noëlle Stenegry, Fourth World activist, Rennes (France)

Pedagogical team
Claude Ferrand, Fourth World volunteer corps member (project coordinator)
Daniel Cornerotte, graduate in Labor Science, Faculty of Economic and Social Policy, Catholic University of Louvain la Neuve (educational advisor)
Françoise Ferrand, Fourth World volunteer corps member (pedagogical counselor)
Pascal Galvani, Doctor in Education, European Professional University, Tours (educational advisor)
Patrick Brun, Doctor of Education, AFDI-IFRADE, Angers (evaluator)

Academic Panel
Matéo Alaluf, President of the Institute of Labor, Free University of Brussels
Jean Germain, President of the European University, Tours
Xavier Godinot, Director of the ATD Fourth World Research and Training Institute
Louis Join-Lambert, Director of the *Revue Quart Monde*
Georges Liénard, Director of the Faculty of Economic and Social Policy, Catholic University of Louvain-la-Neuve
René Rémond, President of the French National Foundation of Political Science and Member of the Académie Française
Michel Serres, philosopher and Member of the Académie Française

Foreword

This work is the result of a research experiment carried out jointly over a two-year period by university professors and researchers in different disciplines (law, economics, history, psychology, physics, education, sociology and others) and members of ATD Fourth World (people living in extreme poverty and members of the Fourth World volunteer corps).

The introduction presents the context, issues and objectives of the project, the participants and the methodology which they had to devise with the aid of a pedagogical team to successfully meet the challenge they had been set: to share and combine different forms of knowledge and learning and in order to think together.

The bulk of this book is composed of five memoirs written by the participants in the Fourth World–University project. They depict the ways in which the participants together arrived at a new kind of knowledge and wrote it up in a joint report. Each memoir must therefore be read as a piece of research and a team effort.

The final part of the book details the views of the Academic Panel, which oversaw and approved the project, and a short evaluation giving the participants' feedback on the project.

Our societies need radically new approaches such as that taken by the participants in this project to eradicate extreme poverty. The participants hope that others will be encouraged to follow in their wake as a result.

Preface

Over ten years have passed since the first research–action–training project was organized by ATD Fourth World, following a long period of reflection on the concept.

For this project, the merging of knowledge ceased to be an intellectual process, instead reinventing itself as an experimental project.

The endorsement of this work by an Academic Panel, and the various evaluations carried out over the last decade demonstrate today just how original and fertile this project was.

Let us begin with its originality. At a first glance, bringing together academics from a wide range of disciplines and people from extremely poor backgrounds in order to work together may seem an insurmountable challenge. Whether due to lack of availability or possessing different means of expression, the obstacles faced could only be overcome with the help of an innovative organization, capable of combining the reference to common ethical principles and the use of structuring educational methods.

The story of the two years during which the initial challenge was overcome merits the publication of this book alone, with its depiction of the procedure and outcome of the project.

Yet the years following the initial French-language publication of the book have also borne witness to the project's fruitfulness, as it extends its scope to further fields.

One example of this was a second project entitled "Fourth World Partner", which came to fruition between May 2000 and December 2001, following in the wake of the "Fourth World–University project". "Fourth World Partner" brought together activists fighting against poverty, professionals, practitioners and educators, such as social workers, magistrates, doctors, teachers, police officers etc.

The objective of this process of "mutual learning" was to encourage interaction between the life knowledge of people living in extreme poverty and difficult conditions, and the action knowledge of professionals working in various sectors of society.

The success of this second project, whose methodology and contents were monitored by a Franco–Belgian Advisory Council, has justified the work carried out since then by the research–action–training group involved in this new line of action.

People from extremely diverse backgrounds are now turning their attention towards it.

For example, the lessons given at the higher education institute, Collège de France, in 2005–2006, devoted to reorganizing powers at a time of internationalization of law, specifically referred to the notion of merging of knowledge ventured during the two ATD Fourth World projects.

Therefore, the core message is gradually getting through to all levels. Merging academic, life and action knowledge makes it possible to link this combined knowledge with the powers that be and the means to guarantee a lively democracy.

Respecting the equal dignity of all citizens requires the experience of those who have been considered to have "no voice" for far too long to be taken into account. This must be the first precondition for "participative democracy".

May reading this book convince all readers!

> Paul Bouchet
> Honorary State Advisor
> Former President of the French National Advisory
> Commission on Human Rights
> Paris, July 2006

ACKNOWLEDGMENTS

We would like to thank the following for their financial support:

Belgium
• The Communauté Française
Ministry of Culture and Vocational Training
Ministry of Education, Research and Training (academic research department)
• The Commission Communautaire Française
Department of Socio-cultural Affairs and Vocational Training
• The Walloon government
Ministry of Social Affairs, Housing and Health
• The National Lottery
• Texas Instruments

France
• European Social Fund
• Ministry of Employment and Social Affairs
• Ministry of Culture
• Ministry of Education
• Caisse d'Épargne Foundation
• Flanders Caisse d'Épargne
• Social Action Fund
• Northern France Regional Authority
• The city councils of Caen, Lille and Rennes
• Microsoft

Notice
A single asterisk (*) indicates that the term is explained in the glossary at the back of the book.
A double asterisk (**) indicates discussions within individual research groups.

GENERAL INTRODUCTION

The five memoirs in this book are the result of a joint training, action and re-search project carried out by the Fourth World in collaboration with the Academic World. By way of introduction we should consider the background to this experiment and examine how it came about, as well as the resources used.

THE GENESIS OF THE FOURTH WORLD–UNIVERSITY PROJECT AND THE ISSUES INVOLVED
by Claude Ferrand

History

The idea for this project grew out of a process of learning, partnership and representation set in motion by Joseph Wresinski* in conjunction with very deprived citizens.

It all started in 1957, when Wresinski arrived at the "homeless camp" in Noisy-le-Grand, near Paris. He had experienced the humiliation of poverty and exclusion during his own childhood, and in this overlooked and forsaken spot, he felt among "his own people". He chose to share their life, to work alongside them to build a better future with them, making them the artisans of a society in which human rights would be respected and protected, and from which extreme poverty and exclusion would be banished. With the help of families in the shanty-town, some friends actively involved in social issues and a handful of people who came and joined him, he created an association known as "Aide à Toute Détresse" or "Help to All in Distress", which later became the International Movement ATD Fourth World*.

In 1960, Joseph Wresinski gave one of the first full-time members of the Fourth World volunteer corps*, Ms Alwine de Vos Van Steenwijk, the task of setting up a Center for Social Research[1]. ATD Fourth World aimed to become a current of thought and a life choice, forming a bulwark against permanent welfare dependency in a society incapable of liberating itself from chronic poverty. An intimate knowledge of poverty, a life of activism shared with the poorest members of society, reflection, research and training were all integral features. They were to lead to a new way of thinking and were the prerequisite for authentic involvement of the poor in all the spheres of individual and social activity. The Center's role was to mobilize researchers and activists, and to organize colloquia, seminars and study groups in order to develop a rigorous academic understanding of poverty, its causes, manifestations and consequences.

Three types of—often silent—resistance displayed by the very poor form the founding principles of ATD Fourth World. These are resistance to the notion that poverty is ineluctable, resistance to the notion that poverty is the fault of the poor, and resistance to the spiritual and human wastage engendered by a society that chooses to deprive itself of the experience its poorest members can offer.

To begin with, a housing project was designed and built on the site of the Noisy-le-Grand shanty-town, subsequently receiving official recognition. Its task was to foster family life and social and cultural development for families which had been—or were in danger of being—split up because of their extreme poverty. This project was the "homeland", the crucible of ATD Fourth World. It was there that, in partnership with very deprived families, ATD Fourth World patiently and diligently experimented with giving everyone fundamental rights and responsibilities, starting with young children and community development. Fifty years after its foundation, this experiment is still ongoing, with new families living in poverty today.

On the November 17, 1977 in Paris, Joseph Wresinski made a public appeal to the French Government and all French citizens for solidarity with the very poor. On that occasion, he announced to the Fourth World activists and delegates that "For the next ten years it must be our goal that no one among us be illiterate, that every child not only attend school, but not fail at school either. Of course, we need help from others to accomplish this, but we can also play our part. Let those who can read and write teach their neighbors. Each of us must take responsibility, to educate not only ourselves, but also those around us." And addressing the whole of society, he added: "This, then, is an alliance between those who are excluded and those who are not, an alliance that must change human relations, politics and the thinking of our time."

In 1987, two events paved the way for public involvement in the fight against poverty:

– The publication of the report on "Chronic Poverty and Lack of Basic Security" by the Economic and Social Council of France (reporter Joseph Wresinski). This report provided a new definition of extreme poverty, which would later gain wide currency: "Lack of basic security is the absence of one or more factors that enable individuals and families to assume basic responsibilities and to enjoy fundamental rights. Such a situation may become more extended and lead to more serious and permanent consequences. Chronic poverty results when the lack of basic security simultaneously affects several aspects of people's lives, when it is prolonged, and when it severely compromises people's chances of regaining their rights and of reassuming their responsibilities in the foreseeable future." This report offered a comprehensive, consistent and viable plan for combating extreme poverty[2].

– The inauguration of a stone honoring the victims of poverty on the Plaza of Liberties and Human Rights in Paris with the following inscription: "Wherever men and women are condemned to live in extreme poverty, human rights are violated. To come together to ensure that these rights be respected is our solemn duty."

By 1971, Joseph Wresinski had already created what were to become the Fourth World People's Universities*. He wanted people living in extreme poverty to be considered not simply as people to be taught, but also as a source of knowledge which could enrich, and be enriched by, that possessed by other members of society. Dialogue could only become possible if the "experts" let themselves be educated by those who, at the time, were regarded as "ignorant". This started at the Fourth World People's Universities, where people living in situations of extreme poverty shared the knowledge acquired from their life experiences with those who had never experienced poverty. Together they were able to produce new ways of thinking and acting.

In 1980, at a meeting of an international committee of academics whom ATD Fourth World had brought together at UNESCO, Joseph Wresinski spoke of the "role and duty of university researchers dealing with research on poverty." First he recalled the twofold need:

– "To make room for the knowledge the very poor and excluded have of their own situation and the world that imposes it upon them, to re-evaluate this knowledge as unique, indispensable, autonomous and a complement to all other forms of knowledge, and to help develop it. . . . "

– "To consolidate the knowledge that those who live and work among the very poor may have."

And he added: "In addition to these two parts of an overall body of knowledge, there is the third part, the researcher's knowledge, that of the external observer. Academic knowledge only tells one part of the story. It can only be indirect knowledge, informative and explanatory. It lacks that firm footing in raw reality that turns knowledge into a mobilizing force capable of leading to action."[3]

Three years later, in 1983, in a lecture at the Sorbonne in Paris attended by Fourth World families and academics, Joseph Wresinski once again repeated his challenge to the Academic World. He told the story of a very poor family that he knew well and demonstrated their understanding and knowledge of their own situation and of society in general. Specifically, he declared that "moral and political responsibility, as well as academic rigor, demand that universities turn their attention to the Fourth World, not in the first instance to teach, but to engage in a dialogue and to learn from it. By 'universities' I also mean all their institutions and subdivisions. I also mean all members of universities who in one way or another possess a part of common knowledge. It is time to acknowledge the reciprocity of knowledge, that is, reciprocity between all those who know and those who have been excluded. That means asking that part of the population which is on the bottom rung of the social ladder to give us the benefit of their thoughts and what they alone know."[4]

And he addressed the academics: "You scholars, you who are recognized as the keepers of knowledge, you must ensure that the thoughts and views of the poorest are recognized as valid. Without you, their validity is constantly challenged and denied; nobody listens to the poorest. Instead, we impose outside interpretations on them that prevent them from thinking about their own lives."

One of the specific objectives of ATD Fourth World is both to give the poor a sense of their own history and to make this story known to society in general. ATD Fourth World organized an academic colloquium at the University of Caen in October 1989 as part of the bicentenary of the French Revolution and the Declaration of the Rights of Man and of the Citizen. The topic was "From the Fourth Order to the Fourth World. The Representation of the Poorest in Democracy." The colloquium examined the place of the poorest in history and the role of collections of their testimonies and thoughts, and was followed by a debate between delegates of the Fourth World People's Universities and historians. When asked, "What can the universities do with regard to the Fourth World?" Professor Marcela David said: "In the '50s, some academics took the initiative of opening up universities to one group of that decade's poor, the working class. They proposed that workers' representatives meet with universities to get to know and understand each other, to speak on equal terms and to address some issues together. The Workers' Institutes did this at many different universities. What can we academics do? We can campaign to create a structure of equal partnership between the poor and academics."[5]

Finally, in June 1993, at ATD Fourth World's initiative, a working group was formed between academics and members of ATD Fourth World (members of the Fourth World volunteer corps and activists from impoverished backgrounds). Its goal was to establish conditions for an experimental project intended to create a dialogue and a reciprocal relationship between the three types of knowledge identified by the founder of ATD Fourth World: the knowledge of those who have lived in extreme poverty and exclusion, the knowledge of those who have committed themselves to working with the poor and academic knowledge.

Drawing up an agenda

The working group spent two years between 1993 and 1995 familiarizing itself with the history of ATD Fourth World, particularly that of Fourth World People's Universities, and engaging with the issues facing universities and those working with ATD Fourth World to arrive at an experimental "training, action and research" project between the Fourth World and the Academic World. Its aim was to "produce a new form of knowledge and understanding of extreme poverty and attempts to combat it."

The group worked on the basis of two *a priori* with regard to the exclusive nature of knowledge. On the one hand, the Academic World is very influential. It determines a society's "intelligence", setting the cultural framework within which political discourse gains legitimacy. On the other hand, the existence of extreme poverty does not fall into any particular field of study in our society and is not really perceived as calling into question issues such as the rule of law or citizenship.

The working group organized a day of experimental dialogue between activists, Fourth World volunteer corps members and academics within the context of developing and producing new knowledge. The topic chosen was citizenship: "What does living as a citizen and a responsible human being mean to you?" Before the discussion proper, each participant wrote a short answer to this question. The aim of working in this way was to encourage individual expression and facilitate the arrival at a common statement.

Evaluations of the day demonstrated:

– the usefulness of a method that combined working alone, working in small groups and working in a large group, thus requiring the participants to negotiate a common conclusion, a synthesis arrived at from their different standpoints

– the value and difficulties of a dialogue involving these three groups

– the specificity of each group's contribution to the discussion. The activists described situations, types of response and strategies—knowledge born of experience. The academics dealt with questions on a more conceptual level, analyzing and drawing on references. The Fourth World volunteer corps members further explained the context of the activists' statements and highlighted the lessons to be drawn from ATD Fourth World's experience.

The day was useful in drawing up a profile of the project's goals, participants and approach, as well as clarifying the composition and mission of both the pedagogical team and the Academic Panel, examining financial resources etc.

THE EXPERIMENTAL TRAINING, ACTION AND RESEARCH PROJECT
by Claude Ferrand

The project was a Franco-Belgian undertaking. Administration was overseen by the ATD Fourth World Research and Training Institute.
A common protocol was agreed upon by all participants. It set out:
– the ultimate purpose, operational objectives and methods;
– the organization, missions and tasks of the various participants;
– the ethical standards which all participants undertook to respect;
– the work schedule.

Agent-authors

In order to test the approach based on autonomy and reciprocity between different forms of knowledge (knowledge gained from direct experience of extreme poverty, knowledge born of active involvement and academic knowledge) the pilot project required a team of "agent-authors". The number was very soon fixed at thirty, all French-speakers.

Fourth World activists were chosen to represent knowledge gained from direct experience of extreme poverty. There were fifteen of these, nine French and six Belgians[6]. They had lived in and suffered the consequences of poverty, either on their own or with their families. Many still lived in such conditions. All had been involved with Fourth World People's Universities for many years, where they had acquired listening and public speaking skills. In order to be agent-authors, they required basic literacy skills. They had to be available to work 3/4 time. If they had a family, their spouse had to agree to their taking part and be prepared to provide moral support. They received a salary established on the basis of their position and living situation. The final deciding factor was geographical location. In order to be able to carry out the required work in the allotted two-year period, they had to be able to work together in groups of two or three. Five regions were thus established: Brittany, Normandy, and the North for France; Brussels and Hainault for Belgium.

– *Researchers and professors* in different disciplines from several universities in France and Belgium were chosen to represent academic knowledge. Four were already members of the preparatory work group and were instrumental in recruiting the others. The academics had to be willing to make time for the project and relatively certain of being able to take an active part on a regular basis. Twelve academics agreed to take part (two working together from the same discipline). Nine were still in post (three researchers and six mainly occupied in teaching) and three were emeritus. They came from ten different universities, most obtaining the agreement of their university chancellor or rector and a letter of support. The disciplines represented were law, economics, education, medicine, physics, criminology, history and sociology.

– *Fourth World volunteer corps members* represented knowledge born of action with the most deprived people (it was decided not to involve any working people from outside so as to keep the focus on the priority aspect, the Fourth World–University dialogue). The five members of the Fourth World volunteer corps constituted the smallest group in number. They were required to be available on a part-time basis (1/3 time) and to have experience working with the very poor (children, teenagers or adults). To maintain a balance, they were selected from a variety of cultural and professional backgrounds, and had differing outlooks on life. Before becoming members of the Fourth World volunteer corps, they had all worked in different professional and social spheres. They all have different roles within in ATD Fourth World.

In total, there were thirty-two agent-authors: fifteen Fourth World activists, twelve academics and five Fourth World volunteer corps members.[7]

Carrying out the project

Group Work

The training, action and research part of the project was spread over two years (from March 1, 1996 to March 1, 1998) as follows:

– The groundwork was laid by the Fourth World activists. In subgroups of three, they worked three days a week for twenty-two months. The groups in France met in Caen, Rennes and Lille-Paris, and the groups in Belgium met in Brussels and La Louvière. For half a day a week, each subgroup was supported by a volunteer resource person (a teacher not actively involved with ATD Fourth World)[x].

– Group work on selected topics was carried out by all the agent-authors together. This took the form of a three-day seminar every two months (ten seminars in all) at the Les Fontaines Cultural Centre in Chantilly (France).

– Production of the memoirs was carried out in groups by theme, with the Fourth World activists, academics and Fourth World volunteer corps members working jointly on topics agreed between them. Each group met locally for a full day every other month, alternating with the months in which there were seminars.

The Pedagogical Team

A reliable pedagogical team was necessary to bring the project to a successful conclusion. Its role was to oversee and organize the knowledge-production process, and to prepare and direct the three-day seminars. This team[9] was made up of:

– The program director, whose task was to ensure that the goals and ultimate purpose of the program were respected, and to direct the project as a whole.

– Two academics, both trained counselors, employed part-time to advise the academics and Fourth World volunteer corps members.

– A pedagogical counselor, employed part-time to coach the Fourth World activists. Because this was an important project and the method had never been tried before, the pedagogical counselor was also the educational resource person for the program as a whole.

– An academic evaluator, employed part-time, whose task was to assemble the knowledge drawn from the training, action and research project throughout the process and to evaluate the various aspects thereof.

On average, the pedagogical team met for one day every fifteen days, that is, thirty-three times over the two years of the program.

The Academic Panel

In order to examine and validate the method and content of the research, a team of distinguished Belgian and French academics were asked to form an Academic Panel[10]. The Panel met twice a year and was invited to participate in some of the seminars. It was also asked to help organize a colloquium of European universities whose aim was to examine the results of the project and their influence on the content and methods of university teaching and research, as well as on initial training.

Common ethical standards

In view of the diverse backgrounds of the participants, their differences and the project's goals, the participants agreed to respect certain fundamental principles, which comprised a kind of ethical rule-book regulating the relationships between them.

Applying the principle of reciprocity to one's own knowledge

Each participant was both supplying and receiving knowledge. The main aim was not to teach, but to be taught. The knowledge offered was a form of personal expression. There was no other way of accessing it than through mutual recognition and respect between all concerned. Knowledge (*connaissance*) thus became a symbolic mutual awakening (*co-naissance*), resulting in joint production of knowledge.

Listening

Listening to another person and accepting all their differences entailed analyzing how one's own understanding was affected by the other person's knowledge. Each party's truth was intertwined with that of the other and involved a reciprocal listening process that linked them together as a pair.

Discretion

People's lives are sensitive matters and must be respected. That is why everything the participants said or wrote, if it has not been published, is confidential and may not be quoted or used at any time.

Collective Property

The memoirs are the collective property of their authors and are published in this book. However, the research data (interviews, hearings, transcription of group exchanges, etc) are not public property. They were archived at the end of the project. All the participants have been expressly requested not to prolong the research themselves and therefore to destroy their data.

METHODOLOGY

by Daniel Cornerotte, Françoise Ferrand and Pascal Galvani

To create a more sophisticated understanding of extreme poverty and attempts to eradicate it, the experimental Fourth World–University project endeavored to bring together various kinds of knowledge and agents in a dialogue. To bring about such knowledge-merging and knowledge-creation, the project required consistent goals and considerable financial support. It was also necessary to create a working method capable of adequately supporting both the project as a whole as well as the agents themselves on a daily basis. The issues arising from the cross-fertilization of knowledge could not be dealt with *ad hoc*. It would not suffice simply to bring together Fourth World activists, members of the Fourth World volunteer corps and academics from different disciplines and let them create a project. Hence, it is useful for the reader to have a description of the conditions necessary for such an experiment. What is "research-action-training"? How can such a project be organized? How can knowledge be formalized and shared between agent-authors, given their differences? How can both reciprocity of understanding and collective intellectual production be achieved?

How to achieve reciprocal understanding:

– Allow each participant to construct their own way of thinking: This was particularly the case for Fourth World activists and Fourth World volunteer corps members. Indeed, knowledge gained from experience, like knowledge born of action, is essentially linked to personal life. Both are less formalized than academic knowledge. They need to be put into more formal frameworks before any attempt is made to recognize or share them. The structure of academic knowledge also has to be reworked to be communicable to and analyzable by the other agent-authors.

– Find fair means of expression: Both equal speaking-time and words and vocabulary of equal weight were necessary for reciprocal discussion. Different forms of expression had to be combined: visual, written, accounts of personal experience, debates, interviews, analyses etc. The administrative team also had to regulate and reformulate modes of expression, even intervene with suggestions for new approaches if subgroups became caught up in misunderstandings. To give everyone the chance to reflect on what had been said and assimilate it for themselves, all the discussions were recorded and transcribed. Different types of subgroups were created in order to allow discussion between all 32 agent-authors.

How to think collectively

– Match stages of training with stages of research: Throughout the two-year period, the pedagogical team was constantly juggling with time-schedules so that each subgroup could make headway. Each period of work had to correspond to one of the stages necessary in research: choice of topic/s, identification of issues, overview of current thought, collection of data, analyses, writing-up etc.

– Suggest methods that allow for collective and equal knowledge-production: The research guidelines had to be adapted to groups made up of people with very different kinds of knowledge.

The three educational advisors had to draw on their experience to find a suitable methodology and adapt it to the situation in order to achieve these aims. They examined the following areas: Fourth World People's Universities as means of expression and dialogue[11]; production of knowledge[12] as the pedagogical aim of adult training; and research guidance for professionals in continuing university training[13]. From their first meetings onwards, the combination of the different abilities of the pedagogical team enabled them to define the project's working method.

To enable the different groups of agent-authors to dialogue and collectively define the research project in question, the pedagogical team itself had to combine its different kinds of knowledge. In this fashion, the team was able to create a methodology that enabled each group of agents to contribute its own knowledge on a given subject to the project in its own way.

A learning-based approach

It was the pedagogical team's task to suggest approaches appropriate to the aims of the project as it developed. Three different steps were necessary:

– Formulation of research questions
– Analysis of collected data
– Writing of memoirs

From the agents' first meetings to the formulation of a research subject

There was no clear way forward at the start of the project. The pedagogical team could not take its direction from any past experience that was directly applicable to the situation at hand, though some pedagogical approaches could be adapted. The success of the first meetings was instrumental in determining what followed.

The "coats of arms meeting"

Along with the joy felt at finally seeing the project become a reality, the pedagogical team also felt great apprehension, since they were responsible for the project's success. Three days of work were necessary just to formulate a first definition of the team's role and to prepare the first seminar. This seminar was carried out with the sole purpose of bringing together not only people from different backgrounds, but also different types of knowledge.

Before the agents could combine their existing knowledge to produce new knowledge, they needed to meet each other. It was also necessary to begin identifying their different ways of thinking. The coat of arms approach, which had already been used in research and trainingal contexts[14], allows each person to depict what about their personal and intellectual background they deem relevant to the present context. Everyone was invited to make a Fourth-World-University Project coat of arms, based on the following model:

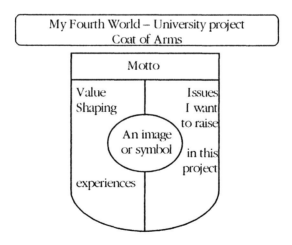

For two hours, everyone was allowed to work alone and create a personal coat of arms on a large sheet of paper. Afterwards, these sheets were posted up behind the participants' places around the conference table. The concentration, focus and quality of attention that characterized this moment are difficult to put into words. This kind of activity cannot be reduced to a "technical procedure" or an "exercise". Everyone was invited to present and comment on their coat of arms. The chair specified that there was to be no criticism or psychological interpretation of anyone else's coat of arms[15]. Slowly, in a hushed atmosphere of sympathy, emotion and attention, everyone laid bare their experiences and questions.

As well as bringing about interpersonal recognition, this meeting focused on the questions and thoughts expressed by the participants. It is from this collection of data that a first thematic basis was constructed to which the participants would later return. By doing this and contextualizing everyone's experience and knowledge of extreme poverty, a collective mode of questioning could then be established. Taking this as a point of reference, the five research themes could then be agreed upon.

The different modes of interaction between participants

The constraints of the present work do not permit us to describe every last detail of the project. Thus, a broad outline will be given of the different ways participants interacted and combined their knowledge, under the guidance of the pedagogical team. By working in and moving between subgroups for varying periods of time, all the participants were able to take part all the time. Most of these subgroups were created in the first months of the project and were operative for the full two years.

The **"thematic" groups** were the five subgroups each allotted one of the research themes defined during the second seminar: History, Family, Knowledge, Work and Human Activity, and Citizenship. The number of groups was determined with regard to geographical constraints that kept the number of participants to six or seven (three activists, one member of the Fourth World volunteer corps, two or three academics). It was in these groups that the research thematics[16], the analyses and the memoirs that make up this work were written. The thematic groups were the principal place where the three kinds of agents shared their different types of knowledge.

The **"agent" groups** (one for the activists, one for the academics and one for the Fourth World volunteer corps members) had one work period set aside for them at each seminar. These groups had several objectives:

– Monitor work in progress according to participants' individual priorities and ensure their contribution was respected;

– Allow agents from similar backgrounds to provide mutual support and to reformulate certain issues in their own words;

– More effectively evaluate work in progress. This entailed keeping in mind the different ways of thinking underlying academic knowledge, knowledge gained from experience and knowledge born of action.

The **"mixed" groups** were picked at random and were made up of academics, activists and members of the Fourth World volunteer corps, without regard to the research themes each was personally involved in. Their goal was to help the participants keep in mind the more general aims of the project, enhancing their own research through engagement with the other research themes.

The "turtle": all the participants gathered together in a plenary assembly for discussion.

For the plenary assemblies, the pedagogical team had to come up with a procedure that would prevent meetings degenerating into debates between a few more articulate or monopolistic speakers. The procedure needed to allow all thirty-two participants to think collectively and progressively. The sessions also had to alternate between plenary and one-to-one discussion, brain-storming in mixed groups and in groups of participants.

Having clearly identified the objectives and criteria to which the procedure had to conform, the pedagogical team finally opted for a group procedure called "the turtle"[17]. They adapted this model to the conditions of the experimental project.

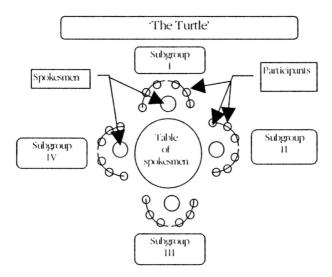

From building a framework to analysis undertaken from a multiplicity of angles

Though the research process can be broken down into successive steps (defining the subject, formulating hypotheses, constructing interpretive models, presenting facts etc.) it is still a journey into the unknown. The role of the pedagogical team was to mark the way and provide an operative structure.

Initial Procedures

There can be no discovery without a question, but asking this question is itself far from simple. It is an intellectual process requiring research in its turn.

Having established its research subject and aim, each thematic group (History, Family, Knowledge, Work and Human Activity, and Citizenship) attempted to formulate its research project by way of an **opening question** that most clearly expressed what the group was looking to discover, elucidate or better understand. This central question was in one way or another the touchstone of the research project and was subsequently reworked. All other questions were offshoots of the central question. The reworking of the question allowed a **framework** to be gradually constructed **within which the question could be addressed**.

This was far from a formal process, but forced the group to clarify its intentions in a useful way. Questions were not always immediately formulated in a fashion which precisely addressed the problem or covered all the angles, but sometimes needed to be deconstructed then reconstructed. There were moments of doubt, but a path had to be found. A description of the passionate discussions which occurred when addressing these questions can be found in the first chapter of each group of agent-authors' memoirs (see the "Methods" chapters).

In order to gradually create an operative structure, it was particularly useful to use pedagogical techniques (approaching things from different angles, experimentation, collecting and analyzing information etc). This "approach" comprised various interdependent stages which formed a consistent whole. These stages were formalized in a schematic procedure by the pedagogical team (central question, hypotheses, verification, understanding and analysis of results etc) in the following way:

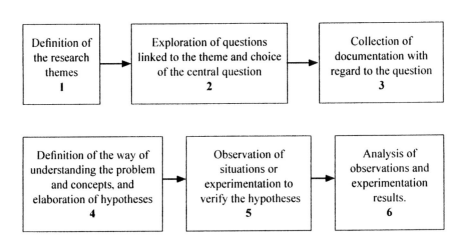

Underlying principles and in-depth exploration of the questions

Many methods were experimented with to help the groups refine their research frameworks. For example, at the seminar in November 1996, each thematic group presented the various parts of its research procedure to the plenary assembly. This was carried out through **mini-conferences** (presentation, Q & A and discussion sessions). The aim of these mini-conferences was to subject the content and methods of research to constructive criticism by the rest of the group of agent-authors. Over the next few days, the thematic groups were asked to take into account the comments, questions and suggestions given during the mini-conferences. In some cases, this meant a complete reworking of their initial question.

Three **lectures** were given by guest speakers who recounted their personal and social experiences with regard to the five research themes. The speakers were Lucie Ribert[18], a Fourth World activist, Emile Creutz, a Doctor of Physics, and Emilie Bourtet[19], a member of the Fourth World volunteer corps. These moments spurred the groups on in their thinking, for they sparked an awareness of the multiplicity of interconnected aspects encountered in all poverty situations. The lectures were thought-provoking and helped put some flesh on the bones of the groups' research frameworks[20].

Each thematic group was also asked to draw up a **research brief** to formalize the structural elements of its research: What is the research subject? What are the key concepts? How will the research be carried out? First, a provisional brief was drawn up including key words, the central question, sub-questions and a hypothesis. This preliminary brief served to refine the research framework; that is, what the group was looking for, and how it would research it. Amongst other things, each group had to justify the relevance of its questions to the subject, the way in which it would verify the hypotheses posited, and the specific "areas" it had chosen for observation. Each participant also had to present the group's research file to a smaller number of members of other thematic groups. This helped to maintain communication between the five research groups.

The collection and analysis of data

Having defined its framework, each research group then defined the data useful in establishing whether its hypotheses were correct. They chose a field of study and appropriate "tools" for their research. Some tools would have to be refined, reviewed or corrected to do the subject justice or to overcome unforeseen difficulties.

To verify their hypotheses, the five thematic groups collected observational data and then analyzed and interpreted their results. In this fashion they brought together different types of information, both pre-established and collected specifically for the purposes of this research. Interviews and transcriptions/decipherings of group discussions were used by all five research groups.

Interviews were mostly carried out by the activists. They approached families living in extreme poverty and asked whether they could make recordings. These interviews were often carried out in their neighborhood, at the families' homes, during which time the Fourth World–University project was explained to them. They were also told that the recorded interviews would help to bring about a better understanding of the living conditions of the very poor. The transcriptions of these interviews were subsequently given to the interviewees for them to correct as they saw necessary to allow them to keep a measure of control over their words and thoughts.

Two thematic groups chose to have interviews carried out by each group member. Each interview was recorded, transcribed by its authors, and analyzed by the group.

Deciphering (recordings and transcriptions of group discussions) was another type of data collection used by all the groups. Each thematic group used the dialogue and deciphering method, which is not a common technique in academic research. Every stage of the research was carried out as a dialogue amongst the group members, from deciding on the theme and verifying hypotheses right through to writing up the final research papers. For this reason, each meeting was recorded, "deciphered," and a copy was given to the participants very shortly afterwards. The word "deciphering" is used here to clarify that the transcription was not intended as linguistic research; a deciphering was a tool for the agent-authors to use. They might use it to return to matters that were too complex or passed over too quickly in meetings, to complete some unfinished analysis, or to remind themselves of a particularly fruitful line of questioning or the precise way a thought had been formulated. They were the only means of guaranteeing equality between the participants throughout the process of research and writing. It was only with the help of these decipherings that the activists, who were not used to taking notes and long periods of concentration, were able to return to the debates they had missed, note[21] an important point, and rekindle discussion of these points at subsequent meetings.

All the data collected (interviews, decipherings of the meetings, readings) were analyzed within and across each of the groups.

From analysis to writing the memoirs

In committing to the project, each participant knew that the final research product was to be a piece of written work, a memoir that would eventually be published in this book.

Right from the start of the project many written works were produced by each thematic group: personal contributions on the theme, transcribed interviews, decipherings of group meetings etc. Each document was catalogued and all agent-authors were given copies of all the documents relative to their research group. This entailed about eighty documents per group of between one and fifty pages in length. This meant that even before the actual memoir-writing phase of the project could begin, each participant had large quantities of written material to go through. For the academics, writing was a part of their job. They had learnt how to write while studying and had already published many written works[21]. The Fourth World volunteer corps members could write, but had rarely written anything for publication. For most of the activists, writing was agony and uncharted territory.

The outlines of the memoirs

An initial data classification was carried out collectively in each group. The activists then took over the process of classification, rereading all the decipherings of group meetings and the interviews, and classifying them using an analytical model decided on by the group. Modification of the model was sometimes necessary. Using the model and the research file as a starting point, a preliminary outline was drawn up for each memoir, specifying the framework and timeline of the writing process. These preliminary outlines were subsequently corrected and refined, taking account of the most recent data brought in by research, the reworking of analytical models in the light of the first writings, which were starting to take shape, and complementary information required as the research proceeded.

All groups have a "Methodology" or "Approach" chapter which deals with the debates within each group. These throw light on the procedure, the agents' expectations of one another and the difficulties and successes which arose in their interaction. It may seem surprising to begin the reading of a memoir with a chapter explaining "How the research was carried out", but because of the experimental nature of combining different types of knowledge, each group became aware that the "how" was an integral part of the content of the research. The reader's understanding of the "how" is thus necessary to their understanding subsequent chapters, since procedure was a decisive factor in research results. In this way, much of the activists' thought could only develop and be written down because of previous contributions by other groups of agent-authors and collective analysis. Similarly, many of the writings of the academics and Fourth World volunteer corps members were only made possible following contributions made by activists. The drafts of the five memoirs, as well as the ordering of chapter sections, conformed to this process of knowledge-merging.

Collaborative writing

The aim of this exercise, proposed by the pedagogical team, was to see whether a collaborative form of writing was possible within each thematic group, presupposing that the data would be read and interpreted in the same way, though allowance was made for potential differences of opinion. To this end, each thematic group was asked to select one key idea from its research. Then, each group of agent-authors (the three activists, the two or three academics and the member of the Fourth World volunteer corps) wrote one page on this key idea, based on the discussions that had already taken place within their groups[22].

This first exercise determined the conditions that would enable the writing of the memoirs. In each thematic group, the three activists were able to present a joint text that they had put a lot of work into composed from texts they had written individually. The pedagogical counselor helped draw conclusions and sum up. The Fourth World volunteer corps member wrote an individual text. The academics, not used to working together or in a cross-disciplinary context, presented unfinished texts within which it had been difficult for them to come to any kind of common agreement. It was concluded from this that, while the activists were capable of group writing, geographical and time constraints made the collaboration between academics very difficult. Also, the Fourth World volunteer corps members asked for more support in their writing.

The aim of this exercise was to create a collaborative text from initial texts written by the different groups of agent-authors which respected the points of view of each group. In one working day, each group managed only a few linesor, at best, half a page!

This exercise also showed how important the writing part of the project was. As a result of this, two groups modified their memoir outlines, shifting the emphasis. It also showed that the writing part of the project needed to begin relatively early. To allow everyone to participate, it could not be left to the final months of the project. Lastly, it seemed impossible to write the entire memoir in this fashion, the method being far too laborious.

The writing of the memoirs

The five research papers were written in parallel, each thematic group concentrating its attention on its own writing. The procedure suggested was that, firstly, the materials for each chapter (decipherings, interviews, readings etc.), would be catalogued and reread and the most detailed outline possible drawn up for the writing of the respective chapters. There were therefore written materials that had to be kept in mind for the composition of each section. Extracts from the decipherings of group discussions were often used as a basis for a first written draft.

Since everyone knew that they were not writing purely in their own names, it was generally accepted that texts would be reread and critiqued by other members of the group. Each text was thus subjected to several group revisions before it was accepted in its final form. The writing guidelines were to write the texts using the information collected and worked on in the group, so that everyone could remain a part of the final written product. As a result of this, no references to authors or works that had not been studied collectively were allowed.

Writing methods and speeds varied greatly from one group of agent-authors to another, as well as within each group.

Everyone was asked to send in their texts a few days prior to the group meetings to allow time for the texts to be understood, checked and amended. The meeting schedule did not always fit this process perfectly. Thus, some groups had to plan extra days of group work for the final product to be a truly collaborative effort.

When fundamental disagreements arose, it was agreed that these disagreements would be mentioned in the final written version so as to respect all points of view.

On several occasions, the composition of a chapter or a section thereof was entrusted to a group of agents that had not originally contributed to that part of the research, demonstrating the efficacy of knowledge-merging. Each memoir's table of contents indicates the person or people responsible for the writing of each section.

Certain sections, especially the introductions and the conclusions of the memoirs, were the subject of much group writing and discussion. Here it was important to reach agreements and negotiate, without giving way on points which agent-authors perceived as vital. It is thus difficult to say exactly who is responsible for the final product. They are really and truly joint efforts, as mentioned and demonstrated in the tables of contents.

Lastly, many of the texts come directly from group discussions, being extracts from the decipherings. These are referred to as internal documents.

The frequent meetings of the pedagogical team allowed for regular monitoring of the works in progress, discussion of difficulties encountered and agreement on adjustments needed to meet the deadline.

The order of the five memoirs presented in this book was decided upon at the end of the project, with the agreement of all the agent-authors. Even though each memoir was written independently of the others and can thus stand on its own, the reader is encouraged to read them in the following order: starting with the bigger picture, that of one group (History: "From Shame to Pride"); then progressing to that of the family (Family: "Time and the Family Project"); followed by the memoirs on the different types of knowledge and skills (Knowledge: "Freeing Knowledge!"; Work and Human Activity: "Hidden Talents"); and ending with the political dimension (Citizenship: "Representation and Extreme Poverty").

Pedagogical issues and concerns

The pedagogical team's role in the Fourth World–University project was to direct individual and collective production. There were three principles to the procedure they used:

– A comprehension-based approach, where everything expressed must be reformulated to ensure understanding between academics, Fourth World volunteer corps members and activists;

– A constructivist approach, where issues arising from agents' experience are used as starting points from which to build a framework and carry out analysis;

– An interactionist (interactive) approach, where all stages of research progress together in and by means of dialogue

Comprehension-related issues and procedures

The pedagogical team needed to ensure that a balance was struck in the research between inter-subjective understanding and the construction of structured thought. In the early seminars, the priority was to aim for reciprocity of understanding in order to create a strong group dynamic. Later on in the project, however, emphasis shifted to a purely intellectual approach to the issue addressed by each group. This balance was essential to a working process where life experience had to be included without forcing activists to discuss their private lives and without creating a teacher-student relationship between the academics and the members of the Fourth World volunteer corps and activists. The goal of mutual understanding aimed to avoid this twofold pitfall: It demanded that everyone involved be scrupulously respected and recognized as an important contributor to research, both seeking and producing knowledge.

The problems which occur in all group work were here exacerbated by the heterogeneity of the people involved, their cultural and linguistic circles and, consequently, their ways of thinking. As the project progressed, the pedagogical team intervened regularly in response to difficulties encountered or requests from the agent-authors, suggesting new approaches when a lack of understanding seriously impeded progress in a group. The potential for mutual understanding between agents was of prime importance in producing the consistent collective intellectual effort required. The thirty agent-authors taking part in the project were not just a group of people with different experiences. Psycho-sociological and socio-cultural factors influenced interaction between agents, each having a different perception of the aim of the project and the research, of training and of activism. All the procedures envisaged by the pedagogical team had to further the aim of reciprocity of understanding and had to create a form of dialogue and debate in which each group of agents could fully participate.

The pedagogical procedures aimed to bring out and develop an attitude in the agents which would help them understand and interpret what other agents brought to the table. This exploratory form of interpretation, where each sought to comprehend the knowledge contribution of the other, was necessary to the project's success.

However, this comprehensive attitude was not sufficient alone. It was necessary, but could have impeded progress if it had become the only mode of dialogue. It only made sense in a broader context of comparing ideas and different types of knowledge, in the same way as comparing analyses without interpretation would quickly have come to a dead end.

In view of the collected testimonies and especially the diversity of the groups, the procedure became one of comprehension and interpretation of the collected materials. For the academics, the procedure could be seen as one of comprehension-based sociology, for although it was based on real facts, the research was concerned with the meaning and significance of events. The data was not collected in order to establish statistics. It was to be expected that there would be moments of disagreement. What was seen as affirmation by some was for others nothing more than a hypothesis in need of verification. The activists were not used to using precise language. Academic language, on the other hand, was often too opaque. All participants were required to listen attentively to avoid making over-swift interpretations of what others thought. The same was true of collaborative work on the understanding of events and interpretation of materials (interviews, lectures, theories etc.).

Research-related issues and procedures

Since the pedagogical team's role was to ensure that research procedures remained collective, they had to create pedagogical aids (described above) to do so, using methodological techniques widely used in social sciences research. The team's job could almost be seen as providing methodological advice and guidance in research. However, its main function was not to provide direct methodological advice (aiding to formulate concepts or the field of research), since the groups were already able to do this. Their main aim was rather to put forward ways of interaction that would help the agents to formulate and negotiate the different stages of research collectively (framework, concept, analysis of content etc.). This process was one of constant movement from considered experience to critical analysis. The disinterested standpoint that is usually required from the start of such research was established progressively in this case, through considering the experience of the agents in each subgroup. Carrying out research meant collectively establishing "proximity and distance" with regard to the subject. This meant not allowing oneself to be guided by one's own emotions, feelings and values, and accepting debate and dispute on the data each member of the group brought to the table.

This comprehension-based approach was complemented at times by a "structuralist" approach. Schemas were drawn up following intensive questioning within each group. These schemas were structures of the thought process that enables complex concepts to be broken down (for example: people, time, representation etc.) and different ways of thinking to be understood. These schemas described more precisely the objectives and goals of research and the ways of achieving them discovered during the project. Drawing up these schemas was an essential stage of research in each group which came about as a product of knowledge-merging, and they therefore figure in this work.

Issues and procedures relative to inter-subjective dialogue

Where differing views and interpretations conflicted, the pedagogical team had to intervene and regulate the inter-subjective dialogue, though they had to avoid merely juxtaposing different points of view and giving a spurious agreement between agents.

Even if the project had the equality of different types of knowledge as its working hypothesis, establishing a truly egalitarian dialogue between them was not easy. Before they could be expressed in dialogue, the different types of knowledge had to be formulated properly and recognized as representing a form of intelligence relevant to the research subject. Even with the best of intentions, this was not straightforward for the activists and Fourth World volunteer corps members, their knowledge being garnered from experience and activism. It was not enough to listen attentively and politely; what was said had to be seen as knowledge worthy of understanding. It is easier to make this effort when listening to the obscure words of an academic. "Naturally", one thinks, one lacks the knowledge required to understand ideas which are beyond one. One wants to learn, research and question. This is the kind of attitude that everyone needed to have toward the other in a project of this nature. It is not so straightforward to adopt it when one does not understand what an activist is saying. It is easier to think it is they who have not understood, who are off-beam or who are engaging in ideological discourse, because they do not formulate their thoughts in the accepted fashion.

Theoretical knowledge is by definition a form of knowledge which has already been formulated and objectified. It can easily be gathered and transmitted to others. It is a knowledge-object[23]. Knowledge gained from experience or born of activism is a much more integral part of the person who holds it. It is difficult to become aware of it and express it without preliminary work[24].

In view of these difficulties, the pedagogical team had to create several means of intervention, based on the use of decipherings and altering time-schedules and forms of dialogue as described above.

Mediation

Mediation in coaching the academics

At the beginning of the project, attention was mainly paid to coaching the activists. Coaching procedures for the academics and Fourth World volunteer corps members were developed on an *ad hoc* basis in response to issues as they arose.

The nature of the project meant that the two educational counselors had no points of reference to guide them concerning the difficulties the academics would encounter. One tends to think of academics as being fully equipped to deal with intellectual exchange, without thinking that they too might need training for this type of experience. How was one to know beforehand that they too would need help understanding, expressing themselves or working in groups? It was these types of problems that every participant in the Fourth World–University project was faced with.

Dealing with problems of understanding

The academics had trouble understanding the ways the activists and Fourth World volunteer corps members expressed themselves. The counselors' first task was to identify where difficulties arose and attempt different modes of intervention. To this end, the pedagogical team had to be made up of both Fourth World volunteer corps members and academics, each having an insight into the different kinds of difficulties the different groups might face. This combination of different types of knowledge within the team helped in analyzing and finding solutions to the problems. The academics' problems of understanding should not be overlooked. The ways activists and Fourth World volunteer corps members expressed knowledge gained from experience and knowledge born of action were just as foreign to the academics as the ways of expressing theoretical or academic knowledge were to the activists. For example, during a debate between two academics over the definition of a concept, an activist told the story of an event he had recently witnessed. One of the academics told him he was speaking out of context and that the group was trying to define a concept. To solve the problem and translate the situation into language that everyone could understand, the intervention of the counselor present was needed. This only happened after much persistence on the part of the activists. As a result, the group realized that the seemingly "out of context" anecdote of the activist offered precisely what was needed to define the concept under discussion. In this case, the thought and conceptual intelligence of the activist was not recognized because it came from knowledge gained from experience and was expressed in an unusual way. To facilitate understanding, the activist should have introduced his story by saying that it fell precisely within the sphere of the concept under discussion, but it seemed obvious to him that this was the case!

The vigilance the team had to demonstrate in order for knowledge gained from experience and knowledge born of action to be acknowledged in a comprehensible form gradually proved to be as important as the conception and creation of procedures allowing the collective project to advance.

Dealing with difficulties of expression

It was also difficult to imagine that academics, in their capacity as speakers and writers, would have difficulty expressing themselves, or that they would also need assistance in doing so. However, this issue was raised several times at academics' meetings. Their role was to provide the theoretical or academic knowledge relevant to the research being done in their respective group. Such knowledge is usually expressed in formal conceptual language, using complicated words, some of which cannot even be found in a dictionary. The question arose of how to express this knowledge in an accessible way. And it was not just a question of words. The style and structure of the texts were also an issue. For example, the very length of the sentences was a real problem for many. It was only by organizing writing workshops for the academics that the difficulties were finally identified and dealt with. Writing in short sentences dealing with one idea at a time takes nothing away from the quality and complexity of an analysis. This is, however, a method of writing that few academics are well versed in.

Academic workgroups

Like the activists, the academics from each thematic group also needed time and assistance to work together and analyze the work in progress. Another problem was the fact that the academics were not used to working in groups, but this was at least partially dealt with through academic meetings, which provided the necessary setting for them to discuss their issues.

Mediation and coaching for the Fourth World volunteer corps members

Both the participants and the pedagogical team quickly became aware of how difficult it was for the Fourth World volunteer corps members to find a role in the debates between activists and academics. This difficulty can partly be explained by the fact that the project brought the two groups of participants with the most marked differences between them, activists and academics, into immediate debate with each other. The Fourth World volunteer corps members had less cause for dispute with the activists and were also interested by the activist-academic debates. Another obstacle made expression difficult for the Fourth World volunteer corps members, namely that their contribution to their groups was to be what they had learned in their work with the poorest. The problem was that knowledge born of action is often inextricably linked to personal experience, and time is needed for contemplation and analysis in order to understand, make explicit and formulate this kind of knowledge for communication. This being the case, half-day training sessions[25] directed by an educational counselor were established for the Fourth World volunteer corps members, taking place before each seminar.

Mediation and coaching for the activists

Through their involvement in ATD Fourth World, the activists had already gained experience of meeting people who had not lived in poverty and are well placed to testify to the importance of this. The project aimed to bring them together with people recognized in society as "experts" on an intellectual level (professors and university researchers), with the aim of carrying out collaborative research where each participant would be a researcher and an actor-agent. The first hurdle was on the level of vocabulary and working methods: how could the different participants arrive at a mutual understanding and how could they perceive the complementary nature of their different forms of knowledge without being forced into a mold that they did not fit?

Structuring one's personal reflections

The first concern was to give the activists the self-confidence to help some of them overcome their fear that "I can't speak", "I can't write", "I don't understand anything", and to give to others the confidence to say, "I don't understand", instead of pretending that they did. This required making them aware that they did have the ability to think and that, as often than not, their thoughts were very accurate. Self-confidence cannot come from outside, one has to experience it in oneself. Each activist had to prove to themselves—quickly—that they were able to think and that their thoughts were valuable to the group. The pedagogical counselor thus had to find specific ways to ensure that each person's thoughts would not be smothered by the rest of the group.

One of the means used throughout the project was preparation in advance. For example, we knew that the first seminar would be set aside for meeting and introducing oneself to the others. Over several days, each activist had prepared a written personal introduction and issues that they wanted the project to address. On the first day of the seminar, when the pedagogical team suggested that everyone make a coat of arms, the activists were on equal footing with the other agent-authors since they were able to adapt what they had already written to the form suggested. The same procedure was used throughout the project for drawing up the outlines, cataloguing research materials, writing etc .This preparation was the only way to allow everyone their own time and pace to formulate and properly express thoughts before meeting with other participants.

Allowing each participant to work at their own pace

A second issue very quickly arose. The aim of the project was to show universities that they would be missing something vital if they ignored the knowledge of the poorest. The activists were not recruited through any kind of competition; their teams of three were heterogeneous, and their levels of oral and written expression were varied. What they had in common was having lived in poverty, having been close to families living in poverty and having been involved with ATD Fourth World. Those activists who were most comfortable with the means of expression used in the project began to dominate each thematic group while others became spectators or passive agents. It was easy to accuse the latter of "being too slow", of "holding up the group", of "not following" etc. Allowing everyone the time and space to think, especially those for whom each word was important, was not taking pity on the slower participants. On the contrary, it meant remaining true to the spirit of the project and listening to new questions or ideas that might help the group to progress or find a new angle. This procedure was experimented with, first in activist groups, then in the thematic groups. It required effort on the part of all participants, but it was also the mark of the project's fresh approach.

Reconciling the project with the participants' lives

Most of the activists involved in the project were still experiencing difficult circumstances such as insufficient financial resources (though the project offered financial security to all the participants, this was minimal and the money had to go towards covering old debts before all else), youth unemployment, difficulties in school for the children, some children were living in care, and the precarious and sometimes distressing situation of older children placed in care etc. Years of living in poverty had also adversely affected their health. What kind of moral and physical support did the activists need if they were to be able to keep up with the work schedule set out for the two years of the project? How could they be assured of having the intellectual space away from their everyday lives which was necessary for the thought and reflection that this project demanded of them? And, finally, how was the pedagogical team to ensure that the project did not just become a means of escape for them, a refuge from the difficult family problems they had to shoulder?

From the outset, the families, close friends or relatives, and/or groups to which the activists belonged—the different Fourth World People's Universities the activists came from in this case—were made aware of the challenge the project would represent. This was done in order to ensure that the activists would be supported in doing what was asked of them. The group sessions that took place three times a week also gave the activists a place where they could find a sympathetic ear, share their problems and find the encouragement they needed if necessary.

Combining different kinds of knowledge

There remained the intellectual challenge of the work. The regular attendance of a resource person in each group of activists—one half-day a week for a year and a half—provided a sense of stability. The task of this resource person26 was to give the activists basic methodological skills with regard to judgment, criticism, expression and writing. Because the tasks of the resource people and the pedagogical counselor to some extent overlapped, the counselor was able to concentrate primarily on the contributions the activists wanted to make to their research groups.

As the project progressed, particularly when the writing process began, it became apparent that everyone's attention had to be brought to bear on all the written texts. The activists thus had some responsibility for the writings of the Fourth World volunteer corps members and the academics. Knowledge-merging, and hence, knowledge-enrichment, could only come about if everyone respected the knowledge and abilities of other participants. No one was treated as the sole authority on any one area—this would have defeated the aim of the project—but to ensure that different types of knowledge were successfully integrated, everyone had to recognize that other people's roles were complementary to their own and that these roles were not interchangeable.

This complementarity was initially experienced within the pedagogical team, which is doubtless the reason it could be applied within the agent-author groups.

TOWARDS A MERGING OF KNOWLEDGE
by Patrick Brun

In 1965, J Wresinski wrote: "The poor person who is not considered in man's thinking will have no place in their communities." This prophetic statement could have served as the motto of the Fourth World–University project—as long as it is understood correctly. This project did not aim to bring learning to the very poor. Nor did it wish to educate them in the sense of cultivating their intellect according to fixed educational standards. The following statement serves to clarify: *As long as the poor are not listened to, as long as community planners do not learn from the poor and the world they live in, the measures taken to alleviate their situation will be erratic, superficial and short-term*[26]. This was not the kind of attention usually paid to the very poor, nor the usual way of listening to them. It was no longer a question of collecting their testimonies, nor of establishing some kind of diagnosis of their situation in order to help them. It was more to do with letting them speak to us in the fullest sense, of being moved by their words, of letting established "intelligence" be tested. It was about breaking down prejudice and letting the intellect, thoughts and points of view of the very poor re-educate society from the inside, of letting the poor express their own perception of humanity and the state of the world. This is what the History group called *turnaround.*

Turnaround is a deepening of the relation between society and the poor to form a new and more inclusive society of which they are a part (and no longer merely related to). As one of the Fourth World activists put it: "If universities do not open their doors to the views of the very poor, they are the poorer for it."

Thus, we all began a process of mutual questioning which lasted twenty-four months: academics, activists, Fourth World volunteer corps members and members of the pedagogical team (itself a microcosm of debates and the sounding board of the three other groups).

This taught us lessons that must be shared in a time when social divisions are roundly criticized.

To begin with, there can be no meeting between the three strands of knowledge[27]—that gained from life experience, that born of activism and that of academia—which is not a meeting of common human experience. Had we had started by discussing our differences, and attempted to communicate over the gap between us, we could not have agreed on definitions and analyses of situations. The time spent together, particularly during the seminars, allowed all the participants to discover their common fundamental human experiences. In this way, many academics re-remembered long-forgotten family troubles and experiences of feeling uprooted, personal trials and past commitments.

It was only then that the imagined preconceptions which the activists and academics in particular had erected between one another like screens could be lowered. In this context, the task of the pedagogical team was to create favorable conditions for meeting and provide catalysts for debate. Still, the principal difficulties remained: how could we come up with a common language and space within which each agent could feel comfortable and communicate their own experiences and reflections?

This was only possible through a process of simultaneous rapprochement and distancing which underlay the rhythms, rituals and procedures used for the production of knowledge and the writing process. The materials each participant brought became input into a melting-pot where different types of knowledge and interpretation could combine and define one another. By returning to their respective communities, each participant could revise the output and put it into their own words, allowing them to prepare future contributions. This was particularly relevant to the activists. Communication between participants, which was often threatened by unavoidable crises, was kept in motion by the pedagogical team. The importance of the pedagogical counselor who assisted the Fourth World activists can hardly be emphasized enough.

The most difficult stage, however, was still to come: putting down in writing each participant's contributions in a joint piece of work. The writing of the work became the crucible in which the different opinions and contributions of each participant or group thereof were to be forged into one, all the while remaining discernable as such. "A hundred times to the task (*Cent fois sur le métier*)"— Boileau's counsel was a relevant one in this instance. The texts had to be reread and rewritten many times, and corrected together and individually before arriving at the final product collected here.

The final product, unfortunately, cannot but reduce to an extent the differences between speech and writing. Writing often "smoothes out" the inherent roughness of the spoken word. No one felt, however, that they had been represented unjustly. Further attestation of this is that much of the synthesis of texts was done by the Fourth World activists, who showed an ability to integrate the thoughts of the other two groups without putting aside their own (although one might have bet on precisely the opposite occurring).

It was here that the pedagogical team played a most influential role. By creating a procedure that could be adjusted as the work progressed, they were able to intervene at the right moments in the transition from the spoken to the written word and in bringing together individual texts into a common written work.

"For once, they have not written about us without us," concluded one Fourth World activist. Now, the final test is to see whether the groups represented in this collaborative effort recognize their own priorities and values reflected in the pages of these memoirs.

It is hoped that this book will not simply stop here, but that the debates and discussions it provokes will be further developed within communities, schools and universities.

After all, is not the aim to create a more universal way of thinking, and thereby a more just society, where recognition of the Other becomes an integral part of the self? We hope this book and the experiences collected therein will contribute to furthering this aim.

Notes

1. The Center for Social Research would later become the Research and Training Institute.
2. Following this report, in 1995 the Roi Baudouin Foundation in Belgium compiled the General Report on Poverty commissioned by the federal government, in collaboration with the Union of Belgian Cities and Communes (CPAS and ATD Fourth World divisions). It was part of a process of mobilization and dialogue between those for whom poverty was an everyday reality, and those who came into contact with poverty and exclusion through their work.
3. J. Wresinski, *The thinking of the poor in a knowledge that leads to combat, 1980*, see annex p.
4. Cahiers de Baillet, J. Wresinski, *Echec à la misère*.
5. *Démocratie et Pauvreté*, Du Quatrième Ordre au Quart Monde, published by Editions Quart Monde, Albin Michel, 1991.
6. For family reasons, one female activist withdrew after a year.
7. See list of agent-authors, p. 8.
8. Pascale Cauchy (Caen), Josette David (Rennes), Josette Delmoitié (Brussels), Jean Dorzée (La Louvière) and Simone Noël (Lille)
9. c.f. list of members of the pedagogical team, p. 8.
10. c.f. list of members of the academic panel, p. 8.
11. Francoise Ferrand, *Et vous, que pensez vous? L'Université populaire Quart Monde*, published by Editions Quart Monde, 1996, 285 pp.
12. This refers more specifically to production of knowledge in the context of self-teaching or co-teaching: Courtois & Pineau, *La formation expérientielle des adultes*, published by La Documentation Française, 1991; Chartier & Lerbet, *La formation par production de savoirs*, published by L'Harmattan, 1993, 265 pp; *L'autoformation en chantiers*, in Revue Education Permanente, no. 122, 1995-1.
13. Quivy & Van Campenhoudt, *Manuel de recherche en Sciences Sociales*, published by Dunod, 1988.
14. Pascal Galvani, *Quête de sens et formation: anthropologie du blason et de l'autoformation*, published by L'Harmattan, 1997, 229 pp.
15. For more information about the *coat of arms meeting*, see P. Galvani, *Ibid.*, chapter two.
16. The framework was constructed around a central question. It consisted of research hypotheses and an analytical framework suitable for the chosen domain of study which would direct empirical research.
17. For more information on this procedure, see Peretti, Legrand and Boniface: *Techniques pour communiquer*, published by Hachette, 1994, pp. 64-67.
18. Lucie Ribert is an alias.
19. Emilie Bourtet is an alias.
20. The lectures discussed in each thematic group, keeping in mind the central research question. Certain excerpts were extracted and used.
21. Many examples of this are given in the "Methodology and Approach" chapters of the five memoirs: On many occasions, the activists instigated essential developments in research af-

ter having reread the decipherings of meetings.

22. See the chapters on Methodology for the central points dealt with in this exercise.
23. Bernard Charlot: *Du rapport au Savoir*, published by Anthropos, 1997, pp. 80-85.
24. Pineau & Legrand: *Les histoires de vie*, published by PUF, 1993, chapitre VII.; Schoen: *Le Praticien réflexif*, Montréal published by Logiques, 1994.
25. The procedure for these sessions was inspired by the following works: Donald Schoen: *Le tournant réflexif*, published by Logiques, 1966; Pierre Vemersch: *L'entretien d'explication*, published by. ESF, 1994.
26. All quotations taken from the Revue Quart Monde, No. 163, February 1998, pp. 2-4.
27. Knowledge that could be defined here as helping people to structure their thoughts and express them in a balanced way.

I

HISTORY:
FROM SHAME TO PRIDE

The journey from the shame of living in extreme poverty to the pride of belonging to a People

by Léon Cassiers, Françoise Digneffe, Daniel Le Breton,
Danielle Lebrun and Marie Jeanne Notermans
with help from Noëlle Stenegry
and the collaboration of
Françoise Ferrand and Pascal Galvani.

HISTORY: FROM SHAME TO PRIDE

Introduction

At the very beginning of this project, many participants insisted on the importance of the subject of history. Has a history of the poorest ever been written? Has the time come for the poorest to write it themselves? By trying to put down in writing some of the aspects of this history together, we understood that the poor were not the only ones involved.

Our approach was to try and understand what people living in poverty have to go through and to find out what gives their lives meaning. Societies are not made up of individuals simply living beside one another; they need meaning so that people can live together. During our research, we tried to establish how this meaning is derived for people living in poverty. We did not wish to assess the number of poor who have escaped poverty or those who are still living in it; nor did we want to investigate how long it takes to escape extreme poverty.

The history we wanted to write aims to understand how shame can turn into pride. We called this transition a "turnaround". Through readings, conducting and analyzing interviews and many hours of group discussions and contemplation, we have attempted to demonstrate the various stages of this turnaround, both on an individual and collective level. Not only have these efforts of understanding and consideration produced a piece of research, but they have also led to a change in all those involved.

Each "agent-author's" views on the chosen subject altered in the course of the research, action and training project. Each of us was forced to reconsider our relationships with others and with society in general. Our text aims to involve its readers in this turnaround too, making them active participants so that they can react to and feel part of the history that we experienced when researching and writing it.

In Chapter 1, we set out our research, providing some information about the way it was conducted. We describe the process and techniques that were used and point out some of the issues raised during the research period. Chapter 2 is devoted to a brief analysis of how the poorest have been regarded throughout history and how they are seen today, describing academics' views as well as those of people helping the poorest. We end the chapter by highlighting the consequences of these (mostly negative) views on the poorest themselves. Chapter 3 is entirely devoted to an understanding of poverty as expressed by the poorest themselves: their

experience of pain, shame and humiliation along with their strengths and qualities, evident in many of the testimonies collected. The fourth chapter represents
the core of our research. By looking at a number of experiences of poverty on an
individual level and in the family, we seek to highlight the importance of roots and
an awareness of one's origins in forming one's identity. We then analyze the various steps of turnaround that lead from shame to the pride of belonging to a people. This chapter also relates key moments in some of the Fourth World volunteer
corps members' own experience of turnaround (taken from accounts of their involvement) together with the turnaround of the academics taking part in the project. The fifth and final chapter focuses on the idea of a People and its significance
in the history of poverty. Based on a study of nineteenth century populist writers,
the activists drew a diagram explaining how a continuous and repeated transformation can lead people out of poverty to become the People of the Fourth World.

Chapter 1

THE GROUP'S APPROACH

The composition of our group and the goals we had set ourselves led us to come up with an original approach together which also conformed to academic norms. In this chapter we shall see how we defined our research subject and memoir outline and how we carried out the interviews and approached reading matter, both of which helped a great deal in testing our hypotheses and understanding some basic ideas, such as that of the People. We will end by saying a few words about the fundamental issues raised by members of our group which sparked important discussions and debates which were sometimes difficult and painful.

Defining the research subject

The need to investigate the history of the poor became immediately apparent so that this history could, for once, be written **with the poor**, in order for them to be able to give their point of view and research their own history. This was a recurring theme in most of the activists'* "coats of arms"*. As such, the issue of history immediately arose as a point of interest, all the more so because the two other groups of participants acknowledged its importance.

The two basic tasks were to explore the conditions and factors in the **journey from the shame of poverty to the pride of belonging to a people**, and the meaning which we would give to the word *people*, with relation to how the word is used within ATD Fourth World and also, in a broader sense, in the history of the poor. We hypothesized that understanding this **journey** and belonging to a **people** was intrinsic to understanding the history of the poorest.

The research brief

The aim of the research brief was twofold. First of all, it was important for all the participants to agree on the questions we had decided to tackle. In the draft research brief, the title was simply *From the shame of poverty to the pride of belonging to a people*. The words *History of a journey* were then added following questions from other groups. The changing of the central question concerning work from: *Does the experience of living in poverty allow us to be proud of belonging to a people?* to: *Does the people of poverty have a history which it can be proud of?* shows that what is important to us was really understanding how and in what ways the poor can gain dignity, pride and recognition. This question was reworded again in the final research brief, becoming: *How, under what conditions and in what stages, has the journey from the shame of poverty to the pride of belonging to the People of the Fourth World taken place?* The idea of belonging to the People of the Fourth World without knowing precisely what that meant was also more explicitly expressed at this juncture.

We decided upon six pairs of key-words: exclusion-belonging, contempt-dignity, shame-pride, injustice-justice, people-aspiration and view-turnaround. These words are opposite or complementary in meaning and give a sense of the direction of the research, of an evolution we shall try and describe, of an encounter which took place within the groups and three sub-groups of participants. In other words, what is described in the research also took place in the microcosm (or mini-world) of the History group.

Drawing up the memoir outline

The outline for our research was put together gradually in order to gain a deeper understanding of complex ideas such as that of *turnaround*, *of belonging to a People* and of shame and pride. Our goal was to render the experience of people living in extreme poverty both comprehensible and credible, since this experience shapes their lives. A further goal was to demonstrate how and why it is justified to speak of this experience in terms of belonging to a People. Finally, we aimed to investigate the meaning and constituent elements of the term *People* which, as we quickly realized, has numerous meanings.

It was also necessary to take account of the backgrounds in our working group itself. Relationships between group members and contrasting points of view made us aware of some aspects of the history of the poorest and their place in society. The final outline was thus the result of a series of proposals made by one of the academics as well as the activists, which were reviewed and discussed within the group and reformulated with the help of the pedagogical team.

Any consistency in the work now which was absent a year ago is thanks to the effort each individual participant undertook to enter into discussion, to make themselves understood by the other members, to find the right words and to develop ideas and the tools necessary for others to understand. In this respect, a defining moment in the research was the activists' work in formalizing their depiction of the People.

From the beginning of the project, one theme recurred in discussion. The activists stressed their belonging to a People of poverty or of the Fourth World (they recognized and resembled each other regardless of their various nationalities, languages etc.). The Fourth World volunteer corps member* also professed to belong to this People. The academics, for their part, asked for the specific nature of this idea of a People to be demonstrated in relation to the idea of social class. What is this feeling of belonging and identity based on? Who can say who belongs to which People? Following the lecture by Lucie Ribert (who spoke of her awareness of belonging to a People), the group discussions and in particular re-reading of the decipherings of group meetings, the activists made a distinction in their analysis between the *People of poverty* and the *People of the Fourth World.* The final chapter of our memoir recounts the analysis of this fundamental discovery.

Choosing and collecting data

The objective basis of the research was provided by several types of data: the method of working with dialogue and deciphering[2], the interviews[3], the individual accounts of turnaround and various texts dealing with the idea of the People.

Accounts of turnaround

On our first day together, the academics asked the other members of the group "What does being an activist mean to you?" The activists agreed to write an account of their own experiences of turnaround; that is, the moment(s) in their lives when they gained self-confidence and wanted to fight alongside others, those who were poor like they were. After writing this down, the academics and the Fourth World volunteer corps member volunteered to describe their own moments of turnaround; that is, the momentous events in their lives that had shaped them. Recounting personal life stories allowed us to feel on an equal footing within the group and served as a bonding experience ahead of the research we would carry out together. One activist later said: *It was then that I felt that everyone had something about them to discover, whatever background they were from. That was what created a great feeling of trust between us and made it possible for us to speak freely as a result.* These written accounts helped the group to work together freely and think collectively in spite of moments of disagreement on the research.

Researching the People

In June 1996, the activists wrote an initial text called: *What is it that enables us to recognize each other as People of the Fourth World?* In it they spoke of *the same suffering, the same humiliation, the same daily struggle and the opportunity to speak out.* From the very first day that the History group met, one of the key words in our subject was the term People. One academic suggested investigating why Father Joseph Wresinski* used the word People. The group as a whole progressed to a more in-depth understanding of the word. One academic suggested looking in history books, and the activists asked the people they interviewed if they felt they belonged to a People. The Fourth World volunteer corps member chose to apply her reading of the philosopher Lévinas to the question of what the Other means and belonging to one and the same humanity.

In November 1996, one academic discovered Alain Pessin's book *The Myth of the People and French Society in the Nineteenth Century*. She wrote a summary of it which she gave to the other members of the group. They worked with Pessin's text many times. The activists wrote their reactions to it. The group then produced a text on the idea of the People. Conceptions of the People as expressed by Pessin and Wresinski were then explored in tandem. The activists continued to work by drawing on life experiences and interviews to arrive at a precise definition of what the word *People* meant to them. At the January 1997 seminar, all the participants in the project were asked: *What does the word "People" mean to you?* The responses to this question helped the activists write another text on the definition of the word *People*, and this was discussed within the group. At the same time, a member of the Fourth World volunteer corps from another group gave us some research she had carried out on the vocabulary used by ATD Fourth World since its founding to describe very poor families.

Fundamental issues raised by the research

Our group was made up of three sub-groups: the activists, the Fourth World volunteer corps member and the academics. All members were agent-authors. We researched and we wrote together. Not only did we have to understand one another and express our beliefs, but each sub-group had to be able to take the memoir we had written together back to their peers and communicate it to them—to other academics, students, poor families and members of the Fourth World volunteer corps.

Understanding one another

Everyone had the chance to express themselves from the first meeting onwards. Our different life experiences were both a fertile resource and a difficulty in dialoguing. One academic set out some rules for group discussion:

> There is something very important between us. We must be able to say what bothers us, but we must also make a distinction between "That bothers me emotionally and I want to react" and "Why do I want to react in this way?" That is the work of the intellect, having a sense of distance between what bothers people and why this is so.

The activists asked the Fourth World volunteer corps member and academics to make their written texts readable and understandable. Time was allotted at each meeting to discuss the texts. Everyone had to make the effort to put themselves in the other's shoes. Our aim was that together we would be able to write something that could be understood by others. In understanding one another within the group, we were halfway there. From the beginning of the project, the relations between the activists and academics were established. The role of the Fourth World volunteer corps member in the group was tackled later.

Tensions between different experiences of poverty

The activists' contribution was based on poverty experienced from within. They live in poverty all year round and have often done so for generations. They know about the suffering caused by poverty and how the poor help one another. The Fourth World volunteer corps member contributed an understanding of what poor families told her and what she had seen herself. She was not a mere observer, but had also experienced and internalized what she had seen and observed with the poor. The academics gave the knowledge they had gained through their studies and professions. Tensions arose on three issues: who is entitled to speak about poverty? Does the way poverty is discussed vary depending on the audience? Who do we mean when we say *People*? The activists contradicted the academics' and Fourth World volunteer corps member's assertions on several occasions. For example, they disagreed with the ideas that the poor are not aware of the injustices they suffer and that the poor consider the rich as role models. They also objected to too many comparisons being made with the world of psychiatry.

Conflicts over the written texts

From the outset, everyone in the group was aware that the aim was to write a memoir. Everyone knew that writing is valuable, and that while spoken words are lost, written words remain. The activists said that it was the first time that the poor had written alongside academics using their own words and their own ideas drawn from their own experience.

The first conflicts in the group arose when comparing each member's written texts. For example, there was a disagreement with the definition of the word *People* given by one of the activists, and several times there were problems with the way poverty was described by an academic and the Fourth World volunteer corps member. The activists were bothered by the way the details of people's lives were discussed. *It strips them bare*, they said, *Do we really need to reveal everything about these people to understand poverty?* The activists said that it should be up to them to decide whether they wanted to discuss their lives in the context of the project. They had made a commitment to it, and were thus obliged to talk about their and their families' lives, but they did not feel able to do the same with other people's lives. In the interviews they carried out, they captured what the interviewees wanted to have expressed. One activist reacted to a text that had been written about her family written some time previously and which had offended her. *It is up to us to write what we want to, it's our lives,* she said. The Fourth World volunteer corps member felt this was due to a misunderstanding. As a member of the Fourth World volunteer corps, she had given an account of what she had seen and experienced. It is her responsibility to do so. It is her job to say that beyond the visible poverty in which so many families remain trapped and which cuts them off from other people, there is a humanity which allows us to realize that we are all part of the same family, the human race. The Fourth World volunteer corps member said that when she gave her accounts in public, she never did so without the permission of the family involved. She is involved with and committed to that family. The discussion was long and painful. Out of respect for the activists' feelings and her own views, she decided to withdraw a text she had written. The question of who is entitled to speak and write about poverty, and how, became a fundamental issue. It is directly related to our group's subject, it prompted much discussion and will be explored in more depth within this memoir.

We hope that the texts we present in this memoir are sufficiently compelling for the reader to feel something of what we experienced when carrying out the research, and that this will play its part in restoring dignity to the poor. In order to better convey this experience, the text is constructed in a non-traditional format, juxtaposing different writing styles such as informative, analytical, reflective, narrative, and even poetic on occasion. The use of the pronoun "we" is reserved to denote the group as the collective identity which we formed over the two years.

Notes
1. Lucie Ribert, see General Introduction.
2. Deciphering, see General Introduction.
3. Interviews, see General Introduction and Annex p.140.

Chapter 2

DIFFERENT VIEWPOINTS

The second chapter deals with the different external perceptions of the poorest; that is, the views shared by those who aid and assist them and by academics, both historically and today. We will develop this idea in order to consider the effects of these views on the poorest themselves.

How the poor have been viewed throughout history

Since this chapter deals with the ways in which the poor are perceived in our western societies, we will limit our remarks to some of the most striking features which can help us understand the way the poorest have been considered. Particular attention will be paid to those views which have most affected the poor themselves, which have left them feeling belittled or, on the other hand, accepted. Essentially, therefore, it is the depiction of them as symbols of exclusion, and more rarely dignity, which we have attempted to pinpoint throughout history[1].

Poverty is often said to have been exalted in the Middle Ages. In reality, it was a voluntary form of poverty that was held in high esteem, such as that of St Francis of Assisi. But involuntary poverty was already regarded with contempt, even by a writer like St Augustine, who writes of the poor "who have no shame, not even to beg[2]". In paintings and images, the poor were always depicted on the rich man's doorstep, humble and beseeching. Castel writes that from the fourteenth to the eighteenth centuries, the poor and beggars were given names brimming with contempt and rejection: in French they were "gueux», in English «rogues», in German «abenteurer", and in Spanish „picaros", and rascals, villains, whores, etc. All these names were attributed to wanderers, criminals, and prostitutes. These individuals formed the most vulnerable group in society and yet could not gain the recognition of the society of the day.

In the eighteenth and nineteenth centuries, a new society emerged and the poor essentially became the superfluous workers, those, as Marx would say, "whose strength was not necessary to the development of capitalism". They were in a state of chronic poverty, the underbelly of society, the "Lumpenproletariat" (the proletariat in rags).

They were seen as dangerous individuals, as potential criminals, and as "ignorant and vicious". Poverty was said to turn people back into a wild state, to affect not only their bodies but their souls as well. In this context, where poverty was associated with vice, nineteenth century philanthropists, instead of acknowledging the real causes of poverty and undertaking to struggle against them, attempted to "moralize" this population and make them accept their lot in life[3]. The result of this was that a gap grew between the good poor, who were submissive, docile and often physically disabled, and the bad poor, who refused this label and treatment, and who in one way or another rebelled against them.

During the nineteenth century, another social group, though not poor economically speaking, was subject to less attention, but was nevertheless treated with contempt. These were people who made a living as rag-and-bone men, collectors of cigar-ends, chickweed pickers etc. These trades endured for some time alongside industrialization, and were practiced by those on the margins of society who, though not necessarily poor, were devoid of any status, power or dignity. Labbens writes that: They belonged to another people who made a living out of society's waste, and were considered as scrap by that very same society[4].

By the 1960s and 70s, the poor in an allegedly affluent society had lost these jobs, which were no longer economically viable, and found themselves deprived of finances, status and power. Though they had begun accumulating certain rights, they were moved to shanty-towns which were soon replaced by temporary residences for those who did not have access to social housing. They remained on the margins of society, dependent on the good will of the benefit system to have their rights respected. All the while, the same discriminating way of viewing the poor persisted: the submissive poor, those who accepted submission and humiliation, were seen as the good poor and though they were still treated with contempt, they were at least granted some attention. Those that did not fall into this category, on the other hand, were seen to represent insecurity. They were feared, and were to be watched and controlled. Their children were taken into care, the authorities hoping thereby to neutralize them as a potential threat.

In today's society, people tend to be separated into winners and losers[5]. This cult of achievement results in the exclusion of those who do not find a role in modern society, yet the number of people living in poverty is increasing, along with the number of the marginalized (poor and newly poor people). This could well destabilize society itself, and force it to concede the existence of values besides those of success and achievement[6].

Though today we are campaigning for the poorest to be accorded dignity so that they may be given a place in society, one must bear in mind that since the birth of democracy, the French Revolution, they have not been granted this place.

Only a few have demanded it. One of these was Dufourny de Villiers, who wondered, "why the poor are not considered among us as human beings, brothers, Frenchmen"[7]. In this way, even before the populists (who we will discuss later), De Villiers insisted on the role of the poorest and on society's obligation to acknowledge their dignity.

How the poor are viewed in today's society

It would seem impossible to speak of the way in which the poor are viewed by today's ("successful") society without surveying, even briefly, our values system.

The dominant culture

The recent fall of Communism has brought to an end a century in which collectivist ideologies subsumed the individual in pursuing the goals of the whole of society. We no longer have a plan for the ideal society; no utopia seems worthy of devoting or even sacrificing our lives for. Instead, the ideal has become individual fulfillment, success in one's own life. There are positive aspects to this development: human rights, the dignity of the individual, and a democratic political system, which are all to be lauded; but there are also negative sides to a win-at-all-costs capitalism which exalts personal initiative, physical health, intellectual mettle, output, efficiency and competitiveness. According to this way of thinking, human success is judged by visible, material success. This lesson is drummed into us daily by the intense media coverage of celebrities.

The priority paid to all that is measurable and scientifically identified compounds this vision of humanity. It becomes difficult, in this context, to demonstrate or defend values such as emotion, an inner life or spirituality (whether religious or not). It is even more difficult to praise the values specific to poverty.

Someone who is poor is a weakling who has failed, liable to be seen as physically and especially mentally deficient: lacking ability, lacking enterprise, neither intellectually nor economically capable, the opposite of a "winner". The prevailing culture regards this as economically, socially, physically and sometimes even genetically inevitable. Moreover, the sight of the poor in adversity is frightening and their potential for violence is feared. At best, those images can make the prosperous feel they have a duty to take charge of those who are weaker than themselves. But this again consigns the poor to an image of powerlessness. How could they possibly not feel ashamed at this?

This short sketch is very broad in scope and should, ideally, be both bolstered with examples and further developed, but this would go beyond the scope of the subject. It nevertheless seemed necessary to us to provide this general social backdrop to our writing. We believe that readers will have no problems identifying various illustrations of this in their own lives.

How the poor are viewed by those who help them

Society's view of the poorest and most deprived people essentially focuses on what they lack: their lack of money, food, clothing, decent housing, education, participation in public life; the list goes on. Above all, it is these shortcomings which make the poor appear as failures and on a lower level than that of the observer.

This perception is obviously not without effect, and the most appropriate response always seems to be assistance and aid, whether professional or not. The fact remains that this response merely conforms to the dynamic of the relationship as it is perceived. The relationship between poor people who lack what others have and an individual or institution which comes to their aid is essentially unequal. It is not surprising that on the whole, our western societies have so often acted rather paternalistically, even if, under the influence of new disciplines such as human sciences, psychologists and psychiatrists have often replaced policemen and jailers.

In this context, relationships are unequal and the main movement is from the haves towards the have-nots, from those who know to those who do not, from the strong to the weak, etc. Thus, in the field of aid and assistance, the 'restos du cœur' are the contemporary equivalent of the soup-kitchen a hundred years ago. One activist told us: "Though I go to the 'restos du cœur', I do it because I have to. I don't like going."

> In counterpoint to this, in a bitingly ironic text, Frédérich Dard writes[8]:
> Patient is the poor man, he expects nothing.
> Doesn't laugh much, for he's hopeless.
> Lives in the present, no future or past to speak of.
> Just like a sea-lion, he'll clap his paws if you throw him a dried fish
> Asks for nothing from those who have everything, and just a bit of bread from those with a little
> He is so undemanding that any abandoned porch or any metro corridor
> will do for the night.
> The night is his bedroom, and the street is his dining room.
> He's best at going unnoticed, but if you do happen to see him, he doesn't mind
> Posing for an "authentic" photo.
> . . .

How the poor are viewed by academics

We do not intend to examine here every academic hypothesis in order to try and explain poverty or to describe the characteristics of the poorest. Our focus is on the "view" underpinning most of these studies; that is, the presuppositions or even prejudices that guide them. Indeed, it is this very view that directly concerns our subject.

It is well known that sociological or psychological studies carry a risk of conveying a determinist and mechanistic image of human beings, as if they were objects, and this has often been heavily criticized. Observations, questionnaires and statistics highlight various factors that "force" their subjects to think and act in various ways. For example, such studies show that extreme poverty alters one's sense of time and long-term planning, or that it engenders inconsistent behavior, violence and alcoholism etc. There are very few researchers who, like Paugam or Charlot, endeavor to show how individuals facing the real adversity of poverty react according to their own freedom and values, to protect their fundamental dignity.

This applies more widely to the poor than to the rich, for the former are more often the subjects of studies. As Paugam says: These mechanisms can more easily be observed and understood by sociologists in the case of economically and socially deprived populations given that their inferiority and failures are acknowledged by specialized institutions. That is to say, institutions founded and run by the more affluent part of society. Thus, the poor are more often presented by academics as lacking freedom—and therefore dignity—than the rich.

In the same way, most studies, even the best-intentioned, frequently use what we call the vocabulary of misfortune. They speak of fragility, dependence, marginality, social misfits and exclusion. Indeed, in trying to help the poorest, one naturally uses words that describe them as weak and disabled without realizing that this maintains an exclusively negative image of poverty and of the poorest. The activists in our group took offence several times at the one-sided language used to describe the poorest.

This was something Father Joseph Wresinski understood well. He was fully aware of the suffering and needs engendered by poverty. He hoped that academics would help him understand how to combat it and the damage it does. Yet he was exasperated by the words used to describe the poorest and the names they were given, and by the misunderstanding that these words revealed.

This is a misunderstanding on two counts. Firstly, it often fails to comprehend the **deeper significance of behavior** that is usually disapproved of by the middle class. And secondly, beyond sufferings and needs, it completely excludes the **positive aspect of the poor**. It is testament to Father Joseph Wresinski's originality of thinking that he avoided falling into either of these traps.

The deeper significance of people's behavior. Many of those features which researchers and the middle classes (from which they generally come) see as pointing to a lack of consistency, intelligence and even morality amongst the poor can—when we listen to those directly concerned—be understood as means of personal or collective survival mechanisms, and often the only option possible. Spending time with and listening to people facing poverty makes it possible to understand that they lack neither intelligence nor moral principles; in fact quite the contrary is true. Those who provide this kind of support are unanimous on this, but it is very rare that academic studies are based on such close proximity.

The criteria upon which the poorest are judged remain those of the middle classes, inevitably creating a negative image of the poorest in studies, which, however well-intentioned, continue to stigmatize them.

The positive aspect of the poor. In most studies, any focus on poverty is usually restricted to the damage that it can wreak on individuals and on their behavior, and there does not seem to be any positive dimension. While we may sometimes talk about solidarity amongst the poorest—the power and complexity of which are often misunderstood—we hardly ever talk about their energy and their resilience in the face of constant precariousness, their ingenuity, their own positive way of interpreting family values, their children, sexuality, money, or their social relationships etc. Few researchers recognize their own failure to understand the language, customs, world-vision and what we could call philosophy of the poor. Instead, they base their research on their own ideas, never thinking that they might actually have something to learn from the poor. We may be wrong on this, but it seems to us that too few studies aim to teach those from affluent backgrounds what it means to live in enduring poverty.

Finally, we must consider the question of why these studies are carried out and who the target audience is. It is evident that research is almost always carried out by and for the middle classes. Although the use made of them is in the interests of the poor, the latter have no involvement or input in either the process or on its consequences. Traditional research thus keeps the poor in a state of dependency on the well-to-do regarding the intellectual view of their destiny. We emphasize this since it is precisely one of the achievements of this project that every stage of this research was carried out with the active, even dominant participation of people who had lived in poverty.

In short, we think that, although they unquestionably raise some interesting points in various fields, most academic studies on poverty and the poor are characterized by the mistake of exclusively describing an outside perception of poverty without giving sufficient regard to how the poor understand their own situation. These studies therefore unconsciously emphasize the undignified image of inferiority in which the poor are trapped.

We also encountered this issue in what throughout our work we have called knowledge-merging between activists, members of the Fourth World volunteer corps and academics. The issues above arose within our discussions and in many hours of group work. We had to revise our views of one another and dismantle numerous prejudices which we were unaware we had in order to experience a human relationship within which each of us had something to learn from the other on an equal footing.

The effects of these views on the poorest

We frequently hear comments in this vein: It's not just that they're poor, but the father drinks as well, and they shout, and their children steal and their eldest smokes. . . .

Taking children into care

From the outside, the simplest and most effective solution to protect children may appear to be to remove them from the family circle. However, once deprived of affection from their parents or brothers and sisters, children do not understand what is happening to them and, to conceal their vulnerability, often withdraw into their shells or become aggressive towards those around them. Whilst growing up, the other children in care become their role models. Petty thievery, such as shoplifting, becomes their way of escaping the overly-rigid life deprived of affection that has been imposed on them. It does not take long before they and their friends have dealings with the law. Rebellion sometimes progresses to stealing mopeds, then cars, and then come jail sentences. Sometimes, children are returned to their parents as teenagers, the most difficult age, having lost all emotional ties to them. They live with their parents for a while, but then living under the same roof soon becomes unbearable. They find themselves on the streets and quickly move in with somebody else. Very often, this person has also spent time in care and the pair of them soon come under fire for not being able to run a household, but this itself is a consequence of having spent time in care.

In the event of a care order, parents, deprived of their children, lose heart and then break down, all the more reason for social services not to listen to them. Alcohol is often the only refuge that enables them to forget all the troubles they cannot share with anybody. If their family situation does not improve, their daily alcohol consumption increases to the point where it becomes an illness.

Scant financial resources are often not enough to pay the bills—rent, electricity, water etc. When the bailiff comes to repossess their property, physical or verbal aggression is their only option. This results in admission to a psychiatric hospital and medical treatment or a prison sentence.

The poor have two options: to shut themselves away or fight

From elementary school onwards, the children of very poor families are often pushed into special schools, where they end up with other children from the same background because they cannot keep up at school, a consequence of their living conditions. The disapproval with which others regard their parents is reflected upon them, and they end up considering themselves incapable of learning like everybody else. Aggression becomes their defense and they grow up expressing this aggression towards society, themselves or their background.

The poorest find it difficult to defend themselves against society. They constantly feel guilty. They have neither the self-confidence nor can they find the right words to explain their situation, even when they are within their rights to do so, be it to their landlord, a teacher or a social worker. *We get carried away, worked up, and we are labeled as coarse people who can't be talked to*[**9].

Disapproving attitudes towards people living in poverty can result in self-destructive behavior, the outward signs of which are alcohol, drugs and self-harm.

Sometimes they even turn their aggression on those closest to them, those weaker than they, which can lead to violence that itself can have tragic consequences. For instance, John let a friend of his son's stay in their home for a while. As the two young men had nothing else to do, they passed the time by drinking. The son's friend often insulted John. One day, when he could no longer put up with this humiliation in front of his own son, John threatened the friend, but to no effect, so John shot him. Grief-stricken at what had happened, and because he had never been a violent man, John gave himself up immediately and received a prison sentence.

Society blames the poorest for their aggression. But it confuses aggression with unmotivated violence. In fact, aggression is the only defense the poorest have, the only way they have left to prove they are alive. When this spark of reaction is gone, shutting themselves away is the only alternative. The fear of being judged paralyzes them. Some mothers of poor families remain shut up indoors for years without going out, seeing only the few people who still visit them.

Sometimes, there are differences in how the different members of a family are viewed. For instance, in one village, while the mother of one very poor family is called "shabby" and the daughters "filthy", the father is perceived as "brave". People always ask him to lend them a hand—setting up stalls for a fete, picking grass, looking after animals. He always does it for free. The family only goes out together after nightfall so as to avoid being stared at.

Notes

1. Works referred to: R Bertaux, Pauvres et marginaux dans la société française, Nancy University Press, Paris, 1994; R Castel, La m étamorphose de la question sociale, Fayard, Paris, 1995; S Paugram (ed.), L'exclusion l'état des savoirs, La Découverte, Paris; J Labbens, Sociologie de la pauvreté, Gallimard, Paris 1978.
2. R Castel, op cit. p. 46.
3. P Buret, de la misère des classes laborieuses en Angleterre et en France, Société typographique Belge, Brussels, adapted by Wahlen and company, 1842.
4. J Labbens op cit. p. 206.
5. V de Gaulejac, I Taboada Léonetti, La lutte des places, Marseille, Hommes et perspectives, Desclée de Brouwer, Paris 1994.
6. R Castel, Les marginaux dans l'histoire, in S Paugam, op cit. p. 38.
7. M Dufourny de Villiers, Cahiers du quatrième ordre, no. 1, 25 April 1789.
8. Preface to F Dard, Portrait des restos du Coeur, edited Pierre Olivieri, 1992.
9. Sentences ending in ** are extracts from group discussions or personal writings.

Chapter 3

UNDERSTANDING POVERTY
FROM WITHIN

In this chapter, another image is presented, that of "poverty seen from within" in all its complexity and richness. Far from seeking pity or assistance, it asks to be recognized for what it is, with its strengths and weaknesses, solidarity and courage. Analysis of interviews and activists' personal experience shows that suffering, shame, humiliation, values and strengths can all be found within poverty.

Suffering

The dictionary definition of suffering is "physical or emotional pain". Suffering is experienced by people from all social backgrounds, for example because of a long illness or the death of a loved one. What kind of suffering are we alluding to when talking about that linked to poverty?

Poor living conditions (housing, resources etc) can cause physical scars from childhood onwards. Lucie Ribert[1] recalled:

> We had to fetch water from a kilometer away. It was OK in summer, but in winter we couldn't get up to the spring because the path was steep. . . . We had to carry water in cans, one in each hand. Washing ourselves and our clothes and going to school was a nightmare. There were times when I didn't go to school because I didn't have any shoes. Other times, we didn't go because we didn't have anything to eat that day. I don't want to sound self-pitying, but that's how it was. That's what it was like for us.

Lucie's family is in no way unique and, even though certain conditions may have been improved, some children and adults still suffer from the cold, hunger and a lack of money. They are tired and worn out by the age of 40 or 50.

The physical suffering caused by poverty is obvious, since poverty is often defined as a lack of material resources, but there are other aspects of poverty that are only known about by those living in such conditions. For example, many women living in poverty devote their whole lives to their children as they know that this is the only way of holding the family together. Unlike the men who sometimes assume this same responsibility, the women often suffer from profound loneliness.

Very poor women cannot imagine life without children. Véronique is from a poor family and learned that she was unable to have children after she was married. She tried her luck with all the medical options, but to no avail. This inability wounded her physically and emotionally, since she knew that because of her social background she would never be allowed to adopt a child. She experienced one bout of depression after another and fell into self-destructive alcohol abuse. Sometimes she said that this pain, added to that of her childhood, was God's punishment. In these tough situations, hardly able to endure this suffering, God seems the only person left to talk to: Why is this happening to me? God, why are you doing this to me?**

Those living in poverty know that it is not simply a question of enduring a painful event once in their lifetime, but of suffering from an accumulation of misfortunes from early childhood onwards, and this is what distinguishes them from people from other backgrounds.

> I reckon I started suffering in my mother's womb. I must have felt the blows she got.**

Another woman looked back at her first childhood memories, of when she was put into care at the age of four:

> I've gone everywhere to try and forget it, but it follows you round all the time. They wanted to show me the place where I was born, where my parents fought to keep me with them. I went there once, I saw the house and I said: "I'll never come here again". It was too painful. My parents put up a fight when "they" (the social services) came to take us away. My mother held me in her arms and yelled. "No, don't take my child away." The more time passes, the more I remember. It's something you never forget[2].

The wounds sustained in childhood never really heal.

> I'll never forget what I had to go through between the ages of 9 and 13. I was lied to, everything fell apart in my head. I knew it was over back then. Nobody had faith in me when I was young, so I lost all faith in myself.**

The man above had been placed in a foster family as a child who considered and treated him like a son. At the age of nine, he was sent on a holiday camp and when he returned he was taken into another foster family without being told why and where he had to slave away on a farm.

Echoing this, one woman related:

> My brothers and sisters and I were lied to. We were taken away in this kind of ambulance. We were all made to lie down, not even allowed to look out the windows.

They told us: "We're taking you to your father's", but we ended up being separated and sent to different homes. I was nine years old. All of a sudden, I had no family life any more. I was cut off from everything.**

A ruined childhood ruins the future adult, who will remain tormented, doubting his own abilities and distrusting other people. This can occur, for example, when social services give the parents a bad name in order to justify care orders. A woman who was taken into care as a child was told that her parents were incapable of taking care of her and her brothers and sisters, whereas she in fact remembers her father as a nature-lover who shared his passion with his children. Because she tried to get back to her father by running away from the boarding house where she had been taken in, she was locked up in a cell for one week in the dark, with an armored door, and I was fed through a trapdoor. I was in quarantine; nobody was allowed to talk to me. All of that was punishment. In addition to being told lies, they break you down.**

A child who has been lied to holds on to these lies deep down inside, and grows up unable to distinguish between right and wrong, truth and lies. They become an adult with two different sides (good and bad) and live in what becomes their own lie with a split personality. This is why people who have experienced poverty are difficult to get to grips with and understand. The part of them which is most visible—their outer appearance—leads to negative judgments. For instance, Lucie said:

My father died in 1973. I need to talk about it today because it's something that's been painful for a long time. He died in a bar, but that was just a coincidence as he'd just stopped by for a glass of wine. He didn't tend to drink much because my grandpa was an alcoholic. He raised his glass, tasted the wine and said he didn't feel well. Then he dropped dead of a heart attack. Afterwards, everyone said that my father died in a bar because he drank too much. I couldn't bear it [3] .

One woman was just as misunderstood while she was alive. Her daughter set things straight:

My mother had an unpleasant appearance. She looked wicked. Her features made her look nasty. She guarded her children like a she-wolf; and wouldn't let anyone touch them. She turned mistrustful. So those who weren't so poor misjudged her. Like the people from every poor family I've known, she wasn't easy to get on with. These families are aggressive so as to protect themselves. They are sparing with their friendship and love.

I remember all this love my mother gave to us, her family, and that we, her children, were the only ones to know about. She used to recite poems by Victor Hugo that I still remember now at 46. She used to cook my mud pies in the oven—it was a game we played, she and I. She liked playing games with us, like dominoes. To make my brother and me go to sleep when it was all grey and dark and cold outside, she would take us in her bed, one of us under each arm, and we would pretend to go on a train journey with her through the imaginary landscapes that she invented. I remember her tenderness when she explained that we children had to love each other. She expected nothing in return and gave the little she had to us and the other poor children. She did it in secret.

I think she must've suffered from being misunderstood, like other poor women—because of the physical poverty that showed in their eyes, their voices and their appearance. Alcohol sometimes made her believe she could forget her cares. I've always liked this kind of woman. When you do get close to them, they are the truest, nicest and most honest with their feelings. People who use a lot of fancy words are always showing off, but when very poor people give you their trust you'll have it forever as long as you respect them. I learned this from my mother. She certainly taught me that the philosophy of the poor is to always remain true.**

Another woman instinctively defended other very poor families' children. In a poor community, suffering is shared secretly since it is experienced by all.

We want to help and support each other but, not knowing our own limits, it often ends up being too much for us. For example, giving some homeless people a room makes our situation worse and leads to more misunderstanding and criticism from people living outside poverty.**

This extreme sensitivity to other people's suffering often has tragic consequences. Having lived in poverty enables one to understand and share with people living in the same conditions, but it does not provide the means to solve problems such as housing, money or employment etc.

We suffer from situations we can't do anything about, either for our children or for others. Although we are aware of the injustice, we feel powerless because of our vulnerability.**

Pains that are deeply graven in poor people's hearts are rarely expressed, or only in veiled terms. Perhaps it was because Father Joseph Wresinski had himself experienced the suffering caused by chronic poverty from his earliest childhood that he wrote that the poor should always be able to say to those who join them in their struggle against poverty that:

You can do all you want, but you will never be able to understand because you haven't experienced what we are going through[4].

Echoing this, an activist[5] testified:

Because we've gone through childhood together, shared friendships, suffering and common values, because we've lived the same sort of life, we usually marry among one another. The poorest marry like this in order to start a home and stop being a burden on their parents, to be free. They love each other. They know that they'd be criticized in other social circles for their lack of culture, knowledge and foresight.

We get married to start a better life than the one we've had so far because of the care orders, separation from our parents and lack of love. Our children are the greatest blessing, so we give them what we didn't have, hoping that things will improve with time. As long as we have the means to think and live, material possessions are not the greatest of our worries.

Our children won't go hungry or cold. And if need be, we'll steal for our kids. We won't criticize our husband even if he gets drunk or has no work, because we're able to understand how hard life is in this world and that, whatever happens, we'll stick together. We also know what we hold dear in life. It's so fragile.

We won't ever try and accumulate wealth, but simply live from day to day, not because we are naive, but because living in a family and keeping it together is a daily struggle in itself, one we are prepared to face together.

We want our children to succeed at school like anybody else, but even this we can't predict, as we never predict anything in advance. We trust one another. That's the way it is.

We know how to accept happiness as well as sorrow. All our life will be a challenge full of joys, sorrows and shortcomings.

Like everyone else, we too wish for happiness, even if it doesn't often knock on our door. We face reality, whatever form it takes.

This is our background and we don't turn our backs on it.

Shame and humiliation

Shame has built up inside me like a kind of education.**

Poverty is humiliating because people from affluent backgrounds, who do not understand us, look down on us.**

Shame is a central theme in our study. It goes hand in hand with the experience of poverty. It is therefore important to explain how it is experienced, why it is in itself a form of suffering that is passed on to others and how it can also impede action to combat poverty.

As we have already seen, poverty itself is a form of suffering in our societies. We can say that shame is an additional form of suffering, which is intimately linked to the way one is perceived by others. Well-to-do people tend to misunderstand, show contempt for and perhaps also fear of poverty, leading them to humiliate those who are not like them, whether they mean to or not.

The *Robert* Dictionary defines "humiliation" as "degrading, crushing, mortifying actions".

In their statements, the people living in poverty explain that since their childhood they have felt crushed for being different to the rest of society, and that this humiliation often engenders shame, a "painful feeling of inferiority and indignity in front of others".

In his book, *The Sources of Shame*, Vincent de Gaulejac[6] devotes a chapter to the relationship between shame and poverty. This chapter, as well as the statements gathered in interviews, gives an understanding of how the feeling of shame can overwhelm poor people's lives from childhood on.

First of all comes the shame of seeing oneself and of being seen by others as someone different because one does not have all that others have.

> What humiliated me was the fact that we couldn't afford to buy white notebooks so Sister Anna made me notebooks out of old grey paper[7].

Children who have no money cannot buy the same things as others and are therefore unable to be like them. Sometimes this shame can be directly triggered by an adult who points out their difference.

> Because we were travelers, the schoolmistress put us at the back of the room. The other children laughed at us. They called us "dirty gypos". My brothers and sisters and I would huddle together to protect ourselves from their attacks. It's really hard for children to brush off such shame and humiliation, they can't just forget it.**

There is also the feeling of being ashamed of loved ones the way others view them.

> I remember this time when I was at the same school as my sister, and the schoolmistress was ill. All the sisters were gathered together but I was crying because all the other girls had gotten their little sisters and mine didn't want to admit that I was her sister because I was badly dressed.
>
> I remember being ashamed of my mother when she came to the school and didn't act her normal self. I shouldn't have been ashamed because I loved her, I really did, but the way other people looked at her changed everything in my head.**

As early as childhood and school, other people's views can crush, shatter and even come between parents and children or brothers and sisters. A perceived difference and a feeling of inferiority can be experienced as exclusion and can have all kinds of consequences which dog those who endure it throughout their lives, such as isolation, fear of others and the feeling of being what others think you are. Children living in poverty soon see their parents presented in a negative light. They are overwhelmed by anger toward the parent, who is despised by others and incapable of protecting the child. At the same time, however, they feel guilty for having these feelings and feel they cannot possibly hate them because they love them.

It is mainly in the way others view you that the esteem in which you are held can be measured[8], writes Vincent de Gaulejac. Children can feel torn in two by the constant fluctuation between their love for their parents and their feeling of shame at other people's views of them.

> – I fought that shame but I was never able to get rid of it. It was as if it was stuck to me.**

> – If poverty was not seen as totally negative, you wouldn't feel the same shame and you wouldn't be ashamed of what your parents or grand-parents did.**

It is not just poverty in itself but, rather, the perception of it that brings shame.

Shame can sometimes lead to violence, fighting or attempts to escape. Sometimes people hide away and become depressed. Shame makes people unhappy, even more so than financial worries.

> When I was a schoolgirl, I wasn't allowed to hang my coat next to the others' in case they caught lice. My peg was the last one. I was ashamed of this, so I was always the very last one to leave the hall. My shame caused me to stay on my own and cut myself off.**

As we have seen, poverty in itself does not cause shame. But in order to survive, poor people are often forced to do humiliating things. Having to depend on others' help, on charity or on the social services causes shame.

> You have to force yourself to go and ask for something, for food or medical care or a free bus pass. It's humiliating for us to be made to beg for help like this.**

What causes shame here—not only in front of other people but actually towards oneself—is a feeling of dependence, a lack of self-sufficiency, a feeling of not being able to get by alone. The poor cannot express their feelings of injustice because they are expected to be grateful and say thank you. Vincent de Gaulejac writes that *All this humiliation assaults children like psychological blows*[9]. Even if the social services in our societies make sure that people do not starve to death and receive a minimum allowance to live on, those people have to queue and jump through all sorts of bureaucratic hoops, all the while suspected of being "moochers".

> Nowadays, when you really need a piece of bread you have to go through a social worker, just for a piece of bread or a jar of jam. Too many people have been abusing the system, so you have to go and see the social worker first[10] .

We have by no means exhausted the list of examples of poverty-related suffering which is principally caused by the perception of poverty by a society which fears it. What is important to remember is that this humiliation and shame causes yet more suffering on top of the difficulties directly linked to living in poverty. This form of suffering is often considered the most difficult to endure. Some speak of "mental poverty" as well as "physical poverty".

The effects of shame are also significant and almost always devastating. Though indignity may spark renewed pride in some and lead them to take up the challenge to do the impossible and fight against it, it may also, as far as isolated individuals or families are concerned, compound their loneliness and force them to hide, lie and avoid being seen by people who view them with contempt. We have observed that people must fight this shame together; that together they must stand up and claim their dignity as human beings. The path that can lead people to be proud of what they are, and the necessary requirements to walk it, will be described in the following chapters.

Values and strengths

The poorest rarely have a chance to express their innermost strengths. For many, these lie within their spirituality. One activist recalls:

My mother was very pious and expressed this within our family. She taught us about the life of Saint Theresa of Lisieux because she was from Normandy and Lisieux was her life. When my sister was in hospital, she told her to "pray, my daughter" and gave her a little medal of Saint Theresa. My parents married in church at the age of 75. My father wanted to give my mother the same union that she had never lost with God. We are very religious too, even if our faith is not always recognized by others. But we don't care because God knows who we are.

We are criticized for not being able to pray with the others, as if faith is something that can be learned. But it's deep inside us, even though our poverty prevents us from expressing it. Maybe most of the other poor people don't know the Gospels either, like me. But they do pray to God every day in times of suffering, and thank Him in times of happiness. This may not be conventional faith, but it is a faith that's deep down in everyone and that we should have the right to express.

Some people say they don't go to church because they feel that the traditional Church isn't for them, especially when it's crowded. Some say, "I pray when the church is empty. I feel closer to God and the Saints, I light a candle for them and we commune together". We can't be with people who aren't from our poor background, as it makes us feel misjudged and out of place.**

The following text is not written in the same way as the rest of our text and analyses, nor is it simply a product of the imagination. When analyzing the transcripts of our discussions, we picked out the words which revealed strengths or values in situations of extreme poverty and put them into the following, rather more poetic register[11] :

Will the whole world ever hear shame and humiliation?
Will it ever see the suffering . . .
The suffering
Of those who *refuse* to let their children go hungry,
Or be condemned to live in poverty?

Will the world ever acknowledge the incessant struggle,
The incessant struggle
Of every man and every woman in extreme poverty,
A struggle hindered by wandering and insolvency,
Hindered by hunger and cold,
Hindered by shabby housing?
Will the world ever believe,
Believe in the love these parents have for their children?
Will it finally recognize the love
In the gestures of these broken families
Who never lose the will to exist?

Gestures of *courage* from mothers and fathers for their children,
With the *hope* deep down,
The hope that gives them the *strength to fight,*
The *strength to survive.*

Gestures of shame and humiliation,
Because they cannot bear
Not being able to give the best of themselves,
Because they are too just and too proud
To tolerate their family having to live in poverty.

Will the world ever hear, ever see?
Children learn to *refuse every day to accept*
The inevitability of poverty.
They learn why you cry,
The reasons why you shout
Their parents teach them what love is
A love which gives the strength to carry on,
A love which tells them not to give up.
The daily fight for survival,
The daily fight for life:
Children to feed, children to clothe,
Children to bring up.
Being exploited, doing odd jobs,
Being driven to let your children beg,
Letting them work too young.
Living on handouts,
Living on cast-offs.
Paying the price for the hunger of their children with tears,
Paying the price for the lives their children lead with sorrow,
Humiliated, but keeping *their pride,*
Tired, but holding up under *their fatigue,*
They are alive and their life is an appeal to humanity.

In the midst of life with nothing but poverty all around,
Where everything is distorted,
Everything hints at a world in search of itself.
Shame is the sign of a forgotten world,
Poverty is an open wound
In a world that has forgotten how to love.

People of the world . . .
Don't they go out of their way to avoid poverty?
And when they do come across it, do they know what to say?
Poverty must be unearthed,
It must be searched for wherever it is:

The poor, the sick, the prisoners,
The tortured, the crushed, the exploited.
They are the ones who will teach us how to love.
Yet these parents across the world go unknown,
Those mothers who can go without food for days
Yet manage to feed their starving children.

We disregard those who have worn
Nothing by hand-me-downs.
Do we know what it means
Never to have chosen the clothes on their backs?
"I sell things to feed my family,
and then, when we were really down,
I rummaged through garbage cans."
To keep the child happy with the little we have,
To hide the husband's *shame* when he can't work.
To shun the family, the children,
Because he can no longer bear being a bad father?
Poor people's humble gestures that we don't know . . .
Finding the *courage* lost the day before,
Rebuilding the family at all costs
When anyone else would have
Given up long ago . . .

The poorest make us feel,
They take us to the very limit of hope,
They hope for a brighter future,
A future which is not broken,
They can still amaze the world,
They can invent
And make us invent ways to free ourselves
If we have the imagination
To assure them that they do count
To assure them that they can teach the world:
Teach men how to agree,
Teach men that honor and dignity count
More than our daily bread.

Father Joseph Wresinski
(From the archives of the
Centre International Joseph Wresinski in Baillet, France)

Notes

1. Lecture.
2. F. Ferrand, *Et vous que pensez-vous?* (What do *you* think?: The Fourth World People's University), Editions Quart Monde, 1996, Mrs. Ligot, p. 106.
3. Lecture.
4. J Wresinski, The Poor are the Church, Twenty-Third Publications 2002, p. 147.
5. Danielle Lebrun.
6. V. de Gaulejac, *Aux sources de la honte* (At the Sources of Shame), Desclée de Brouwer, Paris, 1996.
7. Interview No.10.
8. Ibid., p. 98.
9. Ibid., p. 100.
10. Interview No. 6.
11. Italicized words in the poem are extracts from group discussions or interviews.

Chapter 4

TURNAROUND

This chapter is the fruit of intensive group work, for which each of us had to think very deeply in order to better understand our research subject. Through discussions, re-reading transcripts and profound reflection on the interviews, we were able to identify the moments, stages and conditions of the turnaround from the shame of being poor to the pride of being an individual, a person who lives alongside others and is stronger for it, in spite of daily difficulties. We will also describe the Fourth World volunteer corps members' and the academics' own experiences of this turnaround.

Roots

We did not initially intend to look at the issue of roots as part of our research. Why would belonging to such-and-such a family or group play a part in the *turnaround* from shame to pride or in the feeling of belonging to a People? The issue arose in the course of personal stories and interviews and this is why we feel it is important to mention it here, even if our data on the subject is incomplete.

The further we progressed with the personal stories, the more we perceived the importance of the initial observation that *everybody needs roots*. When people talk about the choices they are making now, their values and their turnaround, they almost always relate them to their personal story, especially their emotional relationship with their parents and family. This observation is not as obvious as it may seem: our group work made us realize just how strong this link is. For example, following these discussions, one of the activists decided to look into her family history on her father's side, something she knew very little about beforehand, and it changed both her view of her family and her relationship with one of her brothers.

That being said, when it came to defining the positive and negative effects of one's roots, we found it difficult to make generalizations, because the individual stories are so different. However, we will now point out a few general trends we were able to observe.

Awareness of being loved by one's parents

The first and main anchor sought by both child and adult seems to be the knowledge that they are loved by their parents. Once they are sure of this, it becomes their *native soil,* as Joseph Wresinski put it, referring to a study by Professor Debuyst: *It is extremely important to be able to recall your native soil and your childhood, to be able to return to your beliefs and values, to rest in times of trouble[1].* This is clearly observable in the case of adopted children, who have problems dealing with the abandonment they endured prior to being adopted, no matter how loving their new family is. In our interviews, we mainly observed this in two ways: first, the frequency with which people mentioned their parents in positive terms and, second, the constant references to the painful separation forced by care orders. It was very rare for interviewees to speak negatively of their parents. We only found two instances of this in our interviews:

– My mother left us when I was born, so my father was forced to put me into care[2].

– To begin with everything was fine. But then one day I started to see that my parents treated me differently from my brothers. That's why I began to kind of hate them[3].

This does not mean they all feel that they had ideal parents. But with time, an image of loving parents appears to prevail over any potential criticism. Accordingly, numerous accounts show that poverty itself does not engender the feeling of having been abandoned or not properly loved by one's parents.

– We did have a very poor childhood, that much is true. But it was rich in love, as none of us were taken into care. I had my grandfather, grandmother, my uncles and aunts and their children. We were one big happy family.[4]

– I knew my parents loved me. When they were allowed to have us for a weekend after several months in care, they went on the run for a year so they could keep us with them. But then afterwards, it wasn't easy seeing my father with the policemen, the handcuffs and the police dogs! But I knew my parents did it because they loved me. They put up with it and faced the consequences.**

– My parents did everything so that we lacked nothing, although it was not easy[5]

One woman spoke of her grandfather who was always away working and rarely at home:

– My dad and his brothers and sisters hardly saw their father. But they spoke of him with respect because he was the breadwinner.**

It would thus appear that the great majority of children from poor backgrounds feel they were loved by their parents. There is nothing to indicate that there is a higher frequency of parents who do not love their children, who beat them or abuse them amongst the poor than amongst the better-off. Disadvantaged children do not blame their parents for their poverty. They say they have witnessed the efforts made to get by and that they are grateful. They even think that because of poverty, they have learned skills that other children do not learn from their parents.

> I feel sorry for those we call the "newly poor". I'm not sure they have the same problems as us, because we've been taught how to get by. . . . They don't have the knowledge we have. We have different ways of surviving in society that our parents have taught us.**

For some, this feeling goes as far as idealizing the poor as a social group or a People of poverty.

> We poor marry among ourselves. We've been marrying among ourselves for generations . . . but it is a bond of pure love. It's nothing to do with material things. It's a real bond of love. It knows no limits. That's why we stay together living amongst ourselves. We have no fear: we bring our love and that's all. We have nothing material to give.**

Uprooting

Though poverty itself does not shake people's faith in their parents' love, a common feature of many poor childhoods is the experience of being uprooted by care orders. This is often a particularly painful experience.

> – The toughest moments in my life were when I was snatched away from my mum and taken into care. Moments like that stay with you forever[6].

> – My mum left when I was born. My dad could not keep me so I ended up in care. When I was nine, my dad re-married and took me back. But because of the nine years in care, there wasn't much of a bond left between us. I turned more towards my two sisters[7].

> – There were eight of us in all, six girls and two boys. All the girls were taken into care. . . . It was a nightmare for my mum, a burden of fear. . . . She never really coped with that fear. She thought they (the social services) were after her all the time. We changed school every year because she was scared that we'd be taken away[8].

We could mention many more stories of children being uprooted, even after having been taken into care; stories about having to change homes or foster families without being given any understandable reason. For example, one of the activists said that he was very young when taken into care by a kind family, to which he became deeply attached. Then, without being told why, he was moved to another family. This was what triggered his life as a delinquent and a runaway that eventually led him to prison. The following is a further example of being uprooted:

> – I was brought up by a nurse. I was three weeks old when I was separated from my mom, and seven years old when I was handed back to her. It was very hard for me

because I'd become attached to my nurse. But still, it was very important for us all to be back together with Mom[9].

Care orders change and even destroy emotional bonds within families.

– I hardly know my sisters. I met up with one of them again but we haven't kept in touch, because she was taken into care. I know where my brothers and sisters are but we don't get on that well. Out of the 16 of them, I only get on with two. Both live in the same sort of conditions as me, the others are better off. Anyway, we were all brought up differently.**

Besides official care orders, other family members such as grandparents sometimes take care of children:

– My brother went to live with my grandma so that he could study. He was lucky. For us it was like he had vanished, we had no feelings for him. My mother always said: "Don't be horrible to him because he was lucky enough to be able to study".**

It is worth noting that things were not necessarily easier for the brother in question, and that he also suffered:

– He still has that feeling of being rejected. . . . We know we're brother and sister. But I can't say that it feels the same as with my brother who I grew up with. There's a rift somewhere. Even though we're related. . . . Things are tricky enough when you end up poor, but when you end up middle class, it's pretty damn hard as well!**

There are many other examples of people who, despite the fact that they have achieved a measure of success through having been in care, still feel deep inside that they have suffered from being uprooted. Being taken into care does not establish real roots compared to the family, and this remains a source of sadness for many that they cannot pin down. Most studies show that this is typical for many adopted children. The relationships formed between children taken into care do not even come close to recreating the emotional bonds of a family:

– I received an education and an upbringing in care, but that didn't keep me from feeling uprooted. . . . You're a child or an adult who has been in care, and that's your identity. You have something in common with others in the same situation, but you're all uprooted people.**

To recap our initial observations: poor children have the same faith in their parents' love as children from wealthier backgrounds. Suffering endured in poverty may well leave its mark on their memories and be part of their psychological roots, but as long as they had parents who fought to escape poverty, even if to no avail, they remain grateful to them and are even quite proud of their childhood struggle. On the other hand, they run a far greater risk of being separated from their parents because of financial difficulties and being taken into care than children from wealthier families.

Whatever material advantages care orders bring, they remain, for most, an enduring source of emotional suffering. They vary for better or worse for each person according to circumstances and personality. It is not an issue of pride or shame here, nor any sense of belonging to a People, but essentially of deep-rooted psychological damage whose scars last a lifetime. This may create feelings of injustice, aggression, suspicion or even deep despair towards this society. Every story is unique and personal but, as one of the activists put it:

> First of all you suffer, then as an adult that suffering becomes a source of endless pain.

Let us now quote two accounts demonstrating that the quality of the relationships forged within ATD Fourth World can sometimes alleviate that suffering:

> – [ATD Fourth World] has given me a lot. It's like having a second family[10].

> – I had never had a place I could call home. . . . Now there's a place where I have good memories. At the [Fourth World] People's University* in Paris, I feel good. I'll be able to tell my grandchildren: "You see, there's a place which was really my home, my background, my family", because I can say that's my family[11].

Family history as "mythical roots"

During the interviews and discussions, we came across a second meaning of the word "roots". It means each person's belonging to a history: that of one's forefathers and, sometimes more broadly, that of one's people. These roots are made up of a collection of narratives, partly historical, partly imaginary, concerning one's family (or people), which provide everyone's personal identity: one's role and position within the family, the values one holds dear and one's aims in life. Because these narratives are partially historical, partially imaginary, and because they relate to the emotional experiences of childhood, we call these roots the "family and personal myth"[12] upon which people build their self-image.

> Everybody needs roots. I understand the point of history. It's about feeling part of a general movement from one place to another.**

We observed the importance of this personal myth in numerous interviews and accounts of turnaround. Its positive function was generally made clear in the Fourth World volunteer corps members' and academics' stories as a reference they used to establish their values. Sometimes the stories revealed a feeling of pride and a kind of motivating force which influences one's aims in life. One man talked of his grandfather's social and political involvement, another recalled the strength his parents and grandparents showed to escape poverty while another talked of his mother's compassion towards the poor, etc. Even if one does not share all the values of one's lineage, it is in relation to them that one's position is defined. Moreover, it is worth noting that these stories are all positive in nature, as if able to sustain their own identity, even providing a kind of impetus to one's chosen aims in life.

Do the poor also possess positive myths concerning their roots? The results of our interviews do not allow us to decisively answer the question of whether coming from a poor background impedes the creation of a personal myth. We did not come across anyone who felt ashamed of their poor origins, though the interviews did not address this question systematically. However, it seems we can say that the poor, just like everyone else, wish to feel part of a history and a positive personal myth which gives them strength and pride, yet this is impossible for many of them because of the care orders and separations that disrupted their childhood.

On the whole, poor people also construct a positive personal myth, which allows them to give sense to their family history, if they know it. Where possible, it is the success rather than the poverty of their antecedents that they retain.

> – I hung on to my mother. Farmers were better than the people back at the Abbé Pierre camp! I was proud of my grandmother who was a cattle breeder.**

This can be true even if parents have fallen further into poverty than previous generations:

> – One of my great-uncles was an instrument-maker. He belonged to the aristocratic side of our family and was well off. We were very poor, though, and they looked down on us a bit. I was sheltered from that, though, by music, and by the identity I adopted for a few years when I just thought: "We're gypsies, and sod everyone else."[13]

> – I'm proud of my roots, because at least I have some, even if they are a bit broken. There are people, though, whose roots are in poverty.**

What seems important is the ability to create one's own personal myth and see it positively, as a strength which reinforces one's own identity. Hence the following remark about gypsy roots:

> We are proud of our lives. We aren't ashamed of being travelers. There've been moments of humiliation: when something was stolen at school, they would always blame me. It was tough, but at the same time I told myself: "I don't care, I'm a gypsy and I do know things."[14]

However, it is not always easy to find roots one can be proud of. Some people want this so much that they invent them:

> My brother has always been proud because he was brought up by my father's side of the family; he thought my grandfather was a minister, but it was all made up.**

However, an entirely fictitious story does not seem to work out well: It makes him sad.

The second observation is, once again, that separations due to care orders have a catastrophic effect on one's ability to create a positive myth.

My husband and I are both from traveler families. We were brought up in care, so we received an education, a steady enough life. But I can see that my older boys have always been torn in two because we claimed that we were settled, yet other people saw the boys as gypsies. They were never able to find an identity: am I settled or am I a gypsy? It was terrible. When you're brought up by social services, you have no roots. I never had a place where I felt at home. I was always pushed from pillar to post. Social services don't give you roots.**

Or if they do, they are painful roots. One man, now a cook, said:

I sometimes make cakes for the kids in the care home. I love them. I get cross with them sometimes, but I do love them. They remind me of what I was like when I was young. We're all the same. We need love, that's it.[15]

Another example is the following statement that one cannot help but feel sad on hearing:

My father was from a farming background. As for my mother, it was different. She was abandoned by her mother, and was brought up by nuns until she was 21. She had very little education. She was brought up to bear children; it was her role, so to speak, to start a family.[16]

To conclude, let us quote this account:

I'm convinced that if you have roots, you're less broken than if you don't. The poorest people are those who don't have roots. They're much more fragile. When we have roots, we're like you: we have them to support us.**

To sum up, as far as the mythical function of roots is concerned, we can say that a family's poor background does not in itself prevent it developing a positive personal myth. But here, just as with the emotional aspect of roots, we can clearly see that poor people are especially exposed to experiences of rupture and uprooting which prevent them from constructing a positive family-based self-image.

The issue of shame

In the light of what has been mentioned above, the shame of living in poverty does not seem to originate principally from the way in which roots (either emotional or mythical) are experienced when living in poverty. The accounts and interviews we have collected frequently mention emotional and sometimes financial difficulties in the family, but not shame. That is not to say that experiences of shame and humiliation do not exist in these stories (far from it), but they result from the attitude of the outside world and not from inside the family circle. One activist who was taken into care remembers: *Our foster mother said to my brother: "Your father is a crook!" But we knew it wasn't true.*** School is also regularly mentioned as a source of shame: *At school they had us sit on separate benches. . . . The teacher used to pay for my sandwich in front of the others. It was kind of her but it made me feel really humiliated[17]. . . . Children from settled backgrounds* *learn better than we do because teachers pay them more attention. It's shameful not being able to read and write, not being educated*[18]. Even the possible shame of belonging to a very poor family comes from the outside world: *Shame is a very heavy burden to bear, one that is passed on from one generation to the next, even in relations with the authorities. Social workers see you in such-and-such a way because that's how your parents were.***

The stages of turnaround

There are events which lead to change in everybody's life: marriage, the birth of a child, moving house, changing jobs, etc. People's paths in life very much depend on their social background and the people they meet. Through examples, we will see some of the stages of "turnaround" as experienced by people "living both in poverty and outside it".

From within poverty

The birth of a child transformed this woman's life:

When I had my daughter Sarah, I experienced an epiphany that changed everything in the way I saw life. I used to be rude, unbalanced, a rebel, but with my child in front of me, the most beautiful thing I'd ever created in my life, I swore to myself that she would never go through misery or poverty. I started working like mad, never turning down overtime. My daughter was certainly a way for me to take revenge on life, on poverty and on the injustice I'd had to go through very early on. I drew from her the strength to fight. I promised myself that Sarah would never lack love or tenderness, that she would be a child like all the others. Even if it was tough sometimes living on my own, Sarah would never be sad for want of anything. She would never go without. Sarah is my reason for living, my pride. She went to school like all the other children. I fought so that she would never experience poverty like I did, and I think succeeded in that. Now she is married and has her own family. She knows where I come from. She has a sense of pride; she does not judge the very poor, for she sees how I fight for them. Now she supports me in combating poverty.**

In two interviews we were able to relive the personal and family lives described below:

Bernard and Madeleine Lemaréchal[19] were born in Rennes. Bernard Lemaréchal was one of four children. He and his sisters were brought up by his mother. His father, a blacksmith, died when Bernard was four. In spite of this, he attended school until the age of 18, obtaining a qualification in carpentry. He was employed on sites far from his home and gradually began to drink. Life then became very tough. He lost his job, divorced and broke off communication with his mother and sisters. Two of his sons, aged three and four, both suffocated to death on the same day. On his own, life was very tough, and he lost his self-confidence. He met Madeleine at work. Their life was very hard. They lived on the street, both separated from their children, both alcoholics. For seven years, they lived in a small van, living on what they found on the rubbish dump. Looking back at that time, Madeleine said: *We didn't believe in anyone or anything. We hated other people. We hated them because we'd fallen into such decline. We didn't want to see anybody. We weren't respected anymore.* They lived near the Noë estate in Rennes, where a Fourth World volunteer corps member was living with poor families. She introduced Madeleine to the ATD Fourth World journal *Feuille de Route* (Road Map), and she began passing it around those she knew. At that time, Bernard was very unhappy and showed no interest. The Rennes Fourth World House was founded in 1981. Bernard was unemployed and agreed to work voluntarily to help renovate it, glad to be able to do some carpentry once more. *It got him back on his feet, he saw he could escape poverty*, Madeleine recalled. She then felt able to take him along to a Fourth World People's University* meeting. Bernard revealed: *Everyone there was like me, people who had been thrown on the scrapheap. Some had managed to get by despite everything, so why couldn't I?*

With the support of a friend* of ATD Fourth World and the help of activists, Bernard and Madeleine fought to give up alcohol for good. They were active participants in Vie Libre (an organization helping alcoholics to give up drink). In 1982, they were re-housed in Vitré and got married. Bernard started working again and they decided to try and win back custody of their children. *I rediscovered what it meant to enjoy life, the pleasure of seeing my children, I rediscovered my dignity*, Bernard said afterwards.

He continued his involvement with ATD Fourth World. He often said that *if I hadn't become involved with ATD [Fourth World], I wouldn't have come this far.* In workshops held during the Summer Street Festival, he made boats in Redon with the children. They went down the river Vilaine on a barge along with their 21 boats, and in the evening villagers came to listen to information about the boats, such as how they were made etc. In the carpentry and painting workshops taking place in Vitré every Sunday, over the course off several years he got families involved and introduced them to ATD Fourth World. He used to say:

> Come to the Fourth World House, you'll see. It's fine and you can talk to people. We wouldn't have the rights we have today if it weren't for ATD [Fourth World], because we didn't know our rights. But we found out what they were. Now we can deal with the authorities without getting angry. We have learned how to talk to the authorities, how to listen to people and keep calm.

Though ill for several years, he still took part in the Fourth World People's University preparatory meetings* that took place in his home, anxious not to miss any of the fruitful discussions. He never let down the families and ATD Fourth World, and before he died, he told Madeleine: *Keep following ATD Fourth World. Don't let them down. Keep going.*

The second interview told the story of Noël Jacques[20]. Noël's father was from a farming background but, after a row with his family, he took to the road, going from one job to another. Noël's mother was brought up by nuns until she was 21. They met at the soup kitchen in Nantes in 1950 and then got married. In 1954, they heard the call of Abbé Pierre. They set out on foot, taking the prams and children with them. Noël never met his six older sisters, who had all been taken into care: *My parents traveled across France on foot, and people saw the children with them on the road. My sisters were taken away from my parents and into the care of social services because of vagrancy, instability and malnutrition.*

They arrived at the camp in Noisy-le-Grand in April 1961. The camp was a shanty-town where 252 families lived in extreme poverty. Noël and his brother were born in the camp. From then on, their parents had to fight constantly to keep their sons. *My parents were always afraid of care orders, especially my mother. It preyed on her mind her whole life. As long as we were minors, the social services could take us at any time. It was a tragedy for my mother, a burden of fear. She never could deal with that fear.* The constant fear of having their youngest children taken away made the family yearn to leave Noisy-le-Grand as soon as possible.

A friend of Father Joseph Wresinski whom they trusted supported them and, in 1967, they went to Brittany to live on some land that he owned. This friend was a rock for the family. But the worries remained. *My mother always thought she was being chased. It had become like a persecution to her. She had lost faith in people, she'd had so many children taken away from her. We were the last, her only ties. She clung to us not realizing we felt smothered, but she did everything she could to keep us.*

For ten years, the family lived alone in the country, in a little house without water or central heating, then in a mobile home. Despite his mother's fears, Noël was enrolled at a boarding school. His brother never left home. He rarely speaks about that period of his life. *At boarding school, you can feel the way others look at you. The nuns didn't understand the background I came from. They should have tried to understand us gradually.*

His parents stayed in touch with some friends of ATD Fourth World. Noël sometimes went to meetings with them. *They loved going to the [Fourth World] People's University. . . . But sometimes I was embarrassed to see my parents so badly dressed and I didn't understand why they went there.*

It was after his parents' death that Noël understood their attachment to ATD Fourth World: *I've since understood that this was my father's driving force, meeting friends, people like him who had become true friends. That gave him a boost. He wasn't alone anymore, he found someone to talk to. Later on I understood that meeting people was really important.* Noël says that he owes his openness towards other people to his father: *he would take us along everywhere he went. He talked to everyone and I think I inherited that from him, the ability to talk to people.*

His parents' relationship with Joseph Wresinski also had a great impact on him: *It was great being with Father Joseph, we never felt lonely. We felt loved by someone, he loved us. And this has been highly valuable to me all my life.* Noël also remembers the Fourth World volunteer corps members he met in Noisy-le-Grand: *They didn't care about my parents' clothes, they respected people.* He especially remembers the foreign members of the Fourth World volunteer corps who celebrated Christmas with them, and one who was very close to his brother: *He often came to see him. He managed to express himself with Jean-Marie, he felt cared for. Since Jean-Marie went abroad, he hasn't got any friends any more, no-one visits him.* Now Noël is the one who encourages his brother to go out and develop his self-confidence.

Noël now shares a mobile-home with his brother. He says this should not be seen as a failure, for he has a home. He works as a maintenance technician. He regularly goes to Paray-le-Monial[21] (a place of pilgrimage): *I share my time with others and feel useful.* For him, it is an extension of what he learned from Father Joseph Wresinski i.e. opening up to the outside world and meeting people. *We are poor on the outside, but rich on the inside. Our hearts are richer than those of the people who have everything.*

Defining turnaround

By turnaround we mean an inner change, a fresh way of viewing life in general and one's own life.

Turnaround means:

– The hope required to pull through by regaining self-confidence and finding the inner strength to fight.

– Realizing there are other people living in poverty, and there are friends to lean on (members of the Fourth World volunteer corps, allies*, friends etc).

– Thinking about those who have tougher lives than one's own and getting involved with them in the fight against poverty.

Meetings as a starting point for turnaround

People living in poverty are conscious of the injustice they face. They fight against it every day. For example, they fight for the benefits they are entitled to and for which they have been waiting for too long; for the child in care who cannot keep up at school; against the mounting debts their meager resources cannot pay, and against the lack of work and training for the young. On their own, there is little chance they can cope with all these problems. The poor know how others view them and the way they judge them. The authorities and the "non-poor" fear them because of their physical appearance and unpredictability. Sometimes, poor people assume full responsibility for their poverty and feel guilty. One injustice after another can lead to a breakdown: *The world is too hard, we can't get by on our own***, said one man, aware of the tremendous effort he is expected to make.

Regaining self-confidence, rediscovering deep inside oneself the strength to fight for a collective eradication of injustice is a real turnaround for the poor. It is another way of seeing their own lives and life in general. To experience this turnaround, it usually takes the support of friends or the occurrence of an important event.

The people interviewed during our research process and the three activists participating in this research defined what happened in their lives to change their way of thinking and cause them to commit themselves to helping others. The starting point was always a meeting. *Someone has to prove to you that you count.*

Father Joseph Wresinski has sometimes been that someone, as Danielle Lebrun recalls:

> Meeting Father Joseph as a child made me an activist forever. I met him in April 1961 and I kept in touch with him until he died. In the camp at Noisy, I found it hard to approach him. It took me a year. I was a lonely child, afraid of other people, regardless of their background. Because I was poor, I always felt out of place. I felt I was a nuisance. I would never take the initiative to talk to another child. I was too used to just staying within my family. I was not open to others. I walked around the cultural center* without ever daring enter, though I really wanted to, to talk to other children and read and draw. Father Joseph started by just watching me, without asking me anything. He would say hello, and I'd run away. Then one day I was outside with my brother, and Father Joseph handed me a brand new book. I didn't take it. Then he said: "If you want to come in, then do. And if you don't want to today, then come back another day." So I went in. I lifted my head for the first time and saw the new books, and Father Joseph said: " Take one, if you want, and read". This changed something in my child's mind: I wasn't treated like a little brat any more. On the contrary, I was part of something outside my family. I felt at that moment that, as Father Joseph welcomed me without judging me on my appearance, I was opening up to the world and other people. He showed me everything a child should have, like books, paints, paper, pencils etc. and, above all, he gave me self-confidence, which I'd never had before. He got me to go on holidays with other children. It was hard to talk my parents into letting me go to the Netherlands. I was afraid but, at last, I was able to leave the camp and see other people. I think in this way, Father Joseph took away my doubts and my fear.
>
> I drew my strength from the way he stuck up for himself and for others. As an adult, he always trusted me, and he became a great friend after my daughter's birth.
>
> I became a committed activist, fighting against the injustice poor people were experiencing. For a few years, I stopped working with ATD [Fourth World], but I never lost touch with Father Joseph. I wrote to him and we used to meet up. He told me of the injustices some families had suffered. He was able to touch my heart and make me react. He would always say: "They are your people and mine. Now that you don't need me anymore, go and fight for others, fight alongside these families. Speak on their behalf, tell people who they are. *You* know them and *you* know what they're going through. They have inner riches that they haven't discovered yet. Spread the

word on behalf of the poorest." Sometimes, I found he became a bit repetitive and I'd say: "No, I won't". But then I'd go to meetings and speak of poor people's suffering and struggles. I strongly believe that he passed his activism on to me and it is now a part of me, like a revolt against injustice.

Sometimes this role is fulfilled by a member of the Fourth World volunteer corps or a friend, as Daniel Le Breton recounts:

I first came into contact with ATD Fourth World on the Noë estate in 1975. My mother lived there, and I returned to live with her after having spent some time in care. I was 25 at the time. I started running the street library for the estate children on Wednesdays, with a [Fourth World volunteer corps member] called Jacques. I didn't have a problem with it because I wasn't working back then and I needed to keep busy. I could have just have messed around like the others did. I could have turned out bad. But I found it helpful. At that time I was a bit of a tearaway, so I said to myself: "Stop messing around." When Jacques suggested I help run the street library, I agreed straight away.

Jacques and two other [Fourth World volunteer corps members] lived on the estate. There was also a building that served as a communal house, where there was a washing machine. Women used to go there to wash their clothes, but some of them also met there for fun, and would bring cakes or sugar or coffee etc. There were parties organized on public holidays, like July 14 or August 15. They were opportunities to get to know some of the families who tended to keep themselves to themselves. The parties helped build friendships between us.

I left ATD Fourth World in 1977 and came back in 1983. I was still poor, but I realized that there were other families living in greater poverty than me.

I wanted to make myself useful and carry on what I had experienced in Noë.

My life is still hard, and that's why I chose a person in my neighborhood that I trust and can talk to, and I know she'll always be there to support me. She gives me the moral support I need and that I can't do without in my everyday life.

But I also need another kind of relationship with people outside my private life, and I find this within ATD Fourth World, where we have a kind of collective, friendly support and where we encourage one another to go and meet other people.

In his account, Daniel says that when living in poverty, people remain fragile, even when they are involved with others in combating poverty. It takes time for a turnaround; for them to gain self-confidence and have trust in others. If someone has been deceived throughout their childhood, they remain mistrustful as an adult.

Lucie Ribert[22], whose family lived in a shack, recounts how one day in 1976, a couple, called Michel and Marie-France, came to their home:

When people came to our house, we didn't like to let them in because it wasn't very clean. It was a bit of a pigsty. But we let *them* in, they looked so friendly and straightforward. . . .

Lucie recounts that her mother offered them coffee, and *"Amazingly, they said yes!"* Michel and Marie-France are both members of the Fourth World volunteer corps. Lucie says: *"They listened to what I said, and that triggered something in me for the first time."*

Danielle defines Fourth World volunteer corps members as follows:

> They don't force themselves on the poor, or presume they will be able to change everything. They just try and listen and understand! But that takes a little while. . . .

Several interviewees said that meeting a member of the Fourth World volunteer corps or a friend of ATD Fourth World in their home was that first "trigger" referred to by Lucie. However, it often takes longer for this to mature, bear fruit and for them to become involved with ATD Fourth World. Noëlle Stenegry explains that in 1989, someone from ATD Fourth World came to her home for the first time, but it was only four years later that she decided to become involved. For four years, the person visited regularly, bringing books for her children: *I didn't feel watched or judged, and I realized we had to stop being ashamed of who we were and show that we were capable of doing things and of thinking.*

Sometimes a neighbor or a parent can take up this role. Bruno is in his twenties, and says that he owes his own involvement to his deceased father, Louis Vanbourgogne: *I come to [Fourth World] People's Universities for my father. Why was it so important to him? He passed it down to me, and now I want to understand myself.*** Two other young people recount that it was their mother who made them want to *better understand how we can eradicate poverty together.*

Sometimes this meeting takes place in the person's neighborhood. For instance, in one area of Brest, there are regular spiritual gatherings, and the locals regularly invite each other to them. These meetings have given birth to a Fourth World People's University preparatory group, to which the locals have kept inviting each other. One woman recalls that it was her neighbor who simply told her: *Come with me and you'll see.* She continues: *I can see that others are more miserable than I am, and they don't dare to speak. They have things to say but they can't express themselves.*[23]

Participation in collective events

The Fourth World People's University is often referred to by the interviewees as a place they can feel comfortable, where they realize that they are not alone. Mrs. Ligot describes it as follows:

> I liked it, I saw people helping each other out. Now that is amazing. Where I live, you don't see that. . . . It's a place where people listen to us, where we're not sent packing like we would be by the authorities. Because a lot of people living in poverty come to the [Fourth World] People's University in Paris, it gives us the confidence to fight harder. We realize there are other people more isolated than we are, then we learn to reach out to others.[24]

The Fourth World People's University is also *an opportunity to talk and express oneself*. Several people said that it was by participating that they realized they were able to speak and make themselves understood, and thus regain the self-confidence they needed for contact with other people. For others, taking part in a rally set things in motion. Indeed, after taking part in an international ATD Fourth World rally, one man wrote:

> I was happy and touched to see that so many people devote their lives to fighting the poverty and injustice suffered by others. Surrounded by all these people, enjoying the day, we (he and his wife) experienced the hope that one day things will change.[25]

Fourth World volunteer corps members introduced Lucie Ribert to ATD Fourth World, but it was during a meeting that she reached an awareness based on her understanding:

> I saw plenty of people like me who spoke, who said powerful things and spoke about their lives. I thought: "Their lives are the same as mine". I could recognize the homelessness, the shame, lots of things like that. That's when something was triggered in me. Then there was Father Joseph's speech. I don't remember the detail, but I realized who he was, that he was like me.[26]

Being accorded responsibilities by other people can also create self-confidence. One woman recalls:

> I had reached the stage where I had lost all self-confidence. I felt capable of doing things, and that I had a contribution to make, but there was no-one to acknowledge it. I regained some of my strength with ATD [Fourth World]. They had faith in me.**

This faith was exemplified when the same woman agreed to publicly testify to her daily struggle against poverty:

> Before becoming involved with ATD Fourth World, if someone had suggested I give a talk on poverty, I would have said: "They're out of their minds if they think I'm going to start talking about myself in public! I've already got enough on my plate!" I found the strength to do so because I wasn't only talking about myself; I could feel all the others behind me. For the first time, I spoke in front of people I didn't know, and I didn't feel ashamed or embarrassed. On the contrary, I felt strong. Something inside me was saying "you have to say it". ATD [Fourth World] gives us the strength to be able to tell other people what we need to say.**

Mr. and Mrs. Combot also confirm how important speaking in public is, the personal pride of being able to say what they think, and the hope of being heard and understood. Speaking in public can be liberating:

> Speaking in public is harrowing. We'd kept it all inside for too long. We found the right place to get it out in the open. It was a great relief. I was liberated from something that was poisoning my life. We felt relieved afterwards.[27]

The consequences of turnaround

Pride in oneself is one of the first consequences of realizing one's own capacities: *We escape extreme poverty through our inner strength, our self-confidence, and support from other people,* says one man, who knows that the first step is to regain self-confidence in oneself. However, turnaround here is not only personal; it is connected to others living in the same situation.

Everyone fights in their everyday lives to remain standing and keep their family together. People living in extreme poverty have to fight every day just to keep their heads above water. The realization that other people are fighting the same fight sparks the first thoughts of activism. These thoughts become a part of life: I'm committed to my own activism on a daily basis, one woman said. She said that in her town, she knows very poor and homeless people. She mentions a woman called Madeleine: I sit with her and talk to her; I ask how the children are getting on. That is activism, it is very simple, it's not being afraid of taboos**. A more visible form of activism is when the poor stand up and assert themselves by speaking in public. But what these two forms of activism have in common is that they are a commitment to all those who still live in poverty. A young woman sums this up by saying: *Poverty must be unearthed. We must seek it out and fight it. We mustn't allow people to lie down and succumb to it.*[28]

One ever-present risk is that those who have learned to "be articulate" are pushed forward.

> You must not take the place of the poorest. They are the ones who need recognition. When people asked me to "speak for them", while they remained silent, I thought "That's enough!" I didn't always want to be the center of attention.**

Is turnaround permanent for the poor?

In spite of their sincere commitment, the precariousness of their daily lives and poor health often mean that turnaround is not permanent. Since everyday life is too difficult, they sometimes withdraw into themselves, not wanting to see or hear from anybody any more. They concentrate all their strength on fighting for themselves and their own family.

However, some people stick together to fight the poverty they see around them. At some point in their life, they get their breath back, they come out of their shell, their life becomes steadier and then they can be freer to become involved alongside others. Poor people's active involvement is never permanent. Their life means it cannot be otherwise.

From outside of poverty

Fourth World volunteer corps members' experiences of turnaround[29]

> I felt at once that I was in the presence of my people. I cannot explain it. That's how it was. From that moment, my life took a turn. . . . The blinding poverty that lay be-

fore me in stifling heat and absolute silence had me caught in a trap.[30]

This was how Father Joseph described his arrival in Noisy-le-Grand, on July 14, 1956. Later, he says:

> The idea of a volunteer corps followed almost immediately. Without this volunteer corps, born in the midst of misery in the Noisy-le-Grand camp, nothing could have been achieved. What could the families and I do, if men and women who wanted what we wanted—to destroy extreme poverty and its shame—had not come forward to join us?[31]

He then mentions the Fourth World volunteer corps members again, saying that:

> They answered my call; but I was separate from them, and they had to build themselves up.[32]

Today, we have around 300 members of the Fourth World volunteer corps across the world. There is not a great deal we can say about them. They are a group in perpetual flux. The creation of the Fourth World volunteer corps represents an innovation in combating poverty.

Fourth World volunteer corps members come from very different historical, socio-economic, political, cultural, philosophical and religious backgrounds. Therefore they differ in how they became involved with the poor and Father Joseph Wresinski. There is no "typical" Fourth World volunteer corps member. Each step of their own turnaround(s) can be combined and re-enacted every day. The following is merely for information.

The meaning of turnaround for Fourth World volunteer corps members

By turnaround, we mean an inner change, another way of seeing one's own life and life in general, the activists tell us. So far, the definition is general enough to be applicable all members of ATD Fourth World: underprivileged families, allies and Fourth World volunteer corps members. What then is specific to the turnaround in a Fourth World volunteer corps member's life? Perhaps the philosopher Lévinas can help us understand some of the stages of turnaround. He emphasizes that to *be human* is to *be responsible*. He attempts to discern the bases of responsibility and the demands of justice. We are responsible not only for ourselves, but for *the Other* also, by virtue of their being *Other*. Not only are we responsible *for* them, we are also responsible *because of* them.

Lévinas writes a great deal on the meaning of the *countenance* of *the Other* and on how we encounter one another through this *countenance*. It tells us that *the Other* is a human like ourselves, a fellow human, and yet an *Other*. This means that our responsibility as humans drives us to explore how we can embrace and make our own the aims of *the Other*, because their aims are also ours. For Lévinas, *the Other* who involves us is the most vulnerable and suffers the most.

For Father Joseph, this *Other* refers to the poorest.

Let us return to the definition of turnaround as experienced by members of the Fourth World volunteer corps.

– Prompted by a sense of justice and responsibility, Fourth World volunteer corps members are used to encountering the poorest at some point. They feel compelled to discover and understand the poorest by the *look* they have seen in their eyes, which speaks of all they have known.

– Fourth World volunteer corps members have also "met" Father Joseph. Some met him in person and, since his death, others have come to know him through his writings and ATD Fourth World, which he founded.

Father Joseph experienced extreme poverty. He calls on every human being, including the poor themselves, to fight to eliminate it, because he is convinced that fundamentally, every person bears a responsibility. Thanks to him, in their dealings with both the poor and the society they live in, the members of the Fourth World volunteer corps have realized their responsibility and the demands of a new type of justice

– A third reality exists in Fourth World volunteer corps members' lives. Meeting *the Other*, i.e. the poorest, takes place all over the world. The poorest do not belong to one neighborhood, town or country. They are everywhere on earth, similar in appearance, with the same life stories, all suffering from the same forms of exclusion. All humanity is represented within this *Other* that Fourth World volunteer corps members meet. It presents them with a challenge to broaden the scope of their responsibility until it becomes universal.

Turnaround in Fourth World volunteer corps members' lives by necessity leads them to share the hopes, thoughts and actions of the poorest. It becomes vital for them in their new conception of peace and human brotherhood. Members of the Fourth World volunteer corps allow themselves to be taught about life and the world by the most excluded.

The stages of turnaround

Each member of the Fourth World volunteer corps has his or her own reasons for becoming one. Some had already encountered poverty, a few had personally experienced it. Others were not aware of poverty in their country or did not refer to in such terms. Some already knew about the world's injustices, the exclusion suffered by some of our fellow citizens. A few had become involved with groups to fight against injustice.

Each of their lives had been spent engaged in social, political, religious, philosophical or professional activity. This had brought them into contact with people living in extreme poverty, either in a professional context or simply on a person-to-person basis.

– The roots of my commitment, like those of all the commitments adults make, go back to my childhood, to the surroundings in which I grew up. Happy or unhappy experiences as children and teenagers shape the way we live within a family, the way we are with our children, our position in society.

– I think that at the beginning it was not as a Fourth World volunteer corps member that I refused injustice, inequality, suffering and poverty. I learned a lot from working as an activist in trade unions for ten years.

– I was a teacher for eight years. And in the different places I went to, both in Africa and in France, meeting migrants or working people, I must admit I've always sought out people who were very different from me, sometimes the complete opposite, because I've always thought that it is through this kind of meeting that we discover who we are, by discovering the other.

– Before becoming a Fourth World volunteer corps member, I was a primary school teacher. There were always a few children who struggled and who did not work. My family always said "There aren't any poor people in France", I grew up with that. I never called the children who were bottom of the class and who came from underprivileged areas "poor". I just thought they were not very intelligent; I never thought it might be their background that stopped them from keeping up at school.

Someone, however, had to show that extreme poverty was the highest form of injustice. Father Joseph Wresinski holds a special place for all involved, for it was from him that this message emanated. He was driven by a desire for his people to regain their proper place and to change our attitudes as a consequence.

As he himself said:

I did not choose the first men and women who joined me. They were workers, teachers, engineers. All they had to offer was their refusal to accept poverty, their trades, and their heart. I asked them to place the poorest families at the center of their lives and to agree to question everything they had learnt until then concerning brotherhood, truth and justice.[33]

He succeeded in passing his feeling of outrage on to Fourth World volunteer corps members, who have taken it on board. To them, the outrage has become just as unbearable and prompts them to action. One member of the Fourth World volunteer corps told us:

We met Father Joseph and he welcomed us with open arms, telling us the Fourth World was waiting for us; we believed in what he said about the Fourth World waiting for us, and we came.

From the very beginning, Father Joseph's call has been passed on from the initial few to others. The Fourth World volunteer corps he founded has itself become a source of turnaround. He continues to shape and share this new attitude towards humanity and extreme poverty.

– When I became a Fourth World volunteer corps member, the story of Joseph Wresinski, the families, the Fourth World volunteer corps members and the allies revealed to me that every human being was a citizen of the world and should be respected.

– The poor have changed my way of seeing humanity thanks to Father Joseph.

Meeting Father Joseph while he was alive was a source of turnaround. He knew how to commit to and support those who joined him. With them, he continued to engage with the world of poverty all his life. All these encounters gave rise to a new way of understanding the poorest and humanity. This knowledge is all the more radical because it came from Father Joseph, himself a poor man, along with all the poor families who joined him. In what sense is this new knowledge a source of turnaround?

One Fourth World volunteer corps member tells us that if one does not come from a poor background, one usually considers the poor with unconcerned and distant eyes:

> Thousands of miles away from poverty, and yet so close, every effort was made to stop me encountering it or seeing it. Every effort was made to make me despise people living in poverty. I had always thought they were responsible for their problems, or even guilty. All they needed to do was go to work, take their children to school, be more sociable, more civilized; I wasn't concerned with their lives.

Yet this attitude can change under the influence of a personal encounter. One member of the Fourth World volunteer corps tells us that before becoming part of ATD Fourth World, she was a teacher. She was convinced that children's and teenagers' lives could be changed, but as far as adults were concerned, it was too late. She thought the only way they could be helped was by educating their children, but that left them out to some extent.

> When I said this to Father Joseph, he strongly criticized this attitude. It was not only that which convinced me I was wrong, time did as well: the adults' efforts, Mrs. N's transformation from aggressive to welcoming, the way children and young people love their parents.

Daily contact with the families, either by living near them or through projects carried out in poor neighborhoods, leads to an awareness of the reality on the ground. Fourth World volunteer corps members witness values and strengths that allow men and women to keep standing despite everything. Two members of the Fourth World volunteer corps told us:

> – Meeting Mr. and Mrs. E. was the beginning of an inner understanding for me. I witnessed gestures of love, gestures expressing the extent of their love and forgiveness, which is so necessary in persistent poverty. I also discovered Mr. E.'s way of thinking. His blunt way of getting straight to the point made him a laughing stock when he said "We're all brothers" or "What keeps me going is thinking about those I love and have cared for." However, I heard in his words all the troubles he had seen.

> – A terrible injustice prevented them from living family life as they would have liked. Sharing this life under the same roof as them every day revolutionized our

own lives. We witnessed their courage every day. We shared their rebellion, their tears, their anger and, sometimes, their inability to cope.

Individual contact is not the only source of turnaround. ATD Fourth World meetings are also occasions for important discoveries. Poor families learn how to express themselves collectively and communicate with the outside world. Fourth World volunteer corps members witness the poorest people's words and pride:

> At the Fourth World People's University I found out about a whole world, a whole community. People were learning to speak in public, listen to each other, and dialogue with others. This period had a great impact on me. Together, they denounced the same injustices, revealed the same aspirations, and shared the same life experiences. My awareness went beyond the boundaries. The families shared a common will to fight for their children to have the same opportunities and the same rights as all other children.

The Fourth World volunteer corps members believe that a life lived together often helps build solidarity. The core of this solidarity is shaped by a common sense of humanity.

> I lived in H., where we accommodated very poor families and it wasn't always easy. However, I was glad to share their life, live next to them and feel that we shared a common humanity.

Father Joseph always fought to remove the divisions among people. For him, it was not rich versus poor or vice versa. Together with the Fourth World volunteer corps members, he devoted his life to reconciling the two groups: *The day when free and educated men join the Fourth World, extreme poverty will have been eradicated.*[34]

Following this process of change in attitudes and behavior, members of the Fourth World volunteer corps transform the way they view underprivileged families. One describes a future full of promise inspired by these changes:

> I drew a boat on my coat of arms*. A boat is for going on an adventure, so it needs a propeller. It needs to call at ports along the way, so it needs an anchor. People on board this boat come from various places and neighborhoods. This boat exists in Paris too. We have had meetings and rallies there for young people. We feel strong together. By meeting one another, people can gain the strength to go out and conquer the world.

But no battle is won once and for all. Turnaround requires daily encounters to continue. It can never occur without *the Other*. It must be a shared experience because it demonstrates that everything can change:

> Being a Fourth World volunteer corps member is something you choose every morning when you wake up. It's also a way of life, a commitment alongside others. A long-term intellectual project that matures, and that gives us hope for important, decisive moments through the people we meet.

The academics' view of turnaround[35]

The academics involved in this project have agreed to give their point of view on the way they experienced this training, action and research project, given their own backgrounds. For several of them, the project was another point of entry into the world of poverty, which they had already experienced in one way or another.

> – My stance towards the poorest was determined before I went to university. I was fortunate enough to live on a working-class housing estate with my parents, who passed on to me their sympathy towards those suffering, as well as a feeling of self-confidence in front of people who have more than I do.

> – My father told me he had to go and fetch packs of food for his family and himself before school. He was embarrassed to have to do this. He said that they were poor and ashamed of it.

> – My family was not poor, but we always had less than my cousins and most of the other children at school.

These situations are far from being comparable with those experienced by people living in extreme poverty since they are not permanent and do not concern all aspects of life. However, they do show a certain sensitivity linked to personal memories which have shaped them as people. For several of them, their parents' attitudes appear to be an important influence on the way they consider others.

> – My parents always told us that people weren't worth more just because they had money. They showed us that money can keep people from seeing reality as it is, and sometimes make children unhappy.

> – My mother always helped people in trouble when I was a child, and that has helped me be more aware of the destitution some people are in.

> – I was very moved and influenced by my mother's attention and care towards my poorest friends.

What does "turnaround" mean to academics?

Most of the academics participating in this project agreed to talk about their turnaround, meaning that the word meant something to them and conveyed a particular experience. It cannot be conceived of as a parallel experience to that of the activists, as *a journey from shame to pride*. And yet some of them did not hesitate to talk about their *journey from the shame (of belonging to exclusive organizations and systems) to the pride (of taking part in collectively creating something)*.

The experience of producing knowledge with the poorest is an opportunity to break with previous practice and to change attitudes, which concern both head and heart. It is an intellectual, but also existential, experience.

From the accounts collected, we have the impression that this experience proceeds in steps, represents an endless path, is difficult and raises questions.

Seeing without understanding

It is generally thought that academics are people whose job is to understand, or at least research the world in order to know more about it, and to exercise a certain degree of control over events. By taking part in this project, most of them thought they would be able to do this easily. They thought their task would mostly be to explain to and teach the poorest and the Fourth World volunteer corps members how to produce knowledge, how to follow working methods and how to share knowledge, since that was the aim. Many had probably never read or had forgotten Father Joseph's words at the Sorbonne in 1983:

> Men of learning—take to the streets, not to research . . . but to be taught and corrected, be prepared to challenge not only your knowledge but also the foundations, the method and the meaning of knowledge. . . . This is what turnaround means.[36]

Today, after 18 months working together, several of them admit that changes occurred in them and in their understanding of the way the poorest think.

Here are a few examples of their "failure to understand" what they thought they already knew:

> – An important step is to become aware of our own failure to understand an activist or their way of thinking. It is amazing to find yourself deaf and blind. It is essential to realize and accept our own ignorance in order to learn how the other thinks.

> – Little by little, I realized that their (the activists') way of speaking was not clumsy at all, that they simply expressed ideas and feelings that I misunderstood because I had no idea of what they were all about.

> – What we see is the suffering of poverty, not its philosophy. As intellectuals, we are used to separating the world of emotions from the world of intellectual work. . . . The process of knowledge-merging with activists forces us to rethink this distinction.

In the beginning, the activists' words were listened to with disbelief, skeptically and carefully. *We are a People, it's obvious*, activists say. Hearing this assertion, skepticism leads to think that *they have swallowed ATD Fourth World buzzwords wholesale, and they want to get us using them. Although we can undoubtedly acknowledge that the activists believe in what they say, that they speak of a reality they have experienced, it doesn't sound like it's related to knowledge, but only to belief and credence.*

Events which change attitudes

As the project and group-work progressed, attitudes changed and new demands were made on participants.

One of the academics said that he thought he would be able to know and understand the point of view of the poor by putting himself in their place. *I have put myself in others' shoes and seen others do so hundreds of times. Alright, it may not always be a success, but it almost always works. We can try doing it, even with the poor.*

And yet, after several months of discussion and debate, this belief changed, and meeting *the Other* began to be understood in a different light:

> We cannot put ourselves in the place of *the Other*. It is their place and we cannot take it from them.
>
> We cannot talk about this place, even if they don't talk about it themselves. Doing so would be stealing it from them.
>
> But can't we simply select a few "pearls" from what somebody says to make our own necklace?
>
> No you mustn't, just as you are forbidden to pick a bunch of edelweiss: you must leave them in their place in their natural surroundings.
>
> We cannot see through somebody else's eyes; it is an illusion, it is impossible. Our eyes are those of a person from an affluent background.
>
> We can't. It is impossible and forbidden, and I can understand why. I mean, just put yourself in their place!

Another of the academics had a similar experience:

> I sensed that the activists feared that I presumed to understand their own words better than they themselves, and this fear was justified enough. I found that I had to try and reconcile their truly egalitarian words with my own conceptions, and also be prepared to have the latter shattered by them.

Questions which are asked and will continue to be asked

The academics were confronted with numerous issues arising from these experiences. They were of a theoretical or scientific, political and moral nature and cannot always be broken down into discrete spheres. In an effort to divide them, they can be presented as follows.

One issue recurs. It concerns the way the poorest and poverty are spoken of, and the legitimacy of what can be said.

> One significant moment was when they refused to acknowledge "the shortcomings caused by poverty", although I was only quoting Father Joseph's own words. It took me a long time to understand that they hadn't been denying those "shortcomings" but that they did not tolerate me as an outsider talking about them. The text they wrote about suffering from extreme poverty was a revelation to me because there I found that they themselves had written all the things that I had thought they had been denying up until then. I then came up against the whole question of knowing who is entitled to speak about suffering and the problems it causes to the people affected.

And this issue is vital to academics because it can challenge the foundations of a whole series of studies. Indeed, another writes:

Encounters under the conditions of group-work (and not in a research context with interviews for instance, where the researcher is always in a "privileged position") lead to changes in the way situations are perceived and, therefore, in the way they are spoken of.

Can we say that existential experience is excluded from academic discourse since we always have to deal with words and concepts? Or does the academic world have room for different types of knowledge? Finally, another academic adds:

I haven't finished thinking about this issue, because I still feel that their wanting to be the only ones to talk about their suffering is somehow absolutely right, even epistemologically speaking (according to theories of knowledge), and yet perhaps a little excessive. Can we talk intellectually about life experience that we haven't experienced? And why should it be illegitimate to do so?

We live in a world in which knowledge has been defined through criteria that are very different from those we are trying to draw up together. An encounter and an egalitarian relationship were necessary to challenge the conviction that, *after listening to them, I would be able to intellectually express the ideas that they could only formulate clumsily because of their lack of training. I thought I knew them, and hadn't imagined that they could show me a new vision of the world.*

Along with the experiences that changed the academics' ways of seeing and thinking, there was also the question of changes to their working practices:

– What is the value and meaning of such a breakthrough in my commitment to my academic work? If there is no tangible consequence for me, then I will not have learned or "turned around" much.

– This project has taught me that we could do much more to acknowledge and involve everybody in training.

One of them wonders how to continue working as an academic:

Either I leave academia or I fight to achieve something meaningful and which involves other people. How can I pass on something I have learnt in this project and find the best words to do so?

To which one answer is:

It is not through linguistic conventions and academic practices that we will convince our colleagues: a speech will not do. It is rather through the things you say and what you believe in, and then all of a sudden someone gets into it, or is moved by what they've read, and then it is worth it. . . . When you see them catch on to something, you're absolutely stunned because it always exceeds your expectations.

Also, it may be that *if you want to pass on your life experience it is better to use poetic rather than academic language.* It is no doubt a vital issue which invites considerable further discussion, and which shows the limits of intellectuals' knowledge and maybe also the limits of the means they have at their disposal.

Notes

1. J Wresinski, *Écrits et Paroles aux volontaires* (Words for Fourth World volunteer corps Members), Editions St Paul-Quart Monde, 1992, p. 139.
2. Interview no. 11.
3. Interview no. 9 (man).
4. Interview no. 10.
5. Interview no. 9 (woman).
6. Interview no. 4.
7. Interview no. 11.
8. Interview no. 17.
9. Interview no. 7.
10. Interview no. 6.
11. Fr. Ferrand, *Et vous que pensez-vous?* (What do *you* Think?: The Fourth World People's University), Editions Quart Monde, 1996, Mrs. Ligot, p. 113.
12. The idea of the myth is developed from p. 112 onwards.
13. Lecture.
14. Lecture.
15. Interview no. 11.
16. Interview no. 17.
17. Lecture.
18. Interview no. 14.
19. Interview no. 3.
20. Interview no. 17.
21. A place of pilgrimage run by a community of the Charismatic Renewal.
22. Lecture.
23. Interview no. 8.
24. Op. Cit., p. 101.
25. Op. Cit., M Russel, p. 216.
26. Lecture.
27. Interview no. 9.
28. Interview no. 4.
29. The quotations in this section are composed of extracts from Fourth World volunteer corps member Emilie Bourtet's lecture and the accounts of five Fourth World volunteer corps members taking part in the Fourth World–University project.
30. J Wresinski, The Poor are the Church, Twenty-Third Publications 2002, p. 49.
31. Ibid., p. 111.
32. Ibid., p. 123.
33. J Wresinski, *Échec à la misère* (Overcoming Poverty), Lecture at the Sorbonne, Editions Quart Monde, 1996.
34. Ibid.
35. The quotations in this section are extracts from the accounts given by the academics taking part in the Fourth World–University project.
36. Ibid.

Chapter 5

FROM THE PEOPLE OF EXTREME POVERTY TO THE PEOPLE OF THE FOURTH WORLD

Through the individual and family lives of people living in extreme poverty, we realized the importance of meetings, groups and gatherings. We realized that pride comes from not feeling alone and from the ability to form bonds with other people; to feel a member of a family, community, even a People. The word 'People' crops up in several interviews and was often used by Joseph Wresinski when speaking about the Fourth World. This is why we have decided to devote the last chapter of this research to in-depth analysis of the terms "People" and "Fourth World". Firstly, we will give a dictionary definition of the word "People" and examine the way it is used in different cultures. Secondly, we will present the notion of "People" as it was used by nineteenth century populists, with reference to the work of Pessin. Then we will deal with the meanings of the term "Fourth World" as the term has been used by ATD Fourth World at different times during its history. Lastly, we will present a diagram explaining the myth of the People of the Fourth World.

The meanings of the word *People*

The notion of People means different thing to each of the three groups participating in the project[1]. What first comes to mind when talking about a People is the first definition of the word in dictionaries: we all belong to a particular country with a common history and language, and with an identifiable culture of its own—although this can become rather cliched.

This notion of a People allows individuals to see themselves as such in the society they live in. The sense of belonging to a People varies in intensity from one person and country to another. We observed that for the poor, this feeling of belonging to the same culture is not experienced in the same way by all of them. On the whole, it does not prevail and is replaced by another sense of the word that we shall observe later. One of the Fourth World activists told us: Isn't this because of an underlying problem? To him, the People is abandoned, forgotten, and unacknowledged.

A People as a "cultural and historical" group

In some cultures, however, even the poor have not lost the feeling of belonging to a particular culture. They are part of it and remain proud of that fact. Take for example gypsies, of peoples like those of Haiti or Reunion Island. Before telling us about her experience of extreme poverty, Lucie Ribert proudly declared: *My parents are gypsies.* One Fourth World volunteer corps member who has lived in Haiti told us:

> When I first arrived in Haiti, it was a shock to me. The poverty there is tremendous; the vast majority of Haitians live below the poverty line. Shanty-towns stand next to luxury homes. When I think about Haitian families, I think not only of the word "courage", but also staying power, even a struggle against poverty. As well as political repression and state violence, there has been extreme poverty for generations. Slavery has left its mark on them. They are proud of having driven out the colonists and having proclaimed the world's first black republic in 1804.[2]

An "abandoned" People

Let us go back to the *People (who is) abandoned, forgotten and unacknowledged.* Listening to the activists, this People emerges as a People of shame and suffering.

I'd say there is one People in the world, and within this People there are those who are pushed aside because they don't fit the typical picture of a normal person.

Historically speaking, activists see themselves as belonging to the "*lower classes*", and as "*beggars*". *Throughout history, we talk about the People, or the masses in derogatory terms.*

Then there is the notion of a People being a People because it shares similar life experiences.

> We have suffered from care orders in the same way, with the ensuing shame and humiliation. We are citizens of the same world, we endure the same struggle. The poorest recognize one another and also the way others view them.

A People "at the core of humanity"

Finally, there is the idea of a People whose natural position is at the core of humanity and of the world. One activist said:

> Since [ATD Fourth World] has existed—and ATD Fourth World knows no borders—we have felt part of one People. We call ourselves a People because we live on the same earth and we all live in poverty.

Another activist went even further:

We are all one People. All human beings living on the earth are one People. For me, a People is the whole of society. I see no difference between white, black, or yellow, Indians, the disabled; for me they are all human beings. In the word "People", there is one section for the poor who are set aside, and another for the rest of society.

We can conclude with this activist's definition:

The People shall be the concern of those who agree to stand by the excluded, to throw their lot in with theirs, and sometimes to leave everything behind to share their lives. This is the only way to belong to a People and be acknowledged as such. In the years I have been participating in the October 17* commemorations, I have observed that there are more and more of us, from all races. This is the "People".

"God's people"

One member of the Fourth World volunteer corps told us:

To my mind, the idea of People makes me think about the biblical sense of the word. It appears at the moment when Moses leads the Hebrews out of Egypt and is thus linked to liberation. A group of slaves becomes a People by liberating themselves. We must not forget our roots. As soon as the Jewish people forgot that they once were slaves, they strayed from the path of liberation.

One activist spoke about this People today:

In 1989, we went to Rome at the Pope's invitation. This encounter was made possible because Father Joseph had told us: "One day, I will see you ascend the steps of the Vatican. You will be the most important, your place is there." Families from the four continents and of all religions and faiths came to participate in this meeting. Families from far, remote countries had arrived one week before. And when European families arrived, poor families from the third world welcomed them under a porch decorated with flowers, singing and dancing. They were joyous, smiling broadly. God and men were one. We sang together, we hugged those we had never met before. Annick and I from the Brittany group cried. We had never been so moved. Together, we were God's people and nobody could deny it.

The notion of "People" within the project

One of the academics, a sociologist, tried to reach a clearer picture of what we mean when talking about a People in the Fourth World–University project:

In the context of the project, when we talk about People, we mean a group of persons. We must be careful because there is a choice to be made: do we mean a Fourth World People with objective features like the Jewish people or the Armenian people, or do we mean a collection of individuals? Let me say what I understand about this word "People". It is a group of individuals united by a common awareness. An awareness of having experienced situations of extreme poverty, suffered deep inside, and of having found the will to stand up and declare their dignity, seeking a way to do so. The People is a group of individuals who have stood alongside one another. It is a community that incorporates the individual. The individual belongs to a People.

Another academic, a historian, added:

I would add that the idea of life experience is important to prevent the People from being defined on one criterion, racial or other, which conveys exclusion rather than a community or common experience. We must make cautious use of this notion. The idea of a People must be understood and defended openly and forcefully to avoid falling into a trap. For me, a People is a group of individuals whose experiences or living conditions are similar, and who share a common history. They recognize this social, cultural and historical identity as well as a common desire or project. A People doesn't exist as a given, as a kind of historical destiny, but remains under construction, leading towards the future and what it will become. A People then is not a rigid code of belonging like race, ethnicity or social class, but a memory of deeds, aware of itself, in a process of transformation. It seems to me that it is in these conditions that we can happily use the notion of People—by defining it we avoid falling into a trap. I speak of a memory of deeds, because the People is where past, present and future combine. The People is a destination and not a prison. Two reasons lead me to assert this: I fear anything stigmatizing people and labeling them, and also, through the project, academics feel they have been partly adopted by this Fourth World People. Here too, there is a unit, and I would fear being totally excluded from it.

One Fourth World volunteer corps member cast the word "People" in another light:

"People" does not cover any particular category, a highly restricted group such as "the poorest", even though they are at its core. The meaning of "People" that I feel in ATD Fourth World is that of Father Joseph's prophetic vision, a vision that gains a physical dimension and takes a shape. Very poor families are the core. It is around them that the People gathers, for they were the first to make a stand. This notion of "People" also covers those who want to work towards this liberation. They are individuals who join together and share a common aim. Their goal is to eradicate poverty. This means they must first explore their own roots. They have a common future; they build it together because it doesn't exist yet. They create rituals and a culture. This is how families understand the word "People" when it is used in the context of the "Fourth World". In no way do they use it in a sociological sense. When we knock on their door, they ask: "Who's there? Is it the Fourth World?", so we are also identified as the Fourth World, this is what they very often call us.

We could conclude with another Fourth World volunteer corps member, who said:

A new meaning of the word "People" was born and has developed as I discovered the poor and the new light that Father Joseph cast on their lives. Until then, I used to categorize people in society. Now, to me the poor and the poorest mean more than simply those at the end of my street or in an area people avoid. They are everywhere. The Fourth World People knows no boundaries. And looking at the history of humanity, we see they have always existed. The People encompasses all those who listen to the poor so that unity between people is possible.

The myth of the People: A dynamic vision of history

Our group discovered Alain Pessin's book, *The Myth of the People and French Society in the Nineteenth Century*[3], which was a real boon to us. It was a boost to our research and enabled us to progress as its object of study directly concerned us. What is striking in the book is that the way it talks about the "People" squares with what we discussed during the Fourth World–University project seminars. Therefore it seemed important to us to sum up its central ideas as we tackled them in our group. These ideas were one of the elements activists incorporated into their diagram showing the path from the People of poverty to the People of the Fourth World.[4]

What is interesting in Pessin's work is his attempt to show that the idea of the People produces a social truth and a new form of politics, within which the People is seen as having a collective experience.

Who were the populists?

In the book, the author analyses works by a number of nineteenth century French writers called "populists". These authors write about the people of their time, their poverty, and their values. They consider the people a central part of nineteenth century society.

The study of the people presented here is not a study of the working-class or poor in the nineteenth century. Rather, it analyses the way writers presented the people as having qualities and features, both real and imaginary. According to Pessin, this is why one can talk of a *myth of the People*, which reveals something fundamental about humanity and society and with which we can all identify.

Populists' thought differed from that of the period's scholars, who wanted objective analyses. Sociology tries to find scientific answers to social problems; it considers that society is based on struggle and tries to determine which social classes and groups need to change to resolve the situation. Populists think differently: they focus on a factor different from those which already exist (group, class, nation etc.). This is the idea of a committed way of thinking. This is why, the author says, the People is more than a social issue, but is related to mythology. Some populists were writers like Victor Hugo, Lamennais, Eugène Sue,

Michelet, George Sand and Louis Blanc etc., while others were painters, such as Delacroix.

How can we define a myth?

According to the dictionary, a myth is "a fabulous story of often popular origin whose characters represent the forces of nature or aspects of the human condition in symbolic form". A myth is a story we tell to give sense to a process of evolution. Some scholars tend to discount this view, considering myths a form of old knowledge which is to be replaced by what they call "true science", which describes and explains reality. However, there are researchers today who think that myths actually play a very important, even essential, role for people and societies.[5] To them, myths are accounts that allow us to *understand* our human condition and that can *give meaning to our acts. Myths allow every community to identify itself, unite and differentiate itself from others in space and time.*[6]

Every society produces its own myths. In today's world, most myths show that desire exceeds the limits of the human condition, as exemplified by the obsession with achievement, success and wealth. The cult of celebrity, cars[7] or the Internet are all examples of this. In this respect, we can say that the myth of the People is something very different.

Pessin attempted to identify the myth of the People in the texts he read, in paintings and also in political acts, then tried to give it meaning. The result of this leads to an understanding of what Pessin calls the *basic structure of populism*, i.e. its main characteristics and how they are connected. In other words, what function does this reference to the People serve, what does this identification with the People mean? On reading and studying these texts, we can observe, according to Pessin, a number of recurring and related subjects. We see how the idea of the People gains meaning in terms of the situation of the poor in the nineteenth century. We also see how it is the People who will succeed in changing society as a whole because the People carries a truth about society. Finally, we understand how these changes can occur. We will now depict this in a number of diagrams describing relationships between the People and other subjects. They show a fluid *history in a never-ending process of evolution.* We will examine each of them in turn and analyze their meaning.

Absence: the relationship between the People and exile

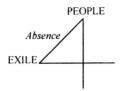

The People is cold and hungry, it suffers: this much is evident. At the beginning of the book, the People is defined as an immense mass of suffering. The problem of the People is first a social and moral one, then a political one. However, to properly understand the People, we need an exact idea of suffering and how it is experienced. We then observe that even before the idea of injustice enters the frame, the People's fundamental problem is not only a social or moral one, but also one of suffering from being abandoned, forgotten, unacknowledged and exiled. This can be expressed in several ways.

The forgotten People: the French Revolution is not over, but remains unfinished. The many people who formed the Fourth Order have been forgotten[8]. The People's life is then defined by a *lack*, because it is ignored and excluded from development and culture.

This ignoring of the People is not transitory, but emanates from the way society is organized.

The People's exile is not only caused by the existence of an upper class and an underclass; but by the existence of a legitimate world which is acknowledged versus an illegitimate world, a world moving forward versus a world on the slippery slope.

The People's life is painful; it has a burden to shoulder. This burden is both social and economic, and is composed of extreme poverty and ignorance. It is a political, economic, judicial and religious burden, none of these fields being more important than another.

Because the People is in exile, there is *an absence* from the very beginning of the book. *The place in society the People ought to occupy is empty. The People cannot be found; there is no People forming a society. There are only individuals deprived of society, left to their own devices.*[9]

Last but not least, in response to this exile, the book shows us that there are two possible solutions. The first solution is that the People is cast further and further adrift and ends up disappearing into the shadows. The second solution is that the People starts to revolt against its situation. It is then defined as a People that stamps its feet, that wears its difference on its sleeve; that changes as it marches. Populism was to follow this second path.

According to populists, this People which arises and marches forward will either take the path leading to peaceful change or the path of revolution. According to Pessin, populists can be divided into two schools of thought between two arguments: which is necessary, reform or revolution? Which must we encourage the People towards, education or political engagement? Non-violence or violence? At first glance, these oppositions seem irreconcilable, but if we explore the question more deeply, we can observe an underlying view which gives rise to what the author calls the *populist dream* or the People's project, and the two schools can be reconciled.

The project: A populist hope and a utopian reflex

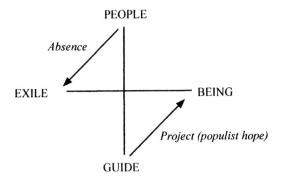

The myth of the People consists in taking the exiled People to a place that does not yet exist. It is therefore a utopian process which is supposed to happen in two stages:

– The first is the dream of a satisfying society for all those who create it in the near future. But as this dream does not seem as though it will come true, different forms of action must be considered, yet these do not seem very effective either. One dreams of an affluent society in which industry works, in which everyone would have a role, in which everyone would be "happy". But the reality is always more extreme poverty, more crime.

– So a second project is started, more humble and more demanding. One dreams of a moment and a place where life would be happy and free. But that place will not appear by itself, it must be created through the "dream of school" or the dream of revolution. There are numerous depictions of the myth of revolution. Revolution is seen as a beginning, as the coming of a new world.

It can be found in Blanqui's texts, in some of George Sand's stories from 1848, and in some paintings by Daumier (*Revolution Scenes*, 1849), Gustave Doré (*Departure Song*, 1870) and Delacroix (*Liberty Guiding the People*, 1830).

Representations of school can be found in populist art because school is seen as a place where a world starts, where the young People builds the future of the world. The teacher's relation to his pupil looks like that of a *guide* to his People. One must bear in mind that at that time, the school teacher was like a symbol of the utopian People. The teacher shared out the best thing he had, his knowledge, his truth, and he also embodied the People because he was poor. *Freedom begins when ignorance ends*, wrote Victor Hugo[10]. Ignorance means being subjected to fate. The schoolteacher, often one of the People by birth, may become a People's guide. This role is embodied by Michelet, who was born to a poor family and who went on to write a history of the People.

Thus we can acknowledge that populist hope is expressed in two different ways: those advocating *revolution*, and those advocating the People's *education* (for example, Blanqui versus Victor Hugo). But if we explore the texts more deeply, we see that education is actually central to all the authors, it prepares the ground for progress. Without education, long-term progress would not be possible. Thus, we see that the guide who will bring the People into existence is in fact the schoolteacher. We also observe that those who claim to want revolution principally want the *revolution's consequences*; they consider the People's liberation as the beginning of progress, they sometimes even think that revolution could be avoided if replaced by universal suffrage or education, for example. The Populist hope is for a People emancipated, free and protected in its freedom. It is the idea that a People will no longer suffer the miseries it has suffered and is still suffering. This longing to *improve the status of the People* is what Pessin also calls a *utopian reflex*.

But what does utopia mean here? Utopia is not something vague and imprecise; neither is it something opposed to science or to ideology. Utopia is a *particular cast of mind*[11] expressing various important things:
– a feeling that truth has departed today's world, that the state of today's world is deceitful and unacceptable;
– that truth can be established within us, within a man or a community, and that even within the prevailing climate of deceit, an "authentic harmony" can be re-established;
– that one must free oneself from the current status quo. The People must accord itself the right to think differently.

In the nineteenth century, utopia was a way for the victims of industrial and political revolution to regain a sense of self. Populism is a commitment to reach something which does not yet exist but which is considered necessary. Populism is *not only* a consequence of acknowledging the People's poverty and the injustice it suffers; it is first and foremost the edification of an idealized form of life, reconciliation, justice and security.[12]

Who is the People and who belongs to the People?

It was by reading Michelet's "*The People*" that we really understood what this People is[13]. According to Pessin, Michelet was the first writer to give the People pride of place and to speak on behalf of the People. Michelet had had a poor childhood, born to a modest family, and his work as a historian was a way to pay his debt to the People from which he came.

> This debt led him to write history as the history of the People, to observe, study and analyze the People. To Michelet, the People writes history.[14]

To him, the notion of People must be carefully differentiated from that of a social class. Making the People into one class or group of classes seems impossible.

The People's thinking is more flexible, it is dynamic and evolving. The idea is that *a part of society, a very mixed group, with no real limits—the humble as a whole—might possess a quality making its members the best representatives of the identity of society as a whole, and which would also guarantee society's future.*[15]

We cannot restrict the People to what were called at that time the plebeians (the poorest); the word must be understood in the broader sense as well. When Michelet spoke of the People, he meant one part which tends to embrace the whole. He thought of something different from race, country, nation or class.

It is not possible to reduce and categorize the People into one or other scientific or sociological concept. The People must be understood as what enables us to go from one part that is promoted and developed (the humble) to the whole. The People is inside each of us (in the sense that we belong to a collective entity), but our individual situations make us feel and experience it to different degrees.

To Michelet, the People could theoretically be everybody. The People is never stronger than when it unites above and beyond the profound class differences that can divide it. In France, the People arises afresh when social classes deny their differences, when worlds begin to meet and acknowledge each other (to the Belgians, it calls to mind what was felt during the "White Walk" in Brussels for the missing children[16]).

With this notion of the People, history unfolds in two stages. There are great moments when the People rediscovers itself and feels the strength of its unity. Then there are other times when the sense of belonging to the People fades in each of us, society grows weaker, oppositions become more marked and mutual misunderstanding and lack of appreciation prevail. To the author's mind, when Michelet writes "the People", one can read *social bond*. Bond in the sense of communitarian relationships, private bonds as well as those in the sense of everyone's attachment to something shared, which is a kind of love. The idea of the People is that of the society that results from human interaction. The question is therefore not to know *who* is the People but rather where is the feeling we call "the People". Who most belongs to the People? Nevertheless for Michelet, though no social group is excluded from the People, one does seem to draw farther and farther away from the People as one reaches higher social classes[17]. The latter have a greater tendency to selfish withdrawal than others. We should also remember Saint Simon's idea, widespread in the nineteenth century, that "the People is the poorest and the most numerous class".

The People is, in a way, the hidden meaning of life and of history. It is also the subject of the history which is yet to be. The People cannot really be recognized or delimited because it is different from observable reality. According to the author, it is a vehicle, something evolving, pointing a way forward.

Birth: The People in exile arises and marches towards existence

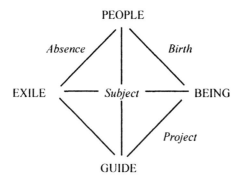

As we have seen, in the beginning the People is in poverty, is exiled, stifled by its extreme poverty most of the time. Something must happen for the People to arise. The circle of exile must be broken. Populists search for that first spark they see as an act of justice and the coming of justice into the world. This justice first takes the form of a *meeting*.

> The future opens up only when there is a harmony between word and deeds, with the certainty that the People's own words and deeds are possible.[18]

A meeting cannot ever be imposed from outside. The People meets the guide. The guide takes the initiative for the meeting. This guide originates from the People but he knows he does not determine the meeting's result.

> He (the guide) talks, acts, multiplies the literature in which the People is invoked and sought; he strives to discover a language the People could understand, strives to formulate the remedy the People could try and use; he constantly conspires, plots and revolutionizes—but we must wait for the People to be born by speaking out and by taking part in the action.[19]

Guides are only messengers who say that a truth is possible and hidden. They await the People, but what are essential are the People's own words. Yet initially the People has no language.

The People is thus born twice:

- There must be a juncture when justice is spoken of. This is done by the guide;

- At the same time, there must be a change in the People. It must go from *exile to existence*. The People can only accomplish its birth alone, but the change can only come about if the strength of the People is revealed to it by the guide.

To conclude, it seems to us that the populists' thinking as analyzed by Pessin allows us to better understand the meaning and implications present when we use the word "People".

The poorest probably best represent the People. But they are not the only People. Thinking about the People is a way of thinking about history and progress in specific terms. Thinking about the People means trying to think about a kind of truth about history that goes beyond that history.

Thinking about the People, in a way, means that one already belongs to it, because it is only possible if one is personally involved, if one goes beyond an objective relationship and if one sets out to discover.

According to Pessin, it is still possible to think of the People at the dawn of the twenty-first century. What the concept of the People keeps on producing in the mind of every rebel in the world, past and present, is the possibility of a different way of thinking.

> The People's thought is one of revolt, hope, sometimes of utopia, and of progress.
> . . . The People's thought is not a timeless concept. It is a form of mythical thought
> employed to save unreasoned times.[20]

Origins of the term "Fourth World"

We felt it would be interesting for us to examine how the words "People" and "Fourth World" have appeared in the thinking of Joseph Wresinski and ATD Fourth World, in order to better understand their full meaning, and relate them to the preceding information.

We started by reading *"Writings and words to the Fourth World volunteer corps members 1960-1967"[21]*. There we find the surviving writings and recordings of meetings in which Joseph Wresinski and members of the Fourth World volunteer corps reflected on their work.

From 1962, we see that he is indignant at the terms used by the worlds of authority and academia to denote the poorest: maladjusted families, problem families, antisocial families and worse. Not only are these words belittling, they also convey the idea that extreme poverty results from the families' own deficiencies instead of from the shame and poverty that society imposes on them. From that time onwards, Father Wresinski most often used the term "families", but in a positive sense: *It is about valuing these families' situations[22]*. This is at the core of his thinking and acts.

Very soon he felt a need to gather these families into a group with its own identity, but he took some time before finding the right words to encapsulate the project. In 1962, he attempted to understand the social bond uniting the families: *By dint of going without the same things and having reacted in the same way, we become to some extent the same People, without means to build anything consistent together; and still in need of others.[23]* He sometimes used the phrase "underclass", but mostly "shanty-towns" or "camps" to describe the group:

(A shanty-town) is like a world, like a group on its own, unaware of its own existence, with no guide nor organization nor centre of activity. . . . A shanty-town is like
a great disaster where extreme poverty alone unites people.[24]

This initial vision of the group is essentially marked by a sense of suffering and
powerlessness. The ensuing logical action was the camps' families trying to leave
and be re-housed elsewhere, scattered. But Father Wresinski saw that this was not
really successful, because though they were better housed, many families did not
adjust and missed the camp at Noisy.

From October 1963[25], a new idea appeared, which he termed *community*. The
latter covers families and members of the Fourth World volunteer corps united in
a *community of destiny* becoming an agent in its own change by staying together. In May 1964, the idea of a community was replaced by that of a *Movement*:
*Striking up personal relations with families and accompanying them as they be-
come part of a Movement.*[26]

Whatever their situations, they (the families) need to know they are part of something bigger, a Movement in which they are together and they find solidarity and
honor.[27]

This is when the word "People" appeared for the first time with a meaning
that has remained ever since: *We have discovered a People that we cannot abandon.*[28]

In the following texts that take us up to the end of 1964, we see the idea of a
People develop its full meaning: those with experience of poverty have their own
values that must be acknowledged. The People and a Movement together form a
project, a campaign:

When we first started out, we didn't know we were faced with a worldwide problem . . . poverty with the same deep-rooted causes everywhere. It was in Noisy-le-
Grand that we discovered the universality of poverty, which always displays the
same problems. . . . Within that poverty, we also discovered the dignity shared by the
poor that entitles them to have their values acknowledged. . . . Thus we embarked
upon a universal struggle. . . . Our organization's aim is to have poor people's hon-
or recognized and for them to re-gain dignity. . . . This task is possible because humankind exists.[29]

The above extracts are accounts of what was said between 1961 and 1965.
Françoise Vedrenne, one of the members of the Fourth World volunteer corps,
researched how the same ideas surfaced in articles written in *Igloos* (an ATD
Fourth World periodical and the forerunner of the *Revue Quart Monde*) between
1961 and 1966. In 1961, families were often described as maladjusted, deprived
or even antisocial (*Igloos* No. 3, 1961). In 1962, *Igloos* No. 7 suggested a variety of terms, showing the near-frantic search for something suitable: families are
described as "socially maladjusted", "segregated", "antisocial" and "poorly inte-

grated", but there is also talk of "shanty-town families" and their "value as human beings". *Igloos* Nos. 8 and 9 spoke of "unhappy", "rejected" or "destitute families". The idea of "maladjusted families" enjoyed a brief resurgence, but in 1963 the term "fragile families" appeared, related to the idea of the families' wounded dignity and family development. In subsequent issues, this term "fragile families" was in turn abandoned, in a return to strictly descriptive designations: "poor", "homeless", and "impoverished families". In 1965, the terms "underprivileged" and "underclass" families were often used (*Igloos* No. 22). The latter expressions gradually disappeared too, undoubtedly more because of the negative ring of the prefix "under" than because of their actual meaning. They were replaced by a much stronger word, "exclusion", found in the title of Klanfer's book "*Social Exclusion*", referred to in *Igloos* No. 24. Also in this issue appeared an expression which has been much-used until the present day, "The poorest populations". In late 1965, a new term appeared in *Igloos* No. 25, that of "People" in "impoverished People" (p 3). At that time, the expression was still only descriptive. The activists Danielle Lebrun and Daniel Le Breton analyzed issues of *Igloos* from 1967 to 1969 (Nos. 33-46). ATD Fourth World, then called "Aide à Toute Détresse/Science et Service", used the expressions "The poor" and "The population". However, in issues 39-40, the word "People" was used more often: *The underclass are not a happy People* (p13), and *A People threatened by police* (p36). And finally: *Our fundamental error is re-housing individuals or small groups which prevents a whole People being inspired to head towards new horizons. This mistake will cost the Nation dear.* Here we clearly see the idea of a People, associated with the idea of this People taking control of its own destiny. This idea was confirmed in the following issues (41-42, May-August 1968): *A People speaks.* It was said that *this People from temporary housing estates and shanty-towns, the People at the bottom of the social ladder, is also the People that bears witness to all of a mechanized society's shortcomings. Do we even know this excluded People which should be the catalyst driving reforms?*

It was in issue No. 44 of *Igloos* in 1969 that the term "Fourth World" was first used to denote the population living in poverty. In the following issue, an article appeared called *What you can do for the Fourth World.* From then on, the term was used more and more to refer to the poor.

Francine de la Gorce, in her work "*A People arises*"[30], quotes Father Joseph Wresinski:

I was not happy with using the word "underclass". It had a Marxist undertone, and I always had in mind the idea of a fourth world. . . . Actually, it came from a conversation with some very dear friends, the Zieglers. One fine day, they gave me a pamphlet on the Fourth Order, which was made up of the lowly and the poor. And it is the Fourth World that we deal with.

Francine de la Gorce continues:

The discovery of the "Notes on the Grievances of the Fourth Order" by Dufourny de Villiers (1789) is almost providential because it returns to families two centuries of history and identity which have been denied them.

The phrase "fourth world", used in 1969 to denote the People of poverty, then became the "Fourth World", with capitals, meaning a People on the move, apparently after having been used as such in the Fourth World People's Universities run by Father Joseph Wresinski in the 1970s.

Another stage, in the 1980s, was expressed by Louis Join-Lambert's definition[31]:

Since the mid-1970s, through the development of community life in poor areas, the term "Fourth World" has allowed this population to identify itself and to be identified as a player and partner in any democratic society. The words "Fourth World" have thus taken on a new tone. They refer less and less to a passive and excluded group. On the contrary, they refer to what the groups can bring us concerning experience, injustice and the hope of justice, the need to be understood, the experience of exclusion and the capacity to participate as social partners in building a democratic society. The phrase "Fourth World" is now addressed to the Fourth World itself. And when the underprivileged say "We, the Fourth World", it is not a target population for the authorities, but rather a People with a cause they share with all those in the world who are excluded and humiliated.

We do not agree with this definition because it is too narrow. It restricts the term "Fourth World" to referring to the poorest. The risk is that this word becomes just one more label to maintain their exclusion. Our research showed us that the People of the Fourth World is a force which concerns more than just the poorest.

From the People of poverty to the People of the Fourth World

Using the analysis of experiences of turnaround (see preceding chapter), of Pessin's works, and of discussions of the meaning of the word "People", activists drew a complex and expressive diagram showing the progression from the People of poverty to the People of the Fourth World. The elements of this diagram are: the realities experienced by the poor, Father Joseph Wresinski's role as a "guide" who is one of the People, the encounters that lead to turnaround and the choice to belong to the People of the Fourth World.

What is common to the People of poverty?

Same suffering
Shame
Humiliation   *Joseph Wresinski*
Same daily struggle
Same life values

Very poor families recognize each other: *We speak the same language; we understand each other by sharing a glance. We are all the same, all equal, we all suffer the same. On the 15th of each month, when everything has been paid for, we have barely 100 francs (*roughly $17) *to live on, and still we need to eat.***

Anyone who lives or has lived in poverty can identify with what this woman says:

> In the shanty-town, everyone was brave. To be honest, they did have a drink from time to time. They would rummage through garbage cans and dumps and pick up rags, scrap metal and old shoes, and burn them to warm themselves. We young people would find all kinds of things, even sweets and cakes, and we'd eat them. We were never ill. We ate everything and anything. We'd take clothes, wash them at the pump, and be happy because they were more fashionable than ours and we went out in them. The parents would go and sell scrap and get 15 or 20 francs a day ($2.5). We were cold, and at night we had to have the little ones with us in bed. The campfire would go out during the night. We were really cold and hungry. This is what it was like: we lived in the cold with a piece of bread and some pâté. But we got on well, we could easily ask our neighbors for some butter or coffee and they would give it to us. We were like brothers and sisters, true friends. We were cold and hungry, true, but we did not lack friendship. We did have friendship and love. Now I have a two-room flat and I'm not too unhappy. I've a friend who lives downstairs and I go down and have coffee, but I can't say I have real friends. We keep ourselves to ourselves. We're too family-oriented. It's not a good thing. We should have other friends, but we can't make any. I don't know why we don't make friends easily. We can talk though, we dress normally, but it's not just about that.[32]

Very poor families recognize one other through the same suffering, the same shame that stays locked inside them, the same daily struggles to feed their family, the same values of love, helping and sharing. This common living experience is what makes them say: we are the same. We are a People, the People of poverty. Can such a common experience in one country be expanded to cover families living in poverty on other continents? To answer this question, our group interviewed Brigitte Seinave, a member of the Fourth World volunteer corps who lived in Haiti for eight years. She tells of a Haitian woman, Rosemarie, and her family who live in one of the lowliest places in the shanty-town. Rosemarie never has a moment's rest. She is on her feet from dawn to dusk to try and find a way of paying the rent, to sell something, to find treatment for a sick child or a place to spend the night etc.

We always wondered where she got her energy. She had her first child when she was still at school. Her mother had already died. She had scarcely given birth when her husband fell ill. "I went through agony to cure him", she says. "Every night at 4 am, I would go to the pump and wash the bedclothes on which he had been sleeping. I'd buy lemon and bleach that I would put on the fabrics before hanging them out to get rid of the smell. When my husband died, everybody abandoned me. I worked as a maid and my baby fell ill, swollen up like a bomb about to explode. I wrapped him in a towel but his body was discharging pus, and flies chased us. I got to the medical centre and they gave me a prescription. I didn't have a nickel. I said to myself: "Where shall I go? This child is mine, he can't be left to die. I would rather beg at the church to have him live". On my way to the church, some of my dad's friends passed me in the street, I hid so that they wouldn't see me with the child. I shook my head, saying to myself: "See what's become of me with this child in my arms!" Every day I went begging with my child."

Then Rosemarie met Philippe, her second husband with whom she had ten children, three of whom died. He was a wood-carver and sold sculptures to tourists in the Dominican Republic. But the wood and all the traveling back and forth became more and more expensive. Rosemarie did everything she could so that her husband wouldn't feel useless and would remain a father to his children. For example, she encouraged him to teach wood-carving to his own children and those from the area. They had to move several times because they could not afford the rent. At the age of 80, her father still broke stones (a common job in Haiti) to help his daughter who lived on a terrace with her children. At that time she heard of another woman living in an arbor with her seven children; every evening she would go down there and make them something to eat.

This woman lived in extreme poverty in one of the world's poorest countries. Although survival conditions are desperate, there are some shared features with the experiences the poorest in developed countries mention: fighting for their children above all else, suffering and shame, a mothers' courage, concern for maintaining the father's dignity in the family and helping other very poor families etc. Early deaths are frequent, but the poorest are often denied the right to rest in peace, whatever the country or continent. Because of their poverty, they cannot afford a plot. Locating a relative's grave is often impossible, since in France the very poor are often buried in communal graves, there is often only a wooden cross with a number on the burial place meaning that parents, brothers and sisters cannot go and contemplate near their deceased relatives, who remain forever dear in their thoughts and hearts.

As a child, Joseph Wresinski underwent the suffering, humiliation, and rebellion that children in poverty experience. He had to take on responsibilities at a very early age. He was a witness to his mother's courage in bringing up five children. He writes[33]:

My earliest childhood memories are of a large hospital ward and of my mother shouting at the nun who was supervising us. As a young boy I suffered from rickets, and I had been hospitalized to have my legs straightened. That day I told my mother that the nun had not let me receive my parcel the previous Sunday. My mother, who obviously had tried hard to gather a few treats, lost her temper. Immediately she wrenched me from the hands of the nuns and brought me back home. My legs have remained bowed ever since. Throughout my childhood, and especially as a teenager, I was subjected to the ridicule and teasing brought on by this handicap—and endured the added embarrassment of a slight limp. . . . At home, my father shouted all the time. He would beat my older brother, much to my mother's despair, as it was always my brother's head that bore the brunt of it. My father frequently cursed my mother, and we lived continually in fear. . . . My parents talked only money. The very people who had no money would forever be arguing because of it. When some money did come into the household, they quarreled about what to spend it on. Later, when my mother was on her own, she would still frequently talk to us about money. . . . I was committed to the fight for food at a very young age. When I was four years old, I was the one who led our goat to the lower meadows. This goat fed all of us children, including my newborn sister. When I took the goat, I would pass the big gate of the Good Shepherd Convent, where a nun would sometimes chat with me. One day she asked whether I would serve Mass every morning. That day I became employed for the first time; and it was real employment as far as I was concerned. In return for serving Mass, I would be entitled to a big bowl of coffee with milk, as well as bread and jam and—on holy days—butter. In addition, I would be given two francs a week. It was those two francs that motivated me to take the job. . . . Every morning for almost eleven years, my mother called me for the seven o'clock Mass. . . . In the winter I was cold and frightened of the dark. . . . I do not remember ever coming home from school and finding my mother happy at home.

Concluding these thoughts on his childhood, he writes:

Joining in the struggle for the excluded is not that simple, however. A person does not become an activist on behalf of individuals scattered here and there: a drunk mother, a fortune teller, or a puny boy. I had to encounter them as one people and to discover I was one of them. As an adult, I had to find myself again the boys who live in the slum housing surrounding our towns and in the unemployed young people who cry with rage. They perpetuate the memory of my miserable childhood, and they remind me that these people in rags have always existed.

I was shocked when I arrived in Noisy-le-Grand

When he was young, Joseph Wresinski encountered Christian Workers' Youth (JOC). Then, as a young man he entered the seminary to become a priest.

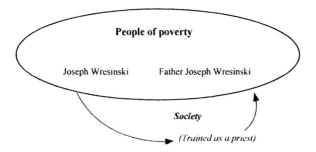

After having sent him to several other parishes, his bishop sent him to the camp at Noisy-le-Grand in 1956.Later, he would write of:

> The shock I experienced upon my arrival at Noisy-le-Grand. Even though I had been brought up in poverty myself and I have seen many poor areas since, Noisy-le-Grand was like a revelation. . . . I felt at once that I was in the presence of my people. I cannot explain it. That's how it was. From that moment, my own life took a turn.[34]

Father Joseph Wresinski was 40 years-old when he arrived in Noisy-le-Grand, home to 252 families. Françoise Lebrun says:

> We arrived in 1961. It wasn't even an estate, it was a camp with chimney stacks everywhere. It was nothing like what we'd experienced until then, it was real poverty. We had seen mild poverty before, but never to such an extent. This was extreme poverty. In the beginning, mothers, girls and even toddlers would go and fetch water from the pump. There were five pumps for 252 of us. It was very tough; we could hardly wash our clothes. [35]

Faced with this situation, Father Joseph's most urgent concern was to ease the mothers' suffering. Together with the men living in the camp, he built a women's club. Françoise Lebrun remembers:

> That was wonderful. There was a place where we could wash clothes, wring and dry them out, for only two francs a week. We could even have a shower. Sometimes, we bumped into Father Joseph and shook hands. He was always surrounded by kids, he would give them sweets, they would talk to him. He laughed with them, he loved children. People liked Father Joseph. He was a wonderful man. He always had something to say to everyone, good or bad. If you didn't go to work, he would call you all the names under the sun. He looked like the people there: if you spoke nicely, so would he, and if you spoke roughly, he would answer roughly too. He didn't mind rolling his sleeves up if things went wrong.

Father Joseph was from the world of poverty. To become a priest, he had to train outside his family circle and his background. Having learnt new things, he chose to come back to his People, the People of poverty. He then became *the guide* of which Pessin writes. He said he was staggered when he arrived at the camp. He sometimes said that on that day he experienced the misery of extreme poverty. He did not go back to his People because of remorse or a sense of debt, or with an agenda. He let himself be inspired by communing with them, as if drawing some hidden potential from each of them, and he formed an alliance with every one of them that he would never break.

The experience he had gained himself, through training, opening up to other environments etc., he passed on to those he met. Everything he did in poor districts was a way of broadening people's horizons. He yearned for all that was best and most technically advanced to be accessible to the poorest. He always encouraged the young people and adults who wanted to commit themselves to their own people (the activists) to undertake the same "return journey" (by means of professional training, encountering other social groups and lifestyles etc.), so as to return to their people freer and more culturally aware and become guides in turn. Passing through other social spheres and returning to the People of poverty is one way of preventing the guide from becoming a leader.

Meetings

Françoise Lebrun explains:

> What I remember about Father Joseph is that he did beautiful things. Not on his own, the poor man couldn't have done all that by himself. He did it with others. People from the camp and the [Fourth World volunteer corps members]. The [Fourth World volunteer corps members] used to bring us our mail. They were brave, poor guys! They were scared of the dogs. They were very kind; they used to stay a while and talk with the moms. We have wonderful memories of them. We were lucky to have them, because we did feel lonely sometimes in the camp.

Meetings happen between people living in poverty and others from different social and professional environments (workers, teachers, executives, the upper classes etc.). No-one is forced to meet anyone else. For the poor, meetings are cherished aspirations because they signify the acknowledgement of a shared humanity, provided both parties share with each other and give each another confidence. Meetings are enriching. They provide a chance to give and receive in exchange. They constitute the gift given and the gift received. These particular meetings, which the poor aspire to and are experienced between the poor and non-poor, are the opposite of what usually happens when poor people are dominated by the rich and educated.

Marie-Jeanne Notermans explains how, as a member of the Fourth World volunteer corps, she experienced her meeting:

As Fourth World volunteer corps members, we're well aware of having weaknesses. But at the same time, we're all trying to progress with you and it is really important that one day a few people say: I'd like to stand by your side and we'll do as best we can. Faced with all your suffering, we feel small but we also grow. But we're human beings, we'll feel we have grown one day and then, the next day we'll feel small again. This path isn't easy, but you've given us new eyes that have enabled us to look differently at society wherever we are.

Meetings can take place in various places. When members of the Fourth World volunteer corps live in poor areas, they share some of the People's *exile*, as Pessin put it. Sometimes, joint action triggers meetings (cultural projects, Fourth World People's Universities, gatherings etc.). Here, the meetings are part of a long-term process; they are not one-off actions. People are not invited to meet isolated individuals, as Father Joseph put it, but rather the People of Poverty.

The People of the Fourth World: A myth

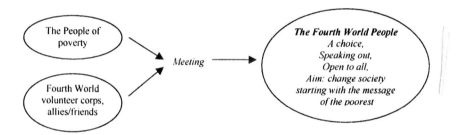

Father Joseph Wresinski writes that when he arrived in Noisy-le-Grand he made a promise to himself:*I vowed that if I stayed, I would see to it that one day these families could go to the Vatican, the Elysée Palace, and the UN. . . . Since then, I have been haunted by the idea that those people would never escape from their poverty as long as they were not welcomed as a whole, as a people, in those places where other people held debates or led struggles. They had to be there, on equal terms, in every place where people discuss and make decisions not only about the present, but also about people's destiny and the future of humanity.*36

Father Joseph never forced the poor to speak—he simply made it possible for them to do so. For the first time, the poorest were seen as having a positive message to deliver, something to say that society could not know without them. However, the People of poverty cannot deliver this message on its own. It must be worked upon with others for it to be understood. This is why the People of the Fourth World is made up of both the poorest and all those joining them in combating poverty; that is to say, all those aware of the injustices suffered by the poorest. The People of the Fourth World is open to anyone who wants to stand up and act together against extreme poverty. Belonging to the People of the Fourth World is a choice everyone can make.

To be able to say "I belong to this People" is something to be proud of. Annick Le Hir says:

> I belong to the People of the Fourth World. It does me good. I have my place within it. Nothing in the world will make me leave my place.[37]

Noël Jacques gives his definition of the People:

> (The poorest) are like a core with the People around it; they dance a farandole and link hands to join together. Together they form the People and fight for just ideas.[38]

Danielle Lebrun defines her place as follows:

> I give all that is dearest to me for the poorest. I still feel flayed alive. I can't help it; it's rooted deep within me. My roots are humiliation. I can say that I'll never feel superior to the poorest. I don't aim to be acknowledged for who I am. Deep down, I'll always belong to the People of poverty.

To belong to the People of the Fourth World is to remain humble. Humble does not mean naïve; on the contrary it means thoughtful, and therefore intelligent.

Marie-Jeanne Notermans talks about belonging to the Fourth World People:

> I remember a conversation I had with Father Joseph and some Fourth World volunteer corps members. We talked about the meaning of the People of the Fourth World. Then I discovered that the Fourth World was not the poor alone, but all of us together. I could then also say that I belong to the Fourth World, though I could not say: I am poor. So the People of the Fourth World has really become my roots too. I must change a little, but then the poor also must change things. We learn from one another. The poorest are the ones who give meaning to the People that we are creating together, the People of destiny.

In this sense, the People of the Fourth World is a myth. A myth with rites such as, for example, gatherings around the stone laid on the Trocadero in Paris, with Father Joseph Wresinski's message:

> "Wherever men and women are condemned to live in extreme poverty, human rights are violated.
> To come together to ensure that these rights be respected is our solemn duty."
> We never would have dreamed of having such a stone. We thought stones were for Presidents.[39]

Brigitte Seinave refers to the celebrations of October 17* all over the world. She experienced gatherings during very violent times in Haiti, when everyone feared for their lives.

Families talked about their situations, but they knew their stories would be recounted to other very poor families all over the world. This is where the notion of the People recurs. They said to other families: we know that you too are living in very tough conditions, this is why we must stand together, it will give us strength even though we don't know one another.

Belonging to the People of the Fourth World is also a form of joint action. Brigitte describes some group initiatives in Haiti:

We sometimes had to stop because the political situation had become too dangerous. We were always guided by the families. They were the ones who told us whenever it was too dangerous. We trained young people to take charge of street libraries. That was when we saw what great unifiers the poorest were. One day, after two women had been evicted, the group said: we can't leave these women and their children homeless. Someone hit on the idea that a permanent room should be built for each of the women. This took time. Allies helped to find the money. For months, families, young people, and friends carried rocks and cement first to build stairs and then the structures. These families, who had been totally rejected from the outset, suddenly found themselves at the center of action.

Group initiatives undertaken on behalf of the People of the Fourth World, whatever the country or continent, always start with the poorest themselves. Everyone has their own place within this People. Father Joseph reminded members of the Fourth World volunteer corps and people involved with the poor as follows:

The great opportunity [ATD Fourth World] offers is that its cause is, at one and same time, individuals who suffer and a people who are on the move, forcing us to move with them. The fact that they are individuals prevents us from making the people into a reason, an excuse, or an alibi for a struggle. Individuals force us to live at their rhythm and to make their heartbeats, their hopes, and their thoughts our own. The fact that they are also a people forces us to stay as we are—men and women to whom the poor can say, "You can do all you want, but you will never be able to understand because you haven't experienced what we are going through." If they couldn't say that to us, we wouldn't be forced to give them the right to speak. The poorest have the right to control and to correct; they can exercise this right only if they and we each stay in our proper place.[40]

The following diagram takes up the constituents previously described and sums up our findings:

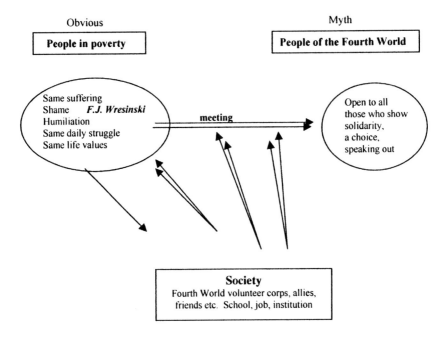

It must be noted that some of the People of poverty, owing to success at school or a professional qualification, acquire a recognized place in society, and some campaign for more justice through their work or in the place they live. This is the meaning of the arrow in the diagram from "The People of poverty" to "Society".

Participating in social change

The People of poverty is always evolving. It evolves towards society in order to have the latter listen to the message of the poorest and participate in determining the future of humanity in every respect. This evolution, this movement, continues so that no-one will be left behind. This is why it remains an active priority to seek out the poorest wherever they are. Extreme poverty must be beaten, and to see this through, the People of the Fourth World must remain ever-vigilant that no-one be in exile and that everybody accept that they belong to one and the same race: humanity.

In continuation of the above diagram, our group produced the following:

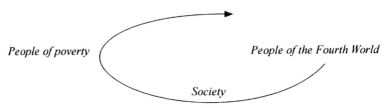

Notes

1. The quotations in this section are not given individual notes. They are extracts from the project participants' answers to the following question asked by the History group in January 1997: "What does the word "people" mean to you?"
2. Fourth World volunteer corps member Brigitte Seinave's lecture to the group.
3. A. Pessin, *Le mythe du peuple et la société française du XIXe siècle* (The Myth of the People and French Society in the Nineteenth Century), PUF, 1992.
4. See the activists' diagram at the end of this chapter.
5. We could quote an increasing number of works on this subject. In French-speaking countries, there is a tradition of research spearheaded by Bachelard, Eliade, Ricoeur, Durand etc. Alain Pessin can be seen as part of this tradition.
6. J.-J. Wunenburger, *L'imagination*, (Imagination) Paris, PUF, "Que sais-je" series, 1991, p. 116.
7. M. Eliade, *Aspects du mythe*, (Aspects of the Myth) Paris, Gallimard, 1963, p. 228.
8. As demonstrated in the *Cahiers du Quatrième Ordre*, in which Dufourny de Villiers demands that the poor have political representation, op. cit.
9. A. Pessin, op. cit., p. 233.
10. V. Hugo, *Le tas de pierres* (Heap of Stones*)*, quoted by A. Pessin, op. cit., p. 90.
11. A. Pessin, op. cit., p. 237.
12. Ibid., p. 239.
13. J. Michelet, *Le peuple* (The People), Paris, Flammarion, 1974. First published 1846.
14. A. Pessin, op. cit., p. 103.
15. Ibid., p. 112.
16. This was a silent demonstration organized in October 1996 by the parents of the children abducted by Marc Dutroux. More than 300,000 people took part, all wearing something white
17. Ibid., p. 114.
18. Ibid., p. 254.
19. Ibid., p. 254.
20. Ibid., p. 269.
21. Father J. Wresinski, *Écrits et Paroles (Words for Fourth World volunteer corps members)*, 1960-1967, Editions St Paul-Quart Monde, Luxembourg, 1992, 574 pp.
22. Ibid., p. 147.
23. Ibid., p. 107.
24. Ibid., p. 165.
25. Ibid., pp. 187 onwards.
26. Ibid., p. 241.
27. Ibid., p. 249.
28. Ibid., p. 247.
29. Ibid., pp. 262-263.
30. Fr. de la Gorce, *Un Peuple se lève* (A People Arises), Editions Quart Monde, Paris, 1995, 316 pp.
31. L. Join-Lambert, *Quart Monde in Universalia*, 1981 supplement to the Encyclopedia Universalis, pp. 341-344.
32. Interview no. 5.
33. J. Wresinski, The Poor are the Church, Twenty-Third Publications 2002, pp. 3-6.
34. Ibid., p. 49.
35. Interview no. 5.

36. Ibid., p. 49.
37. Interview no. 4.
38. Interview no. 17.
39. Interview no. 5.
40. Ibid., pp. 146-147.

CONCLUSION

Summary of research findings

The history that we wanted to write was one of a possible change for the poor and non-poor alike.

By briefly surveying the history of the poor, analyzing their current situation, considering academics' views and activists' accounts, we have shown that the poor have consistently been regarded with contempt. Most often, all that society sees in them is what they lack: material possessions of course, but also education, intelligence, cohesion, a sense of morality etc. The poor trigger reactions of fear and rejection. They are not given the opportunity to speak out.

We therefore wanted to give the poor this opportunity. We could not possibly summarize their accounts: they must be read and digested to perceive the weight of suffering on these lives marked by hunger and cold, money problems of all kinds and, for many, the emotional wrench of care orders. Everywhere they go, they encounter contempt: at school, in the street, by the social services and the authorities, even at church. That contempt shows no awareness of poor people's qualities and strengths: their relentless struggle against insecurity, their ingenuity, their faith in life and in solidarity beyond despair, their love for their partner, their resolute hope for a better future for their children, and the sacrifices they make for them. Yet how can people even realize they have these qualities when they live in the indignity of not having them acknowledged?

Our research then attempted to describe turnaround: the journey from shame to pride. We first examined the different stages starting from within poverty itself. We saw that first of all, meeting someone is very important: Father Joseph Wresinski is this person for some, but it can also be one of our Fourth World volunteer corps members or allies, a friend, neighbor or relative. The respect of another person proves it *is* possible not to be excluded. Then came the awareness of injustice suffered because of extreme poverty, and the awareness of not being alone in that state. Through gatherings and Fourth World People's Universities, those who have encountered ATD Fourth World start to feel confident speaking in public. They feel that they have a cause to fight for, responsibilities to assume, other people they can help, and that they belong to a People in the positive sense of the word: *the People of the Fourth World.*

Our research also showed us that, given the importance of one's view of *the Other*, a similar turnaround must take place in those who are outside poverty. We consider this an important basic premise in our research. This is why we insist on further encounters and *knowledge-merging.*

Finally, we endeavored to use scientific language to describe these experiences of turnaround and to present them in a structured manner. Using Pessin's description of 19th–century populists, activists created a structural diagram which shows the process of turnaround, both for the individual as well as for the group. The activists clearly show that the People of the Fourth World is composed of individuals with a common aim. They also show how this People is dedicated to its main goal which, for the poorest, represents a hope and a path that leads from the shame of poverty to the pride of belonging to this People; and therefore, how it also incorporates all those who are working towards the same goal, even if they have no personal experience of poverty.

The merging of knowledge

The idea of knowledge-merging was decided upon as one of the project's aims. We must admit that initially we were not sure what the term meant. It was only gradually that we were able to fully understand it.

Knowledge-merging is first and foremost an exchange between people, based on mutual respect. This was demonstrated by each of us agreeing to write about the difficult moments in our own lives. What we wrote went no further than our own group. We thus saw that each of us (activists, academics, and members of the Fourth World volunteer corps) bore a hidden burden of suffering.

Merging ideas was also possible, even if we did not always agree, because each of us agreed to learn from the others. The activists had to learn how to learn, and make every effort to change their way of speaking to express themselves more clearly, while retaining the force of what they had to say.

They found writing slightly more difficult because of their low level of schooling and lack of practice. But they had to write down what they expressed in words. For the activists, writing was a talent they discovered within themselves.

The academics, on the other hand, had to learn not to use academic language too much so that the group could understand them and share with them. They had to break free from some of the things they had learned at university or from books in order to hear what was really important to the activists. It was only when they began to understand the activists' point of view that they were able to make a useful contribution. In terms of what they wrote, they accepted that their texts be reread, corrected and sometimes rejected by the rest of the group.

Interaction between the activists and the Fourth World volunteer corps member was different because both are involved in the same struggle against extreme poverty. Their interaction was mainly merging the ideas and knowledge of the poorest. As far as the Fourth World volunteer corps member was concerned, it was difficult for her not to emphasize her beliefs, but to contribute to the research simply based on her life experiences.

Our research has shown us that the conditions for real knowledge-merging are not achieved by merely sharing what we know. What is required—and more difficult—is to know and recognize one another as people, each possessing their own knowledge drawn from their life and perceptions, which others do not know and thus have to learn about. This knowledge-merging is possible only if a real exchange takes place between people, through dialogue and work, but also by eating and laughing together.

Unanswered questions

For the academics

For this research, taking the usual academic approach to human sciences issues such as poverty would have been insufficient, because it does not give priority to the knowledge gained from the experiences of those concerned, but instead generally reinterprets and categorizes this intellectually. The academics therefore had to find a new approach. The best way to describe the approach used in this project would be "a group of co-researchers focusing on a common task together; co-researchers being educated as they discover". This required the use of unusual methods. In this sense, the importance of the transcripts cannot be stressed enough in deepening common thought and knowledge-merging. We also learned that knowledge-merging is an ongoing process. The priority given to the knowledge of those who experience the situations studied, in this instance the poorest, cannot become so exclusive as to say "Only we are entitled to speak about it". If this were the case, there would be no merging of knowledge, but merely juxtaposed monologues.

Giving priority to the poorest means they retain the right to criticize: they must be allowed to correct what academics say, then accept it and find in it new ideas that enrich their own knowledge.

We have yet to find an answer to the question of how the knowledge of the poorest that we have started discovering can be conveyed to that part of the academic world which has not undergone this experience, and how room can be made for it within academia.

For the Fourth World volunteer corps member

One of the fundamental issues raised by knowledge-merging in our research was that of the diversity of the forms of knowledge represented. There is the knowledge of the activists, who have directly experienced extreme poverty and exclusion. There is the Fourth World volunteer corps member's knowledge, acquired through her involvement and her life shared with the poorest. And there is academic knowledge, rigorous and governed by precise rules. There was a constant tension among the group as to the ways of talking about the poorest and poverty, and who is entitled to do so: the question of what is meant by giving priority to the poorest.

By virtue of being human, poor families have values such as justice, solidarity, friendship and love, just like any other family. It is precisely because these values are found in families living in crushing poverty that humanity can be said to be the strongest of all: it resists. This is why activists want to be recognized for their humanity. It is with them and because of them that humanity can make a stand against poverty.

There would be nothing there to save without them, said one activist. Everybody agrees on that point. However, tension arose every time the Fourth World volunteer corps member mentioned *extreme poverty destroying* the humanity of those who suffer it. This notion of *extreme poverty* that *destroys* seems to contradict the notion of a *People* and the activists' pride at belonging to a People. To talk about what poverty destroys in people is to push them further into this poverty. It is a way of speaking that attacks the pride of some activists. Members of the Fourth World volunteer corps and activists belong to the same movement; they are characters in the same story. Joseph Wresinski started things in the camp at Noisy-le-Grand. He created a Fourth World volunteer corps to allow the poorest not only to become a People, but also to become fully aware of being one and acquire the means necessary to be one (solidarity, a sense of distance and a vision of the future). Thus, the question remains in the group: who is entitled to speak about whom and what? Are activists the only ones allowed to talk about poverty?

For the activists

Throughout the project, the activists repeatedly reminded the other participants that they represented not only themselves, but also families living in extreme poverty. This is what kept them going. At the end of the project, their unanswered questions are: How will everything which has been experienced, shared and written down serve future generations? How will it give other people living in poverty the strength to commit themselves in their turn for their People? Who will continue to commit their lives alongside them to have the voice of the poorest heard and listened to respectfully all over the world?

Appendix

The interviews

Our research subject, "History of the journey from the shame of poverty to the pride of belonging to a People" involved, of course, interviewing people who had lived—most of whom were still living—in extreme poverty and who had made this journey.

The group's activists chose people they knew had experienced this. These people agreed to talk about it because they knew the interviewers had shared their experiences and they knew they were taking part in a research project aiming to have the dignity of the poorest recognized. The activists gave them the script of the interview and allowed them to alter it if they wished. They were offered the choice of using either their real name or an alias in order to respect people's right to privacy.

A list of the interviewees and those who provided accounts for activists:

N	M/F	AGE	CHILDREN	HEARD OF ATD FOURTH WORLD?
1	M (deceased)	59	5	Yes
2	F (deceased)	57	2	Yes
3	M (deceased)	58	5	Yes
4	F	68		Yes
5	F	40	4	Yes
6	F	51	5	Yes
7	F	49	5	Yes
8	F	52	5	Yes
9	F	50	5	Yes
10	F	42	7	Yes
11	M	54	4	Yes
12	F	32	0	Yes
13	M	45	0	No
14	M	49	5	Yes
15	F	35	?	No
16	F	?	?	No
17	M	25	0	No
18	F	60	7	No
19	M	60		No
20	M	?	2	No
21	F	96	?	No
22	M	36	0	Yes

22 people, 9 men, 13 women aged:

      60 and over – 4

      50-60 – 7

      40-50 – 5

      under 40 – 4

      age unknown – 2

of the 22 people, 8 had not heard of ATD Fourth World, 14 had heard of ATD Fourth World and 12 described themselves as Fourth World activists

II

FAMILY:
THE FAMILY PLAN AND TIME

by Pierre Fontaine, Marie Jahrling-Apparicio, Pierre Maclouf,
Christian Scribot, Françoise Vedrenne and Paulette Vienne.

With contributions from Daniel Cornerotte, Françoise Ferrand
and Pascal Galvani.

FAMILY: THE FAMILY PLAN AND TIME

Introduction

Does choosing the family as a research topic, just as some Western nations are de-emphasizing it politically, not seem like an attempt to bring back the past? Is wanting to attribute such importance to the family not a bit behind the times? And yet when academics, Fourth World volunteer corps members and activists came together for planning meetings, the family was proposed as a research topic by a large majority of those present. Family life remains a strongly held value in today's society, even if living in one often turns out to be troublesome, disappointing and multiform. No matter what one's viewpoint on it is, the topic of the family quickly becomes inevitable when poverty is concerned, particularly for the very poor.[1] What future plans do the very poor have in mind when they choose to live together, get married and begin having children? The starting point for our hypothesized answer to this question was the idea—subject to lively debate after it was expressed by certain members of the group—that family is a defining value for the very poor. Although it may conflict with contemporary beliefs which maintain that a concern for self-realization comes first, our group retained this view of the family because of the sway it holds in highly disadvantaged circles.

The family may be viewed as a backdrop to love, defined as the action of bringing two people together, but without limiting it to being the sum of two individuals seeking happiness. It marshals the desire which leads them to have children but it cannot simply be reduced to the drive to reproduce. The family not only guarantees security, but offers its members lasting unconditional attachments. Living in a family makes it possible for each member to give of himself, and even demands that he do so.

From amongst the various ways to define family, in particular as a set of relatives or as a couple founded through marriage, the latter was chosen for our purposes here. To be precise, what was discussed was the reproductive family as designated by the couple and their children. When considering the reproductive family from very poor backgrounds, another topic was reformulated during group discussion—looking at family life in terms of recognition of the plans they make. This last notion echoed the idea, also discussed, of the personal responsibility that is evident in taking action to combat poverty, and thus quickly proved susceptible to being elaborated as an object of research.

How and why do very poor people decide to become a couple? Do they view their offspring from this perspective, do their actions seek to breathe life into the family unit? All these different events may be thought together with the help of the concept of a plan. This concept helps us to view the family in terms of actions taken against its own marginalization. It also allows us to talk about poverty while keeping in mind, as is not often done, more than just suffering, and by focusing on the hope that leads us to undertake things no matter what difficulties lie ahead. Planning, a way of making the future happen, invokes man's desire to be considered as a player in society. Thus when plans are being made, the family group as such is not necessarily what is put into play, but the act of committing oneself to something for purposes of self-realization.

Planning for a family is not viewed as a value one holds, but as a kind of practice one engages in by accomplishing two acts: the founding of the family-unit itself, followed by its maintenance, which presupposes the possession of means for constructing a desired future. These two actions take place over time, and the question of time allows for a relationship to be forged between institutions and very poor families.

Time encompasses questions surrounding rhythm, the opening of new perspectives and the closing of horizons. This was the issue whose analysis guided the development of our entire problem-definition.

The topics of planning for a family and poverty are situated on two distinct planes. By deliberately choosing the former, we ran the risk of neglecting the concerns that arise due to the specific problems of extreme poverty. The axis of time brought us back to them.

With this issue we were able to see how very poor people enter into relationships (of dependence, domination, autonomy and emancipation), in particular with social, economic and political institutions, that are lasting in nature. . We also came to grasp another conception of time altogether—theirs and theirs alone. In this way the issue of the conditions of existence for very poor families was reintroduced. These families experience time, but it is as a key source of tension because it is defined, controlled and even imposed by various institutions.

Planning makes it possible to hope, to expect better things to come; whereas the question of time leads one to envision hope as an open—self-assured and risky—relationship with the future. In the end we came to see, even more so than at the outset, the family as a result of time. A result of personal initiatives, that must be undertaken ever anew, viewed as expressions of an action specific to the very poor seeking to forge an opening onto their own future.

The approach we took was to seek to understand the meaning that people in extreme poverty themselves attribute to the creation of their families, and the relationships they establish between their family life and time. Our goals were to effect a change in how the poorest families are viewed, to thereby avoid much suffering, and to sketch out the elements of a family policy that is more just for all.

In Chapter 1 we explain the methodology behind how and why we chose the topic of the family, and how the research question concerning the interstices between planning and time gradually took shape. Chapters 2 and 3 attempt to define the terms and concepts used: family, time, continuance and plan.

Chapter 4 is where we reflect on the seemingly conflictual relationship that exists between short-and long-term timeframes for families in grave difficulty: despite the almost never-ending demands placed upon them by crisis situations, and the stakes these situations raise, how do they manage to continue to maintain long-term plans and put them into effect according to the timing of their own choosing (what we shall call the resourceful-times which stand in stark contrast to the hard-times of their many crises)?

Finally in Chapter 5 we ask ourselves whether planning for a family is, or is not, a stepping stone that very poor families can use for reentering society. We began by thinking together on the different timeframes just mentioned, at which point we began to see that what is essential to building a true partnership is that society maintain a positive view of these families, and that it acknowledge their plans. How can it facilitate the assumption of initiative and responsibility that comes with this type of planning? How can this recognition by institutions and society at large of family plans made by the poorest be situated in relation to the assistance-participation opposition?

Note

1. We are referring here not to poverty in general, but to "extreme poverty" as defined by the Wresinski Report of 1987 and adopted by the Economic and Social Council of France. Chronic Poverty and Lack of Basic Security: The Wresinski Report of the Economic and Social Council of France states: "Chronic poverty results when the lack of basic security simultaneously affects several aspects of people's lives, when it is prolonged, and when it severely compromises people's chances of regaining their rights and of reassuming their responsibilities in the foreseeable future."

Chapter 1

THE GROUP'S APPROACH

Carrying out a research project means being able to stay close to the topic that has been selected while at the same time maintaining a certain distance. This section on methodology depicts the approach, known as merging knowledge, taken by key members of our group while they were defining problem areas for research, gathering and analyzing data, and formulating results.

Defining the research subject

In the first seminar meeting held in March of 1996 each participant raised questions that seemed important to him or her as potential research topics. 21 of the 32 participants came up with a question related to the family, thereby making it a key theme. For example: *Why do families split up? Why does society fail to take into account the efforts made by parents living in subsistence conditions on behalf of their children? How important is the family in the fight against poverty?*

After the first seminar all participants were invited to write about what they thought were the five most important themes mentioned in the meeting and why. This exercise yielded 24 texts on the family. The most recurrent themes included: society's lack of awareness about the poorest families, the fear of having children taken into care; the negative views of the poorest families held by schools, doctors, social workers and neighbors; the lack of housing, resources, health services, advice and counseling; and finally the strengths and values families possess for staying together and fighting poverty.

The research subject

At the first meeting of the Family Group the activists arrived with the following question: *Since all families are of equal worth, why are the families of the poorest not equally recognized?* They asked the academics and Fourth World volunteer corps member to share what they knew about families in their own social milieus in an effort to highlight differences.

One academic insisted the group exchange viewpoints on what it believes *the values and strengths of its families* to be. The Fourth World volunteer corps member wanted us to address the question: *How must society change, and what can be done in order for very poor families to receive recognition?* The words "planning" (*projet*), "family plans," "personal plans" and "family action plans" all appeared during the course of the discussion. By the end of the day the group had written-up two ways of expressing its subject of research:
– family plans to combat poverty
– the fight against poverty goes hand-in-hand with the recognition of each family's equal worth.

Following this first meeting the activists conducted their first interviews. Plans to start a family repeatedly figured as a vital concern for the poorest: *What matters most is being with my children and doing whatever I can to give them a better life than I had. . . .*[1] *Children bring the warmth back into living. . . .*[2]

At the seminar meeting held in September 1996, the Family Group presented its problem-area of research, "Family plans and their recognition in the fight against poverty," to the other thematic groups. There were numerous reactions to the presentation: *Do all families have plans for the future? What defines a family, given there have never before been so many broken homes? To win recognition for these families we would have to know their struggles. How will you treat the issue of child-placement in your research? Do all the members of your group agree on the use of the word "plans?"*

The research brief

During the November 1996 Seminar we compiled a research brief to present our research subject. The brief was written following much discussion and disagreement between the members of our group. It was difficult for the other groups to grasp for several reasons. Firstly, we had de-emphasized the words *family plans*,because what was at issue for us was no longer society's recognition of the plans made by families, but the recognition of the plans of individuals within the families. Secondly, *recognition* no longer appeared amongst our keywords. There was no hypothesis. The other groups' comments helped us to refocus our research.

The activists continued to conduct interviews, and put forward the idea that *starting a family is the most essential life-plan very poor people can make*. The Fourth World volunteer corps member seconded this statement based on personal experience. The academics warned the activists against becoming too wedded to the truth of this assertion, and advised them not to depart too readily from their experience, because in science nothing can be said to be proven until it has been borne out through experimentation. After clarifying the terms a new research brief was compiled with the following key question: What meaning does the plan to start a family and live in one hold for poor people? The accent was placed on how the family plan led to being recognized and accepted into society, and also how it allowed individuals to become part of something lasting. The hypothesis was as follows: for the poorest, plans to engage in family life, despite the obstacles raised in their paths, are an initial stepping stone for giving their lives meaning (continuance, socialization, etc.). Based on an academic's presentation entitled "The role of time in the life of families," and also thanks to numerous other contributions including interviews, conversations and lectures, the group finalized its research subject: The family plan and time.

Drawing up the memoir outline

The activists proposed an initial outline for our memoir based on the work they had completed in the decipherings[3] of the Family Group meetings, the interviews they had conducted, as well as on other texts. The outline differentiated between the family plan, which deals with things that last, like starting a family and keeping it together; and family action-plans, which are frequently undertaken in crisis situations. They also proposed a section devoted to making people understand what really transpires between very poor families and the society in which they live. Their intent was to write about the fights and struggles of very poor families and the views that are held of them. The outline was discussed again at the June 1997 seminar and modified slightly, with the aim of further emphasizing the notions of time and continuance in the family life of the very poor.

Research methods used: Contributions

The methods used for research included interviews[4], lectures[5], books, texts, presentations and debates held between members of our group. From the outset of the program the theme of the family, common to everyone's experience, provoked numerous propositions and strong reactions from the activists. The sheer ubiquity of these spontaneous expressions rendered the task of developing a concrete research strategy even more difficult. Progress was made along two lines: The first followed a presentation by one of the academics on the subject of how to conduct systematic research, including the theoretical bases of his methods for working with, studying and thinking about families. The second followed a presentation by another academic, this time on potential ways of conceptualizing the family through current trends in sociology. Similar progress was made on the notions of planning[6] and time.[7] One academic suggested that they study the book *Vie de familles*[8] (Family Life), from which the group's Fourth World volunteer corps member had brought in an excerpt, in order to shed light on other aspects of poor peoples' experience than those revealed by the activist interviews, and with particular regard to the relationship between family plans and time. The Fourth World volunteer corps member also brought along numerous other texts on Father Joseph Wresinksi's views on the family, the homeless camp in Noisy-le-Grand*, the way in which the very poor were classified in the 1960s, and on Frimhurst Family House in Great Britain*.

Working method: Merging knowledge

Merging knowledge took place throughout the entire course of this research project. Whenever one of us effected some kind of personal work he or she would present it to the others for group discussion.

Interview analysis

Early interviews by the activists were analyzed by the group as a whole with a view toward isolating their unique themes. This generated the need to deepen our understanding of where these families came from, where they were then and where they were going. The interviews aided our understanding of the living conditions for some families. At times the activists were obliged to go back to certain people's homes in order to glean a more complete picture.

An example of merging knowledge based on contributions from multiple sources

The academics gave a presentation on two chapters from *Vies de familles*,[9] the analysis of which brought to light the fear of destiny and carrying out plans. This sparked debate between the members of the group, because one of the female activists seized on the way a woman was portrayed in the book, claiming to identify with her and taking issue with how she was analyzed. The activists pointed to the anxieties very poor families feel about taking certain steps and the time needed to see their plans through to completion. The debate also emphasized how the facts as expressed by people actually living in poverty are the not the same as they appear in the writings of "experts." The activists furnished examples where the facts stemming from the experience of living in a very poor family's neighborhood were not taken into account.

After an academic gave a talk on the subject of "Planning and Time," the activists reworked their contribution based on a written version of the presentation and pointed out that their analysis was different from the one presented. Based on their interviews and direct experiences they felt authorized to assert that "circular time"[10] is not only negative and "linear time" is not only positive, and furthermore that poor people are not mired in repetitive, circular time only. Based on the idea that both times are needed if one is to find one's bearings in life, they came up with a third kind of time which they called "looped time"[11]—a combination of both circular and linear times wherein the past binds people to their roots, but sometimes, for very poor families, time itself seems to stand still when hardships become too great. Often, however, all that is needed in moments like these is some sort of event or encounter to turn them around and move their plans forward. The activists brought their written reflections on this to the group so that they could be incorporated into research.

The practice of collaborative writing

The topic our group chose for this exercise in collaborative writing[12] was: "The family plan and time." The first stage involved each person gaining a better understanding of the texts written by the others through modifications, explications and critiques issuing in:

– requests to simplify language, (since some words and expressions were still too hard to understand);

– more profound revisions, for example the activists and Fourth World volunteer corps member were struck by the absence of the word "we" to define "family" in the text written by the academics, who defined it exclusively using *I, you, and it*. For the activists the family was about 'we' or 'us', the couple and the children.

The academics responded by being more specific: *When we spoke of "corporative entities," i.e. the idea that the family forms a body, we were thinking first and foremost in the second person plural. Nonetheless our primary emphasis, more so than the activists, was indeed on individuals and interpersonal relationships.*

– highly-focused discussions concerning the vision the group members held of the question of time in very poor families. The activists would not allow very poor families to be depicted as having no notion of time. They had to explain that for very poor people the family is by definition an inscription in something that lasts, no matter how hard things get. If they were obliged to live in the short-term this was only due to the difficult living conditions they found themselves in, and this is what they were being reproached for as if it were a choice on their part.

We managed to draw up a group text composed of a few lines.

Notes

1. Interview no. 2.
2. Interview no. 3.
3. On "decipherings," see the General Introduction.
4. Interviews, see Annex, p. 240.
5. Lecture by Lucie Ribert, Emilie Bourtet, Emile Creutz, see the General Introduction, and for lecture of Mrs. Codaccioni, see Annex, p. 242.
6. Based on the work by J.P. Boutinet, *Anthropologie du projet* (*The Anthropology of Plans*), Paris, PUF, 1996 (1st Edition. 1990).
7. Based on the work by P. Fontaine, *Le temps et les familles sous-prolétaires* (*Time and Lower-Class Working Families*), "Family Therapy," Genève, 1992, vol. 13, pp. 297-326 ; and N. Elias, *Du temps* (*On Time*), Paris, Fayard, 1996 (1st Edition. 1984).
8. M. Titran, T. Potekov, *Vies de familles* (*Family Life*), Paris, Gallimard, 1996.
9. *Ibid.*
10. On circular time and linear time see Chapter 3, p. 166.
11. Cf. Chapter 3, p. 168.
12. On exercises in collaborative writing, see the General Introduction.

Chapter 2

THE FAMILY

The theme of the family affects us all. This chapter gives an insight into psychologists', sociologists', very poor families' and Father Joseph Wresinksi's views of the family. It ends with the elaboration of certain viewpoints concerning family policies which are evolving in step with transformations occurring within the contemporary family itself.

General definitions

The 1994 edition of the Petit Robert French dictionary defines "family" as follows: "People with a shared lineage living together under the same roof, especially a father, mother and children." Across centuries, countries and cultures, the word family has designated disparate underlying realities which arguably share two fundamental characteristics that would appear essential:

– on the one hand the members of a family are related to one another through kinship (for at least two generations) or marriage,

– on the other hand they live together under the same roof for a relatively long period of time.

By defining "family" this way we distinguished it from *couples*, as they only constitute one generation. We considered the parent-child relationship to be decisive. We also distinguished our definition from *households* in the statistical sense, defined as a domestic group of people residing in the same dwelling, and which may include short-term occupants. Furthermore, whenever the term family was used in the broader sense, we made specific reference to the *extended family* as a way of designating relatives not living under the same roof.

When members of a family unofficially enter or leave the scene for short periods of time, what comes to be perceived as the family and its boundaries becomes in large part a subjective matter that mostly depends on personal experiences. A family member may be temporarily absent, such as a child placed in care or a partner in jail (*I waited for him without getting my hopes up*[1]), temporarily present,

or may have a fuzzy or evolving status. For instance: *Marcel came by to see me .
. . he gradually stayed more and more . . . I didn't know how serious things were
between us. . . . After that he just took a job . . . we didn't talk about marriage . . .
for four years we were together and that was all. . . ., Then we just decided to get
married.*[2]

In Western society today families are primarily conjugal, meaning they tend to
focus around the relations between married couples, and nuclear, meaning they
are limited to a core group comprising couples—the parents, and their child(ren)
(the siblings).

Because of this, Westerners tend to move from living in one type of nuclear
family to another:

– the first is the family of origin or departure that we are born into and grow
up with;

– the second is the reproductive family we start when we are adults by having
and raising children.

Nowadays, families are increasingly single-parent or made up of parents who
have remarried (and thus include children from previous unions). In contemporary society these and other very different kinds of families coexist.

Psychologists' viewpoints on the family

Psychologists generally view the family as an essential human group whose
goal is the mutual satisfaction of the fundamental and complementary needs of
men and women, parents and children. These include physiological needs (food,
warmth, stimulation), security (shelter, order), intimacy (affection), respect (of
oneself and from others), and self-realization. General Systems Theory psychologists[3] regard the family as a system or whole whose individual members (and their
individual fates) are bound to one another, such that a change for one exercises
an influence over the others (for example when one member of the family finds
work or becomes unemployed). From this viewpoint the family is also related to
the global system of society at large, which it interacts with through communica-
tions "portals" and protective "walls." Like a kind of mini-society, family is situated between the individual and society. It is the primary locus of a child's socialization and self-development.

Humans undergo a lengthy childhood which makes it possible for them to
spend a much longer time learning from their parents and adapting to the com-
plexities of human life. Beginning with the care he receives and the vagaries of
daily communal living, the child establishes bonds first with his maternal figure,
followed by the paternal one and then others, become progressively more autonomous until finding his own place in society.

This depiction of childhood development is in tandem with the one adults
go through in becoming parents. Erikson[4] identified the following as virtues or

strengths in this process: *identity, intimacy, generativity and integrity.* (In the next chapter we shall revisit these life-stages, which build on each other and draw the family into the cycle of life).

The family structures the relationships its members enjoy between themselves and with other systems, including school, work, neighborhood and nature, based on rules, roles and functions, beliefs, values and rituals (e.g. meals, holidays, etc.). It creates its own style, influenced by the surrounding culture, how people in the social category it belongs to behave, and the demands of life.

Over the long term, family ensures both continuity and change: enough stability to let us believe we can always go back to it, coupled with the flexibility we need to adapt to internal changes, like new members that come along through birth and adolescence, as well as external ones likemoving house, etc.

The family and sociology

The family is one of the most characteristically human social institutions, and exactly how its core unit is composed is almost as important as the existence of the core unit itself: the nature of a family's alliances (unions) therefore holds the key to explaining the workings of the family institution itself.

Basing themselves on the thought and texts of Emile Durkheim[5], sociologists have identified two ways of depicting the family:

– through marriage—the family is envisaged as being based on a core unit of two parents and their offspring or even adopted children[6]. This is what the US sociologist, T. Parsons, called the "reproductive family."[7]

– through kinship—that is to say the universe of relatives that blood relations, adoption and marriage give to individuals[8]. Since its specific contents vary from one social milieu to another, family designates as much a set of relatives as it does any one real group.

Following T. Parsons' work in the 1950s many were quick to believe that broader kinship structures were disappearing in the wake of industrialization, and the family would be reduced to the conjugal unit with a small number of children. However these kinship structures have become *visible again*[9] in today's society, although their context has changed from what it was traditionally. The domain in which tight-knit family networks appear and persist appears to have shifted to areas such as providing economic aid, helping find work, shelter and homes, etc.

However other sociologists like F. de Singly[10] maintain that today's family serves as a means for realizing individual happiness. Not only is the contemporary family seen as having withdrawn from larger kinship structures, but the bond between family and the individual is also said to have weakened. Indeed autonomy for the individual has become more important than the marriage vow, and the quest for happiness may trump the continuance of the couple. Marriage has begun to shed its dimension as a moral commitment and has become a *contract* entered into like other more freely-formed unions. In France, the number of divorces practically tripled from 1970 to 1990.

These two dimensions of family just mentioned—marriage and kinship—appear clearly in the numerous interviews conducted by our group, insofar as we focused primarily on the study of the nuclear family (parents and children in both their original and reproductive families).

Perceptions of the family by the poorest

Ten of the 15 Fourth World activists who participated in the program were placed in care during their childhood for reasons directly related to their living conditions. Six of the 15 very poor people interviewed for this research were similarly placed in care at some time during childhood. Some of them said their brothers, sisters or spouse were also placed in care.

At home with the interviewees

Our interview with Colette and Jean-Baptiste[11] showed how important the family is to the poorest. Jean-Baptiste was raised by his grandparents from birth. When they died he was placed in care until by the social services until he was 18, when he went to work on a farm. *At that time I started horsing around, stealing. . . . Until I ended up sleeping on the streets.* He spent time in jail.

Colette was one of 11 children, placed in a foster home at the age of 12 because of domestic violence at home. At 15½ she met Jean-Baptiste, who was 24 at the time and had just gotten out of jail. She ran away from her foster home and had her first child at 16. They were married three years later. For several years they lived with their respective families, then they became squatters in abandoned and unsanitary houses. Three years ago they found housing through the PACT program[12]. They now have ten children, aged betwen16 months to 20 years. Jean-Baptiste told us: *Having a family is terrific. Having your family all around you, having our children with us and not shoved from pillar to post . . . means we love them.* Colette added: *We're a little family all together. When the children come home at night they're glad to see Mom and Dad.* Jean-Baptiste added: *It's tough getting put in a home. We went through it so we know what it's like. We wouldn't want that to happen to our kids or anybody else's either.*

Family is first and foremost about being together, united.

As Odile put it: *We weren't rich, but at least we were together*[13], and for Sandrine and Xavier: *The most important thing is for everybody to stay close*[14]. Some of the interviewees lost or never knew these family ties, like Myriam: *In my family we weren't close, it was like I didn't have a family at all*[15]. Lucy's family *broke up. We were not really a family anymore because we all had our separate lives*[16].

For the poorest "we," the entire family together, comes before "I." Everyone is a part of everyone else—everyone is a part of "we" and only exists through this "we".

The family grounds peoples' identities, names and where they came from.
Who am I, where do I come from and where am I going? became Christian's question after he was placed in care at the age of four until he was 18. *Who am I? I often wonder. Where do I come from? I still need to find out everything about my past history. Where am I going? This is what I have to pass on if I want to make sense out of my life***.

Rolande agreed that *children are our goal in life,* and later added during the course of her interview that *Children bring the warmth back into living*[17].

All of those interviewed mentioned how central their children were to their lives, and it was their relationship with their children that dominated their definitions of family, which was inconceivable without them:
– *Our kids are our happiness, our hope and our joy—they are our everything.*
– My *whole life is those children. My kids come before my husband. If my husband ever left, disappeared, I'd be sad, it would be tough, but my kids are my flesh and blood.*
– *I've had to give up a lot for them . . . I would have given up everything.*
– *It's easy to see that for a woman her child is the most precious thing in the world—it's what she wants to give her partner*[18].

In conclusion, the definition of family is perhaps best captured by Rolande's expression: *What really counts is the love and tenderness they bring. The rest doesn't matter.* For the very poor, the family is a lone outpost, a wellspring of love, strength and understanding.

Father Wresinski's views on the family

In his reflections on what family means for people living in poverty, Father Joseph Wresinski refers to it as a *only* (remaining) *refuge when all else fails; it is the only place where a person might still feel a welcome; it is the only place where one can still be 'somebody.' A person finds identity in the family. The children, the spouse, or the companion constitute a person's last refuge of freedom.* Indeed for a very poor person the family is a *last refuge . . . the last line of defense against adversity, humiliation, and self-destruction. It was the final irreducible cell*[19].

Every family plays this role in socializing children, but the *parent-child relationship is not only socializing and formative, it is a life-giving bond that cannot be broken . . . without provoking a profound disequilibrium that will never heal, and which will continue to have repercussions throughout the entire life of the person marked by it*[20].

However in order to fulfill its educational role, this parent-child relationship requires, among other things, reinforcement from the whole environment in which it is immersed, and Father Wresinski soon realized that the families in Noisy-le-Grand, just like in other homeless camps across the world, were families who had *not inherited everything a family needs to raise children . . . and who cannot enjoy all their rights*. And because they cannot do so they become overly dependent on social services and charitable aid. When it is these same social services who are responsible for deeming a child endangered, the family ends up *terrorized that they will take their children away from them and thereby sever them from their only remaining connection to society*[21].

For Father Wresinski it was unthinkable to abandon these families of the Noisy-le-Grand homeless camp, threatened with the prospect of having their children taken into care, and with the chance that all their hopes and even their family itself might be destroyed. He therefore simply *had* to start a Movement. A Movement on behalf of these families, basing itself on the strength of these same families themselves, on tenacious hope and on parents' determination to give their children a better life than theirs. He often said to the members of the Fourth World volunteer corps who joined him that it was extremely difficult to help men (or women) who were alone in the world to get back on their feet, but that with families the opposite was the case because they were so energized, especially by the presence of children, and that it was possible to sustain them, to tap into them and unleash this energy and reinvigorate their transformation.

Thus from its very beginnings, the International Movement ATD Fourth World sought above all to be a movement uniting families suffering under the most extreme conditions in both rich and poor countries with all those who refused to allow poverty to destroy our humanity, and who were prepared to commit some part of themselves to this cause, each in his own way, so that every person and all families may live in dignity.

How other social classes view the family

In the words of a young couple of academics, *the family is the two of us and the kids*[22]. They also repeated the word love often: a love learned in the family of origin and in the throes of youth, a love they wish to share with their children (at least four, more if possible), but also with friends and by giving their time to Third World causes. No matter how in love they are (the wife expressed this most forcefully), they wish to maintain a degree of autonomy, if not outright independence. The wife works part-time, by choice, thus guaranteeing her autonomy and appearing not to conflict with raising several children.

In speaking with a couple from just one generation back however:

For me, starting a family means choosing someone for life. When you decide you're going to spend your life together because you love each other, you have to let your love shine . . . either through kids [they raised four], or through other people. It also means trying to instill the values you are trying to live in your children . . . even if you do it badly[23].

But just deciding to start a family is not enough. To make it through the hard times and still last, young couples, especially young families today, have to be able to count on their families of origin and their friends.

Families that decide to have several children, especially close together, usually experience social approbation, particularly in the moral sphere. When having her third child in the same hospital, one young lower-class woman overheard a nurse say: *Hope you don't end up here again next year!*[24] Despite this discouragement, two more children, both wanted, came along to complete the family.

Reflections on family policies

The family continues to be the primary vehicle for social reproduction via the chains of generations and transmission it builds. But as the German sociologist, Franz Schultheis, once observed, *family reproductive issues are less and less private affairs.* The state has become increasingly involved in them, and particularly in France family affairs are also affairs of the state[25].

The history of family policy in France is shot through with a series of oppositions[26].

Who bears the brunt of responsibility for the family? For some, the principle of individual responsibility is tantamount to the family question, and thus each family's internal family solidarity reigns supreme. Others contend the family depends on the collective responsibility entailed by the social safety net, and hence is the province of the state. What should be the final aim of family policy? Should it "help the child", meaning dole out services to all families regardless of income level? Should it "help the family," meaning formulate a redistributive policy that differs depending on economic situation? In the first instance the policy serves the institution of the family as such, whereas in the second it seeks social justice for certain social classes.

No matter what the case, a sustained period of decreased spending for family benefits in France is readily apparent. Spending on family benefits represented more than 40% of the overall government welfare spending in 1946, but was no more than 11.5% in the early 1990s.[27]

What should be the scope of the state's involvement? According to one school of thought, families should be offered pre-set services furnished outside the home (for example free food in school canteens). The more liberal viewpoint, however, favors allowing individual families to choose for themselves how to dispose of direct family benefits. One example of this are the "school vouchers" in the United States—families receive them directly and select the school of their choice.

Contemporary transformations

The weakening of the family unit

Two important elements attest to a gradual weakening of the family: not only has the number of divorces greatly increased in France over the past quarter-century, as mentioned previously, but they are occurring much sooner after the wedding itself, and the number of single-parent families is steadily increasing. The number of married couple households grew 24% from 1968 to 1990, but the number of single-parent families almost doubled during the same period. Among families with children[28], the proportion with single parents was 16.2% in 1990[29].

According to J. Commaille[30], single-parents are much more likely to live below the poverty level: *The growing destabilization of the institution of the family is associated with increased difficulties entering and staying in the workforce, lower salary levels, and the creation of more and more social problems.*

The family and social inequalities

Despite these modern trends, the status of an individual's family of origin remains a primary determinant: numerous recent studies have shown that social class continues to determine not only success in school but in the professional sphere as well, (a fact echoed by a just-completed study by the French National Institute of Statistics and Economic studies—INSEE[31]).

The family as a plan

The family is also one of the most important stepping stones a person has for integrating with society. Thus there is little reason to see the desire for autonomy and personal growth as conflicting with starting and keeping a family—this is what we mean when we refer to the *family plan*.

Of course today's "reconstituted family" is a far cry from the "domestic community" of yesteryear's peasant societies (composed of the extended patriarchal family). However as R. Boudon and F. Bourricaud have observed, it remains the case today that even though the family has tended to become more dispersed, *it still forges a bond between parents and children whose solidity would seem to be unmatched by any other social relation*[32].

Notes

1. Interview no. 13.
2. *Id.*
3. This approach views its object of study as systems, defined as a set of elements that interact with one another. There is a wide variety of such systems, including the mechanical (e.g. a thermostat), living (cells), economic, etc. Von Bertalanffy developed his *General Systems Theory* (Paris, Dunod, 1973) in 1947, which was applied to the family in around 1970.

4. Erikson, EH, 1950-1966, *Enfance et Société* (Childhood and Society), Neufchatel, Delachaux, pp. 169-180.

5. E. Durkheim, "The Conjugal Family" in Textes, 3: Social and Institutional Functions, Paris, Minuit, 1975, 1e éd. 1892.

6. In the broadest possible sense, since children may belong to the family from previous marriages.

7. T. Parsons, Le système de parenté dans l'Amérique contemporaine (The Kinship System of the Contemporary United States), in *Éléments pour une sociologie de l'action*, Paris, Plon, 1955, pp.129-150.

8. Cf. M. Segalen, *Sociologie de la famille*, (Sociology of the Family) Paris, A. Colin, 1996, p. 60.

9. Rephrasing M. Segalen expression, *op. cit.*, pp. 94-95.

10. F. de Singly, *Le soi, le couple et la famille*, (The Self, the Couple and the Family) Paris, Nathan, 1996.

11. Interview no. 9.

12. Housing Protection, Improvement, Preservation and Transformation (Formerly the Anti-Slum Action Program).

13. Interview no. 4.

14. Interview no. 6.

15. Interview no. 13.

16. Lecture.

17. Interview no. 3.

18. Interviews no. 9, 11, 4 and doc. int.

19. Father J. Wresinski, *The Poor are the Church*, Twenty-Third Publications 2002, pp. 9 and 119.

20. Atd Quart Monde, *Revue IGLOOS* no. 81, 1974, p. 33.

21. Father J. Wresinski, *Écrits et Paroles aux volontaires*, (Words for Fourth World volunteer corps Members) Éd. St Paul/Quart Monde, 1992, pp. 91 and 67.

22. Interview no. 12.

23. Interview no. 14.

24. Interview no. 1.

25. Cf. F. Schultheis et F. de Singly (dir.), *Affaires de famille, affaires d'État*, (Family Affairs, Affairs of State) Nancy, Éd de l'Est, 1991.

26. This is based on the distinctions proposed by J. Commaille, *Misères de la Famille, question d'État*, (Family Poverty: A Question for the State) Paris, Presses de Sciences-Po, 1996, pp. 98ff.

27. Source: P. Steck, *Les prestations familiales*, (Family Welfare Benefits) Paris, PUF, 1993, p. 104.

28. Without respect to the children's ages.

29. Source: INSEE, *La société française, Données sociales*, (Social Statistics on French Society) 1993, p. 576.

30. J. Commaille, *op. cit.*, p. 228.

31. D. Goux, C. Maurin, Destinées sociales, le rôle de l'école et du milieu d'origine, *Économie et statistique*, no. 306, 1997, pp. 13-26; Démocratisation de l'école et persistance des inégalités (The Democratization of School and the Persistence of Inequality); pp. 27-39.

32. *Dictionnaire critique de la sociologie, (Dictionary of Sociology)* Paris, PUF 1986, pp. 256-257.

Chapter 3

TIME AND CONTINUANCE
IN THE FAMILY PLAN

Who am I, where do I come from, and where am I going? is what one father asked in the previous chapter—a series of questions that present us with the elements of past, present and future. Can it be said that the family is a temporal point of reference for the individual? As children grow up, they go through various stages leading to adult life. How are things different for children in very poor families, where some of these stages overlap or at times do not even occur?

It has often been said and written that poverty is a vicious circle that traps people living within its confines. What if the plan to start and raise a family—the family plan—was one of the ways the poorest people break this image of the circle and orient themselves toward the future?

The family plan engages us in the question of time. Time determines whether seeing a project through to completion is at all possible. Indeed when a plan is being formulated the possibility of failure can never be entirely excluded in advance.

Time

In the life of each individual, time may be measured in years, periods, and stages gone through, (childhood, adolescence, etc.), but time is also what lasts, continuance, to inscribe oneself in the time of others.

Life stages

The family is composed of individuals, parents and children, who evolve over time. Erikson[1] studied a variety of human societies and found that human life comprises at least eight stages:

– Infancy (0 to 15 months).

In this stage the person acquires a basic *trust* in those around him, in particular his mother with whom he communicates. The newborn is able to cry, move around and attract attention. Distrust develops in tandem with trust however, and in some children comes to predominate.

– Early childhood (1 to 3 years).

During this *autonomy* stage the small child learns to say "no" and discovers he can contradict his mother and other people. He begins to discover the world around him, in particular material objects. The child must learn to get by on his own when it comes to moving around, eating and going to the bathroom. Sometimes the people around him fail to respect this nascent autonomy and feelings of doubt and shame become prevalent in the child.

– Preschool (3 to 6 years).

This is the age when playing alone and with other children of the same age begins. Thus it is referred to as an *initiative* stage, meaning the child begins to invent himself through the games he makes up. At times these initiatives are discouraged or even repressed, and the child becomes shy and inhibited.

– School-age (6 to 12 years).

As the child grows up he becomes more aware of the demands society places upon him. According to Erikson, in this *industry* stage, children discover the joy to be had in doing good work and the feeling of being useful and having personal worth. If the child believes his work is not valued, he begins to develop feelings of inferiority.

– Adolescence (12 to 18 years).

This is the *identity* stage. Young people seek to know who they are, try to find a place of their own and define their uniqueness vis-à-vis the adult world. This stage is often referred to as the "moratorium phase," when society stands back and tolerates teenagers' strivings to individuate, in addition to trying to help them succeed. This is also a phase for friends and for doing things without the family. If the young person does not have a group of friends to be with, this period will be very hard for him, insofar as it will be difficult for him to secure his identity.

– Young adulthood.

This is a stage of *intimacy* for those who have already found a mate, but it can also be a time for study and choosing a profession. Young adults often become independent of their families at this time as well, and for some, this period of freedom and opening up to the world does not exist because they pass from adolescence directly on to parenthood.

– Adulthood

This is the *generativity* or procreative phase, in the familial, professional and even artistic domains, marked by the realization of the capacity to bring children into the world, to produce works and to take care of them. This capacity needs to be cultivated and considered as socially useful.

– Maturity
In this final phase in the stages of life, the adult can look back with satisfaction or dissatisfaction on the past and feel a sense of fulfillment or despair.

As Erikson explains, the various stages of life are based upon one another and unfold in a logical order. However sometimes circumstances and social injustices (poverty, being removed from home, academic failure) disrupt this schema. What happens to children torn from their parents as soon as they are born and taken into care? When they reach a certain age they will have to pay the price for having had to adapt to life on their own (experiences, identity etc.) and will be very keen to stand on their own two feet. They rush into moving in with a neighbor or friend in the hope of finding a better life. For most of them, given the failures they encounter, their studies and hoped-for professions will seem like little more than distant dreams. The young adult stage will not exist for them because they will have children at a very young age. It is not rare for them to have three or four children at the age of 20 or 21.

The following example illustrates this: A woman who was placed in an orphanage at the age of two until she was 21 told us she soon learned what it takes to make it in life i.e. reading, writing, sewing, cooking, making a budget and cleaning the house. But as an adolescent she still felt like she was missing something fundamental: love, tenderness, someone to listen to her and the dialogue that normally takes place amongst parents and children or siblings. She was extremely isolated and shut away throughout adolescence. As an adult, she moved in with a man who had been in the Algerian War and had returned sick and wounded. His alcoholism weighed heavily on the family finances, and for over 20 years they lived in a one-room apartment with five children. As a couple, there was never a period when they were close. As she put it: *We were like strangers who didn't know a thing about each other.* She attributed the lack of dialogue between them to the fact that she had never experienced it during her childhood: *After not going out all those years I didn't know how to talk to people, I was afraid to talk.* From the age of 8-10 years, her oldest son had to begin helping his mother out by taking on the responsibilities of an adult. He witnessed and experienced his father's violent behavior. He tried to start a family of his own at 17 but could not keep it together. Two of his three children were taken into care, but their grandmother did everything she could to make sure they were not there for long, eventually gaining custody of her three grandchildren**[2].

In very poor environments it is very rare to find a child who will grow up having gone through all the stages described by Erikson.

Nonetheless all children become adults. The people they meet play a decisive role in compensating for some of the chaos of their childhood. Does it not therefore make sense for people who had to make something of themselves, without passing through all the steps of Erikson's logically ordered schema, to benefit from the best our society has to offer in order to compensate for the injustices and disequilibria of their childhood?

Time and continuance

Days and weeks, each of equal length, are linked together in a chain. The stages of life follow one another in succession, normally in a continuous progression. The modern conception of time is linear in nature, meaning it is thought to develop following an unbroken line and does not go backwards, but always from past, to present to future. In modern society, the future is what is most highly valued, yet in the society of worldwide communication made possible by the Internet, the present moment holds sway. This is what is referred to as "real time." The linear concept of time differs from other conceptions, including the circular and cyclical, which are characterized by the repetition of days (for monks for example), and seasons (for farmers).

Linear time

| past | present | future |

grandparents   parents   children   grandchildren

Circular or cyclical time

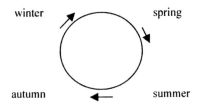

winter   spring

autumn   summer

These concepts distinguish between a *world that is moving forward* (linear time), and a so-called immobile or rigid *tradition* (circular time).

The vicious cycle of poverty depicted by sociologists and economists denotes an inability on the part of a family, community or country to project itself into the future, meaning to move out of circular time and enter into linear time, such that each generation merely reproduces the life of the one that came before it without evolving in any way.

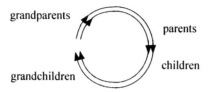

One of the biggest problems families living in poverty are said to have is with planning for the long term. They are considered as being preoccupied solely with their immediate survival. Even some scientists believe this to be the case, including Kluckholn,[3] who distinguishes between Americans: in the US, there are the Hispanic-American poor people (Mexican, Puerto Rican, etc.), depicted as being oriented more towards the present, and their wealthier Anglo- or Euro-American counterparts (of European origin) considered as more future-oriented.

E.T. Hall[4] argues that: *Marginalized families, regardless of their origins, all seem to share in common a complete lack of scheduling and planning*, as if they were totally subject to events as they occur.[5]

However, the poorest themselves do not necessarily hold this conception of time. *Time is something that lasts*, said one woman who had fought for 11 years to get her children back after they were taken into care during a time of acute crisis. Something that lasts between visits with her kids, when the time stretches even longer if the visit did not go well and all she wants to do is hold them in her arms and make the misunderstanding go away. Something that lasts when birthday after birthday goes by and the steps she is taking to get them back have not worked. Something that lasts when it is back-to-school time and she cannot take her kids to the first day of classes, nor is she there to check their homework or sign their grade cards at the end of the term. On the outside, this young woman only seems concerned with the issue of her immediate survival, her day-to-day life that forces her to put on a happy face and focus on not falling into a slump, whereas in reality, all she lives for is the possibility that time will be on her side. To make up for having to wait, she tries to make the time pass more quickly.

The poorest often find their lives have been caught up in this circular time:

– by the importance they place on starting a family and living in one;

– by their living conditions, including housing, work, insufficient resources, etc.;

– as regards children, because of the threat of them being taken into care, setbacks at school or at work;

– by the way they are viewed because of their poverty by neighbors, academic and social institutions, and the aid they receive, including but not limited to welfare benefits.

But these same families are also inscribed in linear time for reasons such as:
– the rights they have won, including family welfare benefits, French minimum income benefits etc.;
– changes in trends in society with respect to moral values on cohabitation, contraception and motherhood etc., and with respect to information (audiovisual communication) and consumption (credit, debt, etc.);
– the creation and mobilization of associations to denounce poverty and the injustices it entails;
– positive trends in youth culture which are leading to increased intercultural mixing, mutual exposure between social strata, but youth culture is also being influenced by phenomena such as drugs etc.

Thinking seriously about the timescale of the poorest entails revisiting the notion of the *vicious circle of poverty*. The poorest are not necessarily caught up in it, time is not only repetitive for them. They are able to plan for the long-term and envision alternate futures. When they consider making new generations and hope for a better life for their children, and take part in collective action to fight for their rights, society begins to be viewed as changeable and worth taking part in.

Furthermore it would appear that all is not negative about circular time, and likewise, linear time is not all positive—both are necessary. Indeed whereas linear time allows for progression to occur, circular time gives us things to hold on to. For example, the importance of family for the poorest is a guidepost for young people amidst an ever-changing society. Every human being needs roots and landmarks. To move forward, we must draw lessons from the past and not just barge on without looking back.

This is why we favor a different way of thinking about time that recognizes the reality of the way linear time emerges from a division within circular time itself. This is what we call **looped time**, which accounts for two temporal aspects: mobility (or moving forward), and returning to fixed points which guarantee the possibility of starting over again after experiencing setbacks.

By focusing our research on how the poorest make *plans*, we are refusing to view them as permanently caught up in the misfortune of a time without future.

The plan

The notion of a plan

The notion of a plan (*projet*) is a mode of mastering time. Planning entails not only having a conception of the future, but also taking concrete steps to make it happen[6]. Planning, in this respect, is different from simply wishing or dreaming, at least in part because it takes possible setbacks into account. Individuals may make plans that reflect their desire for self-realization and, due to modern society's focus on individual happiness, this form of personal planning often comes to predominate. Making plans could be defined as an attempt to follow through on a promise one has made to oneself or others, or may represent a person's concrete commitment to other people.

The family plan

Can the family also be a plan? Today most commentators on the family continually refer to the loss of family ties, the dissolution or erosion of the traditional family model, and thus how uncertain the family institution has become. These transformations are frequently depicted as beneficial insofar as they are often the result of greater freedoms for the individual. Is it therefore reasonable in light of this to expect the family, an institution in crisis, to make it possible for the poorest people to improve their condition?

Various American authors[7] consider one of the primary factors in the persistence of poverty to be precisely this destabilized family situation (missing or unemployed fathers).

The idea of a family plan, as our group has defined it, is in direct opposition to these common notions of personal realization, which portray the desire for self-fulfillment as more important than the ties of belonging to groups and other forms of commitment.

How and why do people today commit to starting a family, defined in terms of a stable plan? How and why today, in the midst of individualistic societies, can self-realization take place *via* a group (family) plan that has succeeded?

Family plan, life plan? The poorest often formulate plans to start a family very early, for reasons stemming from their past. When a child has undergone the ordeal of being taken into care at a very young age, he loses the traces of his roots and enters into a lifelong quest to learn where his name comes from, his origins:

> I was a ward of the state, raised by foster parents in a mining region. For years everybody at school called me a 'bastard,' and every signature on every document was a reminder of the injustice of my situation. I was always having to explain why my name was different from that of my foster family**.

A child raised without the love and tenderness his parents, brothers and sisters can provide will forever seek to understand the reasons why he was taken into care.

Other children raised by their own families live with the same insecurity, related to the never-ending anxiety they feel about being poor. The threat of them being taken into care is ever-present in the minds of their parents, and children are often aware of this. At times living conditions become so difficult (absentee parents, unsanitary or overcrowded housing, scarcity of resources etc.), that the strain becomes unbearable and the family is torn apart. Children also suffer from the looks their parents and older siblings receive, and the way people judge them. Their reputation follows them wherever they go: at school, in the neighborhood, later on when they begin looking for work etc. This lack of confidence which is imposed on them will leave its mark on their entire lives.

For people who have had a difficult childhood, starting a family is a way to defy the past. It is a challenge made on behalf of oneself when it becomes clear life will never get better: *I had nothing left to lose*, said one man who had been placed in care throughout his childhood and viewed his own house as a space of freedom he had never possessed before. For others, starting a family simply means living in society and assuming responsibility for their own lives.

The family plan and time

Starting a family is a way of inscribing oneself in time, despite the setbacks encountered along the way.

The family and time

The family is typically viewed from within the framework of love and happiness. It preserves an essential function: to inscribe people in the succession of generations, which invokes the long-term in two ways: from the past through earlier generations, and towards the future through procreation. When parents bring children into the world and ensure their basic upbringing, they are planning for the future.

Some authors argue that modernity is characterized by the loss of all connection with memory, and thus the present moment always prevails. Planning for the long-term is held to be less important in modern society, dominated as it is by the pursuit of individual happiness, for which the family serves as mere instrument. Others are, conversely, wedded to an idea of the family as an "institution," meaning something that is real, permanent and stable.

The family plan and time for the poorest

The family plan gives life meaning

Although time and means are against them, the family gives the poorest a goal and a reason to live. Despite living in crisis conditions frequently imposed on them, they view their plan for living in a family as a means to project themselves into the long-term. Living in a family is in itself a long-term plan. Indeed children are by their very nature long-term projects, requiring the time of at least one generation, the time to pass on the family name.

Life is the only richness poor people have

Although poor people have little control over their material lives, things are different as concerns life itself, which they hold dear and value despite the hardships and ambushes they encounter along the road. The significance poor people lend to life itself is proven by their deep desire to start families, and thus to have children. Whenever people see a large middle-class family, their reactions are always the same: What a lovely family! But when a large family with low wage-earning parents enters the picture, the reaction always seems to be: "They can't all be from the same father!"[8] as if a five-child family of modest means could only be the result of more than one union. When the family is very poor, the first reaction most social and medical services have to pregnancy is to propose an abortion. This is usually rejected by most women, or else ends up being a very bad experience for them that is often carried out in secret and only chosen out of absolute necessity. They are then quickly admonished to always take precautions not to have any more children. Given the methods of contraception proposed, the decision is often made by the couple and not the woman alone. The need for expensive prescriptions or medical treatments often results in birth control being abandoned in mid-stream. The frequent reactions we heard included: *It's a shame to bring children into the world when you're poor. . . . Don't have children if you can't afford them***.

A pregnant poor woman is never honored and congratulated, even though bringing new life into the world is her reason for being. Each new pregnancy fills her with both anguish and joy. The joy of feeling like being someone, responsible for another life, for protecting the child until it arrives, and hoping its birth will be a new start in life. Anguish for the couple at the prospect of a miscarriage caused by economic and mental hardships, fear the child will eventually be taken into care, concern that they will not be able to assume full responsibility for the coming birth, etc. Various explanations have been offered as to why pregnancies in impoverished environments are typically not neatly laid-out on the calendar: love, chance, and luck, the vagaries of living in poverty mean that poor people's professional and social lives hardly exist if at all, thus reducing most interactions to the level of the couple.

Raising children is a source of happiness and fear

Nothing is worse for a mother than to feel powerless to help her children when they are in pain, to be unable to care for them when they are sick, or feed them when they are hungry. Living in anguish day after day, they agree to countless humiliations in order to keep custody of them, for example** being called a "thief" for having stolen a quart of milk to feed a starving child only to find out 15 years later this "crime" was revealed to one of her sons by the police after having been caught for theft: *It's not surprising, your mother was a thief and the apple never falls far from the tree.* Fathers are also chastised for not providing for their children. They are aware of the situation their families are in, but are unable to find a solution. Judged "unfit and good for nothing", it's up to them to show that there is more to raising children than material sustenance. Nevertheless they take great pride, when the opportunity presents itself, in being able to buy their children little presents with money out of their own pockets, even if it could have gone towards more practical things in the eyes of "society". It is not uncommon for poor parents to neglect their own health and personal appearances, because the children come first.

Keeping the family together is a real challenge for parents

It is the challenge of their lives. When a child falls ill, is puny or too fat, has psychomotor dysfunctions or difficulties with language that appear later in school, when he falls behind in his studies and as an adolescent lacks marketable skills for finding work, his parents are usually blamed. Their whole life as parents becomes devoted therefore to justifying themselves against reproaches from all sides. The children themselves are what give them the strength to hold it together and muddle through. Their presence is an almost unimaginable source of strength for negotiating life's ambushes and in looking forward to the future.

In short, the family plan is located in the present, for the future, but with one eye fixed on the past. Its realization however depends on possessing the means, both material and human, that some have and others do not. For very poor families, its realization does not depend on them alone. They encounter obstacles engendered by "circular time" such as poor living conditions, the looks they receive, welfare and other benefits. These are all constraints imposed upon them by society. Both finding a way to survive day-in and day-out and the crisis situations that the very poor often face would appear to contradict with any long-term planning. Very poor families forever live in both crisis-situations and the long-term. This will be the topic of our next chapter.

Whether the plan is seen through to completion depends on what means of support the family ends up unearthing from associations, institutions, people, etc. When a person's upbringing does not take him through the life stages necessary for his development, society should provide supplemental resources to ensure that when he reaches adulthood he is able to realize his plans, in particular his family plans. What are the resources the very poor can use to make their family plan a reality? This question will be dealt with in Chapter 5.

Notes

1. Erikson, *op. cit.*
2. Sentences followed by a double asterisk ** are taken from group discussions or written accounts.
3. F. Kluchohn, in John Spiegel, Transactions. *The interplay between individual, family and society*, New-York, Science House, 1971, pp. 164-165.
4. E. T. Hall, *La danse de la vie. Temps culturel, temps vécu*, (The Dance of Life: The Other Dimension of Time) Paris, Seuil, 1984, p. 251.
5. Other researchers contest this point of view, see in particular Richard, *La culture du pauvre*, (The Culture of the Poor) Paris, Éd. de Minuit, 1970.
6. J. P. Boutinet, *op. cit.*
7. Cf. J. Patterson, *America's struggle against poverty*, 1900-1985, Cambridge, Harvard University Press, 1990.
8. Interview no. 1.

Chapter 4

BETWEEN CRISIS AND PLANNING: A DIVISION WITHIN FAMILY TIME

Time (but which one?) is always at stake when plans are being made. We have seen the limitations of the opposition that tends to be made between *circular* and *linear* time.

Our description of family plans highlighted the fact that the ways of relating to time are not one, but many. This is doubly true when time itself is divided between the long- and short-term, or between the result of choices that are made and moments of duress. Long-term timeframes that harbor our wishes for the future are always present, especially when the question of future generations are concerned. However timeframes can also be quite short when they are the result of adapting to externally-imposed situations. In short-term timeframes, crisis-thinking predominates, forcing us to resign ourselves to small steps forward, stagnation, even having to take steps back.

These temporal divisions can sometimes characterize the same existence. They point to the greater or lesser capacities we possess to formulate a plan and see it through to completion, and at the same time they bring to light the unequal social conditions that contribute to its success or failure. No matter whether a timeframe is long- or short-term, time may often be a hindrance, but can also be a resource.

The ever-present long-term

The lineage between family members always invokes the presence of the long-term, binding individuals to one another in relation to their ancestors, which we will refer to here as "filiation", and binding individuals to one another in relation to the descendants, which we will call "generation". Filiation and generation may be experienced in different ways, raising the question as to what constitutes a threat to long-term timeframes.

"Filiation" and "generation"

What is at stake in filiation and generation is how individual identity becomes inserted into a past defined by the family of origin.

Filiation: being someone's son or daughter

The presence of filiation

Filiation is always present and may involve multiple generations living together. Jean-Baptiste[1] recalled that when he first met his wife, Colette, they lived at his grandfather's *for a while*. It was *at grandpa's* that Olivier, *his oldest*, was born. Cohabitation may also involve younger people: Hélène[2], Pascal's companion, had decided to *get back on track by staying at (her) mother's* place for a while, hence the young couple in their twenties lived with her and Hélène's grandmother.

Filiation is comprised primarily of what parents transmit to their children: Jean-Baptiste said his grandmother, who raised him following numerous family breakups before he was taken into care, *taught me not to get into trouble, to go to school like I should*[3]. Filiation frequently expresses itself most strongly through the memories of those who have passed away.

Xavier[4] barely knew his father, who was in Algeria when he was a child. He had just lost him: *My father was a terrible, brutal man. When I was a kid all he ever did was smack me and whip me over the head with his belt.* Still he was *forthright.* Xavier's partner, Sandrine, furthered that *it's important to hold on to the good stuff. . . . I liked him a lot, my father-in-law. . . . When we messed up, he put us back in line. He was right and that was that.*

The two were supposed to spend Christmas with their two oldest daughters, both in foster homes. *But what can I do, (my father) died.* Gone, but still present: *we spent Christmas with (him).*

This familial presence can also be expressed by mutual aid: parents and in-laws, aunts, uncles and other close relatives all pitch in to help find housing (like Colette's brother[5] and Rolande's godfather did[6]), cover the rent or supply a security deposit (like Lucienne's father-in-law[7]), put on a fresh coat of paint (Jean-Baptiste's father-in-law), or even give shelter under the same roof (Lucienne's father-in-law, Jean-Baptiste's aunt).

The logic of family filiation exercises a strong influence wherever it appears: even though Xavier's family is *scattered all over the place* and only gets together *for unhappy reasons*, he emphasized that for him *the most important thing is to maintain my family ties.* Rolande repeatedly emphasized what the plans she shared with her husband meant for her: *starting a family of our own.* She referred to their differing family backgrounds in order to more precisely characterize the meaning of this phrase for each of them: After pointing out that her husband *grew up in foster homes*, she defined herself as *having grown up in a large family, not rich, but relatively problem-free. . . . Family was sacred.*

Family filiation breakdowns

The importance of family filiation appears even more strongly when we contrast it with the inverse tendency to break a family's lineage apart. Many people have suffered through some sort of separation from their parents, brothers and sisters.

The harshest form of separation is being placed in foster homes, and then moved around from one to the next. Jean-Batiste was raised by his grandmother from birth. When she died he was *put into various foster homes . . . then on a farm until I was 18.* The same went for his brothers and sisters. His wife, Colette, lived with her parents until she was 12. *But I had to be put in a foster home after that because they drank too much.* Sophie[8], separated from her parents at a very young age because of divorce, *was shuffled around between different foster homes* by the social services. Painful frustration was the result: *When I saw my friends with their parents I took it really hard.* Lucienne echoed a certain feeling of rejection that being in care may also engender[9]: *I was raised by the state and then in a foster home. I always felt rejected. I had to content myself with the toys and clothes other people didn't want anymore.* Nadège[10] captured the essence of the matter thus: *Even though I wasn't being beaten anymore, the state was not my family. I still missed my parents' love.*

Being taken into care breaks family lineages apart, including sibling relationships. Jean-Baptiste and Colette could no longer even remember their brothers' and sisters' ages. *I have four older brothers and six older sisters, but now I don't know how old they are* (Colette).

Instances of a lack of educative guidance, though less radical than separation, also contribute to disturbances in family filiation. Jeannette[11], whose fiancé had been put into foster care, was at pains to *make it clear* that her father had not raised her. Her parents were separated and her mother ran the household. She was certainly grateful that her mother had *muddled through in raising us despite all the hardships she had.* But then she admitted what she had missed the most during her childhood was her *mother's help* with school. *I always had to figure out how get by on my own. Whenever I needed my mother, she wasn't there.* Myriam[12] referred to the same problem in her family: *Nobody paid much attention to me. (My parents) pretty much left me in the corner, a small corner.*

The family as a personal torment

Fully-integrated or partially-damaged family lines are two ways the long-term is structured, but family origins may also exercise an influence over an individual's life in the long-term: the family of origin may be present but also may be the cause of suffering, which may assume many guises:

Internal familial strife is the source of one form of personal torment like this. Jeannette's[13] mother had a hard time accepting her daughter's increasing independence, and did not get along well with her daughter's boyfriend. So Jeanette went to live with her stepmother, who *let (her) know she couldn't take (her) in when (she) was pregnant. . . . Her family strongly disapproved of (her having the baby), so much so that I wasn't going to be able to have it.* When Jean-Baptiste and Colette were first married, they lived with her mother, but according to Jean-Baptiste (who was not happy with the arrangement), it *didn't work out, I had to leave, what with the mother and brothers. . . .* On the other hand when he went to get his driver's license it was his own family who discouraged him by saying *you'll never pass, you can't even read or write.* His wife's greatest pride and joy was that *he still wanted to try,* and *managed to get his license anyway.*

At the other end of the spectrum, family filiation can be marked by a lack of love or even hostility on the part of stepfathers (Jeannette) and stepmothers, new arrivals in a household that has been reconstituted after parental separations. Nadège[14], the mother of a two-month old baby, recalled that her stepmother did not love her or her brother: *She left us alone, locked up with no food or water. She did terrible things to us.*

The destructuring of the family may also occur because parents lose control of their impulses: *My parents were always at each others' throats,* said Colette, *when my father would get home from work my mother would already be drunk.* In fact Colette had to be taken into care because of her parents' alcoholism.

Sandrine's[16] father did things to her that she did not want to talk about. She said: *I am able to talk about what my mother was like . . . but if I don't have to talk about my father then I won't.* Hélène[17] *left home at 13,* because her father was *getting her into trouble,* a phrase she repeated several times during the course of the interview, later on adding that *I don't want to talk about it anymore, but it's never far from my mind.*

The other broad dimension we have attributed to the long-term timeframe concerns "generation". Although the people we met endowed this word with some sort of meaning or another, it often remained under threat.

"Generation"

There were cases when the birth of children was depicted as unwanted, even when the children themselves were accepted: *Now that they're here, they're here,* said Colette, (mother of ten), after having first noted that she *never thought she'd have so many.* More often, however, generation is perceived as conveying something else: it constitutes a means for realizing oneself as a person. It may also be viewed as an end in itself, assuming the significance of a "life-event."

Today I have five children, who are teenagers and adults. They grew up in a dirty, two-room apartment, but I was always there for them, close by, ready to help them grow. My wife was as proud of our first grandson as I was. Our oldest daughter just got married a year ago. She has her own life and a home with her husband. They are both making an effort for their son and life is beginning anew in the next generation**.

A child's arrival as the potential for existence

In the most immediate sense, a child may be an intermediary: a means of existence through immediate social recognition. In the longer term he can be a means of self-realization, and in the end makes it possible to give of oneself.

– Social existence

Nadège18 *had to have a baby in order to get money to survive.* Social services have been much more forthcoming since her baby daughter was born. *My daughter's birth changed a lot for me because when you have a child you're better taken care of.* It is the child's presence that has garnered this increased attention: *People are worried about how we'll make out; I know it's about the baby and not me.*

On the downside, because she receives benefits for single-parent families, she and the child's father live apart, *in our own corners.*[18]

– Self-fulfillment

For Xavier[19], starting a family represents a way of *extending myself.*

In fact for Noella[20], even though originally *I had nothing, I couldn't even get food stamps because you have to be 25 to get them,* but her child's presence was not just a means for her to secure vital resources. Having a child helps you to "grow up" by *assuming responsibilities* (Sophie[21]), and even by building a future for yourself. The child is its parents' future.

On another level, the child is a way to complete oneself as a person through love of another person, by unearthing, despite life's misfortunes, what is needed to survive. Beforehand, Nadège[22] *felt totally alone and sick of life*, and had attempted suicide. *A child gives you a taste for life*, one young mother said who herself had been a ward of the state. Children spur us into action: *When I had my son I sprang into action. I had to find us a place to live* (Myriam[23]).

– The child as a potential "gift"

Taking things a bit further, children are the intermediary between what we never received and the wish to give nevertheless: *I needed to have a child in order to be happy and give him the love I had in me* Rolande told us[24]. Today, Sophie[25], who was *separated from her home early because her parents were divorced, and tossed around between different foster homes,* is the mother of a two-year-old, and wants to start a family so she can give her children *all the love I have stored up in me and was never able to give.*

Noella, who had an unhappy childhood with parents (who did not have the time to take care of her and her brother and sister), and who had a hard time at school, made the same observation. When asked why she wanted to have lots of children when she had had such troubles herself, she replied that it was *because she hadn't received much love from (her) parents.*

"Transmission" is not what is at stake here, because we can only transmit what we have first received, but "giving" instead: giving what is in us without our having first received it. But this desire to give, expressed here in terms of love, may also be translated into other registers: for example as a concern that children acquire the social mannerisms that will afford them the opportunity to experience a greater degree of social integration. Hélène[27], mother of four, said she had taught her children *to be polite to people, to act friendly when they walk into a store.* To which she added: *because that's not how we were raised.*

The child as a life-event

– The children's futures
Both Nadège's and Myriam's comments speak to the same point: *The children's futures? Better than mine, at least . . . I want my children to have a better life than I had . . . I don't want them to have the same problems I did*[28].
Rolande was even more emphatic:

> As for the future of my children and grandchildren, I can see it better than my own. I hope they will have more opportunities than I had, more than we had in fact. I want them to be happy in life, for there to be no more wars, that it will be easier for them to make it than it was for us29.

– "Generation" as hope
When Rolande was asked if she "believed in" the hopes she had just invoked she replied: *I have to believe in them. You have to keep hoping, always believing.* For Xavier, hope is defined as *faith in the future*[30], one that generates continuance. Children are associated with the long-term. Despite being separated from two of his daughters, who had been placed in foster care, he nonetheless reiterated: *We had to at least have them, so we could have something to plan for. When you have nothing, what is there to plan for? . . . I can plan with my daughters if they come home . . . there could be a different future in store for us.* Xavier sees his children's presence as his own future: *My children are my future. . . . Without them, what future is there for me?* His wife, Sandrine, was the one who originally defined children as hope.

–The child as his own future
It is easy to imagine creating a future generation as the projection of oneself into the future. But sometimes it is the image of the future itself that assumesprimacy: *I had children . . . so they would have a future*, Sandrine told us. In this instance she was not thinking of her children's future, but of her children as defined in terms of the future. The future is the very definition of this being that comes into the world, engendered so that someone else besides oneself has a future, his own future.

It has already been emphasized that people have children for purposes of self-realization via the act of giving what they have not received. The same is true of bringing someone into the world in order that they have a future one was deprived of. This expectation is never guaranteed, but only hoped for, and may assume several forms.

Uncertainties and the unforeseeable

Here, we will be considering various situations that disrupt long-term continuance, including precarious employment and material conditions, and the threat (sometimes carried out) of child-removal.

Being out of work and endless waiting

Employment, in particular a full-time job, is a way of structuring life over the long-term, even over several decades for those with salaried jobs (or in agricultural or vocational trades). The undeniable long-term continuance that employment provides has a considerable influence on family plans, and vice versa. Indeed the predictable income it affords is a means for them to plan for the future based on the security it provides.

Employment temporality

Some of the people we met, the older ones usually, had experienced this employment temporality, which we took to be a sign they had worked in the industrial sector. This was the case for Odile[31]: *I worked in the textile mill at H. I left home at 5am until 1pm, when I would come home and watch the kids until my husband took over with them around 5.30–6pm.* Later in the interview she cast doubt on her husband's work ethic: *My husband didn't go to work very often. . . . When it was nice out he would go for a walk instead of going to work.* Rolande[32] had the same experience: *My husband always hated getting up early in the morning. Yes, he did work a little, but as for getting up in the morning . . .*

A promotion, an important path to job satisfaction, constitutes another way for people to find long-term continuance, especially insofar as it usually presupposes various kinds of training and professional development.

This was how Germaine[33], whose husband is an unemployed accountant, described the ten years *he took to get it (his diploma) while working at the same time.* This instance, however, is an exception for the community we interviewed; especially insofar as neither member of this couple came from a poor or disadvantaged background.

Endless waiting

The raising of children does not come to figure within a temporality that is exclusively happy and assured of future events, but is instead ever in search of an impossible long-term social continuance. *The future doesn't seem that far off to me,* Jeannette[34] said, *because as they say, when you're unemployed. . . .* The waiting seems endless and the search for new openings is usually in vain, waiting for that promised land where promises are never fulfilled: *Francis*, Jeannette's part-ner, *found temporary work . . . but people were always promising him more, his bosses were always promising him more. . . . He only worked for six months.*

In a sense, time is neither linear nor cyclical, but is instead *looped,* as the Fourth World activists would say, meaning that even steps forward we think we are sure of may eventually lead to a step back. Sometimes it becomes possible to think of a new beginning when the loop "loops" back around, but there are also those loops that do not prove strong enough and the new step forward can no lon-ger be envisioned, at least for a while. Nadine,[35] who seemed incapable of garner-ing even a minimal degree of social recognition before her baby was born, simply said *hoping scares me.* She does not live with the child's father so that she can receive benefits accorded to single-parent families only[36]. To a certain extent this echoes the *depression* suffered by many people we met, including Lucienne[37] and Mrs. Urbain[38].

The inability to see what lies ahead: the difficulty of saving money

Money is not the most important thing to the poorest, but it is certainly a con-stant preoccupation. Low incomes place heavy constraints on short-term options, for example many people have to interrupt the vocational training they are re-ceiving because their funds dry up, or they cannot afford to pay for something as simple as a driver's license, which is a key to finding work. But for many, these deprivations can be muddled through if there is love, which is often present in overabundance. Rolande, a cleaning lady, recounted the many hardships she had weathered, all the while making it clear that *material things didn't really matter, we always had our iron will*[39].

The fact remains however that setting money aside—in the form of savings or, what amounts to the same thing in temporal terms, borrowing money to pay back later—is not just one form of planning that may take place, but is the veritable sign of planning itself. Myriam mentioned that *in just two more pay periods we'll have enough (to make a down payment on a house).* She also *hopes to put some money aside some day*, but at the same time she bemoans the fact that *I can't say I'm doing it right now.*

Noella[40] emphasized that *we can't make plans for the future because we don't have the money.* Not being able to put money away means being condemned *to live from one day to the next,* she said.

When it is impossible to save money, it also becomes impossible to make an investment, over the long-term, in order to realize one's future plans.

Family filiation threatened or monitored

As we have already seen, from amongst the people we interviewed a certain number experienced breakdowns in their family "filiation" due to their having been taken into care away from their families of origin. This experience can take place in the other direction, when familial generations, (and the relationship to the long-term timeframes that they make possible), are perturbed or punctuated by threats whose presence weigh heavily on the people's chances of raising their own children.

For instance Lucienne's custody of her children is monitored by the state: *They are threatening to take my children away from me. . . . I have to go to family court on a regular basis.*

The threat is almost always there, which is how Rolande accounted for the importance she placed on finding decent housing after being evicted: *If I had no-where to live my children would be taken away from me permanently, and that was something I could never let happen.* This experience can even affect people who are not directly concerned: *In my building*, said Sophie[41], *two young couples had their children taken away from them. . . . It's terrible.* Myriam[42] will do anything to avoid this: *I'll never put my kids in foster care.*

As for this threat, which constantly hung over her children's future, Nadège[43] insisted: *My kids will never end up in foster homes and go through what I did.* For some mothers, the threat becomes all too real. For instance when one young woman told her doctor, whom she trusted, that she was pregnant, he reported it to the social services who had taken her other children into care**. How can she be expected to think in the long-term for herself and for her baby when she is constantly threatened with having it taken away any day?

The short-term stranglehold or crisis

Difficult housing and living conditions upset the rhythm of everyday life, and portray families living in crisis situations in ways that may make it seem like they are doing so by choice.

Living conditions lead to crises

Housing

When the families we interviewed spoke of their living conditions, it was almost always the topic of housing they complained about most. Indeed for younger parents the word "housing" all too often means cohabitating with one or the other's parents, despite their desire to be on their own. *For now I live with my mom. There's nine of us living there! . . . Ten if you count my grandmother*[44].

Sometimes it also means sharing a place with another family (which may be that of a brother or sister). Regardless of whether they're sharing with family or not . . . *there are 11 people in a four-room apartment!*[45] Is long-term planning still conceivable when the day-to-day difficulties caused by this kind of overcrowding must first be overcome (including keeping the house in order, avoiding fights, etc.)?

Even when a family does find housing that is not an abandoned and unsanitary property which has been frequented by squatters, it is usually too small and soon fills up with new children. One mother explained that: *I was expecting my fifth child and couldn't stay where I was anymore . . . I only had two rooms, and with five kids it would have been too much of a stretch.*[46]

In situations like these, time becomes time to wait. Realizing other projects is put aside until decent housing can be found. The expectation can enliven a family with moments of hope, but all too often leads to moments of discouragement and despair. And when all certainties dissolve, in particular those related to futureaccommodation, even if everyone in the family has their minds set on the future it is scarcely possible to prepare for it, plan it out or set it down on paper—specific plans become impossible.

One interviewer asked another family: *When there were six of you living in a two-room apartment, how did you set things up?* The reply was a short but palpable description: *I put my bed there and the kids' bed next to it. All in the same bedroom,* the interviewer concluded . . . though he didn't dare ask if the mother of the house had managed to find a space for herself where she could relax and reflect on the future.[47]

Dilapidation often compounds these overcrowded and even unsanitary conditions: *Check out the ceiling. It could fall in at any minute*[48]. *In one small house we lived in there were only two rooms and mice and rats everywhere*[49].

Indeed rats and mice were often seen during these interviews! What other mode could time be in for these families, but the "in-the-now" timing of crisis mode? Constantly worrying about whether the ceiling is about to fall in clearly impedes the time needed for personal development and making plans.

Money and work

Overcrowded, unsanitary and undersized housing conditions are clearly signs a family lacks financial resources, but they rarely need say it out loud. It is not worth mentioning because it is too obvious. On the other hand, when the families we interviewed did speak about money troubles, it was usually in relation to paying the bills or to say that their parents *practically killed themselves to earn peanuts* just to make ends meet[50].

Either at the end of the month, every now and then, or even for significantly longer periods, time itself seems to almost grind to a halt. Until some payment or another comes in, (family benefits, unemployment benefits, or the minimum income benefit in France, or Minimex in Belgium), almost everything becomes impossible: The adults in the family are all semi-paralyzed until the money comes through. And sometimes when there is nothing left at home, the children cannot even go to school!

Job stability was rarely available to the people we interviewed. Jean-Baptiste[51] put it well: *Having what you need means having a job, stable work, and children.*

But when he was asked if he had these things himself, he replied: *No, just odd jobs, temporary stuff and internships.*

The same is true for Lucienne's[52] husband: *He landed a work program job with the city, but it won't last. We'll end up like before. It might take three months, maybe six months, we don't know. . . .* We don't know. This kind of uncertainty often leads to unforeseen events.

For a mother in a very poor family, especially with numerous young children, working often entails additional obstacles and sometimes is not even possible. This was the case for one mother who had to stop working because her son was not being fed well in day care[53]. For heads of households, especially women in this role, time is marked by frequent interruptions to handle crises, including sick children, unforeseen but necessary measures, accidents, etc.

Support, but not always

Some families feel and consider themselves supported by those around them or social and charitable services. *My mother gave us her extra furniture. . . . At first I would eat at the Mission . . . and got benefits from the City*[54].

Unless these pockets of family aid are normal (like the furniture for example), help of this sort severely risks holding the family back in the long-term, because it only helps them to survive, not plan for the future.

At times moral support, offering advice for example, can have long-term beneficial effects that may even last a lifetime: *I really made progress with The F's. . . . And my mother taught me not to waste money. . . .*[55]

More often, however, this kind of aid must be concrete and financial: *We asked L's father, and he lent us the deposit (for a house)*[56]. They also have electricity thanks to him. There is always the chance this kind of support will not last, as was the case for the family whose grandfather helped out with the rent . . . until he died.[57] Unfortunately help and support are not always there when a family needs them. People may not give help because they lack the knowledge or the means to do so, as with Doctor Titran and his team, who were helping a young woman raise her second child herself, but *we couldn't give her all the coaching like we did with Paule (her first child)*.[58]

Financial and moral support may also be quite simply refused, for no reason, as was the case for a thirteen-year-old girl who, on the advice of her grade-school principal no less, applied for a grant to go to middle-school. *There's no point in her applying Mrs. Ribert*, the social worker told her mother, *they're still hiring at the factory and Lucie can definitely get a job there, and that will make for one more income around the house*.[59] Without doubt this would provide extra money right away, but the social worker was standing in the way of this teenager's long-term prospects, essentially tying her to the short-term.

The moral and psychological conditions that keep families in short-term crisis

One activist in our group pointed out that very often only the negative aspects of poor peoples' lives are focused on, at the expense of the more positive elements and the efforts they are making. Besides being painful for those who experience them, these kinds of judgments are another way of holding people back and miring them in the short-term. It is hardly surprising that we find families actually cowering at these sorts of criticisms heaped upon them, and their children in particular.

One woman we interviewed does not dare send her two sons to the local recreational center because they play up too much—one was barred from the school canteen and the other was expelled: *I'm afraid they'll cause trouble for me*[60]. Their exclusion from school and the canteen prevents them from taking advantage of the possibilities for discovery the recreational center has to offer, and hence bars them from a certain kind of future as well. The need to steer clear of any kind of trouble is miring this family into a short-term timeframe and is standing in the way of their access to the medium- and long-term. These kinds of troubles can lead to children being taken into care, which is clearly what these families fear most, sometimes even when the threat is not real. It is a kind of angst that stems from their situation: *I couldn't live without my kids. If they tried to take them from me, I would resort to force. I would be capable of doing anything*[61].

Moments of struggle and discouragement often follow difficult situations such as these.

One family in northern France was being threatened with imminent eviction. Their social worker revealed plans to place their children in foster care permanently, and convinced them that if they turned their children over themselves they would later be able to bring them home as soon as they had found decent housing *without having to go to court*[62]. So the parents sent their children into care for safe-keeping until they found a new home. But getting them back did not turn out to be as easy as they had thought: in fact, they ended up having to go to court even after they had found a new place to live because they had to prove they were capable of holding on to it.

Many parents are capable of acting with vigor even outside of such extreme situations: the everyday things they do prove they have not given up yet. Examples of this are the mother who got organized and found shoes for her children in the store that offered the best price, and who put her children's bed right next to hers in their only bedroom[63], or the father who applied for his driver's license even though he did not know how to read or write.[64] But as the saying goes, there are always those moments *when enough is enough*, and even the strongest feel like hanging their heads in despair.

The consequences of moments of duress and discontinuity

Here, we will first depict situations characterized by moments of extreme duress and discontinuity, when all planning becomes impossible, and then reflect on the feelings they induce. Moments of extreme duress relate to short-term timeframes, whereas periods of discontinuity occur in the medium and long-term, generally concerning stages in the life of a family, and get passed down from generation to generation.

The very short term: moments of duress

Moments of duress are caused by extreme hardship in life that must be struggled against—even though it may feel like trying to plug holes in a dike—a life that is always on the lookout for help.

Moments of duress must be endured because services that help usually have their own schedules: You will have to wait for housing; they will get back to you, you are on the list. Or if you are waiting to get your child back you are told you have to have a suitable place to live. Everything feels squeezed: *For the poorest people, action in crisis-mode is something they must endure, they don't choose it ... they're expected to come up with a plan to get back on their feet in just a few months time***.

One young mother we met had been given custody of her premature baby on a trial-basis by a judge: she had just nine days to prove she was fit to raise it**. The poor are forced to endure other people's time, which may be different from their own.

In order to better understand these moments of duress we must imagine we no longer have a degree of relative control over time and, instead, envision what the consequences of losing this mastery must be—the rhythm of life becomes chaotic. Time may feel like it has simply stopped when the family hunkers down in the struggle to survive. Time may even seem empty sometimes.

– **Being in Control.** After having spoken of his past, one person said:

Now life is better for me, I don't have to go through my change to buy milk or bread for the next day. I don't have to worry about tomorrow because I don't owe anybody for the rent, and I can fill out the paperwork at City Hall to get the kids into the lunch program, take them to school and won't have to feel ashamed about showing my pay slip65.

– **Chaos.** The aforementioned person had a certain degree of financial and social security. But when these resources are lacking, crisis-situations ensue and people are forced to make use of whatever they find wherever it appears, no longer keeping track of hours or even what time it is. Here's how one of activists of the group described it:

Very poor families get caught up in crisis-situations: one day they're at a soup kitchen in one place, the next they have food parcels or vouchers at another, or in a yet another different place they find clothes, store closeouts, etc.; anything to just get by day-to-day. All these measures are taken under the most punishing physical and mental conditions and, above all, prevent them from getting out of poverty because their efforts are not even acknowledged.

– Waiting and hunkering down.

When you are out of work, penniless and with no-one to help you, you tend to hunker down and put everything on hold because of fear and anguish. You don't respond to anything or think like you did before. When these down-times take hold, you start to ask yourself why get up in the morning when you feel so useless, when you know there's nothing to do all day but hang around, or sit in a chair, or mope around the house.

When you don't have enough money but the kids need to be fed and fed and you're waiting for the money to come, sometimes you just stay in bed. When there's no heat, you stay under the covers. You let time slip away. No-one understands what it is like. Shame quickly overtakes these families. Like in Father Joseph's66 story about the bird, time stands still. When you're down and don't have the strength to get back up anymore, you let yourself go. Some families hunker down and wait for better days, for example when a little money comes in. And then, things get going again**.

For Father Wresinski, a state of constant waiting was a defining characteristic of most poor people's modes of being and living. Everybody waits: for a piece of good news they did not dare hope for, a potential new job perhaps . . . but also anxiously awaiting the debt-collector. . . . At first glance, waiting seems like an entirely passive activity, but it is oriented towards something. It is always *waiting for . . . hoping* for. . . . At the same time hunkering down and waiting may be a kind of survival mode in extreme and even inhuman circumstances: we try to spare ourselves suffering by withdrawing, saving our strength by slowing down and hibernating.

– The appearance of dazed withdrawal in extreme situations. Sometimes, the presence of children is not enough to revitalize parents, as happened to one young woman who experienced a series of traumas over the course of several months: her boyfriend's imprisonment and refusal to acknowledge their unborn child, life in the streets and being raped whilst pregnant. Then much later, after she had finally regained her strength, she realized that at that moment wrought with immense difficulties, she was *rejecting the child*67.

I was living in the streets. I slept in the subway for three nights. I ended up in the hospital because I was losing my daughter (she was pregnant). I was completely rudderless, they found me unconscious in the subway . . . They told me my body had been abused. A shelter took me in for a while. I did what they told me to do, but nothing more. I didn't have a job but I didn't give a damn, I wasn't even aware I was going to have a child.

The longer term: periods of discontinuity

Discontinuity may become inscribed in the life-stages of people, families and their chronological relationship to society.

When children arrive at a certain age, they must fend for themselves and adapt to life (experiences, identity). This is most often the case generally, but even more so when they are raised outside the nuclear family or come from a broken home. There is no moratorium phase for them, and their relationships lack intimacy. Because of this, they rarely engage in planning with their partner and procreation ensues almost immediately after adolescence. What were originally short-term solutions to difficult situations become habits that are hard to get rid of—a way of living that can last a lifetime and is passed on to children and grandchildren. There is no other way, it is a part of us now. The concept of time no longer exists. We live from day to day and even meal to meal. As if chaos has become fixation**.

The lack of plans made or carried through

It is frequently asserted in academic literature that poor people do not make plans, or at least make fewer plans which tend to be more focused on the short-term. Diverse ideas are put forward to explain why this might be the case[68], all of which must be questioned and nuanced.

In our interviews it became clear that poor families do indeed make plans, although there were moments when they admitted they did not, and other times when they said they could not under the circumstances. It seemed their plans may not have been recognized as such by the outside world.

Some periods are considered devoid of all undertaking

Myriam, whom we spoke of earlier, related one of her darkest periods to us:

– No, I wasn't even thinking about the next day . . .
– What concept of the future did you hold at that time?
– I expected nothing from the future . . . nothing at all.

However during this same period, which she considered to be devoid of all undertaking, she nonetheless harbored at least one preoccupation—her plan to get the father of her child to recognize the child as soon as possible and of his own accord (15 days after the birth), and this during a period when she felt incapable of doing anything except what others told her to do. *She had my name, I took her to the prison to see her father as the social workers wanted me to.*

Another mother told us how she used to echo the spirit of the age by referring to the numerous children she had in succession when she was younger as "unplanned". But now she realizes that for her in fact, *expecting a child was like a plan, at least unconsciously***, and she was greatly moved when saying so.

We believe we are faced with a phenomenon similar to the one Boutinet[69] described while observing that the concern with planning is relatively recent in historical terms, and is primarily linked to industrialization. People have always sought to expand their lives, but their plans were usually only lived, and not expressly spelled-out.

What follows, by way of a transition, is an extract from our interview with Liliane[70], who spoke at great length about both her concrete plans and the absence of any sense of the future itself on her part. The text demonstrates how the two can coexist in relatively logical fashion. Liliane and her ex-husband *had definitely made plans, yes. But then he had to go and meet that girl, and that was it.* Now she wants to get out of the housing project where she lives: *I'm sick of it after 22 years.* As for work: *I'm looking for sure, but nothing's out there, it sucks right?* She wants to move out of the place where her brother and sister live, both adults, and look for work in Paris. A friend has offered to let her use her place in S.: *in September if all goes well* (in two months time), *but I'll still have to see what happens because I would have to totally redo the place. It's pretty small really, but it would still take a least a whole day to do.*

When asked how she pictured herself in five years:

– I can tell you this much, I don't know! (smiles). Don't have a clue.
– And in one year?
– I don't know either (laughs). Seriously, I don't know.
– And in six months?
– In six months, I don't know either. I can't give you an answer, we'll just have to see! If I find a boyfriend and he says to me: "Let's live together" or whatever, who knows. I can't really tell you.
– But when you think of the future and when you're a parent . . . (she has custody of her son).
– No (silence). *I* don't know. You know, since I lost my mother (four years ago) *I* don't think anymore. I don't think about anything. It's better like that, because it was like I lost a part of myself.

After speaking about her mother and the plans her mother had made for her, Liliane added:

Then again in September I did make some plans. I would like to get some training to become a nurse's aide. Maybe there's a job in that somewhere, I guess we'll see what happens.

She already works in this field on a temporary basis and seems to have made progress and has received good reviews.

Liliane went through a period of transition after her mother died and her partner left her. Naturally this affected her plans: *Ever since my mom died I haven't been able to think straight anymore*, and *we had made plans* [as a couple]. . . . She experienced numerous setbacks and hopes in her search for stable employment. In the end however, *nothing came up, it's discouraging* [looped time]. We observed that she was capable of planning two or three months in advance, but truly could not make out what lay in store for her beyond that. This is why the possibility of finding a new boyfriend six months from now drove her to say *No-one knows. No-one can know* is what the interviewees in the next paragraph say.

Being truly unable to make plans, given the circumstances

When things were going better for her, Myriam said:

> At first we lived from one day to the next, he hadn't found work yet, and so I can't say we had our minds on the future. At any rate I didn't know if it was serious between us, since I had three kids and he had one who was living with his mother . . . I didn't know if he would stay with me or what, so I wasn't able to plan for the future.

After she found out that she was pregnant, and that her boyfriend wanted her to have the baby, she was able to make plans once more:

> One year later I found out I was pregnant. I asked him, "Should I keep it?" He said yes and that's when we really got together. . . . We decided to get married, but we waited a little bit first because we didn't have much money. . . . We had to find work first, and he thought it was better for him to look rather than me.

Another mother said:

> I think he's already starting to talk (her two-year-old son). As for the rest, we'll see how it goes over time. You can't make plans when you're living from one day to the next[71].

Plans recognized as such by society

Plans are sometimes viewed as not being made, when in reality they are simply yet to be realized. An activist in our group explained that:

> Outsiders may think poor families don't make plans simply because these plans are not followed through, and thus they don't see them. But something else is at stake. What we see is that they are not followed through, for example we may see that a certain family has always lived in the slums and therefore they can't have a plan to find housing, but this is not the case. What is lacking is the plan's realization.

Dreams can prove unrealizable. Their plan is understood, but the first reaction is to say: "That's unrealizable for families with limited resources. It's a pipe-dream, an ideal, but not a plan."

> Poor families formulate plans for living an ordinary life like everyone else but are forced to make do at first with whatever they have. In fact they're not dreaming. In

their heads they are never dreaming. A dream doesn't have the same definition as a plan. I looked it up in the dictionary: a plan is something we intend to do, whereas a dream is when we let our imagination run wild. So the two are not the same thing at all. The word dream cannot be used instead of the word plan**.

Sometimes a plan may have been put in place but it cannot truly be called a plan because it has not been thought through as regards its different steps, the ways to set it in motion and the possible risks involved, etc. Poor people lack the experience needed to understand how this process works and thus are like explorers in a foreign land without a good map, knowledge of the language or a guide.

Feelings

These moments of suffering and disturbance, moments of waiting in one place or that repeat themselves, chaotic moments that escape efforts to control them, all give rise to a number of feelings. For example, waiting leads to anxiety, discouragement and also hope. Here, we shall be speaking primarily of shame and indignation.

Shame is tied to the gaze of the other, who do not see you as a subject with desires, but as an object whose usefulness he exposes and pronounces judgment upon. Every time *you have to expose yourself completely, tell your whole life's story if you want to stand even the slightest chance of getting a job**.*

This shame can extend all the way into feelings of guilt that detract from life's meaning:

Outside the Movement, when we were poor and alone, you better believe we felt guilty about being good for nothings, to the point we started wondering why we were even born if we were so bad and wrong as all that. . . . Since I was a parasite, all that was left was for me to do was to put myself out of my misery**.

It can also lead to indignation and revolt:

It took me ten years to find a place that was big enough for ten people. Even after I did everything I was supposed to, seven of us had to live in two rooms, and this shows that society doesn't really have the good will it takes to find a new way of doing things. . . . And I always felt anxious about being judged and being threatened (with having children taken into care). It really got me down**.

Another group activist told how one time at a lecture he was attending,

The speaker was relating how a child should never be separated too quickly from his mother, that great care must be taken in these matters, above all in explaining to him in advance what is going on. . . . When I asked her, "What about when they take our kids from us without advance warning?" She never was able to answer me.

Seeking and choosing the long-term

Willingly getting involved in the long-term is about engaging in acts that point towards the future, like becoming independent, starting and maintaining a family.

The need for independence

When they reach a certain age, sometimes 15, sometimes 20, children from very poor families often have great difficulty putting up with their living conditions. Penniless and unemployed, they often feel like a burden to their parents and their younger brothers and sisters, and may even feel ashamed that they have to be taken care of without being able to help out. Other times their living conditions become unbearable and they start to blame their parents, making their lives together virtually unlivable. This is how it was for Jeannette: *It was hell after my mother got remarried. When my father was alive things were OK, but my stepfather took advantage of me when my father died*[12].

Jeannette left her mother's when she was 18 and pregnant. Another young woman was said to have left home at the age of 13, but she did not want to revisit her childhood because it was too painful for her.

Others who had been placed in foster families or care homes told of wanting to become independent in order to prove to themselves and others that they existed and were able to take care of themselves. Colette explained that she was taken into care when she was 12 because of her parents' drinking, and at 15½ she left the home with her boyfriend.

Finding a place together and having children

Young people living in non-impoverished circumstances frequently gain their independence through their studies or professional careers, and only live with someone much later. For some, family plans and career paths join together, as in the example of a man who was 28-years-old and studying medicine when he met his future wife:

> I was attracted to her at first because she was working in the same field as I wanted to. What I wanted out of getting married was a wife I could share things with, give my love and attention to, and who I could open up to. I needed affection and desired the intimacy that goes with living as a couple, like I saw all around me. I wanted to complete a project with a spouse who understood me professionally. I didn't know what at the time: a practice, a center maybe, but something we could do together**.

At times, plans to start a family are dictated by resource availability. Another young couple met at university, but waited until they had finished their studies before getting engaged. As one of them put it:

We would often joke that we wanted to have children right away. We knew it wouldn't work financially though, because we didn't have jobs and were out looking. . . . For a relationship to last, both people have to guard their autonomy, their independence[73].

Very often a future family cannot even be conceived of without the security a professional career affords. For example the wife of another couple who also met at university told us:

The original reason we wanted to live together was our love for each other and our careers. I pushed him to continue his studies because he hadn't gotten his degree yet. It took him ten years to get it and work at the same time, having four kids. I pushed him because I told myself "we have to secure a future"[74].

Children are what ultimately make a warm, tender and loving home last. This love and tenderness are concretized with a first child's arrival. According to Rolande:

My husband grew up in foster homes. I came from a big family, not rich but relatively trouble-free. For us, family was sacred. We both loved our kids very much. They were our pride and joy, our reason for living. We were living and working for something. Our first was the best present in the world. We made lots of plans for him before he was even born—plans that were never realized[75].

Given enough time, almost any plan to raise a family can be realized, despite all the obstacles. A young woman of 26, separated very early from her parents and shuffled around from home to home, said that her first concern was to find a place of her own. When she was 12 she met the man who would become the father of her children. When she was 13 she got pregnant and miscarried. Since she was so young, her social worker sent her to live in a home 800 km (500 miles) away from her boyfriend. They could not even write each other because their letters were confiscated, but the day she turned 18 she came back and they moved in together:

We decided to start a family. Having kids is what life is all about. I wanted to give them all the love I had stored up inside me and could never give, the warmth of the household I never knew. My husband grew up a lot after our first child was born. He started doing everything he could to make it in life, to find work, keep our son with us, make the tiny place where we were living, and our lives in general, a little better. Children were very important to him. They changed our lives[76].

Housing means security for a family in the present and in the future. Having a place to call its own, an address, is proof a family exists. Even though it means safety in the present, above all else housing makes it possible for a family to have a future, to be imbibed with something that lasts. When a first child arrives, the question of housing arises, even when it is not something that necessarily prevents people from having their baby. Hélène and Claude lived with her grandmother and their two children: *At first we wanted our own place for our own family. Starting a family of our own was important. It was important for us and the kids*[77]. Every poor person we interviewed expressed having a roof over their heads in order to be able to raise and keep children as a constant concern. One young woman[78] related the story of her mother's struggle to lay her hands on *a kind of brick lean-to in the middle of an orchard*. She secured the owner's permission on the condition she did not spoil the fruit trees. This stable home proved insecure, and was followed by years of homelessness.

Housing for large families with modest means was also frequently referred to, for example a family of five whose father was earning the minimum wage. Social housing for large families is usually limited to five rooms (one living room and four bedrooms), and furthermore families need a guarantor. It is hardly surprising therefore to hear one family with four children, whose only income is from the French minimum income payments and family welfare benefits, tell how their struggle to find housing had lasted for years: *You have to wait. They tell us others are worse off than we are, since at least we have a roof over our heads whereas others are sleeping outside*[79]. They have shared a small two-room apartment with their children for several years. A story Myriam told us about a hard time in her life made it clear just how indispensable the security of having a home was to her life plan:

The social worker would come by almost every day. She asked me what I wanted to do, and I told her I wanted to keep the apartment so they wouldn't take my kids away from me[80].

Now that her situation has stabilized, she reiterated that her plan

is still the same, but I don't know if I'll ever see it through. What we would like is to have a house with a yard. You see I picture my daughter all grown up stopping by with her boyfriend and her kids. . . . Still I can't say I'm saving up for it right now, it's just not possible.

Raising children means looking forward. It gives parents a new rhythm to follow, and new responsibilities. Moving in with someone and starting a family changes your life. According to Jeannette:

We got by on our own. We took responsibility, even when times were tough we muddled through. We never had to live in a home or anything like that. We told ourselves: we have a goal, there's going to be three of us now, it's not just the two of us anymore and we've got to make it work so we can take care of them, because it's up to us to raise them, we have to take responsibility for raising them[81].

A child gives parents new energy. Fathers often get back into the rhythm of work, and even find ways to moonlight on the side, selling things or doing odd jobs for neighbors. One young woman who could not read or write said that when she found out she was pregnant she immediately wanted to learn how, because she realized one day she could help her daughter when she started school.

When families suffer the misfortune of being torn apart by poverty, several of the people we interviewed attested to the fact that every effort is made to bring them back together again. When housing and a regular income make it possible to get a child back, parents devote all their love and attention to preparing for their return: fathers will agree to their umpteenth training course, the house is scrubbed and repainted. It is not unheard of to find these hope-filled occasions resulting in the arrival of a newborn as well.

Marriage as an example of seeking and choosing the long-term

One young couple of college students who have been engaged for several years said the following about their marriage:

> We did it in a church and everything. What we really wanted to get across is that couples can't work without the help of their friends. I wanted everyone to know that our love is not just for us, but to share with others as well. . . . All the readings we chose at our wedding ended with the word friendship[82].

Another lower-class couple share this idea of marriage as the sign of a family that welcomes others.

In impoverished circles marriage is a family affair. Hélène and Claude announced during their interview: We're going to get married, but we're waiting until we get housing. We decided to do it that way ourselves so that we can be together[83]. Jean-Baptiste and Colette[84] were married after living together for three years. *We got married because we loved each other*, said Jean-Baptiste, at which point Colette added, *we got married because my son was using my name at school, and his buddies were always asking him why he didn't use his father's name.*

Jean-Baptiste: *I'm their father after all, so it's only right that I give them my name, that I'm there for them, that they know I'm their father at the end of the day.*

Myriam also said that her marriage carried with it the hope of she and her children using the same name as her husband:

> My daughter was using my maiden name, and imagined to herself that she didn't have a father since her brothers were using their father's name. She was disappointed the day we got married and she saw the family register[85].

Children are recognized by their civil status, and naming children is relatively easy for married couples. Even though it is possible for children to use their father's name when their parents are not married, this was one of the main reasons for doing so offered by the poor people we interviewed. Christian added that *Marriage is the way we make our commitment official for the future of our children***.

Marriage can last a lifetime, and thus assumes another meaning, related to the idea of eternity. As Danielle put it:

> My parents were married in church when they were 75. My father wanted to give my mother this wedding ring which, thank God, she had never lost**.

Hardship-time or resource-time

Formulating family plans is a way of choosing to get involved the long-term, but maintaining control of this timeframe raises particular hardships for the very poor.

Time may be a hardship

Time, viewed from the various angles from which we have considered it and regardless of whether it is in the long- or short-term, can constitute a hardship for the poorest.

Longer-term timeframes may, in this respect, turn into the slow-to-heal imprints of harsh events that have marked people's personal histories and whose consequences extend into the present-day, such as being taken in to care or abandoned, having insecure living conditions or extreme hardship. However, not all these situations mean the same thing. A lack of material means may be compensated for, whereas the emotional and symbolic lack caused by the absence of one or both parents engenders more difficult problems.

Furthermore, planning for the future may run up against different kinds of barriers: Being out of work, first of all, and thus not having a stable income. Even though certain minimum living conditions are guaranteed by the social safety net, these always seem susceptible to being taken away.

The interviewees often had difficulty knowing where they would be in the mid-term (five years) or even the short-term. When they referred to future events, it was usually in the form of a wish rather than a "plan" as such. They often carried the scars of their pasts which they had no control over and were thus incapable of leaving their own mark on their lives and futures based on choices made freely. Thus they often felt like they were *taking baby steps*[86]. These difficulties were even more pronounced when their family was unplanned, and one or both parents did not seem to have been in control of the chain of events which had led it to its current condition.

As far as the short-term was concerned, things usually happened in "lurches" that prevented them from getting organized and staying on track. More things happen to us the more we do not make them happen ourselves. Neither the short-nor the long-term are under control.

Time may also be a resource

Long-term timeframes are not always a hardship. For some people, familial commitments seem to come naturally—it is inscribed in the succession of the generations, at the heart of the framework instituted by a family with stable contours. This was the case for Mr. B**, whose entire life was inscribed in this form of time. No doubt this was at least in part related to the fact that his life had been structured by a culture based on the rigidly ordered, patriarchal family (the Mediterranean culture of Mr. B's Tunisian origins). In more general terms, having children is always related to this kind of time, even when the relationship to them is severed due to them being taken into care, because the family's eventual reunification can only be envisioned in the long-term.

Short-term timeframes are not always unpredictable, and may sometimes even be the source of simple pleasures. The worry-free, unproblematic moments life sometimes affords are lived in the short-term—taking the time to walk to the cheapest supermarket and finding a handbag for just 78 francs ($14), strolling along the riverside, watching movies on TV together, welcoming a new baby into the house by assembling its crib and decorating its room. It was with this short-term time in mind that Myriam invoked, with a certain nostalgia for what might have been, various moments she was not able experience with her husband: *he would have come home at night and we would have had dinner by candlelight* . . .

Whether long-term or short, the time of children is never "problematic". In fact time spent with children, both "long" and "short" term, was usually not depicted as divided up at all. Instead it had to do with hope and escaping beyond the currently barred future. From this point of view, one institution in particular played a key role: school. School affords the possibility to get a diploma, and in doing so spans the entire temporal horizon. At issue here is not so much long-term time, which is always present when desiring something, but rather the social conditions of the life in question, which usually hamper a family's plans. Expectations may be adjusted to fit reality in the short-term. For short periods, the very poor are capable of adapting their timeframe to conditions born of crisis situations. Not being able to see the future beyond a limited time, or not wanting to do so, may stem from unhappiness experienced, but does not necessarily mean a person is unhappy in general.

Hope, a major source of strength, is inscribed in the long-term, but does it not gain sustenance from shorter episodes?

> There were moments when I felt really discouraged [Rolande said], because I hung my head when I saw things weren't working out. I would get fed up, I would hang my head, but then a little pixie would always come along to shake me up a little[87].

This little pixie does not speak into Rolande's ear alone. Those fleeting moments when we hear his helpful whisper are the ones when we find the strength to start over anew, get the idea for a plan, or take a few steps forward.

Notes

1. Interview no. 9.
2. Interview no. 8.
3. Interview no. 9.
4. Interview no. 6.
5. Interview no. 9.
6. Interview no. 3.
7. Interview no. 7.
8. Interview no. 5.
9. Interview no. 7.
10. Interview no. 11.
11. Interview no. 2.
12. Interview no. 13.
13. Interview no. 2.
14. Interview no. 11.
15. Interview no. 9.
16. Interview no. 6.
17. Interview no. 8.
18. Interview no. 11.
19. Interview no. 6.
20. Interview no. 10.
21. Interview no. 5.
22. Interview no. 11.
23. Interview no. 12.
24. Interview no. 3.
25. Interview no. 5.
26. Interview no. 10.
27. Interview no. 8.
28. Interviews no. 11, 13.
29. Interview no. 3.
30. Interview no. 6.
31. Interview no. 4.
32. Interview no. 3.
33. Interview no. 14.
34. Interview no. 2.
35. Interview no. 11.
36. This is a benefit (API) which is accorded to anyone in France without means (without work), and who is raising a child younger than three years of age, or with at least three children.
37. Interview no. 7.
38. Interview no. 16.
39. Interview no. 3.
40. Interview no. 10.
41. Interview no. 5.
42. Interview no. 13.
43. Interview no. 11.
44. Interview no. 8.
45. Interview no. 7.

46. Interview no. 10.
47. Interview no. 4.
48. Interview no. 11.
49. Interview no. 9.
50. Interview no. 10.
51. Interview no. 9.
52. Interview no. 7.
53. Interview no. 4.
54. Interview no. 2.
55. Lecture Lucie Ribert, and doc. int.
56. Interview no. 6.
57. Interview no. 9.
58. M. Titran, T. Potekov, *op. cit.*
59. Lecture Lucie Ribert.
60. Interview no. 10.
61. Interview no. 8.
62. Interview no. 3.
63. Interview no. 4.
64. Interview no. 9.
65. Interview no. 13.
66. J. Wresinski, *Paroles pour demain*, (A Compass for Tomorrow) Paris, Desclée de Brouwer, 1986, pp. 135-139. The tale "Jamais plus un oiseau mort comme signe de détresse" (Never again a dead bird as a sign of distress) tells the story of a family that had hunkered down, and for whom time had stopped. They got through it after several days, but in the meantime their canary starved, and thus had become the symbol of the distress they had endured.
67. Interview no. 13.
68. Apathy-futility syndrome (Polansky), external locus of control (Rotter), conformity (Kohn), polychrony (Hall).
69. J. P. Boutinet, op. cit. p. 298.
70. Interview no. 15.
71. Interview no. 5.
72. Interview no. 2.
73. Interview no. 12.
74. Interview no. 14.
75. Interview no. 3.
76. Interview no. 5.
77. Interview no. 8.
78. Lecture Lucie Ribert.
79. Interview no. 7.
80. Interview no. 13.
81. Interview no. 2.
82. Interview no. 12.
83. Interview no. 8.
84. Interview no. 9.
85. Interview no. 13.
86. Interview no. 16.
87. Interview no. 3.

Chapter 5

IS THE FAMILY PLAN A STEPPING STONE TO ENTERING SOCIETY?

Is the family a stepping stone to entering society? Perhaps before answering this question it is worthwhile to ask more specifically for whom it would be a steeping stone. For children, parents, or the family unit as a whole?

When we start a family and bring children into the world, this is a plan in itself. Children cannot be conceived without thinking of their future. What will they be like in five years? Or in fifteen years? What kind of world will they live in? The ultimate aim of the family plan is to steer the child towards autonomy, in order for him to find his own place in society. A newborn child needs certain things to develop: biologically speaking he needs food, air to breathe and the like; and psychologically he needs affectivity and security. From infancy to adulthood, going through the inevitable phase of becoming fully integrated into the family setting always implies affectivity, a key element for personality construction and attaining autonomy. It enables one to feel confident about oneself and thus capable of taking part in social life. Citizens are not born, they are made. The newborn child is first and foremost dependent on others before becoming an autonomous individual. The family is the initial environment that provides for the child's affective and biological needs. Sometimes, however, parents are too possessive—instead of leading their children towards their own autonomy, they generate an inverse tendency.

Are children born to very poor families viewed as "family beings" or "individuals"? Our research has shown that very poor families live with the constant anxiety of being separated from their children, and the one thing they fight for the most is to have their family plans recognized as such. But in order to gain this recognition, do poor parents not first need to be recognized as responsible individuals themselves? Despite the existence of their family plans, society may or may not be able to provide them with the means to live together as a family, such as resources, housing, work and so forth. When these means are not available, families experience grave difficulties surviving, living, and making sure there is enough for today and tomorrow.

Nothing is worse for a family than when its unity is threatened. When decisions are made for them concerning their own children, parents are no longer recognized as responsible individuals. How do very poor people's plans for family life manifest themselves concretely? What social resources do they avail themselves of? Is the family a means for parents and children alike to gain a stepping stone for re-entering society?

Representations of family plans

Being a parent is a lifelong learning process. When starting a family, one can never know in advance how things will turn out. Old habits and lifestyles often change with the birth of a first child:

> We wanted to be very strong, to be able to protect him. We were very aware of those things we didn't have when we were kids and that we wanted to give him. Even though life is really tough, thanks to our kids we are making it through. We need them just as much as they need us**.

Being a parent is a life skill, one father told us—a life skill that is passed down from father to son and mother to daughter. But people who missed out on these points of reference in their own childhoods because they were placed in care are *often thrown into it with no preparation. Forced onto the path of being reproached* despite their plans to start a family and keep it together.

Planning to start a family for personal and mutual well-being

In previous chapters we have quoted a number of different meanings our interviewees have given to their family plans, including:

– *To start a family of our own . . .*
– *We decided to start a family right away. . . . The warmth of a home was something I never had . . .*
– *The most important thing for me was to start a family . . .*
– *At first, we wanted a family of our own . . .*
– *I remember something I always used to say: 'Start a family' . . .*
– *Making a home means having a goal . . . living as a little family all together.*
– *Living together, or at least trying to . . .* [1]

All too often, however, people living below the poverty line have experienced numerous setbacks in childhood and adolescence that cause them to lack self-confidence. When they meet someone they love, this lack of self-confidence may at times get translated into a form of real suffering linked to the fear of losing this loved one. This fear is amplified when periods of separation become necessary. To contain this fear, some couples have children:

He had to do his military service and was afraid I would fool around while he was gone. He couldn't trust people. For him, it was a kind of guarantee.[2]

When separations last longer, children are sometimes born while their fathers are absent. The frustration is terrible, most especially when the father refuses to acknowledge the child:

I couldn't use his name because we weren't married, so I had to give her my maiden name. He completely refused the child, saying she wasn't his daughter anyway, that he didn't want to have anything to do with her and that I should just give my baby up to the social sevices[3].

Myriam, however, did nothing of the sort. They ended up having other children together but the wound never truly healed.

People with very modest means often try to make something of themselves by starting a family:

– Our goal was to live together, be able to have a child and do everything we could to make it happen, to have a normal home, to have something at least. It was so that we would have a goal of some kind. To feel good and be with our family[4].

– My wife and I always dreamed of feeling the warmth of family life. I drew my strength from my relationship with my partner and from my children. I tore down walls of anguish for them**.

Starting a family also gives people the chance to break out of their (physical and mental) solitude:

–Myriam: I was the last of nine kids, my parents didn't take much care of me. They left me on my own in a corner. I was like a little robot. When I met Christian, I was so happy to be with him because he looked after me.

– Social services placed me in the home of a truck farmer. I took off from there and started to run around, living and sleeping in the streets. I met my wife because I knew her brothers. I used to hang out at their place.[5]

– When you're struggling alone, totally by yourself, tenderness is what you crave. This is usually the first thing two people who have lived through the same thing for years plan for. They crave new experiences. Together, they will be stronger**.

The way the family is envisaged is often based on the image of the traditional family founded on separate roles for men and women:

– My husband wanted to have a second child so I would quit working. He wanted his wife to stay at home. Later on, when he was still unemployed, I said, "one of us, either me or you, has to find work." He said he wanted it to be him and not me, as I had enough work taking care of the kids.[6]

– I wanted him to work all day and for me to stay home and take care of the house, to do whatever it took to be a good housewife. . . . He could see things were not headed in that direction, since I was the one working while he stayed at home. He didn't like it. He knew he was the father and that he was the one who should be working, not me.[7]

The simple wish to live together, otherwise quite easy to realize for the vast majority of people, is little more than a far-off dream given the many troubles most poor families must face.

Planning as a way of conforming to social norms

Starting a family is one way poor people aspire to have a normal life, meaning not having to fear for the future and being able to decide their own and their children's fate. Myriam said:

> Now that my husband has a part time job, I feel like I can go down to the courthouse and fill out the paperwork for their school lunches, and be able to take them home from school without feeling ashamed. I don't have to justify myself anymore. They ask me fewer questions.

Over the course of the interview, Myriam repeated several times *I wanted to have a normal life.* She wanted to drive the kids to school *in the morning, no problem,* have a house of her own, not have to scrape the money together to buy milk or bread, be able to give the kids things when they ask for them.

This goal of *living normally* may be what some people have in mind when they decide to get married as well, because it simplifies the administrative hoops they have to jump through and means they exist officially as a family.

When it comes to children, conforming to social norms also frequently comes to the forefront. The parents of very poor families often neglect themselves so that their children can be *like the other kids.* They make untold self-sacrifices so that their children will have nice clothes and most of the other things they need so that they will not unduly suffer from their situation.

It's not healthy. We don't have a bathroom or hot water, or a yard. This young woman felt bad because her daughter's teacher made her cut her child's hair; even though she did everything she could to make sure her children were clean:

> It's the best I can do in the house I have. I'm doing everything I can to feed my children. I'll go without, but I don't want them to suffer. First thing every month I buy milk, diapers and food. That comes before paying the bills[8].

Plans for getting out of poverty

Our interviews made it clear that the interviewees had formulated numerous plans for getting out of poverty. By starting a family, by which we mean having children, they showed their true belief that life could only get better.

Some people have children expecting to receive benefits

All of the people we interviewed said that the first plan they turned into reality was to have kids. The rhythm of their family life itself was centered on expecting children, bringing them home and making plans for their futures. But for some extremely poor people, expecting a child also meant hoping society would recognize them.

When asked why they had had children even though they and their partners were living in the streets, some of the young women said it was because they hoped they would become eligible for public housing. In fact, they ended up living in maternity homes while their partners were left out on the streets.

The example of Nadège, who had a child in order to gain access to the benefits she needed to live more decently, also comes to mind[9].

Finding the housing needed to realize family plans

The topic of housing came up frequently during our interviews. Housing is part and parcel of family life. It is a plan, a condition, a means and a struggle undertaken in order that a family might live together and stay together:

> – Our first concern was finding a place to live, to have a place of our own . . .
> – We're looking everywhere for a house . . . I'm living at my mother's place while we wait and we're looking everywhere . . .
> – If I had a place to live, I would have more children . . .
> – When I finally found a decent place to live, I was able to get my kids back . . .
> – Having a house is a goal . . .
> – What we really want is a house with a garden . . . [10]

Many people told of the battles they had fought to find housing and live as a family:

> – I had two kids, I was evicted but the house was unsanitary anyway. I wrote to the Mayor's wife. She listened to me. I said I had no place to live and that my kids were about to be taken away from me permanently if I didn't find somewhere. I ended up with decent housing[11].

> – When I started having kids, I was still living in an unsanitary two-room apartment. I struggled to make sure my kids would be born and grow up in a decent home. I fought my way into City Hall. I went there with my social worker, we went back there every day[12].

> – We jumped through a bunch of administrative hoops; we went to see the social worker to make her see the state we were living in because, otherwise, nobody would have done anything for us. If we hadn't gone to see her, no-one would have come by to see us. They just forget about you like that[13].

One mother told the story of the battle she was forced to wage to become eligible for public housing:

One winter, after having lived on the streets for three months, sleeping in a train station with my small children, I decided to go to City Hall and try to meet the mayor. I was determined to put a roof over their heads. The mayor didn't see me, instead an employee in his office told me His Honor was not available, that he had more important matters to attend to and that there was absolutely nothing he could do to remedy our situation. Since I was bent on finding housing and keeping my kids from sleeping outside, I got set to stand in his doorway the entire day. Finally a secretary came out and said His Honor felt sorry for us and that we could go to a nearby shelter where they were expecting us. But it was only for a month. In one month to the day we would have to leave, and I would have to find a way to house us on my own. He couldn't, or maybe wouldn't, do anything for us. That's how I lived for 20 years, with five kids, in a shack dating back to the First World War, located right next to a sewage outlet with no water or electricity and not even a bathroom. Only one of the rooms was even habitable. I applied for housing several times at numerous agencies, for social housing and other kinds of housing assistance. Once every six months an employee from City Hall and the housing authority would review my application. My social worker defended us to the mayor. He said the housing authority was refusing to give us a place to live because we didn't have enough income and because I was unfit to keep house, and because they didn't trust us given my husband's background.

The mayor always argued against us with the housing authority, but then would claim that they were the ones who were rejecting our application. Then the whole song and dance would start over again. In 1987 I managed to secure decent housing from the local authorities with ATD Fourth World's help, via an agency that was willing to rent houses to poor people**.

The consequences of 20 years of poverty for a family, and the education of its children, are considerable. All poor families know that without the security decent housing affords, they will never be able to realize their plans for their children's futures. *There's lots of empty houses out there. If this keeps up I'm going to squat in one soon*, Pascal told us[14].

Future plans for children

The following line from Sophie's interview more or less sums up the wish expressed by all the parents we interviewed: *A better life than mine, always*[15]. Others stated that:

– I am hoping that my children and grandchildren will have more opportunities than I had . . . I always wanted my kids to be better off than me. . . . Just because I didn't make it doesn't mean they can't. . . .

– I hope they won't experience the same hardships I have[16].

Hope for a better life first and foremost means staying together, but it also means doing well in school, despite relations with schools that are not always easy. Hope often resides in the very young: *I know he'll get by in school better than I did*, said Sophie, whose two-year-old had just started preschool. But with older children, parents are often left with little more than their wishes: *I'd love it if they would just settle down and work harder at school, so that they would do better*, Noella told us[17]. Sometimes school is little more than a place where teachers and other parents heap reproaches upon very poor families. One father explained the troubles poor people have establishing smooth relations with schools:

> It's because of the problems we have helping our kids get through school. Since we didn't receive much education when we were kids, we have a harder time fitting in with the other parents, and being a part of the school as a whole. Still it doesn't mean we don't have ideas in our heads like the other parents do**.

One father agreed to run a stand selling French fries at his children's school fundraisers in order to be accepted by the other parents who, after several years, ended up electing him as one of their representatives:

> If you're not a member of the PTA, you'll never get anywhere in terms of making people understand the obstacles your kids face because of their living conditions. There has to be dialogue between the family, teachers and children.

But keeping kids on track at school and steering them towards a good profession in life is hard. Many years of study was perceived as normal by the non-poor families interviewed: *They're all at school right now. . . . Their studies are important, that's their future. . . . Our plans are to make sure the kids finish school. . . . Our financial plans have always put the children's education first. . . .* [18] For poor families on the other hand, hopes for a future profession are perhaps best captured by the following statement: *I hope they'll at least find jobs*[19].

Plans to ensure a family's survival

Having sufficient resources to keep the family alive is a constant worry for poor families. *I had to sell my car to have enough money to pay the deposit and first month's rent*[20].

Every member of the family becomes caught up in the quest for money. One mother told us how her oldest son helped the family get by:

> When Pierre was ten, he would wake up early and see that, like the night before, his little brothers and sisters had nothing to eat, that the baby was crying about having to drink a bottle filled with water instead of milk. He saw that his mother was desperate and powerless to change the situation, so do you know what he got it into his little head to do? He would leave for school earlier than usual and instead of going to classes he would rush over to the supermarket and beg for a little work. He would spend the entire morning there while his mother thought he was at school and, when he got home, he would account for the money he brought home by saying he had helped out a little after classes got out. He would immediately offer his mother the

meager coins he earned so she could buy a liter of milk, a loaf of bread or a few potatoes, and convinced himself he had managed to take on a few of her worries for her. His family's survival was more important to him than school. The same story would repeat itself towards the end of each month when the family's resources were diminished.

Sometimes he would rummage through the refuse piles at the market stands for perishables that hadn't been sold (fish, vegetables, fruit that was going off).

Occasionally, he would even get up very late at night when his brothers and sisters were asleep and sort through garbage cans and dumpsters to find items others no longer wanted that he could sell and make a little money out of. His entire life was disturbed because of what he had to endure when he was a child**.

A job remains the primary objective in keeping a family alive. Benefits and handouts only help it to survive in the short term:

– Family welfare benefits won't help us live a normal life. I wish they would help Christian get on the right track for finding a job like other fathers have. . . . I want to go back to work as soon as my youngest is old enough . . .
– We're trying to find a stable environment, a job . . .
– A job is what I need to make it through . . .
– Being out of work is like having a hole in my life . . . [21]

The men we interviewed had all tried to get vocational training:

My husband tried to get his commercial vehicle license so it would be easier for him to find work. He had to quit the training program because we didn't have enough money.[22]

New plans are hatched when regular income from work resumes. For example a plan to find dental care, in order *to get new teeth.*

My daughter always used to get into fights at school because I didn't have any teeth. Last week she pulled out all the stops to be home on time, so she could find out whether I was going to get my new teeth or not[23].

Family plans as a means for repairing the damage caused by poverty

Family plans are frequently experienced as a chance that must not slip by, because without them, family poverty will continue to cause damage. One woman recounted her struggle to retain custody of her two grandchildren, which was all the more important to her in that it concerned the children of her oldest son, Pierre, whom she told us about earlier**.

When the judge decided to place my two grandchildren in foster homes, they and their parents were living with me. The decision was made because I could no longer support them and their parents, and so an attendant in their daycare center notified a social worker, who turned them over to a childcare agent. I immediately realized that the children's place was in their family and that they would always be better off there than with strangers. I decided there and then to get them back and living with me so that I could raise them myself, but I had to fight tooth and nail for two years to see this plan through. When the day finally arrived, they practically threw the two oldest kids at me without the slightest concern for whether I could cover their needs (the third was born after the first two had already been put into homes). Since I was on a welfare-to-work program to receive the French minimum income payment, I had to sign a contract every two years to the effect that I was following a plan for re-entering the workforce after completing some vocational training. But since I now had three children on my hands, including one who was less than a year old, I was no longer free to complete the training and so I couldn't sign it. It was really tough for me to make the people in the agency understand what I was trying to say: that raising my grandchildren was my way of re-entering the workforce. In the beginning, they categorically refused me any benefits. I was told that things had never been done that way before and that, if I wanted to keep my grandchildren, I needed to train to become a childcare worker and get money from the social services. Then my welfare payments were suspended. I held my ground at the various agencies, though.

With the help of friends, and by carefully reading the local authorities' bulletin on the workforce re-integration program, this woman won her case and was able to raise her children while receiving her French minimum income benefit.

But even when nestled in the heart of our families, nothing can replace individual initiative. Myriam told us of the many things she had done to help her husband make it through. She went with him to many of the places where he worked, and she undertook numerous initiatives to help him fight his alcoholism, including going with him to Alcoholics Anonymous (*Vie Libre*) meetings. *In the end, he's the one who couldn't make it through*[24].

Living family life in connection with others

The family can also be a stepping stone for entering society when it makes it possible for its members to come together with others, adults and children, by enjoying a position of recognition and respect.

For some people, the plan to start a family is an opportunity to share their happiness with others. *We wanted to make it clear that a couple doesn't work except thanks to the friends they have*, one young academic couple told us[25]. An older couple said they took part in a discussion group that *helped us keep going and sometimes know which was the right path to take, whether we should stay on it or not, and always steered us in the right direction*[26].

Getting close to others can sometimes feel like a challenge. One activist engaged in the Fourth World–University project wrote a motto for her coat of arms*: *Learn to observe your neighbor if you seek to know yourself*. She explained her motto in the following way:

I wrote it because I had suffered a lot from the looks others gave me; and I know that many other people suffer from this at that moment. Out of pure defiance, I decided to teach the catechism myself, since my own children had been prevented from going to catechism school because the parents of the well-off families didn't want the children of poor families to attend and potentially be on an equal footing with their own children. As a challenge, I agreed to teach the catechism to the children of these well-off families. The experience made me realize how important it was to be amongst people of different backgrounds and cultures because it was enriching, and it proved I was just as capable as they were. Working together to turn a plan into a reality is crucial.

The logo she designed on the coat of arms included a pair of eyes *that never look away when faced with poverty, nor judge without understanding.* ATD Fourth World may also be a space of meeting and recognition:

> ATD Fourth World made it possible for me to meet other families living in poverty and other people who wanted it to end. It freed me from my feelings of guilt and made me dream of a better life for my children—a dream I shared with others to build a world where the suffering caused by marginalization would be no more, a world where human rights would be enshrined in law**.

A different activist explained why he enrolled in the Fourth World–University project as follows:

> I had already experienced the deep wounds incurred when a family is split up. The wound caused by a separation stays with you for life, for both parents and kids. People have to become aware of our struggle against poverty. We love our children deeply, and we don't want them to suffer the same poverty we did**.

The values and the strengths acquired in the family equip us with what we need to take our place in society. The child is first a family being. His parents are his true starting point in life. In order to grow up, he needs his parents and needs to feel loved by them. Without this familial love, how can we be ourselves? When children are separated from their parents and placed in institutions, they are no longer surrounded by the models they need to shape their personality. Living in a family is itself already like beginning to live in a tiny society. The family provides the basics for society.

Without exception, the family plans poor people make include the goals of maintaining unity and ensuring the children will know a better life. But making these plans work often depends on the support or resistance of institutions and the people who represent them.

Demands and conditions

A plan can only take shape and be realized based on conditions relating to the planners themselves and their social surroundings.

The strengths a family must possess

What makes it possible for a family to formulate a plan and turn it into a reality is having an impetus or goal. One young mother spoke to her interviewers of the time when she was pregnant with her oldest son:

> At three months we told ourselves we would muddle through, to make sure when we brought him home he wouldn't have to sleep on the floor like we had seen in other people's homes. He would have a bed and his own dresser[27].

She then added that she probably already knew how to assume responsibility for raising her child because of the previous experience she has had in this domain. *After all, my mom and I both raised the last two* [of my sisters] *together.* In the same interview she returned once more to the value this experience held for her, even if it was more "familial" than "personal". When asked: *What was the most important thing you learned while living with your parents?*, she replied: *The way my mother muddled through raising us, despite all the troubles she had.* In order for parents to be able to formulate and realize plans in a sustained way, it is equally indispensable for them to have had positive experiences with respect to past projects of their own. One slightly older mother admitted that she no longer makes plans. . . . *I made them when we first got married, but* [they] *fizzled out*[28].

Experiencing success truly does provide the minimum of psychological security without which all plans seem impossible. When we asked a young woman who had spent her childhood in care what kinds of plans she and her partner made when they first met, she evoked her history of exclusion: *It's hard* [to say what we planned]. *I was raised as a ward of the state and then in a foster family. From the beginning I felt like a reject*[29].

We all share, therefore, a need for inner security, but also a need to feel certain about what will happen to us in the future. Jeannette acknowledged that in the beginning of her pregnancy she did not *make many plans because you never know, something can always happen!*[30]

The demands of society

Very often, in order to keep their children or get them back, families must prove they have decent housing. Rolande told us her two children were *taken into care because the house was unsanitary*, but that she later got them back when she *moved into a decent place*[31].

Although the requirement for sanitary living conditions may be justified; other demands seem totally contrary to family dignity. For instance, one young woman complained that social services refused to help her because she was too proud: *They told me that if I don't make it in to collect my food stamps I must not need them*[32].

Another woman made clear just how far the demands of society may sometimes be taken:

I was pregnant with my first daughter while I was still living with this [foster] family. When I turned 18, they kicked me and my baby out. In fact, it was my current husband who picked us up on the side of the highway and took us to the house of one of his sisters. The social worker and the judge both required me to get married if I wanted to keep my child and have a stable situation[33].

This intrusion into her private life took place in the 1990s, not in a time when raising children alone was terribly difficult.

The obstacles the families encounter in trying to make their plans a reality are increasing as current budgetary restrictions take effect, as the following mother of a disabled child made bitterly clear:

I had my son in a rehabilitation program. He was supposed to receive an artificial hand, but they stopped paying the cab fare and I had to give it up, even though I know that hand would have been helpful to him the following year in gradeschool[34].

At times it may even seem like a kind of resistance is propelling certain institutions forward by the force of their own inertia, without taking into account the individuals they are serving and their original mandates. One activist recalled his numerous attempts to carry out his plans to get vocational training:

I had been in a welfare-to-work program since 1988; I had a plan, but it failed every time because the State hadn't budgeted for that training course. . . . I wanted to learn commercial gardening and flower farming. In the beginning, this was a family plan**.

Despite repeated applications, this father never managed to secure the training he needed to make his plans a reality. *My plans were doomed to failure,* he repeated with a tinge of nostalgia.

One of the women mentioned earlier also described the obstacles, raised by the various social services she had to deal with, before winning the right to raise her grandchildren herself after their mother left. Her plan was to see to the upbringing of her oldest son's children, as any grandmother would want to, in order to secure the integrity of her family's unity. The social services planned for her to become a licensed childcare worker so that she would be able to raise them in this official capacity. She had to fight tooth and nail to have her rights as a grandmother recognized as such.

Very often, situations can become highly complicated for families in distress: the demands of society, the incomprehension of people charged with intervening and whatever else may come along are all heaped on top of the various other obstacles in their path which they must find the strength to overcome, in addition to their personal fears.

For approximately two years, a Fourth World volunteer corps member named Emilie[35] conducted a pre-school for the two children of a family living in a trailer in the middle of the woods outside a far-flung Parisian suburb. She went there every week and, over the course of several months, a level of trust was established between her and the children's young parents such that she felt able to formulate plans with them to relocate to another region. Naturally these plans were made in conjunction with the family itself, which was at the end of its rope, living in total discomfort and out of reach from everybody and everything. Everything was arranged for the family to take up residence in the village it was slated to move into, but when the moving van arrived at the family trailer, only the father was to be found. Faced with the prospect of moving to the south of France, the mother had panicked and taken off with the children. The fear of the unknown had proved stronger than the desire to have a house. When the time had come to leave for the south, the small number of guarantees that had been acquired in the woods outweighed the will to secure a better future for the children. In light of this setback it would be easy, but wrong, to say that this mother did not want to make it out of the woods. Indeed, the family had already taken a number of steps that showed her agreement with the relocation plan and her genuine wish to make it out.

The problem was that even though these plans had been formulated properly, clearly this young woman needed more time to fully internalize them, and hence a much more patient approach on the part of those charged with helping see them through was necessary. Nobody, not the social services, friends, nor Fourth World volunteer corps members, is innocent of this desire to rush a plan laid out with a family through to completion. But with destitute families this is the quickest route to failure. Knowing how to give the parents the time they need is the key to success!

Social recognition

Poor families need to find recognition in the eyes of others and of society as a whole. But recognition for what? For their family plans. They are demanding recognition for their struggles and their dynamism, because they are fighting with very few means. They are saying: *We harbor an unacknowledged dynamism, and we're working our fingers to the bone. That's what's really crushing.*

> Xavier said: You can't hang your head in defeat. You've got to fight and keep on fighting even when you're poor. . . . You've got to try and help others. . . . Sandrine said: "October 17* is the day they have dedicated to stopping poverty, but the fight doesn't stop there. Xavier said: It's not about stopping poverty, it's about fighting agcainst it. We're the ones who are poor. We have to fight the battle (together) and help one another show the outside world it's possible[36].

The definition of what constitutes non-recognition, recognition and sympathy will be explored in the following section.

Social non-recognition and misunderstanding

Our first step entails identifying what society is in concrete terms, meaning examining non-recognition as it occurs in the ever-expanding circles that compose it, and from which it is expected. Following this we take a look at the obstacles that may arise in each of the different social circles.

Society

– **The inner circle** is composed of the family first and foremost, including the members of the family we live in (the reproductive family), the one we came from (the family of origin) and the extended family as well. Neighbors may be elected into this circle at times as well.

– **The intermediary circle** which surrounds the inner one is comprised of so-called "first-line" institutions and organizations because they are the first ones we enter into directly. First-line institutions are represented by people who may come and go, but whom we can still know and be known to on a personal basis. Examples include teachers in schools, employers and colleagues at work, the social worker in an aid organization, the police, child services personnel and members or directors of associations we take part in.

– Lastly there is **overall society** which influences us, but in anonymous fashion. It comprises the large-scale components of the state, including the legislative, administration, laws, social security and employment policies. We recognize prominent figures we see in the media, but they do not recognize us. Despite this, as members of various groups we aspire to being recognized.

Inner circle obstacles

– The original or reproductive family. The family plan is born and finds its strongest support in a family setting, but this is not always the case. One example of this was Myriam, referred to above, whose husband refused to recognize their daughter. They lived together with the child despite this until her husband's death. Another woman who was deeply hurt when her spouse left her told us, *What are men good for anyway? Nothing. I'd just as soon raise them alone* (laughs), *I'd be better off*[37]. For now, she does not see anything positive in their having a relationship with him, nor in the role played by the father in general

– The family of origin. A 20-year-old woman told us:

> I was 18 and pregnant with a baby my family didn't want. My mother wanted to make me get an abortion. I would have liked to have finished my studies to become a childcare worker, but with a child that was no longer possible. . . . My husband was living in a dormitory. As we had a child, we had a goal. I felt able to start a family and raise children (she had raised her two sisters). I didn't expect a baby so soon but I accepted him right away[38].

This young woman possessed a maturity that her mother failed to recognize. When Myriam, homeless, moved back into her parent's house with two children:

> They welcomed me back for about a week, but then my mother . . . started taking care of the children as if they were hers. She would say to me, "you should stop breast feeding him. He's not a baby anymore." In other words, I couldn't do what I wanted to anymore and I allowed her to completely take control over me. The day after we arrived, she took me to the salon because I had long hair. It was terrible. . . . At first I was pleased, but when I saw she was taking over the kids for me, I started to feel like something was wrong. She was calling the shots for me. She couldn't see that I had grown up and become a mother myself—that was something she just couldn't sympathize with. And then there was the fact that she didn't approve of Charles [her husband].

– Neighbors. Some neighbors advised one mother to keep her own children and other troubled youths out of her house. They didn't recognize or sympathize with her long-term plans, nor the value a mother possesses to receive and welcome: *I wanted them to make it and I was doing everything I could for them***. Another example of this is as follows:

> – Question: Do the people living around you sympathize with your problems?
> – Lucienne: Not at all. Social workers are constantly receiving letters tipping them off about me. Whenever my daughter cries, they imagine it's because I hit her but, in fact, she couldn't be less abused. But then the social workers arrive, or I'm called in for a court appearance, and I have to go down to SRS (PMI) or else they'll threaten to take my kids away. My oldest daughter is already under supervision and I talk to the judge regularly. I know I didn't do anything wrong, though[39].

Intermediary circle obstacles

Social services do not consider people needy unless they are on food stamps. Their quest for dignity remains unseen.

> I tried to make it on my own until finally I couldn't do it anymore. I had my pride. I didn't contact a social worker because I knew what the consequences would be. They monitored me throughout practically my entire childhood[40].

Lucienne spoke of the lack of understanding she perceived:

> When I can't make the bills because they're too high, I ask for a delay and pay them in installments. I run around from office to office but they never sympathize with me, they say I'm always trying to get out of paying.

Difficulties at the level of overall society

An activist analyzed these difficulties as follows:

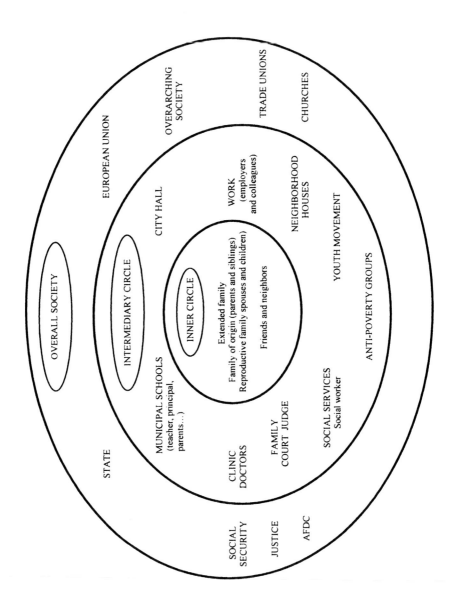

OVERALL SOCIETY

INTERMEDIARY CIRCLE

INNER CIRCLE

Extended family
Family of origin (parents and siblings)
Reproductive family spouses and children)

Friends and neighbors

EUROPEAN UNION

OVERARCHING SOCIETY

TRADE UNIONS

CHURCHES

CITY HALL

WORK
(employers
and colleagues)

NEIGHBORHOOD HOUSES

YOUTH MOVEMENT

ANTI-POVERTY GROUPS

MUNICIPAL SCHOOLS
(teacher, principal,
parents...)

CLINIC DOCTORS

FAMILY COURT JUDGE

SOCIAL SERVICES
Social worker

STATE

SOCIAL SECURITY

JUSTICE

AFDC

Society makes laws for the middle-class population and everyone who falls below that level becomes marginalized. The Minimum Income Bill (RMI) was never really deepened into a plan that would take the intended commitment and training all the way by incorporating the plans of the entire family, by incorporating each member's viewpoint, and by making each member a full-partner**.

In their struggles to get out of poverty, very poor families feel disconnected from, and hence not recognized by, many of the formal measures that have been taken.

The stepping stones society affords

All the people we interviewed reminded us in one way or another that very poor families make plans for their futures and those of their children just like any other family. However they sometimes encountered insurmountable obstacles. The ensuing waste of human potential, unbearable for the families themselves and highly debilitating to society as a whole, is a provocation and a challenge raised to all people of good will. Professionals go above and beyond the line of duty to meet these families' needs, as we saw in the case of Doctor Titran and his team. Other associations are being created in an effort to find new ways to help the parents of families in distress realize their plans to live together as a family despite everything. In 1957, in England, two women opened a homecalled Frimhurst, southwest of London, for families debilitated by poverty. Frimhurst Family House[41] was devoted to helping families get away from the "educational" plans laid out for them by the social service agencies and become able to formulate life plans for themselves. *The insistence on the role of education presupposed that the goal was to impose our personal visions on the families. However, Mrs. Goodman was always concerned first and foremost with the individual plans of each family*[42].

Françoise, a member of the Fourth World volunteer corps, recounted that:

I first came to Frimhurst in 1985. At that time, it focused on primarily housing families whose children had been taken into care. After these families had overcome the initial shock of having their children taken away, and in the interest of getting them back, they had forged a series of plans to promote themselves in the eyes of the social services who had ordered their children to be taken into care. The condition for getting their children back was that they agree to leave their homes and hometowns, and come live for 6 to 12 months along with other families and a team of Fourth World volunteer corps members . . . which they were just finding out about. What an adventure**.

An initial workshop (in woodworking) made it possible for the heads of the households to learn a trade and rediscover their pride as fathers and workingmen. During the weekly meetings of the adults in the house, the people who were more heavily involved in the working world (men and women) encouraged those who were less so to take part in this workshop and, if need be, cajoled their wives into letting them put six hours per day into it. *You'll get into fewer fights at home*, they would say in order to convince those who were hesitant about participating. And the wife who was most troubled at seeing her husband leave her for several hours per day ended up acknowledging, after a few weeks, that *when he comes back we have more things to talk about.*

The people who were encouraging their neighbors to participate in the wood-working workshop in this way had clearly understood that, for the team, the support that poor families convey amongst themselves, (above all, and quite naturally so, between families with shared affinities), needs to extend to watching over the weakest links in the chain and, if necessary, matching everyone else's rhythm to theirs. For the men and women of Frimhurst, this concern for the poorest among them, whom they had come to see as their own, was at once a source of constant concern and of pride. Françoise continued:

> This preoccupation with the poorest, and the pride they felt in being part of a community, in being agents of positive change not only for themselves and their own families, but for others who were experiencing the same difficulties as well, was not always understood by the social services. And yet they were the ones who had required these families to stay at Frimhurst in the first place.

In the following example, the looks a young mother received from her social worker prevented her from acquiring enough self-confidence to be able to raise her two little girls at a specific period in her life. Social action had a paralyzing effect on her in particular, but this does not mean we should judge all social workers negatively. For numerous other families, the friendly and willingly optimistic viewpoints their social workers transmitted had an invigorating effect that was invaluable.

Earlier we heard an interviewee affirm, with obvious affection, that her children had not been taken into care, thanks to the support she received from her "darling" social worker. She, however, was not alone, far from it, in recognizing the importance of social workers and the untold value their work possesses.

What follows is the full story we referred to above, as experienced by Françoise:

> Vicky was a young woman with a very strong temperament who was not very prone towards being a "housewife." When she was born, she was placed in a foster home, but her foster mother died when she was 11 or so and since her foster father was sick and in a wheelchair, she had to assume a large portion of the responsibility for the upkeep of the house: such as cleaning, shopping and other chores. It is not surprising, therefore, that she developed a strong aversion to anything that even remotely resembled housework.
>
> As an adult she married or set up house with—which amounts to the same thing—a young man named Morgan. He came from a working-class family and had

strong working-class values, but was also very rigid as concerns the roles of men and women, and could be a bit abusive, especially when he had been drinking. Their first daughter was placed in foster care when she was only two years old and Vicky was pregnant with their second child. The family then got permission from the social services to live in a family home for six months in order to get their oldest daughter back and to keep the one about to be born. That was how Vicky, Morgan and little Clara first came to Frimhurst just two months before the birth of their second child. During her regular visits with Vicky and Morgan, the social worker was particularly interested in the regularity of feedings and on the cleanliness of their housing. It was true that with regard to cleanliness she had some cause for concern. But the two little girls were growing up without difficulties . . . and I saw no need to worry about the feedings. On the cleanliness front, the battle was forever doomed so long as the causes of Vicky's allergy to housekeeping went untreated. This did not stop Ruby, one of the Frimhurst directors, from keeping an eye on her. Ruby was an extraordinary woman, both gentle and firm, who had worked at Frimhurst Family House for more than 25 years, and she was the one who supervised bottle-time as well. For a good number of adults at Frimhurst, if not the majority of them, the fundamental reason behind their difficulties was a lack of self-confidence. In fact, that was even written in many of their case files. We took the following phrase very seriously: rather than "plugging a finger in the hole in the dike", we preferred to help build, or rebuild, this self-confidence. And to do that, we offered the adults a series of activities designed to have nothing to do with the usual "lacks" they were reproached with, such as evening computer courses, for example.

One of the adults living at Frimhurst was always in charge of greeting people from the "outside" at the various meetings that were held at Frimhurst. A Frimhurst adult was equally given the task of delivering the welcome address on the occasion of public events, such as the inauguration of the new woodshop or receiving the mayor. Vicky was given this terrifying role during her stay. When her social worker visited several days after this reception, I enthusiastically told her that Vicky had made a speech in front of 400 people and the mayor! The social worker eked out a few short words of congratulations and then immediately asked her usual questions concerning how regularly the baby was fed.

I was horrified that she displayed so little interest in what Vicky needed to build the gratifying self-image so necessary for a young woman whose mother had not wanted her. "Even when she was pregnant with me my mother tried to pass me off," she had confided in me one day. This is why I was so scandalized by her social worker's reaction and couldn't help returning to this exceptional event in my mind, which seemed to me to have such long-term significance. I had been politely listened to but, really, between the social workers and us, it was baby bottles versus giving someone a voice, short term versus a future. We were completely talking past each other. Since a lack of self-confidence is the primary issue for adults experiencing great difficulties, wasn't anything that might restore this self-confidence the most important and even the most urgent thing called for? And if being part of a group is a value and a source of strength for a family, why limit the plans we make for it to the individual level such that it cannot belong to everyone?

When we stop imposing our visions on them, Vicky's family and many others find the strength they need to meet the demands of family life from within. Fortunately, the vast majority of social workers are prepared to acknowledge the unique vision each family possesses, and this recognition helps transform their situations. In this sense, recognizing a family's plans is in itself a form of action.

An example of a housing plan

We have just seen what a lack of social recognition can mean, as well as some of the stepping stones society has to offer. We shall now introduce the example of one family's struggle to find a large enough house, and look at the ways society helped, failed and opposed this plan[43]. Colette and Jean-Baptiste[44] lived together for 20 years and had several children. When we asked them what their plans were when they first met, housing was the first thing that came up:

Question: Did you have a goal when you got together?
Colette: No.
Jean-Baptiste: We wanted to have a nice place to live, to have something at least . . . a house.

A sizable portion of the interview was devoted to this subject. A summary view of the homes they owned led to a more detailed story about a large house they lived in, which depicts the helps and the hindrances families may encounter as they seek to realize their plans to have a house large enough to meet their needs.

– The **first house** was Colette's mother's place.

JB: I lived at her mother's house, which I didn't like very much but what can you do! Pretty soon things weren't working out. I had to leave, what with the mother-in-law and brothers . . . I moved in with my grandfather.

– The **second house** was the husband's grandfather's, until the time of his death. The City of L., which owned the house, was opposed to the couple staying there and rented it to an uncle instead.

– The **third house:**

JB: After that we found a small, two-room house. It had rats and mice . . .
Q: How did you find it?
JB: Through a landlord who was there and who told me we could go there. Well, he was actually a tenant.
Q: The house was abandoned?
JB: The neighbors said I could go there. Nobody else lived there.
Q: So you squatted in it.
JB: Yes, in fact we squatted in it. . . . It was part of a courtyard. They evicted the entire courtyard and tore it down.

– Fourth house:

> C: We had that house on L. Street.
>
> JB: The house belonged to one of my father's aunts, who I used to visit from time to time. I told her about how badly things were going and all that. She said to me, "Come live here." Later on, after we did move in, she died. The landlady came and asked if I wanted to buy the house. I said yes, and paid three million centimes for it ($5,500). It was the best. . . . It was a huge house.
>
> C: We were in good shape there.
>
> JB: It had a big yard and eight rooms.

The elderly great-aunt opened her home to them. The landlady gave up her house for next to nothing. Perhaps she preferred to see this house lived-in by young people she knew, rather than its being demolished by the real estate speculator who was about to enter the scene—an antique dealer who lived in the same courtyard and wanted the house for himself.

> JB: He came around every day to bother me. He pushed and pushed to have it. Finally we gave in and he got the house. . . . He wanted to own the entire block, that one. He ended up flattening everything and rebuilding. He gave me seven million centimes ($12,700) but I was had. After I paid back the legal fees I only had three million, and less and less . . . two million and eight hundred thousand ($5,000) . . . I ended up with nothing in the end. My father didn't want me to sell it. He was always saying to me: "Don't sell. You'll end up in the streets! Keep that house. You'll never find another one like it at that price." At the time I was selling things and fixing roofs. I was working for a master roofer.

But this bargain house was too costly for him.

> JB: I didn't have enough money to pay for the house either.
>
> C: Plus there were expensive renovations. . . . At the time, his stepfather was doing the work and he had to be paid.
>
> JB: He did the work but we couldn't do it all in one go. We had to stop the work, and that's why I ended up having to sell.
>
> Q: No-one ever made you aware that it was possible to find ways to finance the work or get a loan?
>
> JB: I did apply for loans. I went everywhere but they turned me down. They wouldn't lend to me. We didn't have anyone left. We were doing everything for ourselves.

The neighbors got involved as well.

> JB: Sometimes other members of the family came by. If they had had something to drink, they would make noise in the courtyard and the neighbor would complain. The police would come. So the guy who bought the house pushed the neighbors to lodge a formal complaint. That's how he got the house.
>
> C: Now all we have are regrets, regrets. We were in good shape there.

Colette and Jean-Baptiste's struggle for the house on L. Street

HELPS	HINDRANCES
JB's father's aunt said "Come live with me."	
When the aunt died the landlady asked JB if he wanted to buy the house. He bought the house for three million (centimes) ($5,500)	
	The antique dealer had a real estate project, He stopped by every day to harass JB: He pushed and pushed to get it.
JB: "It was a huge house with eight rooms and a big yard."	
C: "We were in good shape there."	
JB's father would say: "Don't sell, do you want to end up in the streets? You won't find another house at the price."	
JB's stepfather would stop by to help out. He helped work on the house.	
JB: We did all the work ourselves, together.	
	JB: I didn't have enough money. The stepfather had to be paid. We couldn't afford to make the house payments and pay for the materials.
	I applied for loans. I asked everywhere but got turned down. We didn't have any more welfare checks. We didn't have anyone anymore.
	I got (or would have got) seven million (centimes) ($12,700) for the house. He took me on it. I ended up with 2,800,000 ($5,000).
	The antique dealer pushed the neighbors to lodge a complaint. When we had family members over, sometimes they drank. They would make noise. The neighbor would complain. The police would come. That's how he got the house.

Note: We have arranged the facts in chronological order.

On the left we have indicated the various forms of help and recognition their plans received. They all stemmed from their families, with the exception of the landlady. They can be classed together.

On the right we have indicated the hindrances they encountered. One very active agent was the antique dealer who wielded the stick: pressure, worry stemming from the repair work, a lack of money, a lack of awareness concerning loans, isolation, the neighbors. However he also dangled a carrot: Flashing around money that wasn't there: seven million ($12,700) that would end up being reduced to 2.8m ($5,000).

The antique dealer also raised other obstacles including the neighbors, the police and his notary.

From assistance to partnership

To conclude this chapter, we shall attempt to depict how society or the community can help the family plan. Which attitudes and positions vis-à-vis providing help are welcome, and which are not? Various aid models have been developed else where, but here we shall try to remain close to the experiences of the people we interviewed. There are two extreme positions, polar opposites of one another, that families may go through when formulating plans: The first is full autonomy, or at least being able to get by, and is what these families wish for. The second, receiving assistance, is to be avoided when possible. As we shall see, however, it is possible to combine these two extremes into a third position that encompasses cooperation and partnership and allows families to retain their autonomy while at the same time receiving the help they need. Some characteristics of this kind of approach to help will also be elucidated.

The autonomy families wish for

There are two aspects of autonomy that may be distinguished up front: being able to get by on one's own, and having freedom of choice and action.

Getting by

Finding within yourself the necessary means to not be dependent on others. It is very important for young people to leave the nest and have a place of their own, to be independent.

– At first we wanted to have a place of our own and start our own family, because at the moment I'm living with my mother. I wanted to have my own future.
– Starting your own family is important [silence]. It's about my independence.

Pride is taken in being able to succeed on one's own:

Having a little place of our own is still better than having a big place of someone else's. . . . People helped me out with the furniture and all that. But the big thing is that I got by own my own, all by myself.[46]

There is dignity to be found in being independent, even when one has a right to certain benefits.

My mother relied pretty heavily on her social worker. I knew I qualified to have one too, but I wanted to get by on my own for myself. If at the very last minute I really needed to I would have gone to see her, but I saw it was possible to get by on my own[47].

She realized her situation was precarious: *If at the last minute I really needed to* . . . , and that she qualified to receive help, but she chose to get by without a social worker. The importance of this choice will become even more apparent below.

One's own choices and ideas

Lucie Ribert managed to make her own choices after developing her own ideas about how things were for her. She spoke of her mother, who lacked this freedom, and of the battles she fought so that others might be able to make free choices based on a greater understanding of how things really are.

> We didn't have the freedom to choose. My mother didn't have any choices. She didn't have the choice to be able to choose who to vote for, she didn't have the choice to say "No" to people, she didn't have the choice to say "I want my kids to go to school."We don't have the choice to be free and fully independent citizens, with everything we need at our fingertips in order to understand what is going on.
>
> I really want my commitment to help change that, so that we might all become free citizens who can get informed, and learn how to understand how things are.

The following statement, made previously by one of our activists, may also be understood differently given the perspective of choice:

> We don't have access to certain kinds of information, or else we receive canned information that prevents us from exercising our right to say what we want to say. We don't have the right to choose our own program**.

Assistance to be avoided

We shall now depict various forms of providing assistance based on actual situations, including those that saved lives, and others that were deemed not useful and were rejected. There are levels of distinctions to be made between refusing to use food stamp benefits and saying no to the conditions attached to the French minimum income benefit (RMI). Is receiving aid seen as having to run around left, right and center in order to catch the scraps that fall off the table of our consumption-based society? What does "receiving aid" mean?

> When you are part of a society, you seek its recognition of your personal dignity. . . . But society is content with giving me a little something just to keep things quiet. That's what receiving aid means. . . . It's easier to give 2,200 francs ($400) per month to someone than it is to help them make a plan for getting back on their feet . . . and setting it in motion.
>
> Very often the recognition you get is being labeled as someone who is on benefits. That's not what we are looking for. What we want is to be able to say to ourselves: "We exist, have names, a life and dignity." That's what people have to start thinking more about**.

Rather than having recourse to permanent aid that does nothing to help recipients get out of the situation, people should be recognized based on the fact that they have their own plans, names and lives, which presupposes that their plans receive the attention and aid they need to be seen through to completion.

However, the opposite of this approach of autonomy and freedom of choice entails imposing behavior through moral pressure, usually in a paternalistic context, for the person's "own good" as others see it.

Promoting partnership

Poor families have hopes and long-term goals, their wish is to make their family plans a reality. One of life's conditions is that people participate and cooperate with others. One of the most developed and egalitarian forms of cooperation is called partnership. Although this level of cooperation is not always within reach, it is nevertheless useful to know the elements of it, which we shall attempt to extract from the accounts we have heard. This leads to the emergence of a series of elements that constitute a whole, but which are broken up into different parts in the following examples:

– opening up: leaving your preconceptions and habits behind. Opening yourself up to others to see what motivates their wishes and plans ("others" may be a person or a family);

– skills: recognizing that others do not only have wishes, but also the capabilities to realize their plans and to guide themselves towards doing so;

– commitment: if we want to accompany others, we have to walk with them and behind them, and to do so over time, again and again;

– participation: favoring others' creativity and actions;

– reciprocation: defined as equality and complementarity.

Opening up

Lucie Ribert used the words "opening up" to characterize her first schoolteacher's attitude towards her. When she opened up, she evinced an absence of prejudice, she had confidence in Lucie, gave her plans serious attention and, some might even say, "listened."

Another way to depict opening up would be to place this schoolteacher's opening up to Lucie alongside the more limited opening up of Lucie's mother's small-town friends to her. Lucie's father used to know her schoolteacher when he was young: *She was the lady who was there for me and who opened herself up to me, for sure. For me it was great.* This "for sure" would seem to indicate that the schoolteacher's opening up had been highly spontaneous and thus freed up a degree of spontaneity in Lucie as well. Compare this to the description of how her mother's friends opened up:

My mother met two women after walking around and knocking on people's doors. They invited her in, a bit warily at first, but eventually they became her friends. Still, these friends were always protective towards her: to them she was "poor Mrs. Ribert," but everyone liked her because she was honest.

They may have given up their subtle prejudices (*a bit warily at first*), but they remained protective in a way that probably felt infantilizing, and they gave their affection only conditionally: *because she was honest*, which risked making her feel like her honesty was being valued above her as a person.

The way the Fourth World volunteer corps members at the pro-family housing project opened up to Myriam[48] was also highly demonstrative. We were deeply struck by their manifest interest in learning what Myriam wanted, what her plans were. She was viewed as a subject with the freedom to choose:

> If somebody asked us what we wanted, it was in order to help us. . . . People came by all the time to talk to me about it. They were constantly asking me if I agreed. . . . The social worker came by almost every day. She asked me what I wanted to do. . . . D. called me into his office and asked me what I wanted to do.

With this form of aid, everything appears to start with the other, the person in trouble, and tends toward setting their plan in motion. The Fourth World volunteer corps members have confidence in the ability of the person in trouble to guide themselves, which leads us to the next factor.

Uncovering capabilities

Dr. Titran furnished an example of confidence in the ability of young mothers.[49] Indeed, the confidence he displayed was even capable of reawakening capacities that may have become dormant, a condition that may be aggravated by excessive contact between doctors and children. When Fabrice, who was a premature baby, contracted meningitis and had to be hospitalized for a lengthy period of time, the mother-child relationship had to be completely rebuilt. Titran spoke to the distressed child about what he and his mother had gone through, of their fears and woes. The child calmed down,

> and Colette (his mother) gradually regained confidence in Fabrice and in herself. The clinic that had taken care of Fabrice had set up a dozen appointments with specialists to keep track of any relapses and to start his rehabilitation. I canceled all of them because neither Colette nor Fabrice would have gotten anything out of them. It was more urgent to rejuvenate a new kind of capacity in the mother, to restore their relationship, and to stick to the needs of Fabrice's recovery.
>
> As the weather had turned nice, I also suggested Colette and Fabrice live with Ali for a while. He would be proud to have his son back under his roof. They would be living in the slums, but their three hearts would beat as one. A few weeks later, Fabrice was utterly transformed. [A description followed]. This woman evinced a true capacity to hope and overcome all her fears.

Generally speaking, society does not readily believe in the capabilities of mothers from poor backgrounds—one reminder of this was the story of the woman who had to fight for two and a half years in order to be ruled fit to raise her grandchildren.

Commitment

Commitment was evident in the story Odile[50] told us concerning the threat she faced of having her children taken into care: *I had that dear little social worker who always stood behind me.* "*I had*", she said—as if she were a personal possession. Did she get the impression that the social worker had gone beyond her mere professional function and that there was a person-to-person bond between them? The "*dear little*" would seem to indicate affection, and also hinted that the social worker was not looking to control her, as was confirmed by the fact that she "*stood behind*" her. The element of continuity over time was emphasized with the word "*always.*" In our view, this statement may be connected to certain passages where Myriam reflected on her situation:

> They didn't forget about me, they actually worried about me, like before. . . . The social worker came by almost every day. They [Vie Libre] would go to his place [her husband's], they wouldn't leave him alone, they called him every night on the phone.

We believe this element of continuity is important for poor people who have often lived through separations and foster-care placements during their youth, and who harbor fears of rejection.

This same sensitivity to continuous presence was also evident in Liliane[51], with respect to the close presence of her social worker after her mother's death:

> *Question*: Did you receive aid?
> *L*: Well, luckily the social worker was there. And I would really like to thank her because she was always there for me, especially when I lost my mother.

Creative, liberating and active participation

The approach taken towards Myriam at the pro-family housing project, which consisted in always asking her what she wanted to do, had the effect of jumpstarting her ability to dream of a better future and, ultimately, resulted in her making specific and developed plans. On the first day they arrived there, her husband was invited to make a television program:

> It was for ATD Fourth World, so he said he would do it. Since a lot of people had seen us, they called us up and asked us for our address so they could help. I was pleased. A young couple had brought me some dishes.

Later, after her husband died:

> My son contributed to Isabelle's[52] book. That helped him a lot because he had been pretty closed off—he was five when it happened. He didn't understand that was going on because his father had loved him so much.

In the previous section on stepping stones, the attitude adopted by the members of the Fourth World volunteer corps at Frimhurst Family House was described.

They were constantly endeavoring to rebuild self-confidence through all sorts of new activities and success-stories—for example, the way Vicky succeeded in delivering a speech on the occasion of a visit by the Mayor.

Equality and reciprocity

Nothing would seem to be more enjoyable than when aid between neighbors is reciprocal.

> All of us found ourselves in the s . . . at one time or another. If I happened to be out of milk my friend upstairs would give me some. The same went for her when she was in my situation. Though we are poor, even if we are poor, we have friends and we manage to get by[53].

A number of interviewees mentioned, despite themselves at times, a rich network of solidarity. Could this stem from the pleasure we all feel in being able to give, connected to what we feel when we are equal to each other and fair with one another?

At the institutional level, Lucie Ribert noted:

> I believed at one particular point in time that I was helping ATD Fourth World because I was learning lots of things. I had yet to understand that they were learning along with me.

Doctor Titran described his participation in the "Handicraft Tuesdays" as follows[54]:

> I would knit and make upholstery panels. Everybody has something to teach others. The mothers helped me, and gave me pointers on knitting. This kind of sharing of knowledge is very important. It was not just about showing these women that they did possess a little know-how, but that they were also capable of passing it on to their children, to other parents, etc. This way, their families saw them as having skills. The pleasure shared between the professionals, Fourth World volunteer corps members, parents and children in this group was immense.

When we invite poor people to participate in outside projects, we must take care to ensure things are on an equal enough footing to allow them to give their opinions, assume responsibility for tasks and, ultimately, to make decisions. In our study, this involved social services and others taking part in family plans, but the ultimate responsibility for these plans must always lie primarily in the hands of the poor families themselves. Others may offer their opinions, but must ultimately commit to being "behind" them.

Society can sustain families in their efforts to get beyond troubled and chaotic times and enter periods of evolution and change. Institutions can help people get back into a process where things are moving.

Notes

1. Excerpts from interviews no. 3, no. 5, no. 6, no. 8, no. 14, no. 9, no. 11.
2. Interview no. 4.
3. Interview no. 13.
4. Interview no. 11.
5. Interview no. 10.
6. Interview no. 4.
7. Interview no. 13.
8. Interview no. 11.
9. Cf. Chap. 4.
10. Excerpts from interviews no. 5, no. 8, no. 7, no. 3, no. 9, no. 13.
11. Interview no. 3.
12. Interview no. 4.
13. Interview no. 9.
14. Interview no. 7.
15. Interview no. 5.
16. Excerpts from interviews no. 3, no. 13.
17. Interview no. 10.
18. Interview no. 14.
19. Interview no. 3.
20. Interview no. 10.
21. Excerpts from interviews no. 13, no. 2, no. 9, no. 14.
22. Interview no. 9.
23. Interview no. 13.
24. Interview no. 13.
25. Interview no. 12.
26. Interview no. 14.
27. Interview no. 2.
28. Interview no. 3.
29. Interview no. 7.
30. Interview no. 2.
31. Interview no. 3.
32. Interview no. 5.
33. Interview no. 7.
34. Interview no. 10.
35. Lecture Emilie Bourtet
36. Interview no. 6.
37. Interview no. 15.
38. Interview no. 2.
39. Interview no. 7.
40. Interview no. 5.
41. *Igloos Magazine*, no. 27-28, Ed. Science and Service, 1966.
42. Mrs. Goodman, one of the two founders of Frimhurst Family House, was the one who conceived, organized and ran the house, and who ultimately turned it over to ATD Fourth World after having met its founder, Father Joseph Wresinski. *Igloos*, no. 77-78-79, Ed Science and Service, 1985.
43. The following sequence is depicted in the table below.

44. Interview no. 9.

45. Interview no. 8

46. Interview no. 3

47. Interview no. 2.

48. Interview no. 13.

49. M. Titran, T. Potekov, *op. cit.*, pp. 65-71. Text analyzed by the group.

50. Interview no. 4.

51. Interview no. 15.

52. I. Sentilhes, *Parle-moi. Les pré-écoles familiales*, (Speak to Me) Ed. Quart Monde, 1988.

53. Interview no. 16.

54. M. Titran, T. Potekov, *op. cit.*, p. 99.

Conclusion

We have sought to reflect on the manner in which the consensual bond of commitment that ties us to the other develops over time and assumes the form of the family plan: choosing a partner and having children, whose presence creates obligations for their parents.

Starting a family is a force of action

We have not emphasized the disorganization and ruptures, followed by the rebuilding with another partner, that occur in contemporary families where the priority is given to individual choice, which is the primary reason why the bonds between their members are so fragile.

Nor have we met with people who were living alone or on the streets, but primarily with families, albeit very diverse in composition. Sometimes the familial bond had been legalized through marriage and sometimes not, sometimes the parents lived in a stable couple and sometimes not, and sometimes the children all came from the same mother and father, and sometimes not. But none of them had any doubts that they constituted a family. Parents who had lived in the family setting for a certain number of years almost entirely subsumed their plans to the family plan itself, but no matter what the age of the people we interviewed, they all spoke of something on the order of a plan.

At a particular point in their lives, they equated their personal futures with the desire to start a family and they organized their plans in accordance with this commitment.

The importance of the family plan certainly does not mean that family life is nothing but peace and tranquility. To a certain extent, the more a person's individual childhood experiences involved various kinds of abuse, the more he or she would affirm his or her desire to commit to having children and starting a family. More often than not, there exists a continuity between the suffering one lived through as a child and giving life to a child oneself.

Our observations, therefore, do not support a "pro-family" argument stemming from the specifically "traditional" model. Families may be taken apart and put back together; having one last name for children with different fathers is often a problem. And yet this did little to diminish the will, forcefully expressed, to live together as a family. Thus contrary to what certain moralizing discourses might suggest, the family is not weak because it fails to conform to certain norms.

Starting a family is an act—an act that may lead to the reproduction of the conditions of existence each parent knew in his or her family of origin. But it may also make it possible for them to fight against the poverty they have endured. Many people made this clear: the birth of their children drove them to act. Policies that seek to fight economic marginalization must therefore take this action into account.

How can the family plans of the very poor be sustained, if not by channeling the vitality they reveal into the organized frameworks of institutions? First let us consider the former.

The plans made by poor families reveal their capacity for action

Families often regret that their initiatives were not supported or even recognized as such. On the other hand, others deplore solutions that, besides meeting urgent needs, create habits of "dependency".

To avoid this, many contemporary institutions are willingly asking their volunteers to adopt a "planning" approach. Indeed this has often become one of the conditions for fitting in to the institution itself. Does our research shed any new light on this debate? The concept of a "plan" made it possible for us to reflect on the actions taken by very poor families in new ways.

These actions are not only reactions designed to meet the needs of everyday survival. Beyond crisis situations, and even though they are all too often mired in the short-term by the hazards of everyday life, families envision and prepare for the future by inscribing themselves in the long-term—in a word, they make plans.

For example many parents battle fiercely to get their children back. Sometimes they look for alternative housing that is more sanitary and which will make it possible for them to raise their kids with at least a minimum of hygiene. Others enter into vocational training programs.

An image of very poor families quite different from the one most people have in mind arises from this concept of the plan. It becomes possible to see how their situation may change, and is no longer viewed only in a negative light (stemming from a prejudice towards putting them down, or a compassion for their "impoverishment"). The formulation of family plans, or at least the plan to start a family one day, is a means for parents to affirm their responsibilities. It is a way for them to make a commitment to themselves and take others into account as well.

Poor families taking charge of their own time

Plans inscribe us into the future: poor families are not only capable of acting on their own, they take charge of their own time—but in a way that is far from being uniform.

Sometimes their attempts are rather inept and are either misunderstood or completely unnoticed. This lag between the plans families make and how society perceives them, or refuses to perceive them, can only be a source of pain for those who are misjudged in this way and who experience a rejection they cannot understand. On the other hand, when families are respected and understood by those around them, when they know they are being supported and that a true partnership has been instigated between society and themselves, then all their aspirations have the chance to become real, and time is no longer an obstacle in their path but the source of infinite possibilities.

The ways of relating to time are not one, but many. Long-term time may be the framework in which inequalities, perceived to be insurmountable destinies, are reproduced. On the other hand, we may get caught in the grip of the short-term, moments of crisis and uncertainty . . . which only appear to be opposites. Crises provoked by steps that must be taken, or which are necessitated by the hazards of life, inevitably accompany the uncertainty of waiting for something that may never arrive, be it a job, housing, the return of a child, etc. Being very poor means being deprived of more rational approaches to time, for example the ones afforded by having a professional career. It also means being stripped of the cultural resources that make it possible to envision one's existence on a timeline, as people equipped with a stable and satisfying job can do.

However, the ability to manipulate the future is not the only thing that is unequally divided. It is also the potential to inscribe one's personal life in the long-term: the timing of human life itself, the continuance needed to effectuate the future desired in the plan. A great number of people are thus unable to locate themselves on a timeline stretching several years into the future.

Disparities of this sort between very poor people and those who are less marginalized cannot be due to a "cultural inability" to conceive of the passage of time itself. The presence of children makes it possible to envision the long-term, and even dictates it. We have also highlighted how the very poor make use of the *generations* to inscribe themselves in the long-term. We would further emphasize here that this mode of apprehending time through the angle of children is often associated with the wish that they do well in their studies and thus succeed at school. "Generation", as the act of giving birth to children, is also a way of taking part in the continuation of time itself, the (re)creation of the world.

The relationship between the family plan and time and the stakes in the relationship between institutions and the very poor

Family plans are decisively at stake in determining the success of those endeavors which refuse either to leave people in poverty or mire them in a culture of dependency.

As we have already emphasized, planning entails responsibility. Everybody has dreams, but not all dreams have the potential to be realized. The success and failure of these dreams are what are at stake in the relationships between families and institutions. We have already explored this co-responsibility, which is about working together to make plans fail or succeed: a success that everyone will have been a part of, or a failure for which no-one can deny responsibility.

Getting people committed to the family plan calls for a timing that may lead us into the problem of how institutions define and implement goals in the long-term. If the timing they impose is too long, it may not be suited to plans that cannot wait: the excessive distance entailed by the long-term timeline runs the risk of allowing things to come apart and the drive to keep heading towards what is beyond oneself may flag. If, on the other hand, the timeline is too short, the end too near, a family's plan may not even have a chance to get started. In either case, a timeline that is ill-suited to the real conditions of these families' lives, and is imposed on them, should probably be defined as a failure.

Institutions, however, also endow time with a positive aspect. By setting down fixed periods, institutions prevent legitimately recognized benefits from becoming forms of permanent assistance.

Facilitating people's plans does not mean providing them with assistance. It means favoring the self-responsibility we desire for them: families are the only ones capable of formulating plans for themselves. The family plan can only come from individuals, because it is based on the desire for a different future—in this sense it is the opposite of accepting assistance. However, whereas the foundation of all action resides in the individual, nothing is possible without institutions—the opposite of the "laissez-faire" attitude.

Thus family plans do not develop independently of the many ways there are of being integrated into society. Of particular note in this instance are the extreme discrepancies that exist between the will to start a family, the fragility of working and employment situations, and the highly unfavorable division of housing resources with respect to needs.

The very poor family cannot be structured without long-term continuance; all along the way it may need the regular support of someone close to it, such as a social worker or some other official or unofficial person who steps in. The family plan cannot be realized based solely on the efforts of those immediately concerned: in order to succeed, it sometimes calls for a three-pronged commitment to be made by the people who surround it (extended family, friends, neighbors), associations, and institutions.

What are we going to do, each and every one of us, to ensure all families can formulate the plans they make with dignity?

Appendix

The interviews

The activists were the first to conduct the interviews, usually in pairs. Their aim was to interview poor families in various age groups. At the outset many of the activists lacked experience.

The early interviews showed them the ropes, and resulted in the development of an Interview Guide by the Family Group. Over the course of several months the questions were honed to such an extent that some even popped up during the course of conversation, especially since the activists were more at ease in their role and had more self-confidence. When they sensed some questions were causing tension, they did not insist. They also wanted to interview the parents of a well-off family in order to compare what 'family' meant to them, what their plans were and how they would respond to key difficulties such as unemployment. The activists carried out 12 interviews with five couples. Often, only the mother answered the questions because the father was not present for one reason or another. Mothers are more used to talking about the place family holds in their hearts. For example, Myriam's husband was not sure he would be able to control his emotions, and Hélène had to prod Claude into saying things because he was uncomfortable and would place his hand over the microphone so what he said would not be recorded. At Lucienne's house a large part of the meeting was held with her alone—Pascal was surprised to find us there when he got home. Furthermore, in some instances, several generations were living together, rendering the interview process more difficult.

The member of the Fourth World volunteer corps interviewed a married couple of Fourth World volunteer corps members as well. An academic interviewed a young couple of academics who had just finished their studies. Another academic conducted three interviews, including two that were transcribed and thus figure in the grid below.

Number	People interviewed	Age	Children	Knowledge of ATD Fourth World
1	Muriel	40	5	yes
	Marc	43	5	yes
2	Jeannette	22	1	no
3	Rolande	50	5	yes
4	Odile	64	13	yes
5	Sophie	22	1	no
6	Sandrine	40	3	yes
	Xavier	40	3	yes
7	Lucienne	23	4	no
	Pascal	30	4	no
8	Hélène	21	2	no
	Claude	20	2	no
9	Colette	43	10	no
	Jean Baptiste	39	10	no
10	Noëlla	30	5	no
11	Nadège	22	1	no
12	Nicole	24	0	no
	Bernard	24		
13	Myriam	34	5	yes
14	Germaine	50	4	no
	Paul	50	4	no
15	Liliane	25	2	no
16	Mme Urbain	28	2	no
	M. Urbain	30	2	no

Interview Guide

After the initial round of interviews, the activists began to feel the need for a more developed interview guide. This guide was put together in January 1997, while the research subject was still being defined:

– the academics contributed their technical knowledge concerning how to conduct interviews and ask questions with a research goal in mind;

– the activists avoided questions that had already been asked in previous interviews, and were very careful to protect the families' privacy;

– the Fourth World volunteer corps member wanted to ensure the words being used (e.g. help[1]) would have the same meaning for interviewers and interviewees.

Mandatory questions

Age
Gender
Past history: place of birth,
occupations of parents, grandparents, brothers and sisters

Living conditions in which people grew up (e.g. did their parents
  stay together?)
Studies
Vocational training
Work experience
When did they meet their partners?
How did they meet?

Suggested Questions

Suggested "icebreaker" question: When you first moved in together, what did
you want to do, and at the time how did you envision your future?

Jumpstart questions:
– What plans have you made since you first got married?
– Which ones have been the most successful?
>   How did you do it?
>   What made them a success? What did you rely on?
>   What obstacles did you encounter?
– What plans ended in failure, or have yet to succeed?
>   What went wrong?
>   What problems did you encounter?
– How do you see yourself and your family in five years?
>   How do you see your children's future?
– Do you feel part of society?
>   Does being part of a family help you to feel part of society or not? and if
>   so, how?
– What does "family life" mean to you, or based on everything you've said so far,
>   what is the one thing that defines "family life" the most?
– What does the word "hope" mean to you?

Lecture

In March of 1996, during a meeting on a proposed bill to provide counseling to fight marginalization, the Lille activists had the opportunity to meet Mrs.
Codaccioni, Family Secretary in 1995, and the instigator of the Family Law introduced in 1994. They introduced her to the Fourth World–University project,
which was just getting started at the time. Mrs. Codaccioni was very interested in
their work and offered the services of her office. The activists felt she might be
able to contribute additional information they needed in their research on the family, and therefore accepted. In preparation for this meeting the group developed
a series of questions, to help ensure a fruitful dialogue would take place. They
wrote a letter and the meeting took place over two hours, during which we were
able to greatly deepen our understanding of the subject matter at hand.

Note

1. Help: if we were to ask a young couple, "Who helped you," the answer was almost categorically "No-one," because they took us to mean financial aid rather than the moral support, advice, etc. that was also implied by this question.

III

KNOWLEDGE: FREEING KNOWLEDGE!

Life, school and action

by Marie-Hélène Boureau, Carl Havelange,
Martine Le Corre, Jean-Marie Lefevre, Odette Leroy,
Gaston Pineau and Paul Taylor.

With contributions from Françoise Ferrand and Pascal Galvani

KNOWLEDGE: FREEING KNOWLEDGE!

Introduction

Why the subject of knowledge?

The Fourth World–University project is in itself a source and subject of knowledge as it is about sharing knowledge and represents an opportunity for shared experiences and thoughts. We could thus consider that all the agent-authors* of this project deal with knowledge.

When we all met for this first time, 19 of the 32 coats of arms designed raised questions regarding children, school, culture and the sharing of knowledge. It seemed therefore that our research should focus on school, culture and knowledge. How can these issues be addressed? By looking at the school as an institution? By looking at culture? At knowledge sharing? At poor people's knowledge?

The activists* felt that knowledge was closely linked to school and to the refusal to accept failure at school as academic success often leads to social recognition. Their questions were provocative at times: why do we consider that the poor have no mind? In doing so, they hoped to show that people living in extreme poverty are also intelligent people and that because receiving an education at school is never high on the list of priorities in the fight against poverty, society is unaware of poor people's intelligence. For the activists, being able to work, think and write with the academics was a great opportunity which could help to change prejudices and views of poor people.

For the academics, it proved to be an experience which required learning from others. This constituted an opening for them too as several of them often described university as quite a closed environment. For them, poor people also hold knowledge that comes from their life experience that is rarely acknowledged by teachers and researchers and which could be used for reference both in teaching and in research in order to get a real picture of the "truth and reality".

The Fourth World volunteer corps members* also participated in the project on the basis of their commitment to and experience of working with the poorest. Their work usually entails giving the poorest a voice and becoming their partners in the fight against poverty. Their role is also to serve as representatives of the poor and to try and build bridges between society and those who are excluded from it. As part of this project, the Fourth World volunteer corps members had to share the knowledge gleaned from their action and commitment—knowledge which could be discussed and compared with that of the activists and academics. Their situation is also out of the ordinary.

Therefore, the academics, activists and Fourth World volunteer corps members were to exchange their knowledge in order to discover the complementarities and specific features. The subject of knowledge raises many questions: which type of knowledge are we discussing? Is there only one "knowledge", or are there different types of knowledge? What is the difference between knowledge and skills? What is the relationship between view, knowledge and power? Are culture and social background taken into account?

An activist of the Knowledge Group introduced the research to the rest of the group with the following text:

> What do you know about us, about me?
> I know about you because you are right on the stage.
> You have been given a role, a power.
> You are respected, recognized, listened to.
> You surely fought hard to get there.
> Why? How? For what purpose?
> What were your hopes? Desires? Your desire for knowledge?
> I think I can guess.
> I'd also like to share with you
> What it is that enables you to fully exist.
> We are here, I am here, lost on this earth that is yours,
> That is said to be ours,
> That is said to be mine.
> I cannot believe that you don't know
> That we are dying of it,
> That we want to escape this fog,
> That we're living in,
> That I'm living in.
> Not just to meet you, just like that, all very nice,
> But to share things with you.
> Share your keys, the keys to your knowledge, to your know-how, to your
> intellectual knowledge.
> In turn I will give you my keys, the keys to our knowledge of suffering,
> To our knowledge of hope, our poor people's knowledge.
> You know, we know, I know. And what if these keys allowed us to combine our
>   knowledge?
> And what if these keys allowed us to finally open the door of ignorance
> And let all of us discover that knowledge can be shared?

Which type of knowledge are we discussing?

In general, there seems to be a divide between knowledge gained from life experience and intellectual knowledge. Knowledge gained from life experience is often based on emotions but, if emotions are not a source of knowledge in themselves, would they not make a good starting point for our research?

There are two words for knowledge in the French language: *"savoir"* and *"connaissance"*. Regarding the word *"savoir"*, French dictionaries distinguish between the verb and the noun. As a verb, *savoir* means: *to be educated in something—to be able to carry out an activity that one is experienced in—to have the ability, the talent, the means . . .* and as a noun, *savoir* means: *all the knowledge garnered from having studied something.* "La connaissance" is a way of understanding, perceiving. "Les connaissances" are acquired by studying or practicing something.

If we can gain knowledge through experience or practice, thought and study are essential for this knowledge to become a 'savoir' or skill. Thus, the experience of poverty can become a skill if this experience is thought about and put into context with other forms of knowledge.

It seems possible to combine traditional research and thoughts on experience, i.e. to distinguish different types of knowledge:

– the knowledge that comes from education, techniques, of reading, writing, information technology, etc.;

– human knowledge gained from life, personal experience, the family and society, etc.;

– knowledge born of action, of changing the present, looking towards the future, etc.

Is knowledge liberating?

If there is not *one* knowledge as such but *different types* of knowledge, what links can be created so that no type of knowledge is restrictive?

The information acquired at school and from education is a form of knowledge that is essential in order to exist in society. The joy of learning, discovering and writing is something which comes naturally to all those who have had the chance to study. Several of the project's academics talk of this intellectual satisfaction, for example the joy of experiencing life *in the shoes of an author.*

Is this knowledge liberating for the person who experiences it, insofar as it liberates them from constraints? Poor people say they need this type of knowledge to take hold of their lives and of life in general. Yet the knowledge gained from life experience also contains several invaluable lessons, especially with regard to liberation.

In order to define liberating knowledge, we will develop our research around the following three areas:

– academic knowledge or skills. Based on the extremely different academic experience that each of us has had, what are the possibilities granted by school?

– knowledge gained from life experience. Living in extreme poverty throughout one's childhood, youth and adult life, or living in a socially protected environment or living in mixed surroundings give rise to very different forms of knowledge. How can the knowledge gained from living in extreme poverty be taken into account?

–knowledge born of action and commitment. Regardless of their background, people living with others must accept a certain degree of adventure and risk. How can different people's knowledge be combined?

Chapter 1

METHODOLOGICAL APPROACH

This chapter on methodology forms an integral part of our research. Within our group, extremely different approaches to the subject of "knowledge" were offered according to each person's social and professional status. This chapter explains how our research gradually headed towards dealing with "different types of knowledge" and illustrates the debates that were sparked as a result.

The contributions

What knowledge means for each of us

When the Knowledge Group was formed, it was decided that every member would bring something personal relating to the subject of knowledge along to the first meeting. One activist brought along one of her poems entitled *What do you know?*, which is a call for us to combine and share our knowledge; another offered a song that she had written about school and the Fourth World People's University*; the third reflected on *an unrecognized time on earth,* written about a friend who had passed away. The Fourth World volunteer corps member brought along some postcards by the artist Chagall, showing his ability to morph his subjects with his gentle perspective. One academic brought in a book on poetry which struck a chord with him as a poet and writer; another brought a ring which symbolized a meeting between life and death in the desert.

After this, the academics suggested that *everyone write a personal account based on the questions on knowledge that the group was asking.* The activists wrote about school memories; a meeting with an elementary school teacher; and memories of a Christmas evening, amongst other things. One of the academics took this opportunity to write about his family origins, whilst another described the memory of a meeting in Africa, using personal facts and theoretical writings. The Fourth World volunteer corps member wrote about two examples of meeting and working with very poor people with books. A few months later, she wrote more based on examples about her work as a member of the Fourth World volunteer corps.

The interviews

From the beginning, the activists expressed their wish to go and interview others as they did not want to be simply giving their own opinions[1].

One academic wanted the interviews to be carried out within the group. The activists said that for this project, they would prefer to write what they wanted to about their own lives. An academic and Fourth World volunteer corps member discussed the matter together. They helped each other to specify the elements to be shared with the group on the knowledge that they had developed in their different experiences and lives.

The three people who gave lectures[2] to all the project participants dealt with the question of knowledge in particular. Their contributions confirmed and enriched the analyses that resulted from the interviews.

The texts brought in by the academics

The activists wanted to juxtapose the words of the poorest with what has been written about them in the past and in the present. For this request to be realized, the academics brought in texts by different authors, some of which were discussed within the group[3].

The activists' contribution

Following discussions on the texts written by D. Schön[4] and J. Y. Rochex[5], the activists wrote a letter in which they made a distinction between theoretical and practical knowledge. They added a diagram to this which was then discussed once more within the group.

Afterwards, they realized the need to come up with a new diagram of what constituted *liberating knowledge* for them. They gave this basic diagram to the academics and the Fourth World volunteer corps member[6] who incorporated what the activists had drawn up.

Merging knowledge for research purposes

For our group to work well together, we needed members to be straightforward and respectful to one another and for people to help each other to further participation and understanding. We were all demanding with what we required from each other because the issues our work revolved around were important.

We tried to establish together what we understood by merging knowledge. This was not set in stone. We deemed it necessary for everyone to contribute their experiences, thoughts and texts, etc., in order to enrich and enlighten others, and this in turn would enable participants to create more knowledge or types of knowledge together.

Choosing a research subject on knowledge

At the first meeting, the activists asked two questions:

– Why do people consider that the poor don't have a mind? They looked up two words "knowledge" (savoir) and "culture" in the dictionary. Within the word knowledge, the activists understood everything to do with school, training and professions. School, training and know-how were important for them, as was the appeal of beauty, the theatre, dance, music and everything regarding culture.

– Can people escape poverty without having to disown their background? The academics stressed the need for recognizing and valuing the knowledge of the poor, so for them the important question was: *How can we recognize the skills of the poor? The skills and knowledge of the Fourth World activists are not recognized; this is the paradox.* The Fourth World volunteer corps member emphasized the importance of exchanging, sharing and forming relationships for the subject of knowledge.

We agreed on a formulation that would be developed but which sowed the seed of the essential questions on the subject to be researched: *Can people escape poverty, without having to disown their background, by using the knowledge and skills gained and passed on in their surroundings and by learning skills that are recognized?*

Our discussions were based on liberating knowledge. The academics believed that knowledge is most liberating when it is *collective* and *marked with a strong sense of solidarity;* in fact it is more *the process of producing knowledge* that is liberating. The Fourth World volunteer corps member felt that knowledge is liberating when it takes on meaning in other people's lives. The Fourth World activists thought that knowledge is liberating when recognized skills are learned.

The research brief

The research question expressed three points of view: *Can we create links between the knowledge acquired at school and the knowledge gained from life experience in order to escape poverty and to become integrated into society? What are everyone's responsibilities?*

The hypothesis was thus formulated as follows: poor people will be able to escape poverty if they gain recognized skills.

The main preoccupations of all parties can be found in the key words: school, education, academic institutions-recognition-liberating-exist-knowledge, information, skills-intelligence, ignorance and mind.

The secondary questions are based on knowledge: life knowledge? Poor people's knowledge? Academic knowledge? What is liberating knowledge? And who defines intelligence?

Drawing up the memoir outline

After having drawn up the first outline of the memoir, we came up with two hypotheses thanks to the process of collaborative writing[7]: firstly, having access to recognized skills is essential, and secondly, for knowledge to be liberating, it must be linked to values, action and future plans.

The activists drew up a diagram on liberating knowledge based on three axes: academic knowledge, knowledge gained from life experience and knowledge born of action. They suggested using these three axes as a new outline for the memoir. This outline was discussed and accepted by the group.

Issues that arose during the research process

The expectations, reluctance and resistance of each group of agent-authors

The activists thought about the way they envisioned merging knowledge based on everyone's specific characteristics. They had expectations of the academics as concerns literature, research and their academic knowledge; and they had expectations of the Fourth World volunteer corps member as regards her action and commitment. From the moment the group was formed, they asked the academics to bring in existing literature about poor people and the names of the authors. The idea was to share knowledge and for everyone to take it on board.

The activists' account of this expectation

To us, it seemed that the academics' goal was to emphasize the value of the activists' knowledge. The academics considered that the activists' contributions were sufficient and, what is more, they thought that academic knowledge was "not inaccessible" and that "all the activists had to do was to go to the library" to research the necessary information and quench their thirst for knowledge. They were afraid of coming across as teachers.

We told the academics several times that we wanted to get something out of this project and that they possessed a form of knowledge that is gained from books and learning, using methods of working and analysis which were alien to us, and these types of knowledge seemed to be the basis of real sharing. We stated our case to the academics on several occasions and showed them the extent to which our lack of knowledge and literary references hampered us and how important it was for us not to remain trapped in our world but to learn the different points of view of historians, sociologists and educationalists etc. In order to make this exchange possible, we had to ensure that the research was not based exclusively on ourselves and on our interviews.

The academics agreed to bring in texts as a 'favor' to begin with. We made it clear that we were not passive and that we had the ability to reflect on these texts and to decide whether to incorporate them into our way of thinking.

The academics' account

We wanted to base the research on experiences shared within the group and on the discussions that we would hold within it. The request to reciprocate and exchange knowledge did not seem to be compatible with an attitude that we deemed too teacher-like, an attitude that we would not even tend to use in our own practice at university. Our firm belief was that our own knowledge and sensitivity would be more useful to the group, and more freely demonstrated and exchanged, if we did not have recourse to theoretical material. We were hoping that theory would evolve naturally from within the group, based on the exchange of views that everyone could make on knowledge. It was not that we thought that academic knowledge was superfluous, useless or easy to gain but that, for us, fighting poverty in the context of this project was about free and egalitarian thought which was not based on existing theories but based essentially on the life experience of each member of the group.

The Fourth World volunteer corps member's account

At this initial stage, the meeting between the Fourth World activists and the academics and the resulting dialogue seemed to be so crucial that it seemed neither necessary, nor appropriate at that moment, to add a third element to the thought process: a contribution based on knowledge born of action. This found its own place quite naturally in due course.

The debate on "culture vs. poor people's culture"

During our first working day, we debated for the first time on knowledge and culture. The activists considered that knowledge was associated with *poor people's state of mind* and with their desire for access to and participation in general culture i.e. schools, universities, theatres and music, etc. The academics spoke of a common culture belonging to everyone and a *poor people's culture*:

A poor people's culture insofar as they have had experience of being excluded and they have developed a way of living. How can we give value to this way of living, to their values, knowledge and skills? The debate took off: do poor people have their own specific culture? The activists reacted to this by refusing to accept the phrase "poor people's culture": *We do not want a special culture for the poor or a school for the poor. We want to belong to everyone's culture.* The academics protested that they did not wish for the poor to be locked away on the sidelines with a culture which is alien to common culture. Their desire was rather—based on the notion of "culture"—to identify and highlight the values and ways of acting and speaking of the poor as well as the knowledge garnered from a long experience of poverty. The activists did not want the research to revolve around their life of exclusion but, on the contrary, around their desires and convictions regard-

ing the importance of the knowledge and, in particular, the knowledge that comes
from school and studying.

The debate on "academic knowledge vs. knowledge gained from life experience"

The initial conflict, opposition and series of misunderstandings may have been
resolved as far as the idea of culture was concerned, only to rear its ugly head
again when we addressed the issue of which form of knowledge we were dealing
with—academic knowledge or knowledge gained from life experience.

The activists strove to show the importance of academic knowledge for them
and how difficult it is for their children, themselves and people from the same
background to live without the knowledge which would allow them to be recognized and have freedom of choice. The interviews they conducted with the adults
and young people from their background confirmed this idea. They all spoke of
suffering from a lack of knowledge and of their deep-rooted desire to have access
to it, especially for their children.

The activists focused on school, whereas the academics gave priority to non-
formal forms of knowledge—the knowledge gained from the life experience of the
poor. The academics wanted to go on the personal accounts of everyone: *Around
this table there is a great deal of extraordinary experience belonging to each and
every one of us. . . . Can we identify poor people's knowledge? What is poor people's knowledge? To what extent can we describe or identify poor people's knowledge?* When asked these questions, the activists claimed to have no knowledge
that was particular to them, unless they could consider the knowledge of what
they lack, but they did have desires which they all shared, such as, in particular,
access to school and qualifications. *If you don't have such knowledge, you will be
used, you won't have any choices, you'll always be dependent on someone.*

From the debate on "oppressive knowledge vs. liberating knowledge" to forming an analysis

The academics considered that knowledge can be a means of oppressing people. *Knowing how to read in itself is not liberating.* Here, we were sliding into another debate: is knowledge oppressive or liberating?

According to the activists, it is obvious that knowledge is essentially liberating. They strongly believe in this, based on their own experience. The knowledge
gained from school and from education that they lack so much constitutes the basis of freedom for these people. It is what would enable them to feel equal to others, to exist and be recognized. It is hard to imagine the extent to which this lack of
education is a major obstacle to their lives and how much this desire to learn and

succeed for themselves and, above all, for their children, is essential for them not to have to depend on others and to be able to take control of their own lives.

Two examples among many were put forward. One (English-speaking) academic said:

> My daughter's English teacher told her she didn't speak English properly because she spoke like her parents. She was trapped between our authority and that of her teacher. She felt deeply criticized and this view that she now has isn't liberating. The school, the schoolmaster and the teacher used their own knowledge to destabilize my daughter. In this instance, knowledge was oppressive.

The activists provided the example of a woman they interviewed who said:

> I can't read or write, no-one bothers about me no matter where I go. I depend on everyone[8]. They asked : How can it be said that knowledge is not liberating as it is because of knowledge that you can exist, confirm your existence and build your life.

The academics said that people cannot be made to liberate themselves, since liberation can only come from within, and that it is necessary to identify the moment when they have learned something which helps them to liberate themselves. The activists believed that the key to escaping poverty is knowing how to read and write—academic skills. But they were told that these skills could also be used to limit people's horizons and to control people.

As a result of this debate, it was concluded that school can provide people with knowledge and, depending on how this is used, it can either be liberating or not. This brought about our new hypothesis: *academic knowledge is essential for people to escape poverty if it is associated with life values, action and plans for the future.*

Notes

1. Interviews, see annex p. 337.
2. Lectures, see General Introduction.
3. Cf. annex, p. 338.
4. D. Schön, *Le tournant réflexif* (The Reflexive Turning Point), Montréal, Ed. Logiques, 1996.
5. J. Y. Rochex, *C'est de la cité qu'il s'agit* (It's About the Estate), Dialogue, 1996.
6. The two diagrams are featured in the Conclusion p. 333.
7. For collaborative writing exercise, see General Introduction.
8. Interview no. 5.

Chapter 2

ACADEMIC KNOWLEDGE

Should we write or speak about academic knowledge? How should we proceed? How should we tackle the question? It seemed to us that according to our methodology and the very spirit of our approach, the best way to broach the subject would be for everyone to read each of the group members' statements on their school experiences. Here are seven texts personally "representing" each member of the Knowledge Group and attesting to the diversity of the group members' lives. This is the first piece of material that we will be analyzing and which will also allow us to extend our questioning and thoughts to other people outside the group. After this we will explore school and poverty more generally in order to consider the possibilities afforded by schools.

Experiences

Statements

– **Odette Leroy:** What did I learn at school? What were my relations like with school? And my rebellion?

From as young as I can remember, I was schlepped from one convent to another. I don't have any recollection of having written on a blackboard, played in the playground, or of having had my own desk where I could place my own little secrets and school books.

All this is a gaping hole in my mind, everything is black, and yet I can read and write very well. I remember being able to read perfectly at the age of 13 and the nuns asked me to do a reading in the refectory whilst the girls were eating. I did the reading in the chapel during mass, which we had to go to each day. I read the gospel, the epistles. I used to read during sewing lessons too. The nuns felt I had a gift for reading and they enjoyed listening to me sing. I can also do sums, not in my head, but I get by well enough.

I can't say that I had a good relationship with the teachers because I can't remember anything about them, but my relations with the nuns were disastrous!

I rebelled throughout my youth, constantly creating havoc all the time, which sowed the seed for revolt everywhere—in the dorms, in the corridors, in the chapel. When I was 13, I was in the 18-year-old's quarters and I was known as a quick-tempered scrapper who didn't want to follow the rules.

My revolt was the external expression of my deepest feelings—I never saw my mother or my brothers and sisters. The other girls used to go home to their parents' in the holidays, but I got the chance to go out, so I made my resentment felt wherever I could so that people would pay attention to me in any which way.

But now I want to learn and I learn a lot from books. I would like to know loads of things: everything that I can't bring myself to say out loud, I put into songs that I write myself and which I'm proud of when they work.

I can't say any more because school was an enigma to me.

– **Martine Le Corre:** School, my life, my relations there and my rebellion

I left elementary school at the age of 13 after getting my elementary school diploma. I could read, write, do my sums. I hadn't had to re-sit anything. I liked learning and was particularly fond of writing, poetry, history and civics.

I didn't like going to school itself because of what I went through there, as I felt excluded and humiliated there. All that is left is my bitterness and resentment towards my teachers, apart from the one I had in final grade. She was very gentle, very fair. She never humiliated me, on the contrary she often tried to defend me and she encouraged me. She knew that if you looked beyond "my appearance" I had potential. I liked her lots. But I was 13, unfortunately, so it didn't leave a lot of time for me to change my mind about school. What I'd been through was too harsh for the child that I was.

The other teachers' attitudes towards me affected the way my classmates treated me. They also rejected me and excluded me. They would refuse to lend me a pen or a coloring pencil, refuse to play with me or sit by me in case they got nits, probably because they were afraid that they'd be tarred with the same brush as me for being "a poor kid" who was only good for watching over cattle. This is how they saw my future. This is what they used to say about me. But, despite everything, I managed to learn. I wanted to learn, I was able to learn and I showed it. I didn't have any defense or weapon to use when faced with the adults. I was alone. My parents never got involved with my school.

I suffered from this exclusion every day—it killed me inside. My way of resisting was to rally together with those who were like me. I became the "advocate" for all those who were excluded and insulted like me. This gave me a cause to fight for and gave me strength and reassurance at school because my own people recognized me. I was proud of being their leader and I benefited from the friendship and solidarity that we had together.

But I also wanted to be with everyone else. I didn't want to "be different"; I wanted to be "accepted" by the "normal" children.

I had to make some concessions for that. I had to accept to work a bit less in class so the architect's daughter would be top of the class, I would take the blame for others' foolishness, I got into a fight standing up for another girl who was being hassled in recess, and used my parents' account at the bakery to buy a load of sweets and then give them out at school. But finally the others started playing with me a bit and so I existed and I became important to them.

– Jean-Marie Lefevre: What I learned at school, my relations there and my criticisms

Throughout my time at elementary school I was lucky to be able to learn the three Rs, which gave me a good grounding. My relationship with the teachers who took me until I got my school diploma was generally good. All the things I learned at school are useful to me today, such as the short civics lessons we would have each morning to teach us about life. I got on well with my classmates, both the boys and the girls, which was a good job seeing that we were together all term. This helped things go well in class. I don't recall that any of my old classmates were given the chance to stay on at school.

The religious education I received was precious to me as I wanted to become a priest. I didn't end up becoming one because of the studying and I was also told it wouldn't be possible as I didn't realize what I was getting myself into. I did, however, really want to become one but it would have involved years of studying and I only had the bare minimum. I stuck to this idea for quite some time. It was perhaps because of this mindset that I had a good relationship with everyone. I have always been able to share my joys and woes, I had a feel for communication. This was also something that I learned at school as I mixed with children from different families. I learned how to speak in public by reading in mass on Sundays, always held in the boarding house, which was also good for me and was a good life skill.

After my time in the "orphanage", I returned home and went to a private vocational high school, to train to become a plumber, but I don't have very fond memories of it. I couldn't understand why no-one had asked me if I wanted to do this job. This choice must've been made by the social services and the nuns. My parents weren't much use to me at that time.

At home, the electricity was often cut off, Mom was often ill (depression) and Dad was often drunk when he came home from work. I only stayed one term as my parents couldn't afford it. I found myself in the transition class where I was often treated like the son of a garbage man and people would say I came from a flea-bitten part of town. I didn't always have the right shoes but my mom tried her best. I lost count of how many times people pointed at me at school! My teacher would often put things right, and I saw others in my class who were like me and that comforted me. It was really at school that I came across discrimination, with pupils poking fun at each other. I was often insulted by someone or other, but the education I received outweighed this. I left school aged 16.

– Marie-Hélène Boureau: My memories of school

School . . . I could say that "I was born there". My parents were teachers in the village primary school. The two classrooms were joined to our house. My first memories of it are memories of the atmosphere rather than of what I learned—the smell of ink and chalk in my mom's classroom where she would take me from the age of three or four and where I would watch her with pride. Also the smell of the grape harvest at the beginning of the school year and of the lime trees, filled with the promise of the vacation. Children's cries in recess, a symbol of life. School was my daily life.

At the same time it wasn't always easy being a teacher's daughter. I went to an all-girls school. If I did the slightest thing wrong, the slightest silly thing, my parents were told about it by their colleagues. I had the "privilege" (although I would have gladly gone without it) of my life being recorded in a book each day, which showed my parents my many spelling mistakes, my lack of motivation etc., so an extra dictation or a new problem to solve would be waiting for me on my dad's blackboard in the evening.

It was thanks to a history teacher at junior high school that I discovered the pleasure of learning. She had a way of telling us about mythology that was like she was introducing us to life. She also gave me responsibilities even though I was very shy. She aroused my curiosity and I got interested in French and in math.

I wanted to be like her and become a teacher like her. When I got to university, I felt I was being pulled in two different directions: that of my job to pay for my studies and that of university itself, which was completely alien to meand left me feeling unhappy. It was "too intellectual" for me. I stuck with it though so I could become a teacher.

– Gaston Pineau: Combining school and work

What made me leave school, and what lured me back, was the search for a meaning to daily life. After my compulsory education, I stayed on at school to find a meaning to my daily life in the village where I was born. This daily routine, marked by repetitive work without anything special ever happening, seemed to me to be filled with a sense and a meaning that I was trying to understand. And it seemed to me that continuing to go to school could help to contribute to this. So I continued.

I gradually realized that following a traditional course of studies was drawing me further away from my village. It wasn't giving me the tools I needed to work in harmony with it. In fact, it was making me a stranger to it.

When I turned 19, I had an intellectual crisis and decided to stop studying. I said to myself that if intellectual work wouldn't enable me to go back to whatever or whoever I wanted, then maybe manual labor would. And so I started working as a farm laborer. I hardly opened a single book or wrote a single line for the next six years. And my work and travels as a farming migrant gradually removed me further and further from school, destroyed me, killed me. I had lots of experience but no means of expression. It was oppressive; it was repressive. This inability to express myself left me on the verge of depression.

This was when I discovered university and humanities. The discovery of a place for speaking and organized thought: an opening to continue my adventures . . . in alternation with the setting up and running of a meeting and coaching center for young people in search of themselves and a more habitable society. Because university doesn't help you live. It can only help you to find why and how, provided that you can make room for yourself and work on your own raw materials in order to formulate ideas, put them together and make sense of them. The May '68 movement showed me that I wasn't alone. The problems of daily life could finally be expressed and dealt with in university thanks to pressure from adults in ongoing trainingThis is why I am here and working in the Fourth World–University today.

– Paul Taylor: My experience at school
My time at school until I went to university was nothing out of the ordinary. I was an average student, a bit on the lazy side and I hated school as an institution. There was always an unequal conflict between the schools I went to and our family and social values. My parents never really knew how to support us. But everyone knew, in the post-war period, that school was the only way to survive, even for the rich, but especially for the poor.

However, I liked learning in my own way. I sought refuge in reading in order to dream and escape. I read in several languages, and several alphabets, reading being the only means for survival, a great pleasure, always a discovery, always magical. As a student, I did lots of activities outside of uni. I was aware that I was privileged but was always too busy to fully appreciate this. As an Englishman, I had a very different university culture from the one in France. It seems to me that the French system focuses more on failure than success and I know that, personally, I wouldn't have been able to succeed in such an aggressive and conflictual environment.

My university education allowed me, in unlikely circumstances, to find a job in teaching. By looking for a liberating form of "extra institutional" education for and with my students, I liberated myself. I discovered the joy of studying, of reading and, above all, the heady anxiety of writing. The route I took was not conventional, but my education gave me access to people and to ideas that I cherish and that have profoundly changed my life. Maybe it's because I know that I myself am the undreamt-of heir of this marvelous heritage that educating adults motivates me and encourages me so much, despite the oppression, despite the system's deaf ears.

I am aware that the system can be as liberating as it is oppressive, so I have always tried to support and protect my children as best as possible, especially at elementary school.

My experience has taught me to distinguish between education and learning, which is liberating, and the school system, which demands conformity, stifles imagination and makes pupils "docile", i.e. "teachable" and manageable.

– Carl Havelange: Learning and resisting

I had just started at university after hesitating between history or philosophy.

I chose history in the end, thinking that there would be more to ruminate on in studying man's experiences and lives than in studying the simple products of man's thought. We were given our first assignment, to write a paper on our conception of "history". I put my heart into it, forgetting, in my enthusiasm, to read the book that had been suggested we use to find inspiration. I tried to express my most personal ideas, which were undoubtedly extremely naïve, but nevertheless I think I'd still stick by them to this day. I got my work back a few days later with an awful grade and a single comment on it, written in red pen: "too many spelling mistakes!" I experienced a horrible feeling of incomprehension, injustice and humiliation. How could this way of envisioning history, which I believed to be both generous and demanding, fall so utterly flat and inspire such a bad comment by way of verdict?

In the years that followed, I learned to pay closer attention to my spelling, to present my work in an impeccable manner and to read all the books we were recommended from the beginning and many more thanks to which my research would be well-backed up, well-argued and better received. It was in this way that I gradually learned my profession as a historian. I learned to read, understand and write. I took on board all the tools I was given under the guidance of the lecturers who, fortunately, were not all as narrow-minded as my first marker. But I also learned, above all, to remain or rather to become my own master: a master of the ideas and emotions that I cherish, ideas and emotions that the tools I acquired helped me to explore better and stick up for. I learned that school—elementary school, secondary school, and university—is also full of mediocre markers against whom one must learn to defend oneself. I learned to recognize both the worth and the ineptness of my first assignment.

Analysis of the statements

These statements show the diversity of the group members' time spent in school, both in the classroom and in the institution itself.

The Fourth World activists only attended elementary school (one of them does not have any recollection of it) or transition classes; for the others (the member of the Fourth World volunteer corps and academics), the academic experience continued to university level.

Despite these differences, the seven statements reveal some common desires:

– Martine wrote: *I liked learning and was particularly fond of writing, poetry, history and civics.*

– Jean-Marie emphasized *the civics lessons we would have each morning to teach us about life.*

– Paul said that reading *was always a great pleasure, always a discovery, always magical.*

– Gaston wanted traditional studies to help him *find a meaning to daily life in the village where [he] was born.*

– Marie-Hélène discovered *the pleasure of learning.*

– Carl said: *I learned to read, understand and write. I took on board all the tools I was given.*

Odette was the only person who was not able to discover the pleasure of learning until later, due to her situation (we will come back to this later).

The school experience can be a happy one. For the Fourth World volunteer corps member, the experience of school, particularly in first grade, was linked to her daily life. For her, it was natural and logical to be at school and to have a place there. She also met teachers in junior high school who took the place of her parents in supporting her in this happy quest for knowledge.

In the six other statements, there was sometimes a great divide between hope, desire and reality. If people's families do not fully master academic skills and are not immersed in the culture surrounding these, then this can lead to misunderstandings which turn into suffering or crises.

At some point in their academic career, at school or university, the academics experienced some kind of conflict or tension: *There was always an unequal conflict between my schools and our family and social values.* Gaston did not continue studying after his high school diploma: *I gradually realized that following a traditional course of studies was drawing me further away from my village.* Suffering was also caused by being judged on one detail and not the general idea behind it, the personal idea, and this led to *a horrible feeling of incomprehension, injustice and humiliation.*

How did these people manage to make use of the tools offered by university and move away from these crises? Perhaps they could do so because this conflict brought with it resistance and they managed to draw strength from this experience and develop creative skills which could liberate them.

One of the academics is British. Universities in Britain make it possible for students to make their academic knowledge their own and give them renewed opportunities to re-enter the education system at any level.

Throughout their academic career, the academics of the group met people and had the possibility to access knowledge sources which would allow them to understand them, to make sense of them and draw strength from them. It can be noted that their difficulties, their suffering—however serious they may have been—

never came all at once. In the academics' statements it does not seem that society cast any doubt over the family in itself, as their parents were deemed capable of raising their children. Basically they were considered to be "real parents". If the students sometimes felt destabilized by an academic skill linked to a culture that was not their own, then this did not discredit the basic security needed for development.

This is perhaps the main difference from the activists' experience: the extreme poverty that their families were living in affected them at school and elsewhere by provoking negative reactions towards them and their parents, who were considered incapable of caring for their children properly. In this instance, they had nothing they could lean on to help them overcome their obstacles: As Martine wrote: *I didn't have any defense or weapon to use when faced with the adults. I was alone. My parents never got involved with my school.* There was a lack of family assistance for Odette and Jean-Marie as they had been placed in an institution. Jean-Marie spoke of his "orphanage" (how can this word be interpreted given that his parents were still alive?) and Odette remembers having been *schlepped from one convent to another* and thus had no anchor.

All their brainpower was channeled into the fight to exist, leaving little left over for academic learning. Rebelling seemed to be the only form of resistance when faced with the teachers' and classmates' attitude. This was so trying for Odette that all that remains of her school-time memories is a *gaping hole.* She only remembers that her revolt was linked to profound suffering that she could not express. *My revolt was the external expression of my deepest feelings—I never saw my mother or my brothers and sisters.* Martine said: *I suffered from this exclusion every day—it killed me inside.* . In order to resist, she adopted two strategies. The first was *to rally together with those who were like me.* The second was to be accepted by the others, *the normal children,* for which she had to make concessions on the things which were in fact essential for her to do: she accepted to *work a bit less in class so the architect's daughter would be top of the class* She also left school at the age of 14 to work and thus to help her family.

Jean-Marie's sensitivity and hopes were denied him. He was often *insulted by someone or other.* He did not meet anyone to help him realize his dream of becoming a priest. In his case, it was the social services who decided what he was to do without even asking him or his parents: *This choice must've been made by the social services and the nuns.*

In each of the cases, there were moments of confrontation, struggling and fighting. There was Carl's problem fitting into university and Marie-Hélène's soldiering on so that she would be able to do the job she desired. But the ATD Fourth World activists' struggle started in elementary school; the fight against the others to be who they were, a feeling of solitude which weighs heavily on children. This struggle was all the more important for them because, in their lives, school was their only way of gaining access to knowledge. Failing at school (practically) closes the door once and for all to the possibility of catching up later on. They do not have access to other knowledge sources (groups, libraries, etc.).

Another essential fight for them is that of being recognized as someone who is capable of learning in order to manage their lives, to give them freedom.

The interviewees' school experiences

We explored the role that school played in the lives of people from extremely poor backgrounds by interviewing them. These people revealed that their time at school was often cut short. Many of them felt they had only learned a little, if anything. Others, on the other hand, managed to fill this void outside of school while growing up. The younger ones also showed a similar diversity in experience.

I only learned a little at school, if anything

The majority of people said: *I didn't learn anything.* When we asked these people about how they perceived their time at school, it emerged that *I didn't learn anything* actually meant: school didn't equip me for the future; I didn't learn enough to share with others or to enter into relationships with others.

Henri[1] did not know his parents. He was taken into care just a few days after his birth by the welfare services and he does not know why. He remembers having attended school until the age of 14, but not on a regular basis. *I learned how to read, a bit, but not a lot. . . . Those who were abandoned like me, we didn't have a name.* Paule[2] was also sent to boarding school throughout her childhood. She said: *When I was at boarding school, they taught me to read and write but I didn't know how . . . I was at school but I couldn't read or write . . . I struggled to learn, I didn't know anything.* She explained her failure by telling us about her life of poverty and also about her having been sent to a psychiatric hospital and then to a "home" with deaf and dumb people.

Monique[3] is 46. She told us that she had trouble learning. *I am ashamed because I can barely read or write.* She told us how she found it hard when she saw that her friends knew more than her. She was always at the back of the class because she was not able to read or write. She knew what shame was all about.

Carole[4] is 33. She left school aged 16. She said: *I can read and write and do my sums. I get by but I'm not well-educated.* She added: *School didn't interest me. I had too many family problems. It's hard to concentrate at school when you have to do everything at home.* Carole had to assume various responsibilities in her family from the age of nine.

But learning does not stop at school

Some of the interviewees were not able to learn enough when they were young but found the strength to learn more as they grew up and became adults.

Micheline[5] was often absent from school because of illness. After her mother's death she was taken into care. She took her elementary school exams and passed them. This was the end of her time at school, but she was to go on to learn more later on in life. She got her community certificate at the age of 49. She told us that she loves reading and reads everything that she comes across. Like Micheline, Lucie[6] got her elementary school diploma when she was 13, even though she had only started school at the age of nine. She too found the energy to fight and continue learning, as we will see later on.

Carmen[7], who emigrated from Spain as a child, came to France at the age of 13 and started school then. She said that she managed to learn thanks to her teachers, who supported her:

> My teacher would give me French lessons every lunch break. . . . The teachers helped me loads. They never treated me like an idiot and in two years I had already caught up with the others. I passed my diploma with merit at the age of 17.

Her mother also played an important role:

> She gave us a taste of responsibility. She had confidence in us and that was a great help.

At one point or another, Micheline, Carmen and Lucie were listened to, respected and helped by a teacher or a mother who encouraged them and gave them confidence. Such relationships had a crucial effect on the girls' will to learn.

Monique[8], who suffered so much from her lack of knowledge, told us that she is trying to do her utmost to motivate her children to learn. She wants her children to: *succeed at school so as to succeed in life and learn things which will allow them to be free,* and this is the advice that she gives to children.

Young people have the same problems

Laura[9] is living proof that it is possible to learn. She is 19 years old and told us how her mother and step-father, who have since passed away, encouraged her to learn and supported her. Her mother never hid life's difficulties from her. Laura told how her mother would even go without food to make sure that her children did not have to go without. Laura said:

> I think that the most important thing is to stick to going to school because I don't want to go through what my mother went through when I'm older and have to live in poverty. . . . I am the first person to have succeeded at school. . . . I want to be successful and keep going to show my parents because it's all thanks to them. . . . My mother sent me to private school, I guess to protect me, and by doing so she gave me everything. She went without for us, her children. . . . I think I do well because I hide what I have to go through. No-one knows about it. I am worried that people will judge me. . . . I want to do well for my mom, for my children.

We were keen to place those who had trouble learning at the heart of our research. This is why we are going to talk about Marc[10]. He is 27 and is married with three children. He comes from a family of 10. He told us the following about school:

> I didn't learn anything. I don't have any certificates or qualifications. I didn't get on well with the schoolmistresses. . . . That was my doing and that of the teachers: they didn't explain things well. It wasn't that I didn't want to learn; it was that we couldn't understand each other.

Marc did not receive any support. He simply said: *My family was poor*. It is all still much too painful for him to say any more.

Five main questions

Five questions were drawn up by the group following this initial series of questions and Lucie Ribert's lecture. Lucie was also left to fend for herself from a very early age and explained how she had developed by trying her hand at temporary jobs, internships and training programs, and also by taking on commitments in society and her family. After listening to her, the group asked her the following questions on the importance of school, knowledge and training in her life:
  – Does academic knowledge have a detrimental effect on other skills or know-how?
  – Does learning recognized and official skills mean people have to forsake their roots?
  – What conditions must be fulfilled in order for people to learn?
  – How can school be a means for liberation, a place for gaining life experience and somewhere that draws people away from tradition all at once?
  – How can you explain the rift between the constraints of vocational training and the liberty required by and afforded by social and personal training?

School and poverty

Lucie Ribert's experience gives an indication of what enables a child to learn at school and, as a result, helps us to understand why children from poor families succeed or fail at school.

Lucie's school experience

Lucie is 45 years old. She comes from a gypsy family and is the fifth of 11 children. (One of her brothers and an older sister died at a young age). Her parents spent very little time at school and are both illiterate. They earn their living with seasonal work such as making wicker baskets, collecting scrap metal, picking mushrooms, etc. When Lucie was born, her family was staying with her father's grandparents. They were then driven away and wandered from place to place until the day her mother found a brick shack to rent. There was no water or electricity, but it was a start of a more settled life.

Lucie remembers having spoken about school a great deal with her brother, Albert, who was one year older than her. Their dream was to go to school one day. They watched the village school being built. Her brother would say to her: *Just you see, we'll go to that school and I'm going to be the first one to go there.* Lucie said that it was something magical for them and that their mother gave them encouragement. But Albert was struck down with leukemia and died aged six before he was even able to set foot in the school. Lucie said: *If school was a reality for me, then it was thanks to my brother. It was our joint project.*

Four years later, she started school. She was nine years old and in first grade. She was the first member of the family to go to school. Her older sister had already left home, leaving Lucie as the eldest child at home. Life was difficult:

> There were times when I didn't go to school because I didn't have any shoes or because we didn't have anything to eat. We had to fetch water over half a mile away and in winter we couldn't even get to the spring. Sometimes Mom couldn't defrost the washing. We lived a long way from school. That was how it was for us.

She did, however, learn to read and write. She explains this as follows:

> One thing that definitely helped me was that my teacher that year was quite old and she knew my dad and my uncles. She had taught them on the few days they went to school. This lady was receptive to me. It was great.

Lucie recalled some of the more troublesome moments with her teachers:

> I experienced total humiliation at times, like when the schoolmistress paid for my bread roll in front of all the others. It was nice of her, but it embarrassed me. Then, whenever something went missing, I got the blame. They didn't use to call me Lucie, but Ribert, my last name.

Her first friends at school were also children from very poor families, like hers; *we stood together, us poor kids,* she said. As she managed to do well at school, she had the right to *join the clever kids*, as she put it, and from then on she belonged to their group. She was pleased that she was different from the other poor children. During her third year at school, she made friends with two girls about whom she said: *It was our differences that brought us together.* One was repatriated from Algeria with her family and the other had a Gabonese mother. This represented an opening to the world for Lucie. The three of them were the best three of the class. Because of this she was able to renew her ties with the most excluded children.

Her parents were very proud of her success at school. Lucie, the first member of her family to have gone to school, was then able to help them with administrative procedures. Her brothers and sisters had a harder time at school and some of them did not learn to read and write. Their parents never went to any parents evenings. Their mother would drive them to and from school. She used to speak to the teacher who had taught Lucie's dad and uncles. Lucie described these moments as follows:

> I was ashamed when my mom came. I felt rejection, because when you're at school you start realizing the differences.

Lucie took her exams and obtained her elementary school diploma aged 13½. The headmistress encouraged her to stay on at school and said she should apply for a grant to go to junior high. They had to go and see a social worker for this, in order to draw up a file for her. The social worker told Lucie's mother:

> It's not worth her staying on at school. Your daughter could get work in a factory. That would give you an extra salary.

Lucie was disappointed, and, 30 years on, she is still disgusted with this decision. *I wanted to be a teacher*, she said. She did not want to work in a factory. She waited for a miracle to happen for some time but, when she was 16, she ended up taking the factory route.

Many of the issues that Lucie mentioned were echoed in the interviews: living conditions, relations with the other children at school (with the teachers and the other children) and relations between parents and school. These are not things which are unchangeable. The situation could change if there were better understanding and awareness between those living in poverty and schools.

Living conditions

Like Lucie, the interviewees all grew up in very precarious housing conditions, e.g. one couple and their five children in two rooms, one couple and 12 children in three rooms etc.; they often lived in shelters, in urban developments thrown up after the war, or in *a kind of shack with no water, no lighting*. At present, poor families live on the outskirts of cities in social re-housing developments or in public housing. This housing is often overcrowded: Carole lives with her family of five in a 3-room apartment, Monique lives with her six children and another couple and their two children all in a 6-room apartment, and the list goes on. Factors such as the renovation of old quarters and being removed from housing for not having paid the rent or for having a bad reputation mean that very poor families move house more frequently, forcing their children to change schools.

Poverty often splits families up and if given the chance to stay together, the eldest child takes responsibility for the younger ones, especially if the eldest is a girl. This was the case for Carmen: *I raised my sister. I took care of the house when I was nine. My mother worked. She couldn't look after my sister*11.

A family's social and economic situation weighs heavily on the child:

> Our children have it too hard sometimes. Before they go to school they have to think: "How am I going to face up to the teacher and tell her I don't have the money she's asking for?" The kids know what it means to get home from school and have nothing to eat. They know what it means to go without shoes, clothes that fit or that

are fashionable. When the electricity is cut off, if there's no heating, how can the washing be dried and the child sent to school clean**?[12]

Martine described her time at school as follows:

> I come from a large family with a bad reputation. I wasn't always dressed perfect-ly and I often didn't have all my school things or money for the kitty. I had nits, I didn't know what cinemas, museums or vacations were. . . . This is because of my parents' family problems, but at school, when facing the teachers, it was me who was responsible for these shortfalls because I was taunted and mocked by the oth-ers. And it was me who had to stay away during school trips and who was mocked at the doctor's. **

Several of the adults interviewed said that they were often absent from school due to illness, even if they could not name the illnesses they had suffered from.

Because of extremely difficult living conditions, some families dread their child starting school. For example, a young woman was slow to send her 5-year-old son to school. It was the boy's grandmother who intervened: *My daughter didn't dare go there**.*

The child's relations at school

Lucie explained to us that the welcome given by the teacher who knew her par-ents had been a decisive factor in her time at school. Likewise, Carmen told us of her relationship with the teachers. When she arrived in France aged 13, she was put into first grade:

> There was a young teacher who spoke a little Spanish. She would give me French lessons every lunch break. . . . The teachers helped me loads. They never treated me like an idiot . . . they treated me like the others[13].

Several other adults interviewed hold memories of a teacher who viewed them positively:

> I had a nice teacher who spoke to me lots. He made it clear that it wasn't because he was a teacher that he couldn't talk to us poor kids. He really liked us. He tried to make us see this. I remember his name. I'll never forget it because he spoke to me, listened to me. He tried to understand me. I wanted to stay with him[14].

One school principal who accepted children from diverse social backgrounds (poor housing estates, residential areas) said: *Success or failure is closely linked to relations with teachers[15].* These relations, however, often depend on the so-cial position and reputation of the family. Brigitte said: *When I was at school, people thought badly of me. Afterwards, my brothers were seen in the same light.* According to Martine: *Each year at school, one after the other, it would be the same thing. I wasn't known as Martine, a pupil who was good at this or that, but as a member of that family with its problems**.* For the child, school is also about their relations with other children. The aforementioned principal told us:

> When a child enters the school grounds, he automatically becomes a pupil. This is why he needs to be integrated into his class. We often notice that the children who do badly are not well integrated in the group. This observation is especially true for children from (poor) areas.

Whenever asked about their relations with the other children, the interviewees replied: *We stuck together.*

> I remember that people used to call Odile a "gypsy" because she lived in a caravan. She had nits. I went to see her and said, "Don't cry, it may've been me who gave you nits, coz I've got them too"**.

Two teenagers who were at high school at the time of interview said:

> – I don't talk about my family situation to everyone at school. I talk about it mostly with a friend who is in the same situation, but I don't tell those who are too prejudiced. They don't know how hard it is, they can't even imagine. I can't talk to them. I'm not like the others[16].

> – It's hard to say that our parents don't have enough money. I'm afraid that people will judge me. I would like to tell them. Sometimes I feel like I want to pretend to be different. I need to break down my wall and tell people who I really am[17].

The parents' relations with school

Lucie's parents were proud of her academic success but they were not able to form a relationship with the school which would have helped their other children. The principal told us:

> I think that the cultural background that the child experiences makes a difference. .
> . . The "bourgeois" go for walks, take trains, planes, go on vacation, have hobbies, have such enriching experiences! The poorer families want their children to do well but very often these children have not developed the necessary independence to develop successfully in class.
>   Another criticism is the families' attitude towards literature: they hardly read, if at all, and there's no discussion about literature—the children's problem is linked to their parents' problem—hence a lack of identification with the adult reader or scriptwriter. For many poor families, there is a gulf between the common language they use and the language used at school.

Monique confirmed this idea that the parents are not at ease with the teachers: *If you don't know much yourself, then it's hard to go and see them. You don't dare, you are ashamed to speak to them[18].* They are also ashamed of their living conditions which cause concern:

> – My daughter is ashamed of her life and feels helpless when faced with anyone in authority. She feels that her home life should not be mentioned to others. She is

also afraid that if others learn what her life is like with her children, they'll be taken away**.

– I remember the men and women of the estate who would come to a meeting to discuss their child dressed in their Sunday best (said the principal). I was aware that they saw school as a micro-society to which they would not have access unless they looked like the others. As an institution, our relations with poor families are non-existent. Too many parents don't realize the role they could play in school. Personally, I don't see this absence as them wanting to distinguish themselves from school or as a sign of indifference. To me it seems necessary—and this is an understatement—to come to a mutual understanding in order to dispel certain harmful misconceptions. However, the close link between academic failure and social exclusion cannot be ignored. There is no such thing as incapable children. As for the children from poor backgrounds, I'd say that I could have even taught some of them Chinese. . . . It's the children's surroundings that give importance to their knowledge: their family, their school as an institution, their teachers[19].

Thoughts on the possibilities afforded by school

The knowledge that can be learned at school is not a luxury or an "advantage". It is necessary for everyone in order to enjoy one's freedoms and feel connected with others. *What are we if we are not educated ?* asked Odette.

The need for academic skills

Academic skills, or recognized and socially legitimate skills, are one of the starting blocks in our society in order *to become someone, find one's own place,* form free relationships with others and be able to choose in life.

If we don't manage to exist at school and to leave having gained something . . . having learned those skills, we will be nothing because that's what life is like. . . . The others will choose for you and you'll have to put up with it**.

According to the interviewees, academic success is therefore crucial for themselves and for their children. Their relations with school are one of their major preoccupations. Their future depends on them.

There is no such thing as incapable children, said a school principal who teaches in a so-called "disadvantaged" area. And yet the statements reveal painful experiences, academic failure or children's time at school having been cut short. Most of them therefore get the impression that they *aren't intelligent.*

Poverty: an obstacle which cannot be overcome?

What prevents or enables learning? Difficult living conditions, especially the lack of understanding and the exclusion that go hand in hand with them, are an obstacle to learning academic skills.

Many sociologists believe that this is the reason for academic failure: *The parents' differences in social status correspond to the children's differences in school status*[20]. This "reproductive" sociology holds poverty solely responsible for failure at school: if the parent's didn't succeed at school and are very poor, their children will not succeed and will experience the same situation as their parents. The child at school is, therefore, only seen for what he "lacks" as a result of his difficult living conditions. He is even held responsible for it:

*How am I going to face up to the teacher and tell her I don't have the money she's asking for? I'm the one who'll be insulted, mocked***. The gap widens between them and the other children at school and a wall of incomprehension is erected between the teachers and the children. This wall tends to enclose the teachers' negative views of the child's background and thus of the child.

This exclusion is painfully received by the child and his family and induces them to shut themselves away. *Shutting off their minds (is) very often not a sign of a lack of intelligence, but a sign of their clumsy self-defense against exclusion*[21].

Are entire groups being condemned to academic failure?

There are factors other than social status which play a role. According to experts in educational science, although academic failure may be linked to social inequality, it cannot simply boil down to this. They do not deny that parents' contributions play an extremely significant role in the child's success or failure at school but, according to the experts, acquiring academic knowledge is not only connected to this. Other factors also come into play, such as the parents' commitment, which can also constitute a favorable opening.

The family's social status cannot be viewed in simply socio-professional terms. It has been proven that the family culture, religion and political activism can have positive effects on the child's situation at school. Our group's findings confirm that if people commit themselves to others, this leads to their learning and becoming educated. For those who have experienced extreme poverty and academic failure, such a commitment helps them to overcome their fear of being incapable of learning. As parents, they then pass on to their children this strength and determination to act. In this way, they prepare their children to overcome obstacles that they will encounter (in particular regarding their living conditions).

Gaining knowledge: a human adventure

Bernard Charlot also came up with the idea that *human experience is indivisibly linked to oneself, others and the world*[22]. Here, reflection, understanding of family life, events experienced with intensity, solidarity and parents being open to projects are all elements which help children to connect with school and give them the will to succeed.

This can be perceived in the example of Lucie, who was inspired by her and her brother's plan—which became a *promise*—as well as her mother's strong wish. From this she drew the strength to overcome obstacles. She was not, however, able to carry out her plan through to completion because her plan was dependent upon *external support* which did not materialize. Learning always involves entering into a relationship with others. "The others" are the classmates, but also, more importantly, the teachers. Their attitude is essential: *Those who are excluded from knowledge only open up their minds with caution, only if they are certain that their effort to gain knowledge will not result in yet another case of them having their insufficiencies pointed out to them[23].*

In the examples given, we can see how crucial the teacher's role is and how it can pave the way to acquiring knowledge. This was also the case for Carmen, whose teachers' personal contribution made all the difference.

Creating a social partnership

With regard to this idea, the example of the Lille Education Authority is very significant: at a conference held in April 1992, participants gathered the thoughts and experiences resulting from a project carried out in close collaboration with parents, associations and social workers on the theme "All families as partners with school"[24].The aim of this project was to enable the poorest families to become partners with schools. In creating this "partnership", one junior high school principal stressed the importance *first of all, of renewing contact with parents who failed at school themselves before discussing participation* so that when they would begin to dialogue with each other, they would gain confidence in each other and learn to respect and understand each other.

To reach this stage, it was necessary, first of all, to hold informal meetings outside of school. These meetings led to collaboration (between teachers, parents, associations and social services—united in their wish for children to do well at school, each respecting the specific role of each partner). During these meetings, everyone changed:

– the parents began not only to hope but to believe in the role school can play for their children, without fear of being judged. They thus made those efforts that their means allowed them to (for example, they would create a space for their children to work in and pay attention to their work) and this encouraged them to become educated themselves;

– the teachers discovered how enlightening it can be for schools to ask for poor parents' opinions. They saw these parents making an effort and changing their views and the teachers thus changed their attitude towards these parents and their children;

– the associations and the social workers felt the positive effect on the entire family and were able to support them, particularly on a cultural level, with academic support and training for the adults.

The schools which took part in this experiment do not have ready-made formulae but they do have questions and examples of points of view. They found that *only with close collaboration between teachers, schools and families can the child find his place within school and be boosted*[25] and thus learn.

We look for cures
For all our woes.
Listen to us, our
Academic brothers.
It's for our kids' sake
That we're working
ourselves to death,
It's for our kids' sake
That we're hoping.
The Knowledge Group,
Be taken in,
Let's do something
About all forms of exclusion.
A world of joy
Where we have to slave away,
A world of sadness
Where we have to love
The Knowledge Group,
Knowledge,
The Knowledge Group is here.
We are on the railroad,
The train of freedom.
The scrap-metal coaches
Are full of good will
Gaston, Carl and Marie-Hélène,
Paul Taylor, the intellectuals,
Analytical and dynamic,
Competitive,
These are the enlightening words,
Let's start up dialogue
At university
And we will work
Everyone equal
Do you know what I know?
Do you know what *I* know?
I don't know
Everything that *you* know.
Odette Leroy
Caen
February 3, 1997

Learn the elementary things!
For those whose time has come
it is never too late!
Learn the ABC.
It won't be enough,
Learn it! Don't be dismayed by it?
Begin! You must know everything.
You must take over the leadership.
Learn, man in the asylum!
Learn, man in the prison!
Learn, woman in the kitchen!
Learn sixty year olds!
You must take over the leadership.
Seek out the school, you who are
homeless!
Acquire knowledge, you who shiver!
You who are hungry, reach for the
book:
It is a weapon.
You must take over the leadership.
Don't be afraid to ask, comrade!
Don't be talked into anything.
Check for yourself!
What you do not know yourself
You don't know.
Scrutinize the bill,
It is you who must pay it.
Put your finger on each item,
Ask: how did this get there?
You must take over the leadership.
Bertolt Brecht
German author, 1898-1956.
Extract from The Mother

ADDRESS GIVEN BY FEDERICO GARCIA LORCA TO THE PEOPLE OF FUENTES VAQUEROS (GRANADA), in September 1931

When someone goes to the theater, to a concert or to any kind of event, if he likes the show he will immediately think of his loved ones who are not there and lament: "Oh how my sister or my father would have loved that!", and he will experience the rest of the show with a slight feeling of melancholy. It is this melancholy that I feel, not for the members of my family, which would be small-minded of me, but for all those who, for lack of means and because of their own misery, do not benefit from the good that is beauty—beauty which is life, goodness, serenity and passion. . . .

This is why I never have any books. No sooner do I buy one than I give it away. I've given away infinite numbers of them. And this is why it's a great honor for me to be here. I am pleased to inaugurate this public library, which is most probably the first in the entire province of Granada.

Man does not live on bread alone. If I were hungry and found myself with nothing, on the street, I would not ask for a loaf of bread, but for half a loaf and a book. And from this place where we are gathered, I vehemently criticize those who only talk of economic needs without ever mentioning cultural ones. It is the latter that people are shouting for at the top of their voices.

It would be a good thing if everyone had something to eat, but it is necessary for everyone to have access to knowledge so that they can benefit from the product of every human mind because, without this, they will be transformed into machines to serve the state—into slaves of a terrible organization of society.

I feel much sorrier for someone who cannot get access to the knowledge he requires than for someone who goes hungry. Because a hungry person can easily satisfy his hunger with a piece of bread or some fruit. But someone who is thirsty for knowledge and does not have any means suffers from terrible agony because he needs books, books and more books. And where are those books?

Books! Books! This is a magic word which is tantamount to proclaiming "Love, love" and which people should call for, just as they ask for bread or hope for rain to water their seeds. When the renowned Russian writer, Fyodor Dostoyevsky, the father of the Russian Revolution—much more so than Lenin—was a prisoner in Siberia, cut off from the world, enclosed within four walls, surrounded by bleak, snow-covered plains, he wrote a letter to his family far-away asking them for help and saying: "Send me some books, books, lots of books so that my soul does not die!" He was cold, but he didn't ask for fire; he was so thirsty, but he didn't ask for water. Instead, he asked for books, meaning horizons, meaning steps to climb to the top of the mind and the heart. Because the physical, biological and natural agony of the body caused by hunger, thirst or the cold does not last for long, for very long at all, but the agony of a dissatisfied soul lasts a lifetime.

The great Menéndez Pidal—one of the truly great minds of Europe—once said:

"The motto of the Republic should be culture." Culture, because it is the only way of solving the problems faced by people who are full of faith but deprived of enlightenment.

Do not forget that enlightenment is the origin of everything.

Garcia Lorca
A Spanish poet who died in 1936,
shot by one of Franco's bullets.
Address given at the inauguration of the
library in the town where he was born, Fuente de
Vaqueros (Granada)—Sept. 1931

Notes

1. Interview no. 13.
2. Interview no. 11.
3. Interview no. 5.
4. Interview no. 4.
5. Interview no. 9.
6. Lecture Lucie Ribert.
7. Interview no. 18.
8. Interview no. 5.
9. Interview no. 12.
10. Interview no. 3.
11. Interview no. 18.
12. Two asterisks ** denote extracts from group discussions or personal writings.
13. Interview no. 18.
14. Interview no. 7.
15. Interview with an elementary school principal.
16. Interview no. 11.
17. Interview no. 6.
18. Interview no. 5.
19. Interview with an elementary school principal.

20. B. Charlot, *Du rapport au savoir* (The Link to Knowledge), Eds Anthropos, Paris, 1997, pp. 19-20.
21. J. Maisondieu, *Santé et insertion : un défi à l'illettrisme*, (Health and Integration:Challenging Illiteracy) Ed Documentation française, Paris, 1995, p 121. Paris, 1995, p. 121.
22. *Ibid.*, p. 89.
23. J. Maisondieu, *op. cit.*, p 121
24. *Les Cahiers de Lille* (Notes from Lille), no. 2, June 1992, C.R.D.P., Lille.
25. *Ibid.*

Chapter 3

KNOWLEDGE GAINED FROM
LIFE EXPERIENCE

The school experience for people in extreme poverty is often a painful one. Some examples of academic success do not hide the fact that there is an extreme lack of awareness both with the individual and in society in general. Poor people often have a hard time at school; more often than not they leave school after the first few years and this has a knock-on effect to a great extent on the difficulties which they experience in terms of professional and social integration. For those who have suffered such a lack of education, school seems like an opportunity which could enable their children not to have to experience what they themselves went through. But *knowledge,* as we wish to define it, is not simply a matter of education. It is also related to the life experience, sometimes happy and sometimes sad, that individuals hold within them and which shapes and transforms them. Everyone—the activists, Fourth World volunteer corps members and academics—believed that school is the fountain of knowledge, in the fundamental sense of the word. It is by reflecting on our own lives that we truly become masters of ourselves. It is by reflecting on our own lives that we gradually build up the knowledge that will help us to better take hold of our destiny.

Whether it be the interviews with people living in extreme poverty, the group discussions or lectures in Chantilly, the interviews with the Knowledge Group members, the coats of arms* or the initial experiences of the program participants: most of the texts in our body of material bear witness to this very personal aspect of knowledge. We would now like to echo this.

The way poor people's life experience is regarded

In this section on personal life experience and its role in providing liberating knowledge, why do we need to talk about the way in which those who are living in extreme poverty and in difficult situations are regarded ? Because the way they are regarded can reduce them to mere objects or, on the other hand, can enable them to be recognized as people. The way in which people are viewed tells us just as much about the person who is making the judgments as the person being judged.

A look which transforms a person into an object

The Fourth World volunteer corps member in our group has experienced the way that the poor are usually judged. Once when she was with Annick, who had been living on the streets for years, she was forced to take her place

> . . . this one time, Annick asked me to keep an eye on her bags whilst she went to the toilet. So there I was, in a tunnel in the subway, with her bags next to me. I felt pretty uncomfortable and hoped I wouldn't see anyone I knew. . . . I caught the eyes of some of those passing by and saw that some gave me astonished looks, some were distant, others judged me and regarded me with contempt because of these bags which spoke volumes about their owner's life and, at the same time, took over your entire person. Some people's looks made me feel as though I had become those bags. . . . I got a rough idea of the strength that the poor must need in order to distance themselves from the looks they receive from others and to maintain their dignity despite everything.

This experience highlights just how much the way people are looked at can reduce them to the state of their objects: in this case the bags. It shows that one look can weigh a person down and confine them. This look does not try to understand. It says: "There's nothing to be learned here". It does not see the other person as a human being.

A look which judges a group of people and sets them apart

There is also a look which judges. The entry for the word **beggary** in an old medical dictionary distinguishes between the beggars, who are *worthy of our consideration and even of our respect* as they have to experience *the humiliation and shame that an honest man should react to by holding out his hand*, and those who cause trouble. In fact, there is often the suspicion that *laziness is linked to poverty.* Poverty *goes hand in hand with vice.*

This perception raises suspicion. It pigeonholes people. It professes to know without bothering to ask what the people being looked at think.

In this light, extreme poverty equals amorality: *We lived in a poor area and the people were pigeonholed automatically. We couldn't get away from it . . . all the problems in the village came back to us, to the children living there*[1].

Lucie Ribert had the same experience regarding the judgments that people made on the cause of her father's death, who in fact had a heart attack in a café where they had stopped for a rest. Because he belonged to a discredited group, he was described as having been responsible for his own death in the "news in brief" section of the newspaper (he was described as an alcoholic). The journalist's opinion did not take the reality into account (her father did not actually drink) or the burden of the shame that would be added to the family's grief.

A look which confines people to their lack of material goods   ✗

We often consider that the poor do not have a mind. During a meeting, an administrator criticized those who have no money but have a TV and video player at home. One of the activists tried to explain that, for those who do not have the means to learn or become cultivated, a video player is a window to the world and to discovery. It is one way of fulfilling their desire to learn and understand**.

Another example given by the activist was as follows: A social worker who was called upon to help a little girl who was passionate about dance suggested: *How about the local cheerleaders?***

These are two examples of people who are financially dependent and thus their hopes and aspirations are restricted as a result: *When we refer to the poor, we describe them as people who demand the right to food and shelter and that's it***.

Material restrictions may stand in the way of the poor, but they certainly do not curb these people's desire to be recognized as human beings who are capable of thinking, of developing their skills and talents. This view leads to a lack of ambition for the poorest and denies them of any future plans.

What is usually interdependence—as we all need support from others for our own development—becomes dependence and control in all aspects of life.

This is also exemplified by Jean-Marie's plans for the future, which were rejected, and Lucie's plans to stay on at school—as encouraged by her teacher—which were thwarted by the arguments that the social worker gave to her mother: *If she works in the factory, that would give you an extra salary.*

A condescending look   ✗

This look implies that the poor may well have skills to be developed, but that they should stay where they belong. This was how Carmen experienced it[2]. Her mother was a maid who was housed and fed by a well-off family with no children of their own. They wanted to help Carmen and her siblings to turn the corner whilst refusing to acknowledge any of her mother's capabilities:

> They made her feel like she was incapable of raising her own children. . . . They saw it as though they were doing her a huge favor, as though they were bringing them up for her.

The family encouraged Carmen to learn at school:

> It was really ambiguous. When there were people around, she treated us like we were her children . . . and yet we remained the maid's children. . . . She made me feel like I owed my achievements to her, like it was all thanks to her.

A well-meaning look

This look does not make any judgments about the person and enables a child, such as Carmen for example, to start learning at the age of 13 and to make up for lost time.

> It has to be said that everyone thought I was useless and stupid. . . . They put me in first grade, I was 13. There was this young teacher who would give me French lessons every lunch break. She helped me loads. The teachers never treated me like an idiot . . . they treated me like the others.

An acknowledging look

Some looks create a presence. They do not cast judgment or categorize people. They form the basis of a genuine meeting between two people. It is this type of look that helps people stand on their own two feet and come into their own. Odette mentioned this look when speaking of the *Fourth World–University* project: because she felt that she was regarded in a way that did not simply say "you can learn", but also "teach me, share with me what life has taught you and what I don't know", this enabled her to enact with others:

> I realized that I was a somebody, I had my place in this world. . . . On that day I said to myself: "I must get myself going", and that's how I started interacting with those around me—having conversations, forming friendships, acquiring knowledge. . . . I saw that I was put on this earth for a reason.

This is not only acknowledgment of the individual, but also of their families, their roots and their backgrounds. This was something that Lucie Ribert experienced during an ATD Fourth World meeting in Paris[3]:

> I saw other people like me, who said very powerful things, who spoke of their lives. . . . I didn't feel lost. I felt recognized straight away.

This feeling of suddenly existing as a human being and being taken at face value by others enables people to talk about their life experience and background. This means that nothing about their past and what made them the people they are is omitted and thus the life experience they talk of becomes knowledge which can be passed on and is expected. This is an exchange between people living together in interdependence—a source of learning and mutual enrichment.

Thoughts on life experience among the poor

I don't want my children to have to go through what I did. Anyone who has experienced or still lives in poverty will have uttered or thought these words. It is what they desire more than anything in the world. However, adults know from experience that it is easier said than done, their troublesome childhood having left them scarred.

Adults' thoughts on the ups and downs of their childhood

The thing that I missed most in life was not really money, but love**, said one woman who lived in care from the age of 3 to 21. She was starved of love and affection from her parents and siblings and she did not receive the affection from the nuns who raised her that every child is entitled to. This lack of love is manifested by many adults who spent their childhood in care.

Henri, who was taken into care on a farm just a few days after his birth, said the following:

> It was obvious to me that I wasn't spoiled as a child or kissed like the other kids who were with their mothers and fathers. I knew that I was neglected. I cried many times and I never spoke of it[4].

One man, whose parents were looked down upon because they received food vouchers, their electricity was cut off and also because of the drunken state of his father when coming home from his arduous and humiliating job, said:

> My parents weren't able to give us some material things. People could think what they like when they saw the state of our curtains, but if they were to look closer, they would see there was a lot of love. We loved each other lots and we had many happy moments, despite the ups and downs**.

This man passionately evoked the things his father taught him, such as an appetite for reading—as he used to bring the union magazine home each week—and how to make candles by pouring oil and water into a glass, cutting the end off a cork, placing a wick through it and not forgetting to use a piece of gilt paper to insulate it. . . . The dim light it gave off would last for ages. These were the things that went on *behind our curtains,* that no-one would have even imagined, but they did happen, they were real.

I don't want my children to have to wait 30 years to give me a kiss. I don't want to miss out on this time as I did with my dad. It's pointless suffering**, said another woman who could not communicate with her father or show him any emotion because she was forced to defend her mother from a very early age and compensate for her in daily life. It is often the case with poor families that one of the children has to grow up too quickly:

> I learned to take on responsibilities from a very early age. When I was about nine, I already had to do the shopping, the cooking and hide my mother's drinking from my father to prevent any violence. My mom died a painful death due to cancer. She called for me, she needed me, I forgave her everything. I knew that deep down she had always been unhappy and it was that which made me see how much my parents meant to me[5].

Children are also affected by family affairs which have an impact on their lives in one way or another and which they do not always understand:

My mom was in prison when I was about 10. I suffered because of it, it was awful. When she came home after several months, she had changed. This situation caused me terrible humiliation. As a child I wanted to understand what had changed my mom. A child shouldn't have to go through that. And yet I made my own children go through the same thing years later. I don't know if this was conscious or not.**

All the adults spoke of the parents' love being irreplaceable. This was felt most strongly by those who spent their childhood in care and whose main priority is to keep their children in the family. They know that this love is not only shown by acts of tenderness, but also by dialogue, discussion and mutual trust. Yet how can they put this into practice when they had no experience of it during their own childhood? Adults rarely tend to blame the hardships they endured during childhood on their parents. If this does happen, it is because in those families there was so much poverty and consternation that there was no room for dialogue.

Other adults came to the following realization:

I am aware of the hardship my parents endured for my brothers and sisters and me. Their life was too hard for me to simply get over it just like that. I have too much respect for what my parents went through. It must have been so tough**.

Adults' thoughts on their lives as adults

In order to understand and analyze one's life it is necessary to put it into the context of the events which have happened and the people one has encountered.

One woman spoke of what happened to her when, at the age of 21, she had to leave the institution where she had been taken in because she had come of age:

They left me on the sidewalk with my suitcase and my mother's address. I found her in the back of a courtyard without any sun. My mother didn't recognize me. She couldn't take me in. I had to get by own my own. It was on that day that I met the man who was to become my husband**.

This woman in search of love had confidence in life and believed she was sufficiently prepared to live with her partner and start a family. She found the support she needed when the going got tough from a neighbor who was in the same situation: *We supported each other in times of need.*

Many adults spoke of this understanding and support which occurs in poor neighborhoods:

When we were kicked out to go and live in a shanty-town, we found that we were amongst others who had had their fair share of troubles in life. Our neighbors soon accepted us. It was not the coziest of places but we were at home there. We felt we were able to live again**.

Starting a family is something natural for young people from poor backgrounds. They cannot imagine a future without children, regardless of the experiences that they have been through. One young woman said the following:

In a sense, I felt ashamed of my parents because of the way that people saw us. I was only waiting for one thing in life. I used to say to myself: "When I'm 18, I'm getting out of here and I'm going to do something well, better than they did and I'm not going to go through the nightmare that they did". But then, with time, you realize that between getting what you want and achieving what is possible, there's a whole set of obstacles to overcome**

The first obstacle is oneself—to know oneself enough to face up to difficulties confidently as and when they arise, such as loneliness, fear of the unknown, fear of others, fear of failure, etc. This lack of self-confidence sometimes leads people to put up with extreme situations, such as violence. When there is violence in a relationship, it is often due to accumulated suffering, including factors such as the childhood traumas of one of the partners, enduring difficult living conditions, alcohol-related problems, etc. Women living in poverty put up with more than other women would for years and years. They hope that life will change and have trouble accepting that their dream has turned into a nightmare. They cannot talk about it because they are afraid of their children being taken into care or because they believe so strongly in love.

One woman told us that her parents had a violent relationship and that she hated that violence. She vowed that she would never put her own children through the same experience. And yet her relationship turned out to be a violent one:

> It is difficult to put our strongest wishes into practice. When two people get together and both of them have had a childhood affected by loss and humiliation, it is difficult to find a balance. We didn't know how to talk to each other or listen to each other. There were so many unspoken problems gnawing away at each of us that we couldn't really help each other. If your life's been shaped by poverty, you tend to think you can put up with anything. Poverty taught us to have hope and to hold on to this hope in such a difficult situation. We don't have anything other than this**.

Starting a family means the hope of having a home which one is proud of, where one's children can invite their friends round and where everything is clear and as it should be. Parents who can afford to have a house big enough to accommodate the entire family say that it is sometimes hard not to overcompensate for what they went through as a child and not to become obsessed with order. *It goes from one extreme to the other. You just can't seem to find a happy medium***.

What skills and values do parents pass on to their children?

Life teaches adults to stands up for themselves and gives them the desire to pass on to their children the hopes and desires that they find so hard to fulfill themselves.

Their main ambition is for their children to do well at school, where they failed, as they know that school can help their children to develop their minds through education and develop their social skills by enacting with others.

> I support my daughter and reassure her when someone makes a harsh remark about where she lives. I explain to her that she must fight to exist and to be recognized in the eyes of other people. I stay close to her, ready to listen to her and tell her that I'm there and that I believe that she can do well and that she is someone. Just because a child lives in a poor area doesn't mean they are less intelligent**.

This mother suffered herself from not having been given any help with school from her own mother.

In addition, one grandmother encouraged her daughter to go and see her grandson's teacher, *I now try and do the things for my grandchildren that I wasn't able to do with my own children**,* she said.

Many adults have experienced shame and humiliation relating to their families and their neighborhoods. They do not want their own children to have the same experience. In order to transcend their own guilt of still being poor, they often need to have external support from people around them and from people who know them well enough to share with them the strengths and values that they have discovered. For example, it was during a meeting with Father Joseph Wresinski* in her neighborhood that Martine heard someone speak positively of her father.

Being proud of where one comes from means being able to say one day:

> Coming from a poor background is actually a real asset because it means you appreciate the little you do have. Even if it's not much, you appreciate it, you hold on to it and you notice it. I think that passing this on to your children raises them with that awareness. I find that really important. I like to think I manage to get that much over to them**.

These adults do not forget their childhood. They do not want to hide life's difficulties from their children but they have become aware that: *I may have suffered a great deal mentally, but I find that life is worth living**.* One man from a very poor family spoke of wealth:

> The marginalized people who come from poor backgrounds are often very 'rich'. They have acquired a wealth of experience from life's hazards, which they can share in solidarity. Their form of wealth isn't tangible but it is worth much more than material wealth[6].

The young people interviewed as part of this project spoke of what they have learned from their parents. *My mother taught me to like school. She tells me to think hard and concentrate on my work. She keeps an eye on me because she's thinking of my future,* said an eight-year-old child[7].

Those who stay on at school after the age of 16 know how much this is due to their parents' determination. They feel that they had to prove that they were capable of rising to the challenge of doing well at school, despite their difficult social conditions.

– My mom didn't have an easy childhood; she did all she could to make life better for us. So I want to show everyone that, even if I come from a poor background, I am still able to get somewhere in life[8].

– I owe a lot to my parents. My mum fought for us, she went without for us, even without food. My parents taught me that we were more important than anything. So I'm fighting to do well. I want to shout and fight against the unfairness of it all as they did[9].

Several young people said that their parents taught them that they have to fight for things in life and that they should start by relying on their own strengths:

My mom taught me not to let myself be brought down. . . . It's definitely thanks to my mom and my background and what I've been through that I have the strength to want to change things. My mom drummed it into me enough. She made me believe in myself and taught me to make others respect me and, above all, she made me see that money wasn't everything. She taught me not to be ashamed of being unemployed, of having fewer resources and less money. . . . [10]

Changing life experience into knowledge by means of reflection and dialoguing with others

When adults have the pleasure of being able to reflect on their own lives, of learning lessons from it and of dialoguing with others, they can relieve themselves of their guilt and pass on to their children and neighbors that out of poverty comes strength. Reflecting on one's own life is also a means of liberating oneself, because liberating oneself from poverty is putting right a wrong that those living in poverty feel guilty of.

Thoughts on life experience in university

Reflecting on ones' own life is obviously something which is just as necessary for those in the world of university. By confronting their various life experiences as part of the Fourth World–University project, the agent-authors became aware of their differences. Yet looking beyond these differences and the divide which separates those who have experienced extreme poverty and those who have not, we also became aware of a number of beliefs that we had in common. We will now attempt to set out those differences and similarities by looking at the individual statements made by the Knowledge Group members and by a few other academics involved in the project.

Different backgrounds

The activists often spoke of *their background.* The academics, on the other hand, spoke of several different settings where they have lived and which they have experienced. For many of them, the background they came from as a child has little in common with their adult surroundings.

Of all 11 academics participating in the project, only one went through a difficult time with his family, when he was taken into care for a time after the war for financial reasons. Some spoke of coming from a modest background, but this was relative to the more comfortable settings that they had come to find themselves in. They did not come from poor backgrounds as they had the benefit of their parents' cultural openings. For example, one academic spoke of a difficult time when his father found himself unemployed for two years, despite being an electrotechnician—a qualification which is the current equivalent of an expert electronics engineer. His grandfather administered land. Another spoke of his parents who were craftsmen.

Several of the academics spoke of their parents' commitment:

> My dad was one of the very first professors at the National University of Zaire, founded by the Belgian state. They lived a very poor existence. They made a very serious commitment that counted a lot in terms of family life[11].

Another academic said that one of his grandfathers created a law on universal suffrage in Belgium.

All of them were able to complete their schooling and university studies. Their experiences in life and their academic knowledge are the result of a certain number of choices or identity crises which partly account for the reasons why they committed themselves to the project.

Moments of choice or crisis

Crises or moments of serious doubt are often linked to coming into contact with circumstances that seem almost incompatible. This was the case for one academic who chose to work in manual labor after graduating from high school. The world of academia became *more foreign than China* to him. This can lead to the experience of *the night* that he mentioned, and to the experience of losing one's foothold and purpose in life:

> When I was 25 or 26 I took up my studies again, in Paris. The only people I would see every morning would be the garbage collectors and I was jealous of them because at least they knew who they were. . . . When you don't belong to any category, you lose your means of identification.

Another academic explained that he decided to work as a miller's assistant for two years:

> When I did this, I found myself on the "other side", i.e. as a simple laborer, and that's how rich people viewed me and it was a shock.

An academic told us that thanks to what he learned at school, he was able to continue the commitments he took on when he was younger, for example, he was leader of a youth movement:

When I did this, I said to myself "You have to know how to help those people you don't necessarily like".

As a professor, he worked in a cooperation scheme for over 10 years: *It wasn't only about helping people, it was about listening to them, the need to listen to what others need and not just bring along all we have.*

All the academics sought coherence in the world of academia, which they embraced, and wanted to be able to introduce into it the wealth of their past experiences, whether happy or painful—the mysteries of life without which all research and teaching lose their real meaning.

One academic wrote: *After a few years of working at university, I really felt that I had nothing left to say to the students. I didn't really know what I was doing there any more.* Everyone encounters such moments of doubt, to a certain extent, at some point in their lives or career. These crises can be extremely painful and getting through them is no mean feat. The memories they leave behind have a significant impact on future choices.

Influential meetings

We have just seen that family and social status was decisive for many of the academics, one of whom said: *The experiences that shaped me, which made me who I am, were primarily those of meeting various people.* Throughout our lives, particularly with milestones which structure them, we meet people who pass on something essential. These are privileged meetings, full of universal values, which enable us to overcome problems and get through crises.

These key figures are pillars who symbolize the ease of transition between life experience and professional commitment. One of these people was one of the academic's employers, a gardener, who the academic considered to be *the greatest philosopher* that he had ever known and who was the inspiration behind his idea of training adults with a view to their liberation.

These are meetings with people who are trailblazers and who become our models for the rest of our lives.

As luck would have it, I met a number of people who were in the process of setting up a refuge center in Brussels for young people who had left their parents' or foster homes. Another example of such a meeting was given by an academic who quoted the following words that a member of the Fourth World volunteer corps had said to him one day: *poverty doesn't go on vacation.*

Learning from the poor

Many of the project's academics had one of these influential meetings with people from poor backgrounds. Learning from those who are often presumed to have everything to learn themselves is not only the general principle agreed on by all project participants, but is also a shared experience at a particular moment in life.

Memories of childhood or adult lives, as well as meetings with marginalized and very poor people, always seemed to have been decisive. Many such meetings constituted life lessons which had more of an influence on sensitivity, values, beliefs, enthusiasm, refusals and rebellion, i.e. the foundation of all knowledge, than any theory could have done. For one person in our group, such a meeting was with a nomad in the Malian desert, who revealed the true nature of benefaction. For another, it was with a shoe-shiner in Dakar, who explained how to look beyond differences and power struggles. For others, it comes from the lessons they have learned due to their involvement in ATD Fourth World and the Fourth World People's University, where they have learned from poor people.

Life, school and work

The academics do not consider that there is education learned from school on the one hand and from life on the other. School, university and careers provide life experience which the academics address with their personalities and the surroundings they come from.

Of all the statements, Emile Creutz's[12] was the most illuminative with regard to the link between life experience and university. How did he become a committed academic and militant unionist over the years? When listening to him answer questions during one of his lectures, we were struck by the close links between his personal life experience and his academic and professional orientation.

He said, *coming from a working-class background, I obviously put everything into my education because it was the only way of achieving something solid in society.* Despite his difficult time at school he achieved this, mainly thanks to the unflagging strength of will of his mother, who was attentive and determined. The difficulties he encountered formed the basis of his future professional commitment:

> My challenge essentially started with the education system. Throughout my life, I've been really irritated by all the stages and hoops I've had to jump through and which show me how extremely elitist society is and how things aren't for the benefit of local and regional development and even less so for the people themselves.

But it was at the beginning of his secondary education that the open-mindedness of a school principal who actively encouraged pupils to help each other inspired Emile Creutz to support the idea of alternative pedagogy based on "mutual teaching".

Another aspect of his life also became apparent during his talk and could be felt very strongly in the exchanges that followed. This was the movement which led to his fight against what he believes to be unfair and, at the same time, to his research in social and intellectual recognition, without which his fight would not have been possible. An activist said to him: *Throughout your work there is a conflict between the revolt against elitism and injustice and the need for recognition and integration.*

It is this conflict which allowed him to gradually organize a revolt, the result of which was felt very early on. For Emile Creutz, this revolt has always been related to the teaching system, no matter how remotely: *It's true that my life has fed from this revolt against the teaching system, so it's quite clear that I've really had to revolt at each stage.* But this revolt still required organization. He had to obtain the highest university qualification and gain the tools to be able to fight effectively against those aspects of the teaching system which he deemed negative. By doing so, by searching for a delicate balance between recognition and revolt, integration and subversion, he has managed to implement his ideal that science *actually serves the development of society.*

It is without doubt here, at the center of these tightly-woven links between life, school and work, that the determining factor uniting the majority of the academics involved in this project can be found: the feeling of being both "inside and outside" and of dividing their energy between the desire and necessity for recognition and this demand for constructive exposure, without which no social or individual transformation would be possible.

Can life experience change one's life?

One thing is certain: knowledge shapes us. We are who we are thanks to or because of what we may or may not know. But in what way does life experience transform us, change us and makes us develop? In what way does life experience make a difference between not only what we are and what we were, but also between what we are and what we could be?

Life experience in itself does not change us. It can only change us if we reflect on it. If we do not do this, it can have the opposite effect and cement our ways of living, being and thinking. All the statements that we gathered[13] showed the importance of this realization, without which our life experiences, no matter how intense, would not change us.

Life experience raises awareness

When we become aware that we have learned something, we either realize that things have changed or that things should change. We have a different perspective and our experience takes on a different meaning. The statements made it very clear that this catalytic moment is crucial not for changing people's situation but their way of perceiving their own surroundings. For example, the fact that people are aware that they are enduring extreme poverty does not change anything. However, from the moment they start reflecting on their situation and taking a critical stance towards it, they start to form *knowledge which explains their situation, they know that they have become capable of giving answers that (their) parents could not because they hadn't asked "why?".*

This question is essential for both the poor and the non-poor. It is a means of giving meaning to lives which are not only poor in the material sense but also in the intellectual sense. Several academics find themselves confronted with the same problem: *I felt that I had nothing left to say to the students. I didn't really know what I was doing there any more.* Or quite simply, as another said: *One day I became aware of my ignorance.* Faced with this, there is no other solution but to change and to begin living differently.

Life experience fosters solidarity

This feeling of a life without meaning, of having no knowledge and nothing to be able to give in terms of information, experience or one's background, is enough to destabilize anyone, especially young people. The poor know that they are being exploited and excluded and, even if they can explain why this is so, they cannot help but feel a sense of guilt and shame. This was something experienced by the Fourth World volunteer corps member: *I felt uncomfortable and hoped I wouldn't see anyone I knew,* and by one of the academics, who explained that he had experienced what it felt like to be *on the "other side".* These thoughts, initially evoked by this notion of *us* and *the others,* made these people aware that they could not handle the situation alone: knowledge is only liberating when it is collective, when it is shared. Support between families, friends and neighbors is something which is often mentioned in the statements—a support which is based on sharing common values passed on from one generation to the next, such as honesty, generosity, faith in human dignity, justice and fraternity.

Those who have suffered in the same way also have the ability and strength to fight. They learn to resist, to stop blaming themselves and, importantly, not to disown their backgrounds. The academics also learned how important such resistance is, but how? One of the elements which is common to both poor and non-poor families is the influence their parents had on them not in terms of politics or economics but regarding these same fundamental values.

Life experience forges personality

I learned how to be free, said Lucie. What a transformation! There could hardly be a more striking example. Malcolm Knowles also confirmed this with the following remarks: *The (learners) adults are aware that they are responsible for their own decisions and lives. Once they are aware of this, they develop the strong desire to be seen and treated like individuals who are capable of looking after themselves.* This development changes their perceptions. Knowles said: *For the child, the experience is based on what has happened to them. For the adult, it is based on who they are*[14]. Life experience transforms people's relationships with their surroundings and with the world in general because it transforms people's relationships with themselves. *I don't put myself down if I tell people what my social situation is like. I feel comfortable talking about it as I know I have skills.* Thus the conclusion is clear: *it isn't because we come from a certain background that we don't have the right to culture, knowledge and beauty.* The poor also have *a mind which allows them to think, act and reflect on things.* This echoes the words of one of the academics, who said: *you need to question yourselves.* When you question yourself, you find yourself.

Life experience socializes people

This way of thinking, of changing the way we think about the world and knowledge, and where we see ourselves in society corresponds to what Freire calls an *awareness-raising process:* People are with others and not simply alone on this earth. *Those who are labeled as 'marginalized' and who are oppressed have never been 'outside'. They are still part of the world. They are still within the structure which turns them into "beings for others". Their salvation is therefore not a question of becoming integrated . . . into this structure which oppresses them, but to transform it so that they can become "beings for themselves"*[15].

Whatever our background, where we come from forms the basis of each and every one of us: *Without my background, I don't exist.* And as one of the academics pointed out, even when he entered the world of university, *I entered it with the mindset that I was there to hold onto to my links with my background.* There is always the risk of breaking away or becoming distanced from it and a tendency to disassociate oneself from it. These are risks that must be accepted, but this is where a militant organization or movement can step in. It is a real risk which becomes transformed into the strong desire to fight against the exploitation of the poor, either at school, work or at university. One of the academics said *I saw my father's commitment to this . . . this passion to liberate a people.*

Many of the statements showed how this critical way of thinking helps people to demand this fundamental recognition as human beings and to transform their relationships with society. It makes them call for schooling for their children and ongoing training for the adults, either as participants or as trainers. They assert their right to work, to beauty and to quality of life. In other words, the right to escape poverty and to have the necessary means to live in harmony with society.

This knowledge is not idealist or intellectual or academic. It stems from actual experience of daily life. Even if the people who share their social and cultural experiences come from different backgrounds, this knowledge advocates solidarity and can marshal change in society.

Notes

1. Interview no. 18.
2. Interview no. 18.
3. November 17, 1977, ATD Fourth World meeting in Paris.
4. Interview no. 13.
5. Interview no. 4.
6. Interview no. 2.

7. Interview no. 16.
8. Interview no. 6.
9. Interview no. 11.
10. Interview no. 15.
11. The quotes in this section are taken from the presentation of the coats of arms* during the first Fourth World–University project meeting.
12. Lecture Emile Creutz, see General Introduction.
13. This section is entirely based on analysis of the interviews, lectures and coats of arms.
14. M. Knowles, *L'apprenant adulte*, (Adult Learners) Paris, Éd. de l'Organisation, 1990, pp. 71-72.
15. P. Freire, *Pédagogie des opprimés*, (Educating the Oppressed) Paris, Maspéro, 1977, p. 54.

Chapter 4

KNOWLEDGE BORN OF ACTION AND PERSONAL COMMITMENT

In all social or professional situations, people try to change day-to-day life and influence the future. In this chapter we will be studying the work carried out by the poor and those who work with them in order to fight poverty, as well as the work carried out within university. We will then attempt to establish which type of knowledge is linked to work and commitment.

Work carried out by the poor in their surroundings

Poverty is frightening. It traps people and forces them to stay silent, to conceal themselves and to hide their lives. They know that they are labeled as "anti-social", "misfits" and "good-for-nothings", etc. Deep down, they feel that this is unfair but what can they do? Their only negotiating partners are those who represent the law, such as social workers, policemen, bailiffs, etc.

However, commitment and action can exist in areas occupied by the poor. There is mutual aid between poor families, who help each other out in their daily lives if they run out of food or money, or need someone to look after their children, or a place to stay, etc. This aid is essential for their survival but is simply not enough to tackle the root of the problem of poverty.

Meetings which enable commitment and action[1]

Personal commitment and collective action can emerge following meetings which occur outside of the poor's territory. Generally, it is associations which enable such meetings to take place. Our project's activists spoke of their coming into contact with ATD Fourth World as an example of such a meeting. For some people, their meeting was with ATD Fourth World's founder, Father Joseph Wresinski. For others, it was meeting with the Fourth World volunteer corps members or allies* who have adopted the fight against poverty on their own. These meetings are essential, as "the other party" is not there to advise or educate the poor but to learn alongside the poor and, most importantly, to work with them in the long-term. In doing so, the poorest families can regain confidence in themselves and allow themselves to exist fully.

One young woman spoke of her own meeting with the members of the Fourth World volunteer corps. She was 18 at the time. She had just given birth to her first child and was to marry his father—a 21-year-old Algerian—three months later. The marriage announcements had been published and the wedding preparations were underway. Her husband-to-be would go and see her from time to time. The plan was that the young couple would stay at the girl's parents as they did not have their own apartment yet.

> The big day came, but we didn't get married. Meidhi didn't show up. All the dreams I had as a little girl were shattered and I couldn't understand what was happening. Our friends, neighbors and families were there for the wedding, we all started getting annoyed, hatred was in the air. No-one had seen Meidhi and I ended up realizing that our mixed race marriage was unfeasible in the eyes of his family. The locals started talking of my wrecked wedding and some even mocked me openly. It can make you feel better at times to laugh at other people's misfortune; it's a bit like the wheel keeps turning and misfortune chooses another victim. A couple of [Fourth World volunteer corps members] had moved to my estate not long before. We knew each other to look at and to say hello to. They put a little note in my letter box telling me that they shared my despair. Then they would come to my house almost every day. They would come and be with me, sometimes they would sit there, silently, respecting my silence, my fears, my anger, my discouragement. I didn't want there to be any violence or revenge and they supported me in this. Thanks to their knowledge about Arab culture, I was able to see what Meidhi had never dared tell me. This awareness made it possible for me to respect him and his family and to raise my son to respect his father, his culture and traditions. Also, to help me to try and understand, they did what I wasn't able to do, which was to talk to the local families in my area and encourage them to support me and show solidarity towards me. They helped me to face up to my family and, above all, to myself. So I was able to rediscover a taste for life and to hope again. Later on, I found out that as well as being people who lived near me, they were also involved in ATD Fourth World.

Examples of commitment and action

I saw myself in him

Daniel lived with his wife in a little house that was in a sorry state. The roof leaked. They had three children, including a daughter who still lived with them. They lived off the little they had, i.e. the French minimum income benefit, and the leftovers from markets. People poked fun at them and would say that their house was the *drunkards' meeting point*. These jibes and insults did not crush Daniel, who was an upright man. Despite their difficult situation, he was not embittered. One activist, who had been visiting him for several years, said:

> I was so lucky to have met Daniel! He would give of himself, do people favors. He often used to say: "There are people worse off than us". He must've had some kind of secret. I saw myself in him, like I saw many others in life who counted for nothing. We sang a lot together. We forgot the daily grind for a bit.

Poor people who commit themselves to helping others like them draw their strength from people like Daniel. They commune with each other and are so closely connected that their lives seem to become one. Their story becomes one. Even if their commitment is a personal one, they travel the same path together and reassure each other. They bear strength within them for others, in a simple and humble manner.

Cultural work

The Summer Street Festivals* are events organized in poor areas in which artists, professionals and sportspeople can share their passions and skills with the children in the neighborhood. The adults in that area are also invited to share their know-how. This is carried out in the form of street workshops which last at least a week.

During one of these weeks, one resident came up with the idea one afternoon of organizing a drawing competition on the sidewalk in front of the apartment blocks. Around 30 children let their imagination run wild and drew on their own designated patch using colored chalk. The parents came to see the drawings. This moment of freedom of expression was spoiled by the janitor of one of the blocks and a member of staff from the housing office. They were not at all impressed with what had been done as apparently this was going to make the entrances to the apartment blocks dirty when the residents were to enter them. *Who's going to clean up after you?* All the drawings were still admired though, as it was wonderful to see children using their imagination on the sidewalk. One resident dared to attempt an adventure and show that it was possible to forget their worries while expressing themselves on the sidewalk. This resident came to the following conclusion: *the children expressed their dreams on the sidewalk. This was the most important thing for me and I am proud of it.*

Poor families' commitment and action

The Grégoires were very poor and had been rejected by everyone in their local area. The parents barely dared leave their house as they were criticized and mocked so much. Mr. Grégoire would often stand at his window and shout out to his children at the top of his voice. Mrs. Grégoire was obese and found it very hard to get about. She was the laughing stock of the estate. Their six children only ventured out to do some shopping and go to school, but never went outside to play with the other children. In fact, nobody really knew the Grégoire family yet, at the same time, they served as a scapegoat for everyone.

When the Fourth World volunteer corps members left, Father Joseph Wresinski asked two young women who lived on the same estate and who also came from poor backgrounds to take over responsibility for the work: *You and you, you can both take over the work carried out by the Fourth World volunteer corps members. You must organize yourselves as the idea isn't that the Fourth World volunteer corps members stay in your neighborhoods forever. You are capable of this and you are going to show it. . . .*

One of the young women called upon in this meeting said:

> I couldn't believe it. In fact, I was waiting to do something, but if Father Joseph hadn't suggested that I take on this commitment I would never have dared. On that day I was petrified, yet proud and happy that he had confidence in me.

Because of the work already carried out by the members of the Fourth World volunteer corps, the families living on the estate had gotten into the habit of meeting up regularly. They had taken the time to get to know and be thankful for each other. Starting with the two women, a group of families would meet up regularly to prepare for the Fourth World People's University and put together a local newsletter for their estate. The group was up and running.

During a training session in Pierrelaye*, Father Joseph asked the two women to do their utmost to ensure that the very poor families on their estate be included in their work, especially the Grégoires, the most rejected family of them all.

> This was what made us realize how important our commitment was. No sooner had we taken on responsibility to carry out work within our estate than Father Joseph sent us out to the poorest amongst us. This was the key to our mission.

At first, it was difficult for the families who were already in the group to accept the fact that they were no longer the priority. They realized that because the poorest families would be the main recipients of the action, the two young women would not be spending as much time with them. One of these young women said:

> Every day I would go and see the family. I took the time to introduce myself to them, to tell them about myself and to draw connections between my life and theirs. Because of this, they easily agreed to form a relationship with me.

Sometimes the confidence-building process takes more time. The activists also had to be accepted. This was especially true when their work required them to leave their own neighborhood to go to the aid of other poor areas. One example of this is the activist who took over eight months to build up confidence with a marginalized family in a neighborhood close by:

I went to say hello to them every day. We always spoke on the doorstep. One day, it was really cold and rainy outside and they invited me in for a coffee. They kept apologizing for the fact that it was dark indoors because they kept the shutters closed, for fear that someone would break the windows with stones, and because the electricity had been cut off. I was fully aware of what such situations are like as I'd been through them myself, so I was able to relate their situation to my own and to those of other families I knew.

The idea of this work is not to build up an individual rapport between a very poor family and an activist. The main thing is that this family is not excluded from its own neighborhood and can take part in action with everyone else. Mr. and Mrs. Grégoire were extremely afraid of the families on their estate. They felt worthless and undesirable and did not feel that they had anything to say. The young activist recalls that this work was continuing a process that others had allowed her to experience: *They were interested in me without judging me, without giving me advice, they said I was capable. . . .* She would prepare the topics to be dealt with in the Fourth World People's University at Mr. and Mrs. Grégoire's home and would then pass on their thoughts to the rest of the group. A further barrier was overcome when the adults on the estate went with her to the Grégoire's home. Afterwards, it was easier for them to take the final step, in other words to come to the meetings themselves, as they knew that they were expected.

The confidence given to the Grégoire family and this shared commitment enabled the group to draw strength and lessons from it which could be applied elsewhere. For example, at a meeting between two very poor neighborhoods from two towns, one of the groups put on a slide show of the work carried out on their estate. They were proud of their work, proud of sharing it with other families. They put a lot of effort into it and spent several hours preparing it. During their slide show, a man from the estate which was hosting them began causing a scene, he was in a state of insurrection: *It's total bullshit what you're doing . . . it's no use . . . it's all hot air. . . .* The tension mounted immediately as this man's outburst was unbearable. It prompted the following discussion:

What do we do? Should we leave? Should we bar him from our meeting? An activist explained:

> By situating this man's attitude in our own lives, we saw that we have to resist our desire to leave and that we have to stay and show that it's possible to exchange views, even with this man, if we give ourselves the means to do so.

Mr. and Mrs. Grégoire were not present that day but the commitment and work carried out with them enabled people to think before excluding others and to implement the challenge of working from the poorest upwards.

Public action

In 1977, during a working session at Pierrelaye, Fourth World volunteer corps member Henri Bossan spoke of a woman who, according to the press, had deliberately allowed her children to starve to death, locked away in the apartment. The newspapers accused this woman of being a bad mother, of having worked as a prostitute, of alcohol abuse and of living in a bad way. They also described the hell these children had to endure. This had a deep impact on the activists at this session, as anything to do with children is sacred.

First of all, Henri Bossan let them base their thoughts on some press articles. He then showed them other articles in which it emerged that the mother had called for help from the social services and people around her. Father Joseph Wresinski went to the prison to build up a relationship with her. The activists were asked the following questions: Can we show solidarity towards this woman? Would you be able to give her support? Do you feel concerned about this situation? Is it possible to come to the conclusion that exclusion and lack of recognition of poverty can have such tragic consequences? The activists considered these questions: for many, the idea of supporting a mother who had let her children starve to death was intolerable. They understood, having seen all the aspects and information about this case, that it was simply not a question of taking away this woman's responsibilities but that it was necessary to understand what could have pushed her to such an extent. After much hard thinking, the activists took sides and agreed to participate in the petition for support that ATD Fourth World had launched. Following this working session, the activists were responsible for spreading the word in their neighborhood and passing around the petition for support.

In these neighborhoods, the initial reactions were similar to those of the activists. Before adhering to the change of opinion and taking action, several discussions took place. On one estate, the activists decided to go from door to door, in pairs, to ask people to sign the petition. They also went to City Hall and the social services, etc. They were made to leave on more than one occasion, but they stuck to their task and returned to those who had turned them away because they had become involved in the situation: *She had lost hope . . . she was all strung out . . . she was totally demoralized . . . all doors had been closed to her. . . .* This situation enabled the activists to discover the idea of shared responsibility and understood that this woman was not, should not and could not be deemed solely responsible for this tragedy which was the result of extreme poverty. They read what was written in the papers: *This woman is no human being but a walking mass of flesh and bones, an empty shell.* The work carried out involved them making a public commitment and required them to stick firmly to this commitment, even when faced with those who have been rejected by everyone. The petition received strong support from poor families. Father Joseph Wresinski stood as a witness before the Crown Court in February 1978.

A commitment to solidarity across borders

Family days, as organized by ATD Fourth World in various regions, are days for reflection and meeting people, bringing very poor families from a city together with people from all walks of life. These days are divided in two. The morning is a time for discovery and for sharing ideas based on a statement or report etc. on an unfair situation of some sort. The afternoon is a convivial time when participants can share their skills in drama, painting or poetry workshops, to name but a few. One of these days took place in the middle of winter in a big utility room with no heating. It was the only place available. All the participants were frozen. One of the plays looked back over the life of a very poor Guatemalan woman. This woman lived near a railroad, in a shack made of planks which would take off at the slightest gust of wind. She lived in constant fear that one of her children would get hit by a train. One night, a train came off the rails and demolished her shack. She shared her fear with her children and her neighbors. In response to this play, some of the poor families spoke of other similar situations. The cold and windy weather on that day did nothing but enhance the participants' feelings of solidarity towards this woman and all others who live in similar poverty-stricken conditions. A message of solidarity was sent to her in Guatemala. This family day enabled all of the participants to come together and discover poverty across borders and to take into account the international aspect of the fight against poverty.

Other actions and projects are also carried out by poor families in collaboration with Fourth World volunteer corps members, allies and friends, such as manning delegations to meet the mayor, members of parliament or representatives from other associations, from the parish, schools and the media, etc. The goal of this work is always to denounce the unfair situation of the poorest and raise awareness of this in the hope that everyone will accept their responsibilities and take on a role in the fight against poverty.

Knowledge learned from this work

The poorest enable us to see ourselves

It is impossible for someone coming from a poor background and encountering others living in extreme poverty not to make the link between these people's situation and their own lives. Working with the poor is like seeing a mirror-image of their own lives. Work carried out outside of their own family makes it possible for them to take a step back, have patience and listen, which can sometimes prompt the question: why is it easier to be like this with others but not at home? It is easier to be a witness to other people's poverty than an actor in one's own family. It is easier to see what is wrong with others than at home.

Activists who get involved and take action within their own neighborhood cannot come across as *superior* to their neighbors as they are also living in difficult conditions. This is why their work and commitment can sometimes cause new problems for them: they want life to change for others and are fighting for this but, at the same time, they also have their own situation, children and life to worry about, *with all our own inadequacies and failings,* as one of them put it. Awareness is not necessarily the key to happiness.

> My work as an activist helps me to escape from isolation and to be less selfish and think of others. It also helps me to believe in other horizons, to keep my chin up whatever happens, especially when I'm with my children. But sometimes I have doubts because I know how I'm supposed to be, but I don't always know how "to be" and that pains me.

How can the people who work with the poor make use of the knowledge they have learned from doing so? Their work and commitment with the very poor often forces them to work on themselves.

Where does a lack of faith in humankind lead?

This question was raised by an activist who had previously said about his friend Daniel: *He must've had some kind of secret.* One of Daniel's secrets was never to give up hope. Not the hope that life was going to change for him, but hope in the people he met. If we give up on hope and stop believing in others when the going gets tough, then we will never get anywhere. It is because others believed in them that the activists were able to work for people like themselves.

> Those who I meet today, who are considered incapable by everyone, that was me 20 years ago—I was considered to be a passive person who wallowed in poverty. How am I supposed to forget who I was? What would have become of me if no-one had believed in me?

Very poor people are waiting for someone to hold their hand out to them, to see them and to listen to them. They are not looking for compassion; they want to meet people who can help them to stand on their own two feet and discover and express what they are capable of doing. Who would have thought that the Grégoires and so many other poor families could have rallied so many people around them? They were only able to escape their isolation and the exclusion they are trapped in thanks to the committed work carried out with them. This work with the very poor highlights their strengths. It is all a matter of time. It takes time to get to know each other, to find out about each other and learn to like and respect each other. Thanks to the work carried out with them and the courage they showed themselves, Mr. and Mrs. Grégoire made it clear to all those who had rejected them that, deep down in their poverty, they always had hope.

Having faith in humankind also means having hope in people, whether rich or poor. Even those who are well-off need to have time and means and to meet people in order to change and develop.

Twenty years ago I would never have imagined that I would have been able have in-depth conversations with the school principal, teachers, the mayor and social workers, etc. I thought that they weren't at all flexible. The work taught me to have hope in them.

How can they realize this if they always feel blamed and if they never have the chance to explain what they have to go through?

Maintaining hope towards all human beings—this is what can be learned from fighting poverty, for it is not simply something which concerns the poorbut each and every one of us. Nowadays, people from all social circles are joining the poorest in their fight, and their work in schools, associations, administrations etc. is invaluable.

Moving forwards without rejecting one's own

Believing in a very poor person requires courage and the ability to take risks, as this is often something which is criticized. But this is of little importance, *we are motivated by strength, we keep going because we have discovered that our life is worth something. That's our strength,* said one activist.

When a poor person takes on commitment to help other poor people, they end up on the receiving end of a lot of criticism, judgments and advice. Very often, those who get involved with the poor tend to react in such a way that they do all they can to help them escape poverty as soon as possible. Their aid is therefore in the form of individual aid or assistance. They are often told to sever their links with their surroundings: *You can escape, but they can't. . . .You have skills, but they don't. . . . You aren't like the rest. . . .* This is a temptation to seize the opportunity to *escape poverty.* And no-one can hold it against those who are won over by the discourse often heard against the very poor. Being able to resist this call to break away from one's own requires *unflagging energy and strength of character that is greater than oneself and which can only be felt because one is supported by one's people and a movement.*

The work described previously involves solidarity with the poorest, who are sometimes even excluded by other poor people. If the families of the estate where Mr. and Mrs. Grégoire lived did not have the need for peace and justice, if they did not know in their hearts what it felt like to hear the words: *they don't even want to help themselves*—and they would all have heard this at some point or another—then they would not have been able to go and help the poorest and the work would have never even begun. First of all, the activists had to accept criticism from their own estate: *Who does she think she is . . . ? She'll drop us afterwards. . . .* They stuck to their commitment because they knew that welcoming and attending to those who are even poorer than themselves are values which stem from their background. Their commitment has helped them to bring these values out into the open for everyone to see and for everyone on the estate to be proud of.

All work to combat poverty should be supported by the milieu of poverty itself, in harmony with it and legitimized by it. When a very poor family kept their door closed for several months, preventing any form of discussion, an activist had to ask what he could do himself, what support he could find and what would prompt the family to open the door one day without having to force dialogue. One day, he too opened his door.

This earth is full of poverty, but also hope

As well as being a priest, Father Joseph Wresinski also founded a movement which unites people from all religious denominations because the fight against poverty is an issue for all those who believe in humankind. However, he has always advocated that the poor's right to spirituality be recognized alongside all other human rights.

For this reason, after his death, a Fourth World delegation comprising people from all denominations and bearing witness to this possible unity, not only in religious terms but beyond, went to meet the pope. They symbolically presented him with earth gathered from poor places in all four continents. One activist brought him some earth from a shanty town where he had lived and where there were huts especially built for the very poor families who lived there. He said:

> This earth is full of poverty, but also hope. It represents all the suffering and injustice that the poor endure. It represents the numerous people who have disappeared. All the earth collected has been mixed together and given as a gift. Hope is there, the earth is nourishing, and this poor earth can also give life. It is not God who is responsible for our poverty on earth, but the individual and collective selfishness of humankind.

The way society considers and views the poor, and how they are accounted for on an institutional level (in political, legal, religious institutions, etc.), is not making particularly rapid progress. Work and action is teaching people to have hope in others and also in these institutions. When families need support because they have been forced to leave their homes or because their electricity has been cut off, when they need help from social services, the hope they have is sometimes put to the test. *If we don't move, we'll just be crushed,* said one activist. By committing themselves to the fight against poverty, the poor prove that they need to be able to rally together with others for their voices to be heard and their ideas to be understood.

They were associated with the Wresinski Report[2] and with the bill on social cohesion[3] in France. They continue to believe that if everyone rallies behind the poorest, things can change. *I have a gut feeling about it,* one activist said.

Sharing knowledge—the force to act

One activist expressed his relationship with others as follows:

> I try to learn from other peoples because we need others to be able to make knkowledge pour forth for the good of everyone.

The source of knowledge which induces action is made up of various underground rivers which cross paths, intermingle and, finally, merge. Sharing knowledge, based on the idea of the source, is not simply an exchange of knowledge which is directly practical, such as how to cook or write, etc. No. Sharing knowledge, as discussed here, should bring about something new that can belong to everyone and which would not exist if it were not the product of multiple contributions. The work and action described above bear witness to such exchanges of knowledge.

A further example of this is a writing workshop which was held in a town on October 17*. All participants were asked to either write a statement about the fight against poverty or write a tribute to those who are fighting for this cause. One of the activists wrote the following statement:

> I lost someone who I was close to yesterday. I was by her side. Her last words were: "Tell Mom I love her very much", "Thank Michel for all the support he's given me", "Goodbye to this dog's life". Continuing this fight is the greatest tribute that I could pay her, as someone who knew what poverty was all about, and all those who have lived in poverty and have left for other horizons.

This statement was read aloud, but anonymously, to all participants.

The funeral for this woman who had endured such a difficult life was held two days later. The priest gave a very warm and respectful welcome in the church. He prepared the blessing with one of the woman's children and a long-standing friend of ATD Fourth World. This friend pronounced a few words in the church. He made the connection between this woman's life and the World Day to Overcome Extreme Poverty, which had just taken place. With all due respect, he repeated the words that he had heard she had said: *She said, "Goodbye to this dog's life".* The priest continued by deploring the injustice to which the poorest are subjugated and stressed the life-long struggle and courage that this woman had attested to. These were not simply words. He showed the utmost respect towards her and accompanied her coffin as far as the exit of the church, his hand placed upon it. Before leaving for the funeral reception, he reiterated that this woman's life should serve as a symbol of courage for everyone. This life that would have been labeled as *useless,* as *an alcoholic's life,* was in fact valuable thanks to her fight against death, disease and solitude.

This woman's family and loved ones felt honored by this ceremony. All that was shared as a result of this woman's death created a force which everyone could draw from. Not only were emotions shared, but also knowledge: the knowledge of her life, as written in the statement by a family member, the knowledge of her commitment over very many years as mentioned by her friend and the knowledge of the priest who knew how to talk to God whilst taking into account the family and friends who were in the church and who were not necessarily religious but who were present to share their profound grief. This priest, only having been in this parish for three months, knew how to be in communion because of the knowledge which had been passed on to him. Before becoming a priest, he was *like a child* in the eyes of everyone. Knowledge becomes shared when one adopts what one has learned from others and when one has created something new, enriched by everyone's contribution. For this, the different knowledge and skills should learn to join together while respecting the original features of everyone. This is not about personal enrichment, because if everyone makes a contribution, new knowledge can be created for the benefit of everyone. Sharing knowledge between very poor people and people from other social backgrounds is impossible without a joint commitment, because it is not only about sharing knowledge but also information.

Adopting what one has learned from others to create something new takes time. Time (or continuance) is certainly one of the essential conditions for reciprocity to take place. Sharing other people's knowledge means suffering with them, hoping with them, learning with them and making commitments with them. Very often non-poor people say that they discover and learn courage from the poor. On the other hand, the poor say they learn what security means from those who make commitments to them in the long-term.

Security is about more than confidence. Being secure means being sure that you will not be betrayed and that the other party will not use you for their own benefit, and will not use the lives of your loved ones for means that are not theirs or yours. Security is about an equal relationship where all parties can remain true to themselves, using their own words and their own way of thinking. They know that they are accepted for who they are and that they will accept the other, for together they know where they are heading.

The commitment and action of Fourth World volunteer corps members

The work of the Fourth World volunteer corps members aims to give the poorest in our society the chance to express their thoughts and opinions. The Fourth World volunteer corps members allow them to exercise their responsibilities in society, always bearing the very poorest in mind as a point of reference. How do they do this?

– by being present with those who live in extreme poverty and sharing their lives on a daily basis. It is a presence which encourages them to seek out those who are hiding due to poverty. In the logic of giving priority to the poorest, it is the poorest themselves who are the most important—the spearheads of transformation.

– by sharing knowledge and experience of the significant work that affects all areas of life, such as work, health, housing, education, culture and knowledge, etc.

– by carrying out work based on knowledge and shared experience, work that can be called political because it aims to bring about change in society with regard to everyday life, but also with regard to the taking into account of the opinions of the poorest of citizens.

In this type of work, know-how and knowledge are often closely interlinked. Know-how, which is constantly being developed, is based on meeting people. It depends on the other person's awareness of being responsible. Not in the sense of taking charge, but in the sense that the other person's life cannot be something about which I am indifferent because the other person is a human being, similar to me. This is the mindset in which members of the Fourth World volunteer corps carry out their daily work of going to meet the poorest.

The following example aims to illustrate what kind of meeting is being referred to and thus which skills are developed. The experience of this meeting constitutes a sort of crossroads of knowledge drawn from other meetings. This exchange of knowledge takes on a meaning in the life of those who are on the receiving end and thus becomes personal experience—the very source of new transferable skills.

Meeting people

A Fourth World volunteer corps member's tale:

One evening, in one of the outer subway tunnels of a very busy station, I saw a woman aged about 30 or so sitting on the ground on an old beige backpack, crammed full. She lowered her head.

What made me stop next to her from the very first time I saw her? Her face and her whole being reminded me of the mothers I'd known in the two live-in family development camps[4] where I'd worked with the families who'd invited me into their daily lives. I saw their reflection in this woman's face.

I find it hard to see people sitting at my feet like that. I crouched down beside her. I was crouching, not sitting, and this is an important detail to me. I felt that I needed to be physically close to Annick, there where she was, to be with her, to communicate with her through this gesture. But, at the same time, I'm not Annick and it's not up to me try to ape her: I was simply at her side, near and different. If I had sat by her I wouldn't have felt like I was respecting her, as it would have being trying to act like we were the same. As Father Wresinski once wrote[5]: "Regarding poverty, both closeness and distance are necessary".

This initial encounter was brief. I didn't want to ask her questions or make her tell me about her life or lie to me. Nor did I want to take up her precious time. Whilst I was talking to her, no-one gave her any money. I simply gave her a copy of the ATD Fourth World journal *Feuille de Route* (Road Map), with the address of the Fourth World House* in Marseille. I told her that in this journal there were stories about families who have had a very difficult life (I never use the words "poor" or "poverty" when I first meet someone as I never know how this will be received). I added that she would be welcome in the Fourth World House, where she could meet people like me and other families who have a very hard time in life.

What made me want to approach the woman there, where she was, in that way without knowing what would happen? Marie-France, a Fourth World volunteer corps member, affected me a great deal with the insight she had of people who were trapped in great distress. Her way of approaching them, of letting herself go with the flow, without understanding, of entering into a world of unacceptable poverty in order to come out the other side of it with them and thanks to them. This is a compulsory stage for true liberation. Therefore, crouching down next to Annick and doing this enough times so that she would stand up to talk to me (it took about four or five times) was similar to accepting that I was powerless, that I didn't know. I was accepting the wait, not trying to anticipate the moment which would make Annick stand up, not only in the literal sense, but also in the symbolic sense too, and letting her take the initiative. But it was also important for me to be able to pave the way for this initiative. I had to enter into something I didn't understand, into what hurts me, and be crushed so that we could get back up together.

Why did I give her a copy of *Feuille de Route*? This was thanks to Hélène Béranger, an activist from Marseille, who taught me to have one in my bag. She uses *Feuille de Route* to raise awareness about ATD Fourth World and to show people that they are not alone in living in and fighting against poverty. What's more, it doesn't involve asking questions, it's offering something. Anyway, I couldn't deal with people like Annick if I wasn't able to offer them some form of personal relationship, no matter how close. I cannot go about it light-heartedly. I put my whole self into it, but I also open up links to other people too, so they can get to know other committed workers and discover that they belong to something which can liberate them from me, particularly by introducing them to other very poor families.

Discovering their daily lives

The same Fourth World volunteer corps member continues her tale:

So, every day I would stop for a while by Annick's side, sometimes on my own and sometimes with my daughter, Elise. Before long, Annick's partner, Didier, came to join us. I hadn't met him before. He was a beggar at a subway exit that I didn't ever use. Elise's presence reassured them. Maybe she reminded Annick of her two children who had been taken into care in the Paris region. A child has a reassuring effect. Didier and Annick gave her a comic and a pin. One day they told me with great pride that Elise had said hello to them. She had been passing by with a friend and her friend's mother. She went to give Annick a kiss and her friend's mother was astonished and asked her "Do you know her?" Elise had replied "Yes, I know her through my mom".

I had an inkling that they would come to the Fourth World House one day. I had a good idea of the effort that this would require of them: half a day without either of them collecting any money, taking the subway without a ticket, walking a way with heavy bags even though Annick was so tired. It takes half an hour to walk from the nearest subway station to the Fourth World House, and that's without any bags. For Annick and Didier, they had to take the few belongings they had with them wherever they went, which means always carrying bags around with them, everywhere.

Members of the Fourth World volunteer corps develop this type of know-how and knowledge through meeting people. Personal meetings are essential provided that they lead to the possibility of other meetings and that they offer a sharing of experiences and knowledge. It was with this in mind that ATD Fourth World took significant initiatives to provide access to knowledge.

The Fourth World People's Universities

The Fourth World People's Universities were established to give the very poor a voice and give them the opportunity to enter into dialogue with other actors in society[6]. They are a means of introducing these people's worries and suggestions into society. For these Fourth World People's Universities to operate, the Fourth World volunteer corps members developed certain procedures with this sharing of knowledge and experience in mind. The following describes the experience of our group's Fourth World volunteer corps member:

An open letter written with someone who did not know how to read or write . . .

In view of the drafting of the French law on academic reform, a pedagogical counselor and a teacher were invited to the Fourth World People's University. During the discussion, the participants expressed the difficulties they had encountered and what they had done in order to send their children to school in the best conditions. They had already tried writing open letters. It seemed important to them to write one about school. Why an open letter and not a report? Because an open letter formulated thoughts with a view to a discussion (in this case, with the teachers). It was not directed at the participants but at the others, and constituted a means of broadening discussion.

The first stage in the discussion process was made at the Fourth World People's University, which gives priority of expression to the poorest and at which everybody seeks to understand. The open letter served as a second stage, which was to make these people's thoughts understandable for those who were not present but who were affected by the subject addressed. A further advantage of the open letter was that it set out the thoughts and expression of a given moment, without pretending to have said all that there was to say about the subject. It therefore allowed people to experiment with the idea that thoughts are not static but are in constant evolution and deepening. The challenge was also to allow those who cannot read or write to participate in this collaborative writing process. Five people worked on this letter, including one who did not know how to read or write at all. In order for each of them to play an active role, the small group listened to a cassette recording, thus allowing the illiterate member of the group to be on a level playing field with the others. The Fourth World volunteer corps member underlined the chosen sections on the deciphering.

Then, the group carried out a conventional composition process. They grouped together the chosen sections and drew up an outline. The first draft was made by the person who could not read, together with the Fourth World volunteer corps member, then the rest of the group read it through, corrected it and produced the final version.

The personal work carried out with the person who could not read led to an unexpected opening for the Fourth World volunteer corps member:

> During a class at the Fourth World People's University, Mr. Tanguy said: "On our housing estate, there are parents who do not take an interest in their children's school." I understood this to be a judgment of the parents who did not care about their children's future. He insisted that we put this sentence into the open letter. When we were both working on the collaborative writing process, I asked him why this was so and he told me: "Because I don't know how to read and write, so how can I get involved with school?" So I worked together with him to rewrite his sentence and make it understandable for the teachers. He was asking a fundamental question: "How can people play a role in school when they do not know how to read or write?" He would never have been able to ask the teachers this question without the help of the open letter and, in doing so, he was expressing something that did not only involve him.

... And which led to further meetings and training

The Fourth World activists went to their children's school to take this letter to the principals and teachers. The pedagogical counselor also distributed it amongst other people working in education. This letter prompted the request for ATD Fourth World to put on three half-day educational sessions on relations with families in great difficulty. It was understood that the Fourth World volunteer corps member would lead the first two sessions and that for the third, the teachers would come together to learn with the families themselves during a class at the Fourth World People's University. The members of the Fourth World People's University were proud of reversing the roles in this way and receiving 16 teachers, 2 pedagogical counselors and an education inspector. The stakes were high! How could real dialogue take place with these people who were knowledgeable and were used to talking and expressing themselves? What could be done for them to see that they could learn from the parents who do not turn up to school meetings or speak up during them? We decided to opt for a theater forum[7].

The stage was built by a preparation group (the Fourth World People's Universities are set up by small groups of people from the local neighborhood). The scenario was that the parents had received a note from the school principal asking them to come into the school as their child had been absent for the last 15 days! The child said that he had not gone to school because he had been told off by the teacher for having lost his school gear and he knew that his parents could not afford any others, and, in addition, the teacher had smacked him. The parents were furious and went to the school. . . . The members of the Fourth World People's University found it quite easy to play their relevant roles and improvise based on their experience. The teachers found it harder to enter into terrain in which they were not the leaders. They were caught off guard by this way of thinking. They were used to being the ones who made the comments; they wanted to change the scenario by leaving out the smack. The first teacher to act out her role in front of the families and her colleagues showed quite a lot of courage. She managed to find a way out of the situation and establish dialogue with the parents, firstly by not doing away with the infamous smack, but by showing great respect for the parents and, secondly, by not acting in a defensive manner, but by adopting a listening approach. This theater forum was a success in that it showed (not explained) to the teachers that the parents are intelligent. (The person playing the role of the mother could neither read nor write, but impressed everyone with the intelligence of her retorts). The teachers were also able to see that dialogue was possible and enriching, provided certain conditions were met. As for the parents, they were able to overcome their fear of dialoguing with the teachers.

Seizing the historic moment so that the poor assume their place in history

Another Fourth World People's University used a national event as a starting point: the bicentenary of the French Revolution. This was an occasion to reintroduce the poor onto the scene and to understand their present situation by looking at their past. In Marseille, two Fourth World People's Universities were established based on the French Revolution, the main goal being to take history on board in order to find the very poor's place in it, or at the very least a trace of them. A trace of them was found in the *cahier de Doléances du Quatrième Ordre* (Notes on the Grievances of the Fourth Order), found by an ATD member on a second-hand bookstall[8]. It bears witness to the efforts made by the author and Paris architect, Dufourny de Villiers, to give a voice to those who had none. Using these extracts, transposed into modern French, the participants extracted the main ideas (the cover remained in the French of the time so that, with the help of the short text, everyone could see how much the language had evolved throughout history).

Three main points resulted from this study:

– Those with "neither hearth nor home" were not represented by the three other orders.

– Dufourny de Villiers, having had close contact with the poor, attested that what was said about the residents of Paris' poor neighborhoods was not true for everyone and that they held values which were ignored by society.

– He called upon all men of goodwill to listen to the voices of those who were not heard.

These thoughts rang very true to modern-day poor families. At the same time, these families learned something about the history of that period and saw that there was a will to give a voice to everyone, by means of these *cahiers de Doléances*, but that the poorest were forgotten and not represented.

The second objective was to reintroduce poor people's lives into the center of today's society by taking a look at their past. For this objective to be met, a more formal Fourth World People's University session was organized with several significant points. First of all, the chosen location, *"La Vieille Charité"*, was a hospice built in the seventeenth and eighteenth century by a reputed sculpture-architect, Pierre Puget, to "lock up" the poor. What was distinctive about this place was that it almost continuously "housed" the poor until the 1950s. The Fourth World People's University session was due to take place in this building, because of its history and because of what it has become, i.e. a place of culture and reflection. In this vein, it was also hosting an exhibition on the French Revolution at the time.

There were two Fourth World People's University sessions:

– The first consisted of a guided tour of one of the exhibition rooms, containing the *cahiers de Doléances* (in particular of traders), information on the French national anthem *la Marseillaise* and paintings of Marseille in the seventeenth century. The study on the *cahiers des Doléances* was good starting point to get into the exhibition, and the participants took the time to read the *cahiers* and notice the cross-references and differences. They looked for their neighborhoods on the paintings, etc.

– The second session involved giving an address before a representative of the mayor and of the prefect, and a presentation of a copy of the *Cahiers des Doléances* to each participant.

Two activists gave an address in public on behalf of the others. How were the speakers chosen? Mr. Riggi was not the most suitable or deft candidate to give an address. He was hyper-sensitive, a characteristic which sometimes led him into thundering rages against what he deemed unfair or when he was misunderstood. He could barely read and write, his reading being limited to the *menu du jour* at the local eatery. He had always considered himself to be a bit of an *ass*, but he carried other people's poverty within him and had a keen appetite for learning. He took his role very seriously, aware of his difficulties and with the hope that the families would feel honored by his words.

The Fourth World volunteer corps member explained:

> Allowing Mr. Riggi to give an address in public required a lot of individual work with him. First of all I listened to his train of thought. He surprised me by announcing that he wanted to explain the name of ATD Fourth World. I didn't see what he was getting at. By developing this double name *Aide à Toute Détresse-Quart Monde* (Help to All in Distress-Fourth World)—the first part of which we don't tend to

know as well—he developed the transition from shameful poverty that shuts people away and makes people need someone to hold out their hand to the Fourth World (taken from fourth order), where people can come together to fight against poverty.

For him, distress is the state you get into when you're poor, a situation which makes everything pass you by in life. To escape from this, you need people by your side who recognize you as a person—this was what "Help to all in Distress" or "ATD" meant for him. But it doesn't stop there. "Fourth World" expresses what we become when we join the collective fight against poverty. He helped me to rediscover the full meaning of the name.

Working with him meant holding a pencil for him, writing his sentences, highlighting the powerful expressions he used, reformulating them to understand them and to make them understandable and looking for the right words with him that he could utter with ease, naturally. So together we came up with a short text (he wanted to learn it by heart). We typed the text out using a very large font size and marked the silences together. He realized all the work that went into putting an idea into words. Something which seemed to roll off the tongue effortlessly was in fact not an improvisation, and thus his thoughts grew and grew and became deeper. This is the same Mr. Riggi who, at a Fourth World People's University session on the subject of freedom, said to us: "I am free because I have the freedom of thought; I have discovered that a poor person can think just like a rich one. It amounts to the same thing." For me, he entered into a form of freedom that's not easy to gain, but which can be developed by all those who do not accept being trapped in ignorance and poverty.

A new experience . . .
During that afternoon, there were periods of deep internalization, such as the way in which the participants took a walk around the confines of the *Vieille Charité* with their children. It was a moment of peace and harmony within the beauty of these noble and bare surroundings, a moment of communion with all the suffering, love and hope witnessed by those walls. A time for contemplation, for gathering one's strength to face the new and the unknown: everyone together experienced the idea *that we can't love if we don't have the time to look at, understand and pervade things, to discover them in depth, to internalize them. It is time to change ourselves, to become someone new, because we have experienced something new*[9]. The participants were all, both personally and collectively, experiencing something new. History was in the making.

What knowledge is gained from this type of action with the very poor?

The group's Fourth World volunteer corps member came up with the following in this regard:

I originally chose to be a teacher. This profession allowed me to work on something that was important for me, i.e. stimulating intelligence (linked to the development of noble-heartedness). I took an interest in history. Studying the subject showed me various blockages, advances and quests made by human beings in different times and surroundings. My commitment to ATD Fourth World as a member of the Fourth World volunteer corps made me quit my profession, but it enabled me to develop the reason why I chose the profession. Working with the poorest taught me that daring to take academic knowledge on board first of all requires life experience to be recognized as a source of knowledge.

When carrying out work, such as at the Fourth World People's University, with others like me and sharing their experiences, I have learned to create meetings which put very different people in a position to be able to learn from one another.

I've finally learned that to create new experiences where the poor and non-poor meet, understand each other and unite in the fight against poverty and ignorance, a certain amount of work and presence is necessary from day to day and in the long-term. It's also necessary to make the most of events and significant places which make this action more effective and which trigger an awareness of knowledge which leads people to open up their knowledge to others, thus bringing about a new experience.

A commitment within university life

"Marie-Hélène: Do you like what you do at university?
Gaston: Yes I do, thankfully**!"

The researchers and professors participating in the Fourth World–University project are all "recognized academics". They have all studied for many years and gained the qualifications which now enable them to work as academics. Regardless of the diversity of their respective lives, they all had the chance to study and chose to do so for a long time. They teach, give lectures and write books and articles. It goes without saying that none of them currently suffer the ill-effects of poverty or exclusion. In the eyes of society, they possess knowledge that they are to pass on to others and make fruitful by teaching and carrying out research. Everything seems to be nice and simple. And it is true that anyone in their place would share the same enthusiasm to pass on their knowledge, or what they think they know, to their students, and the same enthusiasm to defend their intellectual work and values.

Sometimes, they leave the confines of their ivory towers. The academics participating in our project are living proof of this. What is important for them is to establish links between their academic work and other forms of participation in society. They are, in this respect, committed academics. In other words, they believe that the thoughts they hold—their knowledge and intellectual activity—can lead to various forms of action which, in turn, can change society. Knowing and acting: this could be the motto of these committed academics! Once again, this seems nice and simple. And of course, there is some truth in it.

In this section comprising three subsections, we would like to take our thoughts one step further and show that any form of action or commitment is not simply an "extra part" of an academic's profession, but an essential element of it.

Making a commitment within university

Knowing and acting . . . maybe. But knowing is already acting! Knowledge is not a meteorite which falls from the academic sky into the world. It is part of the world. It is formed by individuals who *act* in their own way, for example by writing books. These academics know more or less how to write the books that they are expected to. They have studied. They know, for example, how to carry out a survey or library research and they know how to read and appreciate academic literature as well as how to expound on the results of their research. They know what they need to do for their books to be accepted by the academic world to which they belong.

But no book presents eternal truths. They are all the product of history, written at a certain moment by a certain person in a given context. No matter how rigorous the methods used and the scale of the documentation used, all books and all research are the result of a certain number of choices, points of view and means of perceiving reality. Writing a book is therefore an action, not only because it is a practical activity, recognized by society and integrated in the field of academic activity, but also because an academic book's purpose is always to explain, suggest or impose a certain way of viewing the world. The truths which are drawn up in an academic book are always the result or product of a certain conception of the world and academia. When these truths become accepted and circulated, they can have a great impact on society. Whether writing a book or carrying out a study, academics are always key players in the society to which they belong. Exercising their thoughts in a university is a social activity in its own right.

The first, and certainly most fundamental, form of commitment for academics is for them to realize the worth of their knowledge in society and to *act* accordingly. They should think very hard about the role they could have amongst their colleagues, readers and students. They should not choose their research subjects at random, but should build on themselves and arouse the intellectual awareness, critical mind and sense of responsibility amongst their students, which would enable them to devote their knowledge to serve a life-long and worthwhile social project. This is one of the most accurate descriptions of a model academic who wishes to get involved in a transformation project on both an individual and collective level. Academic work always aims to achieve something, in one way or another. As a result, carrying out a study, writing a book or teaching always involves a strong commitment: "*Knowledge is neither free nor enslaved: it is what we make of it*", as we mentioned previously.

This ideal is no further removed than the institutional and human reality that is

The word *university* comes from the Latin *universitas,* which primarily referred to a human community or "a community of students and masters" (as the new university institution in Paris was called in 1215)[10]. The lecturers were often itinerants, who would call for a degree to authorize them to teach *omnia omnino omnibus,* i.e. any subject, in any place, to anyone.

With this in mind, the ideal university is both a place for education through solidarity and a "univer-city", a "univer-sal" place where everyone can acquire universal knowledge. Learning is a social act more than a cognitive one: I learn, you teach me, we learn *together omnia omnino omnibus*—everything, everywhere and with everyone.

university. As with knowledge, universities are indeed "within the world". Thus, a commitment taken on within a university can also include another dimension, which was the subject of several discussions within the Knowledge Group. For each of the three academics in the group, university is not simply a privileged place where knowledge can blossom freely, but is also an institution which aims to have a certain form of both intellectual control (in that it formulates truths and values which it holds on to) and social control (as it awards degrees and defines its own academic criteria, for example). What are these truths, values and academic criteria? All too often they seem linked to the conservatism and elitism which, to a certain extent, characterize the university institution. For this reason, the three academics of the Knowledge Group feel that university has become a place of fighting and disputes. They call into question the workings of exclusion that universities implement and sometimes produce, they call into question the power struggles which arise there, not to mention the importance of the hierarchy, power games and the wrongdoings of corporatism which lead people to become withdrawn rather than offering them openings to the world. University may well exercise the ideal of universality, "teaching everything, to everyone, everywhere", but it is also characterized by its traditional practices which are far from ideal, such as selection, division and oppression. This paradox is part of university life, and the following sections intend to illustrate this.

Opening the doors to university

The ideal university does not exist, only the "traditional" university does; part of a social system, a values system, full of power struggles—an accurate portrayal of the society we live in. For as long as knowledge develops and is passed on from one person to another, it will never be a stranger to power or to forces of integration and exclusion—the very fabric of society, for better or worse. Making a commitment within university also means taking a position within this power game.

Universities have become more accessible to new groups of society over the last century. They used to be places which were almost exclusively reserved for the sons of "good" families, representing "the elite of the nation", and have gradually moved towards accepting the daughters of these same families. Women at university: this was a revolution in itself just a few generations ago[11]! Following the Second World War, and in particular since the 1970s, universities have generally become "democratized". There are ever-increasing numbers of students and, socially speaking, they come from a wider range of backgrounds. Despite unemployment, which is increasingly hitting our countries with a vengeance, university still seems to be a privileged tool for moving up the social ladder, the key to a secure and meaningful job.

However, this trend towards democratization within universities does not mean that higher education is open to everyone, in fact, far from it. First and foremost, going to university is expensive. Even when there are no tuition fees as such, families with low incomes still have to make great financial sacrifices to allow their children to study there for four or five years. In addition, the system of examining knowledge is based on a highly competitive selection process, which inevitably leads to exclusion as opposed to solidarity: the "best" benefit from this without there really being the educational means to help those who run into difficulties. There is also the fact that the doors to university remain closed to those who did not have the chance to complete their primary and secondary education in the best possible conditions[12]. This means that the poor's failure to catch up at school is irreversible.

In this respect, the ideal of a truly democratic university, a truly "universal" place, remains a vain hope, far removed from reality. Given the current situation, a large proportion of the population cannot go to university. It is obvious that, once again, the poorest are the first to be excluded, but there are also many other people who, for social, economic, professional or personal reasons, do not have the necessary qualifications to go to university and do not have the necessary means to have a successful university career. University is one of many institutions which, in reflection of the world we live in, remains a place of exclusion as well as a place for training. For two of the academics of the Knowledge Group, *making a commitment* within the world of academia means fighting the numerous barriers which block access to it. The field they work in is ongoing training, i.e. training programs aimed at those who do not have the necessary qualifications (in particular a high school diploma) to get into traditional universities but who are already working and wish to gain a university training. This type of alternative university training, created in France and Belgium in the 1970s, evidently does not resolve all the exclusion problems generated by universities.

Not all subjects are covered by this alternative means, but rather social or cultural ones. (There are no ongoing training programs on nuclear physics or medicine, for example!) In addition, it is a form of training which remains on the sidelines of traditional universities[13] and is only available to those who already have a job[14]. These university networks were born out of the opening up of relations and alliances between some universities and the world of work. An example of this was the founding, in Belgium, of the ISCO (Higher Institute for Educating Workers) and the FOPES (Open University for Economic and Social Politics) by Emile Creutz. At the same time, in France, Marcel David set up the ISTs (Higher Institutes of Labor Studies). In collaboration with social movements, these pioneers created institutes, networks and qualifications which opened up the world of university to new sections of the population[15].

Despite the age-long trend towards democratization, the university institution remains closed to large segments of the population. It continues to generate exclusion and its doors are far from being open wide. The desire to open them wider, by developing the field of ongoing training would involve a great struggle and much commitment. This would be a fight which would partly be against the institution. As one of the group members explained: *we are in a position to create a strong link, not between society and university, but between society and the academics who are committed to their various struggles against social inequality.*

These struggles are both individual and collective. They are always developing. We will now attempt to better understand the possible boundaries and the numerous personal and institutional implications. To do this we will be following one of our group members, Gaston Pineau, who was at the origin of the dissenting and integrating ongoing training movement in France and Quebec. The following text is therefore a personal statement. It is both fragile and risky, and, as with any statement, he tries to find the "right words to express himself". He is essentially trying to establish the link—our main concern here—between academic or professional knowledge, knowledge gained from life experience and knowledge born of action and commitment. In this regard, his statement seems to be more enlightening than any theory and we are thus attributing great value to his words.

Ongoing training: to the borders of individuals and institutions

Gaston Pineau:

My knowledge gained from my commitment to ongoing training in universities can be traced back to my fight against a certain kind of "poverty" or destitution. I want to talk about individuals' lack of power of expression vis-à-vis institutions. This commitment led me and continues to lead me to travel "to the borders of individuals and institutions", to different countries and to different social spheres. But also in my head, my heart, my body. This commitment affects me, drives me and motivates me in several ways, without me really being able to identify them, or understand why and how. And I am in even less of a position to draw any clear or recognized lessons from them.

This is because I'm not a major player in the fight. I am not an officer of any sort.

I am just a militant, fighting on the borders, almost illegally. I go from here to there, mysteriously. More to give a helping hand than to sound off or for any big maneuvers. Not that it's a conscious decision on my part. Even if I'm sometimes led into acting as a volunteer. But more often than not it's the movement which gives the orders. Not the instituted and organized movement. Not really. I am quite far from all that, at the borders, at the tip of the wave—the big wave of anonymous individuals who fight against this lack: this lack of expression which means that their daily life is dominated by all the big institutions. They are dominated by the big information and consumer channels . . . but also crushed by the people with positions, the well-established and instituted ones. They are individuals swamped in their anonymous daily lives. Without a voice, without the right to speak.

This commitment to the borders of individuals and organizations had me carried away from a very early age, from my childhood. It used to make me cry. Study. Work. Get involved in institutions. Get out of them or be excluded from them. Roam about. Discover university. Go there to find the means for expression and the desire to change it in order to perform the most difficult of escape acts: freeing oneself from one's daily routine.

One evening in May 1968, we were 10 or so students and we did a sit-in at the National Pedagogical Institute. It was one of many of the symbolic acts which didn't have any immediate consequences. However, as the student movement continued, the law on ongoing training was drawn up in '71. Ongoing training services were created in universities to make them more democratic by opening them up to adults who hadn't had access to university previously. This difficult opening, which was developed to varying degrees depending on the country, led me to Quebec to help set up a small research team. Working for the university seemed to be a betrayal of my cause to some of my peers. It was the route to a border. It meant I found myself on the other side, in a dominating institution.

This route, which others also took, familiarized me with this field and helped me to open breaches. A few years later, I tried to write an account of this in a book which stirred up fierce debate: *Fighting at the borders of organizations.* This book aimed to link up with other fights led by millions of citizens every day against the organizations in society which enslave them. These fights rarely make the headlines. They rarely form the basis of major social debates. They take place at the borders of these organizations, at ground level, in the shadows. They are individual mini-fights, isolated, suffocated, repressed, receiving little attention or recognition.

In what way can these mini-combats coming from such lowly quarters interest universities—prestigious places for higher education, destined to educate the elite, the organizers and leaders of organizations? This question is formidable. The book asked it directly. It showed how the ongoing training services tried to answer it by introducing new groups (local associations, associations for the elderly, etc.) and new professions (leaders, educators, etc.) into universities. It showed how the action carried out by this service aimed to meet three main objectives: firstly, to bring to the fore what I would call "border-people". These are adult educators, responsible for linking the academic world with social spheres which have little to do with it, and are in fact generally opposed to it, such as the working-class people. Secondly, to encourage development of "partnerships" by setting up and carrying out research-training programs with the people involved. Finally, to engender mediators and allies on both sides of the barrier, i.e. in universities and in society. This means creating new community, family, social and professional areas.

The experience of coming and going between university and the world also enabled me to develop new research processes and new academic viewpoints. These were mainly "life stories" used for research and allowing a meaning to be found in daily life, which is usually deemed insignificant. It is also about the recognition and validation of life experience to allow people who are richer in experience than in material wealth to have access to university. And this is finally the formation of an education theory which recognizes that the most important training is what we teach and create ourselves.

These processes do not go without saying. They require people to think outside of their traditional boxes. They can also cut people off from university. This can reduce tension, but in turn it makes any commitment less effective. Although action carried out privately sometimes allows for commitments that would not be possible otherwise, they are likely to be a lot less effective in mobilizing socio-professional and institutional society. With this in mind, it seems to me that maintaining close ties can lead to effective commitment. This is a dual role assigned to border-people who do not want to be customs officers or smugglers, and to those who transcend or even break down borders in the end.

It is, of course, the idea of this dual role that explains my commitment to the Fourth World–University project. It led me to try and evaluate the knowledge that I had gained from this adventure as a maverick at the borders of individuals and organizations. This brief outline of my time at university allowed me to pinpoint three types of commitment knowledge:

– the first one is **political**: critical situations bring to bear participation as a last resort either in institutions or for individuals, by subordinating and sacrificing each other.

– the second is **strategic**: it involves the means of commitment. It is a question of finding a place and means which are suitable for the objectives being pursued. Borders and crossroads seem to me to be privileged places of action, interaction and transaction.

– the third is **existential**: this can be summed up in three key words: love, co-birth and transformation. "Love": I dare to put this throwaway word, repressed from dominant academic discourse, in first position because love is indeed the only word, in my opinion, which can navigate its way through difficult situations. Love's "link-forming properties" are also beginning to be taken into account in soft sciences. It cannot be disassociated from the recognition of the immense complexity of human and social behavior. Next comes "co-birth", because I refuse to believe that love is blind. It is blind if we make it so. But when we take love as a source of knowledge, the relationship that it enables gives access not only to a specific form of knowledge, but also to a new birth with the person or subject that one is trying to get to know. It is thus a form of co-birth. Finally comes "transformation": this form of knowledge triggers a transformation movement which requires ongoing learning. Training is achieved through an ongoing transformation.

Current European integration is weakening the borders established between individuals and institutions, running the risk of an unprecedented social divide. Academics, whether they like it or not, are involved in this disintegration/reintegration process. Their action or inaction is either contributing to the severity of this divide or creating new places and forging new links. By getting representatives from opposite social spectra to work together, i.e. from the worlds of academia and extreme poverty, this Fourth World–University project is experimenting with a virtually unprecedented partnership. Some people may see it as something which is outrageously against the cultural norms. Others, on the other hand, may feel that it is something which can be traced back to the dynamics of the initial university project, i.e. the universal sharing of all knowledge by everyone, everywhere. Realizing this project without naivety or illusions can lead to political, strategic and existential knowledge which helps us, on a small scale, to achieve what is being pursued. We have to leave something for the others! And learn to find our place in a realistic and optimistic way in the movement at the borders of institutions.

Conclusion

In conclusion to this chapter, we can confirm that action can have just as much an effect, if not more so, on the person carrying out the work as the people on the receiving end.

Commitment and work arise from meetings and very often have a deeper root, stemming back from childhood and the surroundings in which people grew up. Life experience, whether positive or negative, shapes the way people think about and perceive life, as well as how they enter into relationships with others. A meeting which triggers someone's commitment rarely occurs by chance. It is often part of an ongoing process.

Work and action help us to get to know ourselves better

Fighting poverty is no mean feat. You have to fight it so as not to be beaten by it. The knowledge derived from living in poverty incites people to escape it as much as to fight it. The only solution is to act with determined commitment, which requires personal awareness and much perseverance. It is a commitment with others, thought out over the long-term, which gradually moves things ahead as people learn from one another. When people from extremely poor backgrounds get involved in this fight alongside others in their situation, it is as though something finally becomes possible. A foothold is gained, a hope becomes possible. Their commitment allows them to take on a new view of themselves. *I don't see things the same way any more, I've changed my viewpoint and now my life is so worthwhile**!* Thanks to the work carried out by these activists, other very poor people are making commitments too, as they are also regaining hope that life can be different.

By learning alongside the poorest, the Fourth World volunteer corps members made a choice. They discovered that commitment is not easy and that only with time is it possible for people to get to know and appreciate each other. They needed to cast aside any prejudices about the poor and remain true to themselves, as far as possible, so that they could enter in to dialogue with them and share and recognize the aspirations of an entire social group. It is not easy to go from "we have to help the poor", "give them what they don't have", and "change them" to "they can teach me", "they have a mind and thoughts and we have to build on them, together with them".

The problem of recognition of the poorest is not simply one of ignorance, which can be resolved. It is more of a problem of accepting and confronting differences. Becoming committed to the poorest means recognizing their life experience, and being aware of and emphasizing all their moments of survival. At the beginning of all forms of commitment to fight poverty there may well be a dawning of awareness—or sometimes revolt—regarding the extreme injustice that poverty represents, but for it to last in the long-term, it is necessary for everyone to accept involvement in a long adventure where every step throws them off-balance and reveals the unknown, the uncertain and a lack of knowledge, all of which are to be overcome. Accepting this lack of knowledge leads to exchanges with others.

This experience of a lack of knowledge is what led several academics to get involved in the Fourth World–University project. A lack of knowledge which became apparent during meetings with very poor people.

Taking action means having confidence in people and believing that institutions can change

At the root of all action there is the belief that it can bring about change. Otherwise, what would be the point of it ?

The many examples of action which we have looked at in this chapter show that confidence in oneself, in others and in institutions is something which is built up with time. Maintaining hope—this is what the fight against poverty teaches us. The poorest know that for a world that takes them into account, there need to be relationships of trust and respect, and time is needed to discover what the poor really want. But there also needs to be time for them to understand how those with decision-making powers operate. This is why the activists go to meet people from social services, and religious and academic institutions, etc.: so that a true partnership can be forged. Without relationships of trust, how can children, for example, flourish at school and develop their intelligence?

The only way to initiate change is through close collaboration between people themselves and between institutions and people, as this way they accept to learn from one another. Members of the Fourth World volunteer corps and allies often perform this mediatory role within institutions: they prepare for meetings which allow for dialogue to take place with the poorest. This is why the Fourth World volunteer corps members must continue to build bridges between the poorest and society, to lay the foundations for a true partnership.

The academics' field of action is often the place where they work, i.e. university. Some of them make a commitment *to borders*, in other words they enable links to be established between what they have discovered about the poorest, for example, and their students or their academic subject, thus making it possible for the knowledge they hold today to transform the way the poor are regarded by society. It is also this commitment *to borders* which leads some of them to set up training programs for adults in universities.

Everyone needs support from their peers

In order to take action, Fourth World activists need to be recognized, not only by the non-poor but also by the poor themselves—by people from their own backgrounds, neighborhoods and estates. Without this support, they do not even exist. It is the shared knowledge about poverty which brings the poor closer together. This is knowledge which people rarely tend to talk about and which is difficult to express in words, but can be manifested by means of gestures, regards and presences. For the activists, it is manifested by their listening and welcoming skills, but also by their rebellion and commitment. They are given the support they need by their own people, who also suffer from the same injustice and humiliation. No-one can fight poverty single-handedly. It is this confidence their own people have in them which prevents them from having to disown their origins, as they can draw strength from them and be proud of their commitment.

At the same time, members of the Fourth World volunteer corps do not work alone. During her lecture, Emilie Bourtet stressed how important the team of Fourth World volunteer corps members, to which she belonged, was for catching her breath, understanding, taking a step back and simply for having someone to listen to her questions and doubts.

It is possible that this "collective" experience is not as apparent in the world of university, which would explain why some of the academics participating in our project are referred to as "untypical" or "misfits" by their associates. However, they do not work alone either. They recreate new alliances and networks at the borders of their academic community which allow them to see their work through to completion.

Suffering and hope bring people closer together

This world, which we walk upon and in which all of us live, whether rich or poor, is the bearer of our lives full of suffering, happiness and desires. We are more or less armed to fight suffering, everyone having a different endurance threshold. But suffering nevertheless hurts all those who endure it. This is undoubtedly why suffering can bring people closer together. Suffering in itself means nothing. Fighting to ease suffering can unite people. The knowledge gained from living in poverty is derived from a melting pot of suffering and from ordeals which have been overcome. This knowledge prompts people to take action and represents hope—the hope of the poor themselves and the hope that comes from others joining with them to fight poverty. Those who join the fight are not asked to immerse themselves in suffering and unhappiness, as this would not help anything or anyone. The aim of the fight against poverty is to put an end to the suffering caused by poverty.

There is hope in the work and action carried out to enable the poorest to be acknowledged, listened to and recognized.

Notes

1. All examples and quotes in this section were from the activists in our group.
2. *Chronic Poverty and Lack of Basic Security : The Wresinski Report of the Economic and Social Council of France,* first adopted in 1987.
3. Following the Wresinski Report, *Chronic Poverty and Lack of Basic Security: The Wresinski Report of the Economic and Social Council of France,* and the G. de Gaulle Anthonioz-led *Report on the Evaluation of Public Policies on the Fight Against Extreme Poverty* which was adopted by the Economic and Social Council of France in 1995, the French Government drew up draft reform and programming laws on the fight against extreme poverty and exclusion, in cooperation with various institutions, social partners and associations in the country. The reform act on the fight against exclusion was adopted on July 29, 1998.
4. A place for working together with families living in extreme poverty.
5. Father Joseph Wresinski, *The Poor are the Church,* Twenty-Third Publications 2002.
6. Fr Ferrand, *Et vous que pensez-vous? L'université populaire Quart Monde,* (What do *you* Think?: The Fourth World People's University) Éd Quart Monde, Paris, 1996.
7. The theater-forum techniques were invented by A. Boal for use with very poor groups of people in Peru. In Europe, these techniques were developed by the *Centre d'Étude et de Diffusion des Techniques Actives d'Expression.*
8. L. P. Dufourny de Villiers, *Cahiers du Quatrième Ordre (Notes on the Grievances of the Fourth Order),* no. 1, April 25, 1789.
9. Father J. Wresinski, *Écrits et paroles aux volontaires (Words for Fourth World volunteer corps Members),* Éd St Paul-Quart Monde, 1992.
10. Cf. Encyclopedia Universalis, under " Université ".
11. Women at university? This was a question asked at the end of the nineteenth century by a renowned representative of the Royal Academy of Medicine. The answer to this allows us to see how far things have come since then: "Women have many more important things to do in life than study. They have to look after and bring up their children and run the household, activities which are closely connected. This is the reasoning and physiology behind the attribution of traditions to general laws of nature." (*Bulletin de l'Académie Royale de Médecine de Belgique,* 1875, p. 356)
12. And this is even more so as growing student numbers have not led to an increase in the materials and staff available to universities. As a result, there are too few lecturers for too many students. How will universities manage to select its students from those who do not have a

high school diploma, given these difficult conditions?

13. Indeed, it remains largely impossible for those without the necessary qualifications to study, and this is the case despite the fact that in France there is a system which, in theory, allows people without qualifications to receive such a training. This is what is known as the "knowledge validation" process. But this "exceptional entrance" procedure lacks transparency. Its criteria are not clearly defined and only few people take advantage of it. Very often departments of traditional disciplines, which are also the most popular ones, accept this process for first-year diplomas but show strong resistance to it when it comes to higher levels of study (B.A.s or M.A.s).

14. Paul Taylor explains: *In France, a compromise has been made to encourage access not to university itself, but to ongoing training. However, although this training would give rise to more opportunities for action to benefit society, it is difficult to gain access to it. Universities don't ask for any previous qualifications, but they do require students to be employed. So, if you are employed, you can gain access to ongoing training and, as a result, move onwards and upwards. But if you don't have a job, it's almost impossible to enter into the system in order to become employable. It's true that, in this case, the selection process is not carried out by university, but by the employers. Obviously, the young people who have done badly at school, the women who want to take up studying again or find a job and more mature students who are prepared and motivated to following a training program are victims of this two-fold discrimination.*

15. Further reading on this subject: M. David, *Témoins de l'impossible. Militants du monde ouvrier à l'Université*, (Witnesses of the Impossible: Activists from the World of Work at University) Éditions de l'Atelier, Éd. Ouvrières, 1982 ; H. Desroche, *Entreprendre d'apprendre*, (Undertaking Learning) Éditions de l'Atelier, Éd. Ouvrières, 1990 ; B. Schwartz, *Moderniser sans exclure.* (Modernizing Without Excluding) Paris, La Découverte, 1994.

Conclusion

TOWARDS THE LIBERATION
OF KNOWLEDGE

What is knowledge? The question is so vast that it overwhelmed us for a long time! Knowledge comes in multiple forms. There is not only knowledge, but skills. There are "recognized" skills, which are learned at school, at university and in books. And then there are the skills that come from life experience, personal experience or joint action. We had to recognize and consider these different forms of knowledge and skills.

The question also overwhelmed us because it seemed to backfire on itself, as though caught in its own trap: how can we *know* what *knowledge* is? The subject of our research—knowledge and skills—was also what we required to carry it out. Whilst trying to understand, we had to ask ourselves what we were doing, go back over our discussions and our very different ways of tackling the subject. All of us, whether activists, members of the Fourth World volunteer corps or academics, had preconceived ideas and specific expectations. These ideas and expectations had to withstand the test of the group and confrontation, the fruitful test of contradiction.

Our journey was sometimes arduous and sometimes hazy, with the odd bright patch. The further we went, the more we felt that the knowledge on knowledge that we were producing was something which belonged to everyone—a common form of knowledge. It was this that helped us discover and experience what we believed to be an essential idea about knowledge, i.e. that knowledge equals *relationships*. It is formed together with others and exchanged and shared with others.

Naturally, we have not said all there is to say about knowledge! We have chosen and given priority to what seemed to be the most important ideas and which clearly reflected our working hypothesis: *having access to recognized skills is essential, but, for knowledge to be liberating, it must be linked to values, action and future plans.* Can knowledge be *liberating* and, if so, under which conditions?

This question constituted the crux of our memoir, determining its meaning, pace and structure. Knowledge is neither free nor enslaved but what we make of it. As a result, what can be done for it to be liberating and not oppressive, as we would like it to be?

During the first few months, our research hit upon a single and antagonistic representation of knowledge. This was synonymous with academic knowledge, something which the activists overestimated and the academics underestimated. A letter written by the activists to the academics clarified the situation with the help of a diagram setting out the two different types of knowledge—practical and theoretical—and by indicating a third type, which was harder to place within the diagram. This was knowledge born of action, generally associated with the work of the Fourth World volunteer corps members. The aim of the diagram was not only to identify these knowledge types, but also to put them into context together and thus see how they interact and work together.

First diagram based on two forms of knowledge
(letter written by the activists on 5/02/97)

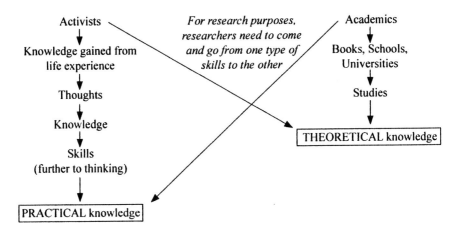

The center of the diagram features the words: *For research purposes, researchers need to come and go from one type of skills to the other*. In the original diagram, this sentence was written along the arrow which goes from the academics to the practical skills, but this coming and going is also true of the activists. In the letter which went with this diagram they wrote the following:

> For us to become researchers, it would seem that we need . . . to be able to access your ground. . . . If we don't use theory, we are not real researchers. This goes both ways. For real knowledge merging to take place, we need reciprocity and acceptance that one group will enter the ground of the other, and vice versa.

The diagram was backed up by relating it to Plato's Myth of the Cave[1].

The difficulty of where to situate the Fourth World volunteer corps member's diagram of knowledge born of action can be seen as the result of a division which is too clear-cut into two opposite poles. The force of one of the two poles hides the importance of a third pole—which is the interaction between them. Forming this third, more mobile pole, required specific knowledge. Little by little, it gradually became a third form of knowledge called knowledge born of commitment. It was an essential form of knowledge as it connected the two other forms.

In addition, two months later, the activists came up with their second diagram which served as an outline for our work and a map to help us guide our way through the research process.

Second diagram on three forms of knowledge
(letter written by the activists on 14/04/1997)

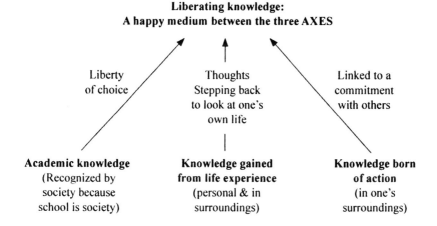

This diagram aims to show:

– that school and recognized skills are essential for the road to liberation (1st axis);

– that personal knowledge gained from experience in one's own surroundings leads people to think about and take a step back to look at their lives (2nd axis);

– that knowledge born of action affords a commitment (or not) with others (3rd axis).

These three elements are essential for there to be such a thing as liberating knowledge. The activists explained this in the accompanying letter to the second diagram:

Harmony between these three forms of knowledge would seem to be the precondition for knowledge to be liberating. This seems to be true for all social spheres, not just for the poorest.

The transition from the first to the second diagram principally represented the transition from two to three forms of knowledge. In the second diagram, even if every group holds more of one type of knowledge or another, the knowledge types are not mutually exclusive. Setting out the relationship between these knowledge types as such, shows that each person can draw on the three in order to take action. The combination of these knowledge types to form liberating knowledge should therefore take place within the individuals, within the groups they belong to and within society as a whole. This threefold challenge means that this combination has a permanent and never-ending role.

By placing the three knowledge types on the same level, the second diagram makes them equal and calls for their full recognition in society. But this does not mean that the social inequality and power struggles which stand in the way of the realization of this ideal should be forgotten. This hierarchy gives social priority to academic knowledge, which is held in higher esteem than the personal knowledge gained from life experience. Therefore, the knowledge born of commitment of those who have academic knowledge and those who have knowledge gained from life experience is not the same. For those with academic knowledge, knowledge born of commitment is about the difficult acquisition of solidarity knowledge. For those who are rich in knowledge gained from life experience but poor in academic knowledge, the knowledge born of commitment is about the equally difficult acquisition of a more abstract type of formal expression. There is thus the need to learn from each other. This would be impossible alone, but possible when encountering a confrontation of knowledge. These differences represent an opportunity and strength because they allow everyone to teach others.

The following words encapsulate our personal and collective attitude based on the research that we have carried out.

> *Knowing ignorance,*
> *Knowing differently,*
> *Different types of knowledge,*
> *Let it out and hold on to it,*
> *Keep going and make your mark!*

Note

1. This myth can be seen as the first attempt at a process of ongoing training. The idea was to free people who were chained up at the back of a cave by creating a long, educational circuit to show them theoretical knowledge, symbolized by the sun. (G. Pineau, *La formation permanente : vie d'un mythe*, (Ongoing Training: The Life of a Myth) in *Éducation Permanente*, 1989, no. 98, pp. 89-99).

Appendix

The interviews

The people interviewed were people who the group's activists knew and who had been told about the Fourth World–University project. The activists sometimes had to go back to the same people on several occasions to ask for further information. 17 interviews were recorded and deciphered. A school principle was also interviewed.

The Fourth World volunteer corps member carried out four interviews: one with a person of Spanish origin who had low school attendance because her family were poor; one with a regional counselor who said that he had learned the importance of knowledge and culture for very poor families; and two with a couple who spoke of their participation in the Fourth World People's University.

No.	First name	Age	No. of children	Socio-professional status	Qualifications
1.	Pierre	46	6	Disabled	Elementary school diploma
2.	Robert	46	2	Disabled	Fishing certificate
3.	Marc	27	3	Temp worker	Painting course certificate
4.	Carole	33	1	Cleaning lady	No qualifications
5.	Monique	46	7	No profession	No qualifications
6.	Muriel	17		At school	
7.	Brigitte	26		No profession	No qualifications
8.	Amar	50	3	Unemployed	
9.	Bernadette	55		Disabled	Elementary school diploma
10.	Paule	57	9	No profession	No qualifications
11.	Laura	19		At school	
12.	André	75	12	Retired	No qualifications
13.	Henri	72	2	Retired	No qualifications
14.	Marie	60	12	No profession	No qualifications
15.	Patricia	14		At school	
16.	Mélaine	7		At school	
17.	Gilles	34		No profession	No qualifications
18.	Carmen	50	3	At-home mother	Sewing course certificate
19.	Hélène	35	3	At-home mother	No qualifications
20.	Francis	60	?	Elected representative	?
21.	Roger	35	3	Unemployed	No qualifications

Texts brought in by the academics

Astolfi, J.-P., *L'école pour apprendre,* Paris, ESF, 1992, pp. 67-71. On the difference between skills information and knowledge.

Dubet, F., "Action et autoréflexion " in *Raisons Pratiques,* 1990, pp. 171-193. A study on the relationship between a researcher and his subjects.

Freire, P., " La conception " bancaire " de l'éducation comme instrument de l'oppression " in *Pédagogie des opprimés,* Paris, Maspero, 1977, pp. 71-81. Criticism on the dehumanizing aspects of education and the possibility of an "awareness-raising education".

Freire, P., "Le dialogue, essence de l'éducation comme pratique de la liberté ", in *Pédagogie des opprimés,* Paris, Maspero, 1977, pp. 71-81. On the relationship between dialogue, knowledge and freedom.

Knowles, M., *L'apprenant adulte,* Paris, Éditions de l'organisation, 1990. The theory of adult learning: andragogy.

Kolb, D., *"Cercle d'apprentissage"* in Experimental learning, PTR Terence Hall, 1976. Modeling technique on the various stages of learning.

Michaux, H., Poteaux d'angle, Paris, Editions Gallimard, 1981. On knowledge-ignorance.

Pineau, G., "Dialectique de lecture en formation permanente" in Masseyforder, J, *Lectures et lecteurs en éducation,* Paris, L'Harmattan, 1993. A personal way of reading and writing words and the world

Rochex, J.-Y., "Ouverture: c'est de la cité qu'il s'agit" in *Savoir et citoyenneté en banlieue, Dialogue,* no. 83-84, 1996, pp. 2-6. Reflections on knowledge, failure at school and collective learning.

Schön, D., *Le tournant réflexif,* Montréal, Éditions Logiques, 1996, pp. 17-36. Or how to help people discover what they already know and they way in which they use their knowledge.

Sugier, C., *Haïti, terre cassée,* Paris, L'Harmattan, 1996, pp. 7-11. An example of thoughts on vital life experience.

Taylor, P., *La méthode Paulo Freire.* A brief introduction to the Freire method and the idea of awareness-raising

Van Turenhoudt, S., *Gérer une pédagogie différenciée,* Bruxelles, De Boeck, 1989. On the hows and whys of working on our representations.

IV

WORK AND HUMAN ACTIVITY: HIDDEN TALENTS

The poorest as workers: Skills that should be known about and recognized

by Didier Clerbois, Marc Couillard, Hector Guichart,
Luigi Mosca, Ides Nicaise, Jacques Ogier
and Jean-Maurice Verdier.

With contributions from Daniel Cornerotte and Françoise Ferrand.

WORK AND HUMAN ACTIVITY: HIDDEN TALENTS

Introduction

Work and the future of work are currently a central topic in debates on the future of society. In developed countries, they are perhaps the essential feature of social issues. Since industrialization, societies in these countries have become salaried societies, constructed on the basis of employers and salaried employees. To a large extent, work even today determines each person's role in society. It gives them a social status, identity and dignity, as well as protection when life takes an unpredictable turn, to the extent that work is the "great integrator", without which one is (or finds oneself) "on the scrapheap".

Work, however, is changing rapidly, shrinking but not disappearing. It is by turns becoming more varied and interesting by combining several discrete tasks, and becoming fragmentary to the point of being "bitty". It is often unstable, linked to production levels which vary with the economic climate or subject to company relocations, all of which goes hand in hand with ever-faster changes in jobs and qualifications. Stable, full-time work is disappearing and being replaced by unstable, short-term or (enforced) part-time jobs.

Job insecurity and unemployment impoverish new generations and marginalize those already rejected by the economic system even more, whereas on the whole, people are wealthier. These two factors also increase the vulnerability of people who are not guaranteed permanent social protection by their work.

Unlawful situations are on the increase, for though the shift from the collective to the individual as the basis of working relations encourages personal initiative and independence, it also favors the strongest.

At the same time, work itself is changing dramatically, away from manufacturing and material services towards relational services. This is less physically demanding but requires higher levels of relational skills and intellectual ability, and therefore training.

What place do the poor occupy against this changing backdrop? Previously, they made up the underclass, manual workers moving from job to job, unqualified and exploited, living on the fringes of industrial society (as flower-sellers, rag-and-bone men, seasonal workers, day laborers, domestic servants etc). We are told that these jobs disappeared because of changes in technology, that the minimum wage made their productivity levels untenable, that their skills had become obsolete. Should we not add to this list at least the phenomenon of the most vulnerable workers losing their jobs to stronger, fitter, better-qualified workers? There is a kind of involuntary competition among those looking for work caused by there not being enough work for everyone.

In spite of rising wealth levels, there is a question mark hanging over the solidarity displayed by the majority who finance income support (the benefits system). The system has been tightened up regarding eligibility for benefits, and people are less certain of being awarded them. Increasingly, eligibility is determined by recipients accepting a variety of non-permanent jobs, such as work placements, apprenticeships, public-private partnership schemes, sheltered workshops. Just how useful these are is not always clear, but they are used, runs the official line, to keep people occupied and stop them playing the system. Opinion is divided on these jobs : for some, they qualify as real jobs and make workers feel empowered members of society; for others, they are just low-paid temping jobs with low status and no prospect of real integration into the working world.

It appears that work will remain, at least for the time being, the basis of one's social status, whether it be salaried or self-employed. Perhaps the idea of work should be expanded to cover a broader range of activities, whether involving a contract or not, which nevertheless are recognized and subject to protection, such as jobs, training, volunteer work etc. In France, this track was partially explored in the Boissonnat Report[1] on the future of work. In this context, how can we ensure that the poorest are not consigned to simply menial jobs?

Let us begin by getting to the crux of the issue. Can we hope the poor will break free of the cycle of unstable jobs, whether these be market-governed or subsidized? Will they be able to regain a footing in trades and sectors with better prospects?

Some think that what is most important is redistributing work fairly throughout all levels of society. If managed correctly, job-sharing could contribute to reducing layoff and lightening the burden on the most vulnerable groups. The 35-hour week, (re)introduced by the French government, was a step in this direction. Could this provide a hope for the poorest?

Others suggest better arming jobseekers to find work, mainly through education/training. The issue then arises of how accessible these training programs are, given that in the past they tended rather to increase inequality since they were too academic in nature. Currently, there is a gradual trend for training programs to make use of what people already know and can do. They are moving away from the purely intellectual knowledge dominated by the middle- and upper-classes. People's personal strengths, such as initiative, adaptability to different situations and ability to care for others and their development are becoming real boons in jobs involving welcome, advising and coaching. New niche sectors are opening up, in which social skills are more highly valued.

Taking due account of all the options put forward, we opted for a third way which we think complements rather than contradicts the others. It involves discovering new jobs and markets based on the skills the poorest already possess. The poor and very poor have always found ways to earn money and build a community allowing them to adapt as best they can to unfavorable circumstances, make ends meet for their families and support their neighbors and friends. To do so, they have come up with or adapted particular skills. People working alongside them bear witness to these skills, sometimes even revealing them to the rest of the world.

What are these skills? We will start by describing the skills revealed through our interviews with people living in extreme poverty and a range of reading material (Chapter 1). These skills will be analyzed in Chapter 2, where we address in particular their specific nature and relationship to experiences of poverty.

In Chapter 3 we will look at issues relating to education and training, without which skills risk being marginalized. How can education and training be made more accessible and more effective?

Finally, Chapter 4 will be dealing with the recognition of these skills at personal, collective and official levels in both formal and informal contexts, both in the world of school and the world of work.

Our analysis is limited to the situation in Belgium and France. Though it is incontestable that the globalization of the labor market is a major factor influencing the situation of the poorest in our countries, and though there are similarities between their skills and those of people in the Third World (for example, scrap metal recovery), nevertheless we had to take into account this project's time constraints and limited funding. We therefore decided not to study the links between the occupations practiced by the poorest outside our own countries.

Note

1. J. Boissonnat. Report of the Committee, *Work in twenty years' time*, General Commissariat, Editions Odile Jacob/La Documentation Française, 1995

Methodology

The choice of methodology was particularly important in our joint research project, our goal being to arrive at a new form of knowledge whose originality lay in bringing together the life experiences of the poorest, the experiences of those who are engaged with them, and a scientific approach.

Everyone was aware of the importance of the method from the outset, though that did not make the problems we encountered any easier to deal with.

Our group's subject was Work and Human Activity. Choosing a specific topic within this main topic (the skills of the poorest in an ever-changing society) required us all to throw our hats into the ring and combine our approaches, which was a rewarding experience for all of us.

Choosing a thematic

Our group, *Work and Human Activity*, was set the task of drawing up a research framework which took into account all the agent-authors'* suggestions: dignity and work; thoughts on human activity and common property; the right to work; the question of whether social recognition linked to salaried or paid employment?

The activists* suggested using the working situations of people they knew as a starting-block. Most are not salaried workers, but do work nevertheless. Using specific examples, they listed the skills of some poor people: recovering scrap metal, recycling, welcome, coaching, amongst others. This was why the activists wanted to use the skills of the poor as a basis for the research. They asked a question to be investigated: *Do the poorest have useful skills (they can practice and pass on to others) in building the society of tomorrow?* One academic suggested: *In a changing society, what are the human activities which are (or should be) recognized, which give people social dignity on an individual and collective level?* Another academic suggested: *Competitiveness or solidarity?* The Fourth World volunteer corps member* put the research question this way:

In a society which can no longer provide paid employment for all, to what means do the poorest have recourse to provide for themselves and their families, and to preserve a sense of personal dignity and public recognition of their acting in the common weal?

The academics took issue with the term *skills,* used by the activists. One academic found the question *interesting but too narrow,* and wished to broaden the research to cover new professions and qualifications. The Fourth World volunteer corps member feared that these would then be restricted to the poor, who would become trapped in marginalized, dead-end jobs. The activists suggested four approaches to their question: seeking out and learning about the skills of the poorest; asking who decides if these skills are useful or not; learning about and understanding the economic context (businesses, financial markets etc); and asking how the skills of the poorest can be exercised and passed on to others.

The key terms used in our research are: skills, usefulness and recognition. The term *skills* was accepted as the starting-block for the research.

After discussions, the research question was formulated thus: *Are the skills of the poorest useful in society and how might they be recognized?* After discussion with the rest of the project participants, we arrived at the following hypothesis: *For the poorest to be recognized as workers, it is necessary for their skills to be known about and included in the new training courses and qualifications which are useful to our changing society.*

Collecting data and research tools

All members of the group took part in collecting data, either in the form of interviews[1], lectures[2] or by contributing articles, journals and mini-presentations[3].

At the start of the research, one academic suggested compiling a fairly systematic bibliography of texts in the area of our research. The activists and the Fourth World volunteer corps member, seeing the scale of the works the academics were quoting, said that such a list was pointless, since they did not have the time to read them and doubted they were up to the task. The bibliography is therefore limited to the works and articles actually used in the research[4].

The same academic suggested the group compile a glossary in order to give precise definitions of the terms used, particularly of the key words *work* (paid or salaried), *human activity, skills, ability, trade/job* etc. He would have liked the group to define these terms together. The point of the research was to use the real life experiences of the poorest as a springboard to thought rather than start from abstract definitions. However, some terms did need to be defined as research progressed.

Conceiving the memoir outline

Our memoir outline was drawn up together on the basis of the fully recorded group discussion exchanges.

Discussion of the data

Data were first presented and analyzed by the person who had collected them (by writing a summary or presenting the main thrust of an article or book, or extracting important passages from an interview). The fruit of their labors was then given to each member of the group. Each member worked individually to analyze the material (except the activists, who always worked together). During subsequent meetings, we compared our points of view and analyses (these discussions were recorded and deciphered[5]). During the debate, we merged our knowledge in a meeting of minds where different interpretations combined, complemented and challenged one another.

Drawing up the memoir outline

Using the analyses we had carried out together, the group as a whole drew up a first draft for the research outline. Then, based on this, we discussed various suggestions for the draft by mail, resulting in a second draft, which defined the subtopics and their interrelations.

Cutting out excerpts from the decipherings (classification)

The recordings and decipherings of our discussions are a written record and served as a support for the sessions where we shared our thoughts. The activists would later take each-one of the decipherings, cut passages out of it and catalogue them in the files according to the overall outline for the memoir. The same passage is sometimes found in several files, since the subjects of the various chapters are not strictly separated.

Together, we subsequently checked the distribution of what had been cut out to ensure that the detailed outline for our memoir corresponded to our question. This allowed us both to make any potential adjustments to the outline and to reclassify passages which were more relevant to a different chapter.

The detailed outline

The detailed chapter-by-chapter outline was then drawn up during the meetings preceding the writing phase, based on the excerpts cut out of the decipherings by the activists. Thus, we were able to add different people's contributions right up until the end of the project.

Collaborative writing

This was probably the part of writing the memoir that was least easy to begin with, compared to the other aspects of our joint project. The three activists started by drawing attention to their unfamiliarity with this kind of exercise. This gave rise to a debate which resurfaced numerous times, and during which it was established that the activists did indeed have experience in writing texts, such as reports or summaries of interviews, and that writing the memoir was the natural continuation of what they had done until then.

The three academics also had problems agreeing on a joint text. The situation was resolved by debating the writing strategy. It changed in a fairly pragmatic way, becoming a very fair sharing-out of the various points in the outline for the memoir (itself written jointly) among the group members for a first draft. The Table of Contents indicates the authors of each section.

This stage of the writing benefited greatly from cutting out excerpts of the decipherings of our group meetings, mentioned above.

Each contribution was then systematically given out to each member of the group to allow everyone to undertake their own critical reading of the text.

During the writing phase, the group experienced some serious and passionate debates. For example, over the word "recognition". Is recognition about seeking out resemblances or accepting differences[6]? Since the activists were in charge of writing the first draft of this section, they opted for the former definition, arguing that in situations of extreme poverty, what people suffer from most is being considered as different. For the academics, recognition was first and foremost synonymous with tolerance and respect for differences, whether cultural, social, racial, etc.

Taking time to discuss all the remarks and suggestions allowed us to proceed to subsequent drafts, and eventually, to the final version of the memoir.

Notes

1. Interviews, see annex p. 425.
2. Lectures by Lucie Ribert, Emile Creutz and Emilie Bourtet. See General Introduction, and group lectures, see annex, p. 423.
3. See annex p.423.
4. See annex p.423.
5. For recordings and decipherings, see General Introduction.
6. This debate is described in Chapter 4, p. 409.

Chapter 1

A DESCRIPTION OF SOME SKILLS

Do people living in extreme poverty have particular skills linked to their life experiences? At first sight, we might assume that their skills are mainly a matter of "getting by", honed through their daily struggle against poverty. Is this always the case, or do they have more original and complex abilities? And even if they are "getting by", can we imagine this becoming a skill they could use at work?

We will first tackle this issue by sketching some portraits of people living in poverty, focusing on describing what they do, whether work- or home-related, or voluntary. We draw our information from the interviews, mainly carried out by the activists amongst people they know, from lectures and from the texts we read. The range of skills described is undoubtedly far from complete, but serves as an example. We simply wanted to reflect a measure of the diversity of skills by sector.

The interviews and texts will form the basis of the analyses in the subsequent chapters.

Scrap metal recovery

Marcel[1] is 56, and lives with his family in a deprived area of Brussels.

His father died when he was 10, and his mother was left alone with three children. Life was tough. He is married and has five children aged between 10 and 29, and six grandchildren. He has worked for two scrap metal merchants. For a while, he worked for the local Highways department.

His grandmother gave him the idea of collecting scrap metal. She used to pick up the empty crates from markets after they had finished, take out the nails and keep them in a box to resell them. She turned the crates into firewood which she sold in bags of 20-25kg (44-55 lbs).

Like all those who collect scrap metal, Marcel is nicknamed *biffin* (rag-and-bone-man). He walks the streets of Brussels all day with his handcart in tow. He collects old refrigerators, washing machines, stoves and metal (copper, zinc, lead, aluminum, iron etc). When he gets home, he strips and sorts the metal. For example, he collects all the electric cables and spools, and lights a fire to burn the casing around the copper insides. This is important because he can sell copper cleaned in this way to the scrap metal merchant for a higher price. Another example is when he is stripping a machine and comes across some mercury, he carefully collects it in a container, and when he has a certain amount, he sells it for a good price (around 100 Belgian Francs (BEF)[2] per kilo, or $ 6.60 per lb).

If he takes an unstripped machine to the scrap metal merchant, it sells for the price of scrap, that is, 2 BEF per kilo. If he strips it down, however, the engine is worth between 3 and 4 BEF per kilo, aluminum between 15 and 18 BEF per kilo, etc.

The price of the metals changes with the going rate on the Stock Exchange, so Marcel follows the market every day.

He has been treading the streets of Brussels for 20 years now. People know him, and call out to him when they have something they want to get rid of. He works with his family, without a truck—just the handcart and his hands.

Scrap metal merchants have been forced to leave central Brussels and set up shop on the outskirts. In order to store his metal, Marcel has to have a skip in his yard, and a truck belonging to the scrap dealer comes and collects it when it is full. He rents the skip.

Previously he used to collect paper and cardboard, but at the moment there is no money in it.

Marcel has friends who collect other things. Some collect objects and sell them on in junk shops. Others collect glass bottles to get the money for returning them.

There are people who collect wood in the streets. For some it is firewood. One man sorts the wood and uses the best bits to make toys and model furniture for children's dolls, reminiscent of the African children who also use what they find (such as jam-jars, iron wire, corks etc) to make toys.

Repairing and mending

Mr. Gérard[3] is 48, married with four children and two grandchildren.

He started work at 14 in the construction industry, then spent eight years in the metalworking trade before moving to Brussels in 1973. He has been unemployed since 1983.

About 20 years ago, one of his children fell ill at the age of two and had to spend time in hospital. When the child returned home, he kept asking for the cartoons he had seen on the television in the hospital crèche. Mr. Gérard could not afford to buy a new television set, so bought a second-hand one which soon stopped working. He could not afford to have it repaired, so tried to do it himself. A television shop owner showed him how to read a diagram and track down the fault.

Now, he collects televisions he finds in garbage cans and skips. People with little money bring their televisions to him to have them repaired. He uses diagrams to find the fault—every brand of television has its own diagram. Mr. Gérard has most of them. *The sound's on one side, the circuit controlling the volume on another, and there's also the high-voltage circuit which controls the picture tube. Everything in a TV set is divided into sectors, you just need to know them.* Using a digital gauge with an instant display, he measures the tension (the voltage), the power, resistance, etc.

He also repairs video recorders, hi-fis and domestic appliances. For example, he found a set of two hot plates in a skip, cleaned them and checked them over. The bigger plate was in good working order, but the smaller one was disconnected. For his own safety, he chose not to reconnect it. He also found a deep-fat fryer in a garbage can, and took it home with him. He took three days to clean and scour it and make it good as new. Afterwards, it worked.

When appliances cannot be repaired, he removes the parts which still work (complete circuits, transistors, diodes, condensers etc) and which can be used elsewhere: *I take out anything with copper in it, too, like transformers, vents, spools or electric wires. I sell the bits to the scrap metal merchant.* He does his repairs and mending at his home, in a cellar which serves as his workshop. One of his sons and a family friend help him.

Gérard says that he does it partly to make ends meet, and also because he is against waste and the consumer society which encourages people to throw things away and buy new things.

There are other types of repair work—for example, one man collects and repairs stoves and gas ovens.

Building and renovation

Building and renovation skills are only explicitly mentioned in one of the interviews, but this example is very interesting and revealing.

Luc Lefevre[4] got straight to the point by describing the way his family's house was built:

> My parents built this house with some friends. It took three years. My father (who was already working at an ironmonger's) worked on the house after his regular job, and he dug the foundations, too. He cut the wood himself for the joinery, and as he was working for G, he stayed friends with him. They took a truck and got the wood my father had cut down, then cut it up to do the joinery.

He continued by developing a reflection on this situation:

> That's why I think that stories of bravery are in the workplaces of the poorest, and also everywhere they fight to survive. Everything which is set-up is a way of fighting poverty. The problem is that these means of fighting poverty aren't recognized— that's the particular knowledge of the poor.

The interview then revealed the multi-faceted and multi-functional nature of the Lefevre household—for example, how welcoming it was: *There were us three children, but there were always more than that in the house because there were always people living with us*; there was a workshop: *we made a forge in the house, with an anvil*; and even small-scale agriculture: *later, we bred chickens . . . the kitchen garden . . . we bought some chicks and my father made incubators with big boxes that had been used to store sauerkraut.*

It was by starting from all this experience, already lived by him when he was young, that Luc Lefevre acquired the skills and beliefs which prompted the "55 affair" and the association which he went on to found, Struggle, Solidarity and Work (LST)[5].

He continued:

> There's loads of social services with big ambitions for poor families to fight poverty, but it's all just hot air because the people who have to fight poverty most are the poor themselves, and that's their most important job which is not recognized . . . but as long as it is not recognized, nothing will be possible. . . .

Out of solidarity, he left to live at *the 55* in Namur, where around 200 very poor people lived until the owner decided to demolish the site. Luc and some others formed LST to oppose the destruction of the *55*.

> So we squatted. We renovated the houses so they were livable as they stood, since we had no more money. We couldn't afford to spend much and we lived in these houses . . . we squatted for five years, which is the time it took for the people to find somewhere else to live. And that's how LST was born. At the same time, we struck up contacts with other families who had been evicted.
>
> After eight years with no legal status, some of the workers said, "we've had it up to here with being treated like idiots by the CPAS[6], we want to prove we're workers, that we can actively show solidarity in our work and training. We want a real wage that entitles us to family allowances and benefits." That's when we decided to become recognized in law, we started a non-profit[7]. Actually, the cooperative wanted to implement our motto "We are workers" by having a business like any ordinary business. . . . In the cooperative statutes, we wrote that the tool we made together is a tool which is not only accessible to the weakest, but also a tool that can be used by the weakest. . . . Out of 11 people we've currently got Pierre working for us, who's trained as an engineer, he's a friend, and Paul, who was long-term unemployed but worked a lot as a plumber earlier on; he's our union rep. The others are people from poor backgrounds who have learned on the hoof working in the cooperative and who have a past of resistance to poverty.

Welcome and coaching

I come from C. and I do nothing, said Jacqueline Meton[8] when asked to introduce herself, before adding, as if by way of excuse, *I've had angina.*

Jacqueline did not really have a childhood. Her parents were constantly at each others' throats. She always felt rejected by everyone. She has not been able to eat properly since she was six. A friend from the Christian Workers' Youth (JOC), whose mother had died, invited her to spend her weekends at her home to give her a hand. Her father was a miner, and there were 10 children in the family. *We laugh about it now, but when I arrived, it was a nightmare and no mistake. We started doing the washing, the ironing and mending when I was 12 and had just taken the JOC promise.* When she was 13, she left school to work as a charlady in a children's care home. Later, she and her husband worked as janitors in a special school, most of whose pupils were poor. Officially she worked three hours a day, but in reality it was more like eight, from washing-up to home visits and watching over the children as they got on the bus. And all the while she had several young children of her own to look after.

Today, the couple receive disability benefit and Jacqueline Meton helps anyone who knocks on her door. *They know that if the light's on, they can ring the bell . . .*: a young homeless man, pushed from one CPAS office to another, a neighbor in conflict with his landlord, a man whose brother had been arrested with no papers, a young mother on her own with nowhere to live and in serious financial difficulty, or a dying woman living in a run-down apartment with her child.

Jacqueline's commitment and activism have won her favor with the social services, even the mayor's office, and often mean she wins her case, though it is not guaranteed. Her husband and children just have to put up with it. Her skills have been gained on the hoof, and they include:

– familiarity with official channels, such as the CPAS, the mayor and the police, and unofficial sources of help, such as networks of relatives and safe houses in the town;

– charisma, negotiating skills: *You need to be able to parley, you see, If that doesn't work, you go up a level.*

– a good helping of psychology:

> Yes, if I don't do it, people stay as they are, they won't move. They'll just get worse. You have to go along with them as soon as they start moving. I don't mind going once or twice, but afterwards you do have to think about it.

These skills are complemented by a strong sense of injustice and if need be a sort of brotherhood -acquired through her own experience of poverty and rejection—and a feeling of civic responsibility: *If they can't go, no one's going to help them. Society won't come and do it for them.*

Jacqueline Meton may be an exception, but she is certainly not alone. Jean[9], an unemployed bachelor with no qualifications, was put in care, saw his parents' marriage break down, has had financial difficulties and has been homeless. Recently he has started volunteering, recruiting children from deprived areas for cultural workshops (cooking, IT, painting etc), as part of a *Summer Street Festival** organized by ATD Fourth World in his town. He went door-to-door asking parents if their children could take part. He justified his doing this by saying that he had no particular skills he could use to run a workshop. However, though he had no family of his own, he had often taken care of his nieces and he felt comfortable *dealing with people*. He said you need *tact, don't interfere in people's private lives, and take your time.*

Today, the *commune* continues to organize these summer activities for children. The organizers are paid, and he is not able to get involved. Workshops no longer take place in the street, but indoors. No one goes door-to-door to recruit children, but Jean still goes to see families in difficult circumstances in his area, so they are not alone.

Paul Linden[10] and some unemployed friends on the minimex[11] or disability benefit started a non-profit organization which provides material aid such as clothes, food and legal advice to the homeless, and which ran an emergency housing center. Paul himself was taken into care and had to leave school at 15:

> My dream was to study law but I wasn't able to stay on at school after 15 for family reasons. Otherwise, all my skills come from my experiences on the ground, because what I know is that people who want to be helped will never come to you. You have to go to them.

His legal knowledge may be less than complete, but his skills are no less developed for that. He has acquired listening and people skills which no university teaches.

> Not everyone finds it easy to listen to those around them and reach out to them when they need it. You need to be a bit of a psychologist for this, and in particular you need to learn on the job. You won't learn what life is really about by sitting on a chair all day long in some office.

Paul Linden has life experience he can draw on. As a father, he found himself on the street with his children after a fire damaged their family home.

His work meets with mixed reactions from those around him. He was refused unemployment benefit for three months because he was working with the non-profit organization as a volunteer. He finally won his case at an industrial tribunal. The housing center was not recognized by the authorities for safety reasons. However, 25 people were put up there in one year, and when the police found someone in the street, they would take them there. The center finally closed on June 30, 1997 for lack of funding. Paul Linden continues his other work helping and coaching people, encouraged by *the children's smiles*.

Mr. Gérard spent part of his life living in slums, shelters and refuges of all kinds. He cannot help himself welcoming anyone who knocks at his door, either.

> We've been there too, we found ourselves on the street when my wife was pregnant. We've been through it, so we understand it better. We can't help ourselves.

Hector[12]** also lived on the street for a while, 15 years ago now. Since then, he has started helping other homeless people at the CPAS to receive housing and the minimex. *I remember where I used to live, I got 27 people in four years.* He goes to the railway station regularly, where the homeless live together and receive the *minimex de rue* (homeless persons' minimex). The *commune* recently appointed two social workers to act as intermediaries, seeking out the homeless on the streets. *They do not know what it's like on the street* says Hector, who advocates that people who have themselves experienced poverty and vagrancy should be employed to do this job. His friend Maurice[13] adds: *200 yards from the CPAS office there are people sleeping on benches during the day and the social workers don't see them.*

Anne[14] is a young mother from a poor background. The nurse in charge of an ONE (Office for Births and Childhood) perinatal consultation center invited her to greet visitors once a week, on a voluntary basis. Anne's job was to create a welcoming atmosphere, especially for families who felt judged, uncomfortable or that they were being "stared at". She greeted them, took their names down in the files, weighed their children and took them back to their parents in the waiting room. She made time to chat to them briefly, in as friendly a tone as she could.

The center manager[15] highlighted the qualities required for this kind of work: reliability, an ability to relate to people and basic administrative skills. It's being able to relate to people that is really important, maybe to make up for the duty doctor, who usually used to greet patients by ringing his bell. And beyond that, people identify with a young mother who has asked herself a thousand questions about her children's health, all the while struggling to get by while living in poverty.

Library outreach workers

Being a library outreach worker was a job experimented with in France in the early 1990s by ATD Fourth World in partnership with the Ministry of Culture, with 16 young people from impoverished, immigrant or Fourth World volunteer corps backgrounds. Claudine and Valérie are both library outreach workers. Claudine is from a family living in poverty, while Valérie is from a working-class family of Spanish immigrants and is a member of the Fourth World volunteer corps.

Claudine: Being a library outreach worker should be about building a bridge between libraries and children and their families in poor areas.

(Poor children) also have the right to read books and use libraries, visit museums where there are fish or things like that, discover all sorts of things. Because most of them stay at home, they don't move, they don't want to go out. They're a bit frightened. Sometimes they're a bit ashamed to go to the library because they can't read. So I tell them when I was their age, I was the same, I didn't dare go to the library, I was afraid, I couldn't read.

Then I learned with them[16].

Valérie: For me, being an outreach worker at the public library is being there for poor and very poor children, young people and adults who don't have access to books. Because most of them aren't used to having books at home. They can't afford them. Or because they're not used to having them, and don't dare go to the library.

You have to be welcoming: make yourself available, listen, adapt to the situation, try and do what people want, etc. And you have to constantly ask yourself: are the poorest children, young people or adults coming? What can we do to welcome them, make them feel comfortable and at ease and make them want to come back again?[17]

Being a library outreach worker is also about:
– making books and the other services offered by libraries more accessible to the poorest children;
– encouraging these children to look at and read factual or story books;
– inviting them to related activities (e.g. storytelling);
–making reading as simple, enjoyable and enriching an activity as possible;
–making them feel at home in the library and confident in themselves and those around them so that they will eventually enjoy coming and can be as independent as any other member of the library.

The library outreach workers mainly use "street libraries" in their work. This is where children can discover the joys of reading before braving a public library:

Valérie: As soon as the weather was good enough I invited the children to go and sit outside, just outside the building. We benefited from some of the plus points of street libraries that are lost when you're inside, for example the children feel freer to stay or leave as they please. Whereas inside, you have to open and shut the door, and then you're inside afterwards. That makes a big difference for the children. When you're outside, you're somewhere you know and feel at home[18].

Claudine: I started working with children from the local area. It didn't go very well at first because they didn't know me from Adam. It was only to be expected that they and their families should be suspicious. I had no contact with their families. It was quite hard with the children. But by being there every day, seeing the children, trying to start running the street libraries to be outside with them, being just next to the library but also right near where they lived, our rapport improved.

The hardest thing was to get children from the estate behind the library and children from P Street to come together, because they couldn't stand each other. They never stopped fighting and exchanging insults. Even their parents were the same with one other. But I managed to get the kids together. I managed it in time for the *Summer Street Festival** by getting them to put on a short play together. And after that they started to get on better and do things together[19].

But library outreach workers really come into their own in terms of using knowledge garnered from their own experience and personal background:

Sylvie is 11, from a very poor French family. I could see that she was quite poor from her clothes, the way she behaved and mainly from her face, which already bore the marks of a difficult life. When Sylvie was living in B, she used to come to the public library from time to time. She had no library card, but she came with her friend who borrowed books. While her friend Christine was choosing books to borrow, Sylvie would be looking at the books on the shelves. She would take one or two down, flick through them and put them back again. When she saw me, she avoided meeting my eye. She knew I worked in the library—maybe that was why she was afraid of me and avoided me every time. I tried to speak to her several times. I didn't have much success to begin with. Then one day she was feeling more confident, and after three or four weeks she talked to me. I was so happy to be able to tell her about how the books were shelved and where they were put, and I felt that was one of the jobs of a library outreach worker[20].

Experts by experience[21]

Inspired by the De Cirkel association, at the end of 1992 the European Commission Horizon program began funding a successful experiment in Anvers (Belgium) with Kind en Gezin[22], a public service responsible for child benefit and parental support, organizing consultations and home visits, with particular focus on families in difficulty. The Kind en Gezin manager, who was opposed to children being put into care, participated enthusiastically in the project.

There were two goals. One was to better adapt the service to the real needs of the poorest families by improving communication between them and nursing social workers, with the help of women from poor backgrounds who knew how poor families felt, what their ambitions were and how they survived. The other was to offer them the opportunity for professional training courses selected and paid for by Kind en Gezin. The women accepted the offer because as one of them said: *it was mainly to show I won't be beaten by the injustice I've suffered* and because she has *had so much experience with this service*[23].

Ten women were therefore recruited to take part in the program. They had few or no professional qualifications and were long-term unemployed who lived in or were familiar enough with a poor neighborhood, but capable of distancing themselves enough from their own situations and thinking about them. They were taken on at two-thirds time.

They completed a twelve-week training course designed to complement their life experiences, and so help them work as mediators between families and nurses, by teaching them about preventative care, the work of medical-social workers, situations of poverty and the help families can receive with.

This was carried out in tandem with the Kind en Gezin nursing social workers, and the results are already visible: knowledge and skills were shared between people with a lot of experiences and professional nursing social workers, and the women who took part could live more securely on what they were paid—eight of them in fact now work with Kind en Gezin. Most of all, there was a marked improvement in the relationships between the families and the social services, who were often dreaded in the past, but who no longer provoked the same fear as they once did, due to their better understanding of the families' situations, their needs and their fear of their children being taken into care. This improved understanding was due to the women from poor backgrounds. The families' trust in the women meant the latter could more easily teach the mothers how to look after and raise their children and avoid having them taken into care, even if one did say *being taken into care isn't always necessarily a bad thing for a child* and added *social workers have to be more diplomatic when giving someone bad news for example—though we can* be more direct because we're closer to them[24].

We should not underestimate some people's reluctance to accept "experts by experience", who are closer to their "clients" and inclined to mix their work and their personal lives. The opposite is also true, there being a risk that the experts gradually become more and more distanced from their roots. But the experiment was judged sufficiently successful by some of the participants that it seemed a good idea to extend the project to men. The nursing social workers were satisfied with the contribution made by the women experts, on the whole. The families themselves appreciated the latter, since they could have more straightforward relationships with them and often felt more confident with the social services through their contact with the experts. For example, one *mother at the start was always upset when an electricity bill arrived. She would put the bill in a drawer and close it. Now, she does something about it, on her own*[25].

These results prompted a second project, still at the conception stage, in which 15 people will follow a course, 10 of whom will be employed afterwards, possibly full-time. They will have the same duties as before, plus they will help run courses for young and future mothers.

The job of an "expert by experience" will thus be incorporated into other institutions in Anvers and elsewhere. There is even a cooperative project on the cards involving experts from Romania.

Mediators on public transport and in neighborhoods

The three or four experimental mediation projects in disadvantaged or problem neighborhoods or on public transport leading to, from or through these areas were all based on a common principle: the ability of often young, most often unemployed people from poor backgrounds to communicate, understand and dialogue with other young (even very young) or older people who live in the same areas and who share or at least know about the precariousness and insecurity of their lives, their hopes and dreams, their responses, etc.

One of them said:

It's been more than a year now since I've been working as an AMIS[26] on the buses in Lyon. My job is in a new sector they call "proximity work". Jobs like mine are meant to respond to the demands of modern society and show that creating more humanity and better social bonds is a matter of urgency, it is vital. Public transport is somewhere that communication no longer exists between people encountering one another on the buses or subways. There are increasing problems between people from poor areas, the suburbs and public transport staff. The idea of AMIS is to fill this need—we see how necessary our work is every day**.

These skills are applied in various places, such as a large estate ("La Noé" in Chanteloup-les-Vignes in France); big conurbations in Belgium; on buses (the Lyon Public Transport authority, TCL) for the "AMIS"; the eastern and western suburban lines around Paris for the French National Railway (SNCF) etc. The experiments are sufficiently advanced for results to be available for the "Urban protection officers" of the La Noé estate, whose work has already been extended to buses and trains, "Protection and security workers" (Belgium), the "AMIS" (TCL) and the "Surroundings and protection officers" (SNCF, east Paris).

The initiative can come from young people aware of the urgency and seriousness of situations they feel they can and should tackle. It may also come from a local authority or a company which sees involving itself with young or long-term unemployed people as a way a solving problems they encounter in particular areas or on particular routes. Sometimes an association is founded to facilitate organizing the young people involved and ease their relations with the local authorities or partner company. One example is the association started in Chanteloup-les-Vignes, called *Les Messagers* ("The Messengers") which is made up of young people.

In the case of this association, the initiative came from young adults aged 18-25 because they had realized that most of the troublemakers harassing people were pre-teens aged between 9-13 who were classed as failures and rejected by those in authority. As "big brothers," the young adults felt they would be more accepted as "advisers" than older people, particularly those representing outside institutions such as the city council, the police or social services etc.

Their mediation was based on using the experience of young people, both paid and volunteer staff, and their knowledge of the background they too came from. They established a presence, and were able to dialogue with people such as residents of the neighborhood or estate, public transport users and employees such as drivers, conductors etc.

When they were looking for people to work as AMIS two years ago, they didn't go and look for people from the top schools, but for people who lived in disadvantaged areas and people who had been unemployed for more than a year. People like us know what the suburbs are like. You need to know this world if you're going to do this job. For me, being an "AMIS" is a real job. You're a social worker and bodyguard, protecting the surroundings and welcoming people all at the same time.

I feel they're using our skills to get to know the suburbs to stop these problems on public transport. We can make society a better place by improving people's interaction on the buses in our work. I try to get people to see they're not alone. I give them responsibilities, I challenge them to live with other people. That's what we mean when we say "making society a better place"**.

Young people working on the eastern suburban lines in Paris said: *the first few days, people were pretty curious and suspicious. But when we explained to people why we were there, they congratulated us*[27].

Their presence, contact and dialogue with people allowed them to reassure and help travelers, provide them with information (sometimes about their rights), prevent aggressive behavior and incitements to violence, vandalism to buildings and property, and also to report incidents to the people in charge of the estate, the neighborhood or the transport company.

In the case of the La Noé estate in Chanteloup-les-Vignes, it was principally young preteens going off the rails with no role models to guide them that the "Urban protection officers" from the *Les Messagers* association tried to contact and advise. For example, they talked to them about their own previous experiences and tried to supervise them and channel their energy into constructive outlets. The young people were recruited on a fixed-term contract, and were paid directly by the local authority or transport company, or by the association they had founded. They were not always happy with the situation.

One said: *The status we've been given is not satisfactory. We have a one-year contract. 30 hours per week, renewable for one year. Our official employer isn't the TCL, it's an association started by the department.*

They were given a uniform by which people and passengers could identify them, without making them look like inspectors or police, though in the beginning, people sometimes thought they were. *When we started, lots of the passengers stubbed out their cigarettes and took their feet off the seats* said one young man who works on train lines in the east Paris suburbs. *People were even giving us their tickets or ID cards. But it's exactly the opposite. We're more mediators. Our only weapon is dialogue.*

These young people all received training designed as a vital complement to their experience, skills and abilities to help them make the most of these, stopping them becoming a sort of parallel militia (at least in the case of *Les Messagers* in Chanteloup-les-Vignes).

They were still not satisfied with things, but some appreciated the training they received on conflict management, which helped them find the right words in tricky situations.

The result, though in some instances it is still provisional, already seems to the authorities to be a clear success. Some of the young people taken on did have problems "sticking to the rules" particularly concerning working regular hours and being punctual. But most gained a renewed sense of self-confidence and hoped to continue doing the same job after the project finished, or at least find another job more easily: *even if I end up working somewhere else, it's a good calling card, it gives a real example of our dialogue skills* said the young people working on the east Parisian suburban trains.

Most of them won the trust of the residents, the public transport users and the partners providing financial backing who continue to require their help, though some think they were sometimes seen as "servants" or that they were not trusted, or feel there was no dialogue.

At the end of the day, it was noted that there were demonstrably fewer petty incidents, fewer people traveling without tickets and a reduction in vandalism and violence on public transport, as well as an increase in people taking the lines the young people worked on and a decrease in feelings of insecurity amongst residents of the neighborhoods and public transport users. A follow-up to the experiment is envisaged.

Other jobs

The jobs described thus far represent only (an admittedly significant) portion of the skills of the poorest. It would be difficult to give a general overview, but our research showed us a very broad range of jobs in which the poorest workers seem primarily represented. The list below aims to give an indication of some of these, without being exhaustive.

In **primary industry** (agriculture, forestry, fishing):

– *pigouillers* who work at ports during the night, unloading fish from ships' holds. There is a knack to doing this with a spade without ruining the fish;

– many poor families breed domestic animals and small livestock such as dogs, birds, chicks and rabbits, sometimes selling them door-to-door, or often as a source of cheap meat;

– some garden to grow themselves a source of food. Gardening and market gardening (e.g. growing chicory) require specific skills, some of which can be gained through experience or in informal contexts. This is of course seasonal work in the same way as agricultural labor.

– in forested areas, young people spend their holidays pruning trees in fir plantations to get a bit of pocket money. The methods they use are sometimes primitive, but no less effective for it. For example, Luc Lefevre described how during icy spells he and his cousins would check to see if the trees' branches were hard enough. Then they would hit them with crowbars to break off several branches in one go. During the 1980s, the job of pruner was expanded in France as part of the "New Qualifications" scheme, training young people to appreciate the trees and providing them with a basic grounding in ecology, etc.

Workers from poor backgrounds also work in the **services industry**, especially the hospitality industry[28] as dishwashers, kitchen-hands, waiting staff and chambermaids and cleaning and personal services such as charladies and home helps. As the skills required for these occupations do not seem to be based in any knowledge or experience garnered from living in poverty, we do not intend to dwell on them.

Poor workers also work in the **road transport sector** as truck drivers. Since this sector is booming, companies do not demand much in the way of qualifications or experience, provided candidates can afford to take a truck driver's license or have been able to take it in the army. Other workers are employed in express delivery companies. They are paid on commission and have to pay for their own gas and vehicle upkeep. Here again, these are jobs the very poor do rather than ones in which they can put their life experiences to use.

Finally, let us look at a range of jobs very much linked to the lifestyles of **travelers**. These are itinerant, ancient jobs, some of which are disappearing, such as knife-grinders, saddlers, tinkers, chair-bottomers, basket-makers etc. Lucie Ribert[29], whose family no longer lives on the road, does not seem to mourn their passing, remembering the less romantic aspects of the trades:

> When my mother used to go and sell baskets, I often went with her and there was this scorn. . . . I was really ashamed that my mother sold baskets, I can't say otherwise. We were looked down upon, especially when she couldn't sell any and I knew how much work went into them, it ruined her hands and I was ashamed about it for a long time. I think school made us want to live differently.

Notes

1. Interview no. 5.
2. 100 BEF = $ 2.99—prices are as of January 1998.
3. Interview no. 3.
4. Interview no. 10.
5. The LST Cooperative was founded in 1984 and in accordance with Article 4 of its constitution *promotes labor and more humane working conditions with a view to all its members developing their community.* It is active in the construction industry: building shells, coverings, finishing, electrics, sanitation and heating, applying these skills to both renovation work and building new houses. The LST Cooperative does compete with other construction companies, but its main aim as a company is to train less qualified workers by giving them on-the-job experience. In the ten years from 1984 to 1994, LST provided this training and experience for 27 people.
6. CPAS = *(Centre public d'Aide Sociale)* Public Center for Social Aid.
7. A non-profit organization, known in Belgium as an ASBL or an *association sans but lucrative* and regulated in France by the Associations Act 1901.
8. Interview no. 4.
9. Interview no. 1.
10. Interview no. 2.
11. Belgian benefit providing the minimum required to survive.
12. Two asterisks ** denote extracts from group discussions or personal writings.
13. Interview no. 6.

14. Interview no. 11.
15. Interview no. 12.
16. Interview no. 8.
17. Interview no. 14.
18. Interview no. 14.
19. Interview no. 8.
20. Interview no. 14.
21. Ervaringsdeskundigen in Flemish.
22. Flemish for "child and family".
23. Interview no. 18.
24. Interview no. 18.
25. Interview no. 18.
26. AMIS = (*Agents de Médiation, d'Information et de Service*) Mediation, Information and Service Officers.
27. Article from *Le Parisien SNCF*, a newspaper given out free on Parisian suburban trains.
28. Hotels, restaurants and cafés.
29. Lecture.

Chapter 2

SKILLS ANALYSIS

The skills which emerge from the interviews require analysis. But first of all, one preliminary remark: the professional skills the interviewees possess are often mixed with relational skills which are sometimes even dominant, and which always play a vital role in making what they do so individual and different.

Equally, these skills should not be confused with the need for something to do when unemployment forces inactivity upon people, nor with getting by, nor with DIY activities, which are practiced in their spare time by many people who have never encountered poverty in their lives.

We are talking here about the often unique activities or relational skills which very poor people develop because of their difficult living conditions (in which they did not choose to live!)

Differences and points in common

Does someone who collects scrap or repairs used appliances have anything in common with someone who provides social coaching for poor people?

Manual skills and relational skills

Two types of skills emerge from what we have just described. One kind might be called *manual* or *practical* skills and relates to mainly physical work. For example, collecting scrap (especially metal), recycling, repairing or mending, renovating buildings, gardening, market gardening, pruning, breeding small livestock, working in restaurants, driving vehicles, itinerant jobs etc. The other type of skills is primarily based on one's relationships with other people and involves hospitality, accommodation, social coaching, representing people to the authorities or social services, mediating on behalf of poor families, children, young people, public transport users or residents of problem estates or neighborhoods.

The skills of the poorest, contrary to popular perceptions, fall not just into the first category but into the second as well.

Realizing this led us to the following two observations:

Points in common between the two types of skills

Firstly, there is the sense of pride which comes through in the interviews. This is felt by those who do purely practical or manual work. It might often be in very difficult conditions, but at least it allows them to be less dependent on benefits. It is also felt by those who work in hospitality, coaching, support or mediation, who are driven by the urge to show solidarity with those as poor as (or even poorer than) themselves and the desire to help them and their children escape poverty.

Almost all the skills of the poorest just described were acquired through their backgrounds, from their parents or prompted by their experience of poverty and the problems encountered by families or children at school or elsewhere. There are too many examples to list here, but they relate to the whole range of skills.

Most of these skills, including the manual ones, demonstrate observation skills, intelligence, often a degree of astuteness, as well as a skill which can be acquired "on the hoof" or via a structured training course which provides or complements it.

It was by observation that Marcel[1] realized that the price of the metals he collected each day was dependent on the Stock Market, so he started following the share prices. It was by observation that Mr. Gérard[2] learned that each brand of television he repairs has its own diagram, that he needs to know what parts a particular model has and that he must measure the voltage, power and resistance. Jacqueline Meton[3] learned about the social services' work all on her own in order to help other people. On the other hand, Luc Lefevre[4] trained as a social worker to help him in setting up his association LST, and trained as a heating engineer to be allowed to train other people to renovate buildings.

Different prospects for the future

This is observable between manual and relational skills. Some manual skills are at risk of being threatened by the appearance or development of new technology or means of production used by companies in these sectors, employing people who generally do not have these skills. On the other hand, there seems to be more of a future in relational skills, since these are dependent on the ability to establish a bond or rapport in welcome, coaching or mediation. They form part of the important social or personal services industry which is currently trying to expand to meet growing, though largely unsatisfied, demand.

Individual, collective and institutionalized skills

Most of these skills are linked to an individual job which is independent or voluntary. The job can be physical, like scrap collection, repairing or mending televisions, videos or hi-fis or informal work like gardening, market gardening, washing up, express delivery services or itinerant jobs. But it can also be welcome or coaching services delivered in a neighborhood or in a hospital, even in a railway station.

Other skills are linked to a job working with other people, often with a salary, with organizations or institutions which can be outside institutions, local authorities or companies, as is the case for the AMIS and the protection, surroundings and security officers. They can also be specialist institutions such as local libraries for library outreach workers or the Office of Births and Children, or public social services in the case of the "experts by experience". ATD Fourth World also qualifies as such. But in several cases we looked at, the institution was created by someone who felt that their skills and commitment would be more effective in a structured group. This was what prompted Luc Lefevre to found his non-profit organization, *Lutte Solidarité Travail* (struggle, solidarity and work), in which he and others renovate buildings threatened with being pulled down. Paul Linden[5] founded a non-profit association in which he provides the homeless with financial, legal and administrative assistance.

Motivation and the meaning of skills

What do the skills the poor possess mean to them? What drives them to be interested in such or such a job, even one which is not paid? The interviews reveal a range of diverse, sometimes unexpected meanings.

It is primarily survival strategies which drive some people to collect or repair what others have thrown out. Mr. Gérard[6] started taking an interest in repairing televisions when his son was taken into hospital and spent his time in there watching TV. When he came out of hospital, he could only afford to buy a second-hand set, which often stopped working. Maurice[7], who went through *garbage cans and junk stores* before concentrating on scrap metal, answered: *When you've got nothing, you still have to find something. And in Brussels, rents are very high and life is very tough.* His inventive approach was therefore simply a way of dealing with poverty.

To some extent the same is true of all the practical jobs the poor do. Thus, the LST Cooperative, which specializes in renovation, was founded to deal with the urgent needs of the homeless. Luc Lefevre used to do the wiring in the rooms his friends were squatting in. When *the 55* was sold, the residents who remained asked if they could be taken on to demolish part of the building to earn a bit of cash. Later, they had to knock down the hovels where they were squatting.

Some people were lucky (or determined?) enough to be able to refuse jobs they did not like and find work which was more fulfilling for them. Lucie Ribert[8] has had a fairly varied career, partly because she could not stand working on a production line. When she worked for a cobbler, however:

> I liked it a lot. It was in a workshop where we were really creating something. I repaired shoes and leather clothing. Leather's great, I loved it, I'm a very manual person.

Claudine[9], a library outreach worker, said:

> But all the jobs I'd done before I hadn't found interesting, I kept getting ripped off
> and anyway I really liked working with children. I've been able to do loads of things
> as a result—write a lot more, discover books at the same time as the children.

Her colleague Valérie[10] even gave up a full-time job as an office worker to
become a member of the Fourth World volunteer corps and library outreach
worker.

However, behind the personal interests also lies a strong social motivation. Mr.
Gérard[11], who collects scrap, inveighs against the wastage of consumer society:

> People chuck things out for nothing sometimes, because they don't like the model
> any more, or because someone's conned them into it. Official, accredited scrap col-
> lectors con people to get them to buy something else, saying it can't be fixed, but I
> want to show that's not true.

For LST, belonging to the world of work, even for those who have lost their
jobs, is a key founding precept of the cooperative:

> We want to prove we're workers. Friends who haven't got any work, who aren't
> looking but who are there to support their friends who are in a bad way—that's work
> too. If you do a job the social services haven't done, you're working. That's our
> identity as workers which binds us together[12].

The feeling of belonging to a bigger social group which is recognized affects
not just workers, but others too. Some of them have joined social movements and
are involved to demonstrate their solidarity.

The dream of being able to eradicate poverty for the generations to come is
shared by nearly all the interviewees, it is like a leitmotif. Paul Linden, Mr. Gérard
and Maurice, who are involved in coaching or sheltering the homeless, all state
that, one way or another, it is their experience of living on the streets that drives
them to save others from this fate. Two of the "experts by experience", of whose
personal lives we know very little, revealed that they had spent time in care and
been abused. The two library outreach workers, Claudine and Valérie, were excluded as children and strive to protect children in the neighborhoods where they
work from feeling inferior in the way they did.

> I was always on my own. The whole time, I saw others ridiculing me, my family, my
> brothers and sisters. It got on my nerves to such an extent that when I got the oppor-
> tunity to work with children from various areas, I thought, I'll have to do all I can to
> make sure none of them are left out[13].

Through their passionate commitment, we can sense a measure of the desire
felt by these damaged individuals to regain dignity both for themselves and for
those around them. It is the same commitment which drives those at LST to have

their identity as workers recognized. And when Lucie Ribert decided to join ATD Fourth World, this is how she described what motivated her:

> We weren't free, we had no freedom to choose. My mother never had the choice, never knew who she was voting for (because she was illiterate), never had the choice of saying yes or no to people. And me, I've got involved—alright, maybe it's a bit selfish, but I really want to do my bit for everyone to become free citizens who can be educated to understand the world from which we're rather excluded.

Acquiring these skills

These skills are acquired essentially by being passed from one member of a community to another, and via people adapting to the situations they live in.

Learning

The way these skills are acquired differs from person to person, and sometimes even with the same person. Mostly they are acquired through "on the ground" experience, traditional school-based forms of professional training only rarely being applied in a direct and specific way, if at all.

This experience on the ground is often extremely deeply rooted in poor people's life experiences, especially those within the family. For example, Marcel[14] learned the basics of scrap collection from his grandmother, and Luc Lefevre observed as a child how his father used all the tricks he knew to get by in tough situations, and remembered them.

The family circle is also where people's moral compass is formed, by witnessing their parents' struggle against poverty and bravery to preserve their dignity at any cost, and their concern for those who are in even worse situations. Two of the most striking examples of this are Lucie Ribert's parents and those of Luc Lefevre. The latter's mother told him:

> You have to make the most of your potential to use it to help others who are weaker than you.

Or, in slightly more colorful language:

> Working isn't about living the life of Riley, it's about doing your bit to help other people[15].

Some people learn their skills through contact with other people from different backgrounds, such as schools and colleges, as in the cases of Mr. Gérard[16], who trained at ORBEM[17] as a mechanic, Luc Lefevre, who trained as an electrical engineer, heating engineer and plumber, and Valérie[18], who did a work placement in IT. Or they can learn their skills from small businesses, as with Marcel, who worked for a scrap metal merchant for two years, and Mr. Gérard (again) who asked a professional television repairman for help several times to help him achieve the same level of skill.

One requirement is highlighted by one young man[19] in particular: you need to be trusted by the employer or trainer. *It was alright for me because at least he trusted me.*

Another way of learning is in the associative sector, where one very good example is that of ATD Fourth World library outreach workers. Valérie told us of her passion for her new vocation after two years of training for it.

> I felt increasingly that I had to be available to greet the children I was waiting for, the ones I really hoped would come. Little by little the children got used to the library and the rules. I also got used to them. With the children I saw most often, I started getting to know their likes and dislikes and their styles. I could suggest books to them that might appeal more, depending on what they were like as people.

Another very important (and older) name in the associative sector is the Christian Workers' Youth (JOC). Several people who do a lot to help the poor, such as Jacqueline Meton and Luc Lefevre's parents, explained to what extent they could trace their roots and their impetus to this movement. Luc Lefevre's father, who had helped found his local JOC, had gained a particularly strong sense of the worth of every and any worker from it, which he passed on to his son, who went on to found LST in his turn. Trade unions and political organizations are also important points of reference and shaping forces.

> My father was a militant trade unionist worker. He was an activist from the age of 14, and never tried to use his position to get on in life. "I'll stay where I was born," he used to say. I was in various movements. I was in some groups with links to the Communist party, when I was still at the ITL[20]. I was in the international movement for reconciliation. The first organizations to fight poverty in an organized way, as a collective, were the trade unions. They were the first to fight for the emancipation of the poorest and say we're fed up of this yoke round our necks—at least in the industrialized world. Like the resistance funds, as they were called when the trade unions were starting out, they were ways of fighting poverty.

There is one more way of acquiring skills we should not forget: teaching oneself. The most striking example of this is that of Maurice[21], who learned to collect metals by their value all on his own, though the same attitude is displayed to varying degrees by all the interviewees.

Adapting

In order to cope with very difficult situations, often alongside others, the very poor[22] possess the ability to adapt. This is mainly evident in what they do in order to provide for themselves or others, but also plays an instructive role which goes beyond coping with emergencies.

Passing on skills

When people learn skills from other poor people in the same situation, they are often passed down from one generation to the next. There are many examples of this: we could cite Mr. Gérard's attitude towards his children and other people with problems regarding television repairs. Or that of Marcel[23], who taught his brother-in-law how to collect scrap. Or that of Luc Lefevre's parents, of whom we have already spoken, concerning the acquisition of skills. Or we might mention once more Lucie Ribert[24], who realized how beautiful the baskets were that her mother used to make and even began making them herself for her own creative fulfillment.

As we have already seen, passing on these skills plays a vital and irreplaceable role in acquiring relational skills and in all probability really enriches the lives of many of the very poor.

One striking example is that of Valérie[25], who bears witness to the open-mindedness, tolerance and sensitivity to those around her, even if they were sometimes hostile and violent, which she learned from her parents, in particular her father. These qualities she would display at a later date when she went on to fight against all odds to reach the poorest children through street libraries and communicate her passion for books to them, so *they could benefit from it and catch up with the other children at school, and so that one day, no child, young person or parent would be excluded or singled out.*

Knowing what it is like to live in poverty

Being from a poor background is the source of some of the skills we have described, but at the same time, being from this background can cause problems.

All the interviewees grew up in poor families, but some were from lower-working class or small-scale agricultural backgrounds, such as Luc Lefevre, Paul Linden, Jacqueline Meton, Valérie and Emile Creutz[26], while others grew up in extreme poverty, such as Claudine, Mr. Gérard, Jean, Marcel and André[27].

Though they are connected, these two backgrounds are not regarded by society in the same way. This is because their living situations are different and the working world is able to define itself as a social class. For example, the people from working-class backgrounds sometimes had the chance to study, allowing them learn a trade and receive a qualification. Valérie is from a family of Spanish immigrants who arrived in France in 1961. Her parents left Spain leaving all they had behind. She went first to a Spanish school, then a French one to learn French. She then attended a *lycée professional* (technical college), but failed her course. Her parents then paid for her to go to a private school for her to learn to be an office worker.

Luc Lefevre is also from a working-class family. His father worked on the railways as a loader and was a trade unionist. His parents received financial help after World War II which enabled them to build their house. They encouraged Luc and his brothers to join youth movements. Luc studied to be an electrical engineer, then trained as a social worker, financing his studies himself by working at the same time. Later he trained as a plumber and heating engineer. His own working-class roots taught him how important manual work is for the poor.

Jacqueline Meton[28] was a member of Patro (a youth movement) from the age of 5½ to 12, when she joined the JOC and recited its pledge:

> Being granted the privilege of wearing the JOC badge, I promise to do my utmost to realize the JOC's ideals every day in my family, my neighborhood, my place of work or school, my free time and in building the world of tomorrow.

People from poor backgrounds tend to have shorter academic careers. For example, Claudine[29] left school at 14. Everyone made fun of her and her family. *If you're all alone, you just retreat into your shell, you don't want to talk to anyone and then you're too scared to talk to anyone, you're too shy.*

Children who grow up in a very poor family know what it is like to be singled out because their hair-style or clothes are not like those of the other children, because they do not have the right books at school or because their family or neighborhood has a bad reputation.

Marcel's[30] father died when he was 10, and his mother was left alone with three children. He remembers his grandmother collecting the crates from markets to pay her gas and electricity bills. He started work at a very young age.

André[31] is 22. He only started school at 12, because his parents had 12 children and only sent the oldest to school. He has problems reading and writing.

Succeeding at school for children from poor backgrounds is a struggle to learn, be accepted by the others, pay for one's studies, etc. For some, this struggle results in failure. This struggle and failure are the lessons they draw from their early lives.

Another example is that of Mr. Gérard[32], who found himself on the street with his wife who was pregnant with their son. Living through this was what prompted him to put up other homeless people later in life, and suffering from a lack of material possessions prompted him to collect and repair used objects for himself and others who lived in similar situations.

People who work with the poor may say that they know about poverty because they have studied it in books or on the ground as part of their work. But the knowledge we are talking about here is that which people living in poverty have acquired themselves through their own experiences.

The opportunities and the problems of being raised in poverty

For using skills

The skills described thus far are individual or collective. We saw that some interviewees from working-class backgrounds, such as Luc Lefevre, Paul Linden and Emile Creutz, have been able to start their own association in order to develop and share their skills and pass them on to others. For her part, Jacqueline

Meton can help people living in poverty since she is familiar with the way society is organized, the rules, people's rights, the bureaucracy etc. Their working-class backgrounds have allowed them all to acquire a knowledge of society and organizational skills. Valérie learned along with her family how to integrate into a new country, so she knows how to be accepted into a foreign environment and this helped her fit in better when working as a secretary.

Jean, Mr. Gérard and Marcel, who are from impoverished backgrounds, have not founded any non-profit organization or cooperative, but have put their skills to work with those around them. They know nothing of employment law and have no referees, nor do they know anything about the bodies making up an organization.

Contact with others living in poverty

Some interviewees have made themselves available to help others who live in poverty. There was Luc Lefevre and the residents of *the 55*, Jacqueline Meton and the people at the central railway station, Paul Linden and the homeless shelter he started, Valérie and Claudine working with children in libraries, Anne helping people at the ONE, Jean and the children taking part in the Summer Street Festivals* etc.

Aged just 13½, Jacqueline[33] started helping a family with a lot of children who had just lost their mother. Later, when she worked in the canteen of a school where poor children made up 70% of pupil numbers, she gave sandwiches to children who did not have any. She also could not bear children being taken into care, and stood up on behalf of the most vulnerable to the principal and teachers.

The experts by experience[34] are familiar with the feelings of pain, torment, uncertainty, heartbreak, impotence and incomprehension that poor families experience. They also know their survival strategies and their hopes and dreams. They protect the interests of these families by helping them dialogue with social workers etc. They are close to poor families, sometimes so close that they lend them things.

Claudine[35] comes into contact with very poor children and families and talks with them. She knows that they need more care and attention, since these children do not have the same opportunities as others. She tries to show them they are like other children by taking them to the library and encouraging them to look at the books. She knows it is important to get them to leave the family home, since otherwise they will remain stuck inside immobile, and will not want to go out because they are afraid. She is in a position to tell them that when she was their age she was just the same, which makes them trust her: *They know that what they say to me wouldn't go down the same way with other people.*

But contact still remains difficult sometimes. Jacqueline Meton said that some people never came to meetings. Valérie[36] spoke of a family who had moved house and whose mother did not want her children to go to the library any more. It was Valérie's persistence in going to see the children at their new home every Saturday that made the mother eventually change her mind. Valérie persisted because she knew that people often need time to make up their minds themselves.

When Claudine started a street library, the parents took no interest at first, though they sent their children along. Claudine managed to bring together children from various neighborhoods who would not otherwise have met one another.

One of the problems encountered by several people who help others despite living in poverty themselves is that their private lives, like those of all poor people, is public property. Sometimes they are criticized for their private lives, even by those of a similar background. This is especially true when they are offended by something and try to make their opinion known in a capacity they are not seen as being entitled to assume, such as when experts of experience lend their personal belongings to families with whom they also work in a professional context.

Contact with the authorities and people working with the poor

The interviews show that contact with the authorities and those working with the poor (such as the *commune*, social services, librarians, doctors, nurses, CPAS etc) is frequent, and people's views of them are often mixed.

Claudine's skills as a library outreach worker were appreciated by the head librarian, as she made other librarians see the importance of seeking out very poor children to show them how to look for a book in a library. At the same time, however, the same head librarian criticized Claudine for *lacking maturity*, that is, arriving late or being absent, and having health problems. Yet all these were actually due to her difficult living conditions.

Jacqueline Meton, Maurice and Luc Lefevre help people with problems to deal with the authorities. By being there for them, they can help them get the results they want more quickly because they are familiar with administrative procedures.

Mr. Gérard's[37] relationship with the working world entails him having to buy his electronic spare parts from resellers, since the parent companies do not consider him a real repairman. In a separate field, Anne[38] entertains friendly relations with an ONE consultant nurse, but is not on such good terms with the other nurses and the doctors[39].

The nurses find that the experts by experience for their part are over-protected, and they are given too much credit. In other cases, it has been remarked that *as the financial situation of the experts by experience improves, so there is a risk of their becoming increasingly removed from their roots[40]*.

The paradox

Clearly, poverty is a blight on our society and should be eradicated—and yet we are saying that those living in poverty acquire unique skills. Is this not a contradiction?

Poverty forces those who endure it to find survival strategies. Some of these become, over time, real skills such as those we have seen. Helping one another also comes as a matter of course for the poor and is part of daily life. This becomes a real skill for people whose lives thereby become a little easier on a material level.

In a report on the experts by experience, some of the nurses said that *it is not enough to know about poverty to be a good expert by experience.* It seems to us that being from a poor background and the intimate knowledge this brings are vital in order to understand and help those in poverty. But this knowledge alone is insufficient, and must be accompanied by some sort of education or training to become a real "profession".

The skills we have analyzed should serve to eradicate poverty—giving children a taste for reading, helping children from different backgrounds to get along and live together, allowing everyone to have access to their rights concerning resources, housing, health, citizenship, education etc, reintroducing the poorest to the world of work (in the construction industry or recycling), believing in and developing the intelligence and abilities of the poorest (experts by experience, or people who know about collecting and mending etc).

In order to eradicate poverty, we need the help of those who have learned to fight it every day of their lives. We need to accept these people as full individuals, accept their good sides as well as the bad, which are due to the ill-effects of poverty.

But in order to avoid going round in circles like in this diagram:

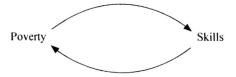

The skills of the poor have to become real trades useful to society as a whole; for example, recycling to protect the environment or the way town or village life is organized etc.

The diagram would then become:

With no education beyond the world of poverty, these skills serve only to keep those who have them and those around them alive. Training programs allow them to consolidate and complement these skills, which thus become real professions useful not just to the poor but to society as a whole.

Manual and relational skills with specific relevance to the poorest

Generally speaking, the jobs which the skills of the poorest tend to suit are or can be done by someone else. These skills, then, are not usually unique in themselves. However, nearly all these skills are remarkable for individual features which may be attributable either to the resilience of the poorest in dealing with major problems in life and the conditions under which they have to work, or to a knowledge of their needs and deeply-held ambitions, both being the result of personal experience of poverty. These specific features may manifest themselves in two ways:

Firstly, in the way they act (or practice their skill), which is different to that of other people with an ability in the same field of work:

– being able to use resources others would consider insufficient, for example in using or collecting scrap metal.

– thinking of making an economical but effective repair, c§hanging only one part which is maybe worn out or defective, when others, especially professional repairmen, can only conceive of changing the entire mechanism, which is costly (in repairing or mending television sets for example);

– introducing people to culture on as personal a basis as possible, meaning very poor people (children) who have thus far been excluded can take part (library outreach workers).

It is also a truly particular ability, a skill which is in some way "unique," to do particular jobs with very poor people, presupposing understanding, communication, even patience, which can only come as a result of an intimate knowledge of life in poverty. This ability is often found in mediation work in neighborhoods, on public transport, in encouraging children and young people to use libraries, in welcome and coaching people and with the benefits services (the experts by experience, Jacqueline Meton, Jean, the library outreach workers etc).

Usefulness in a changing society

To some degree, perceptions of the usefulness of skills are subjective and dependent on how they are analyzed. We or the interviewees can say that such and such a skill is useful. We can even prove how they are useful (which is indeed what we are going to do). But we very quickly run up against the issue of official, social or personal recognition for each and any skill. The issues of usefulness and recognition are linked and it is sometimes difficult to separate the two, so closely are they interconnected.

Manual skills

Here we are talking about skillfully sorting refuse, collecting scrap metal or consumer goods (and repairing them) such as televisions, hot plates etc.

The first way in which these skills are useful is in proving one's abilities to oneself, giving one a sense of self-confidence and a degree of pride in being able to take part in the life of society.

Mr. Gérard[41] helps other people by recovering and repairing things: *It helps people who are a bit less well-off than yourself, who've got nothing.* Marcel[42] pays for the poorest children to go on scout camps. This usefulness is therefore combined with a service.

These are valuable activities in the sense that they try to stop waste and improve quality of life. Mr. Gérard said: *There's pile upon pile of garbage cans. We're trying stop quality of life being eroded in an eco-friendly way, by reducing the number of them. That's one way, maybe just a drop in the ocean, but it's a start.*

Marcel helps people and his *commune* by cleaning their courtyards or the streets of litter which makes the place unclean and unpleasant to live in.

But in doing so, do these people not find themselves in competition with others in official, recognized jobs?

Here are some examples:

– some scrap metal wholesalers (particularly in Belgium) take a very dim view of those who collect scrap with a little handcart, since they tend to drive prices down;

– the automobile industry has introduced systematic recycling of old cars, thus taking away a large part of scrap metal merchants' livelihoods;

– many very poor people *scrape a dime* from the returns on bottles they find in bins. But not only is returning bottles less and less common nowadays, the fact that bottle banks are now a common sight in cities has removed this significant source of income.

Given the changes in society and its economic system, have these skills become redundant or do they have to find other outlets? Here, again, we may run up against the financial clout of certain large companies, such as for example in *tire*[43] recuperation. In Belgium, environmental legislation obliges producers to recuperate their materials. A study showed that it was possible to recuperate more tires by remolding the less worn ones. Measuring, sorting and remolding tires are menial jobs which can employ a lot of people in small local businesses. Transport costs are reduced by decentralizing the recycling centers. However, importers refused to accept this, preferring that large, heavily-mechanized centers be built to re-melt the rubber, since there was a risk of recovered tires competing with imported ones—a big factory suited the importers' interests better.

Is Mr. Gérard, who repaired televisions and domestic appliances for little money, not competing unfairly with official repairmen who pay taxes and professional guild membership? Actually, out of solidarity, he only helps those who do not have the money to go to an official repairman.

Small-scale collectors and repairers are therefore active in sectors of the economy which are not really covered by others, as well as providing a useful service to society as a whole (in improving quality of life) and, especially, to the poorest (helping one another). From a financial point of view, though they pay no taxes or professional membership fees and therefore do not contribute to society, they nevertheless save the authorities money on benefit payouts.

Relational skills

This work involves relating to people, being friendly and mediating, and is done by people working on public transport in several large cities and their suburbs, and on estates, by people providing coaching and welcome in the health and social services, and by library outreach workers.

Regarding public transport, an AMIS[44] explained how necessary it is for them to be able to create a social bond on public transport. Their role is to create an agreeable atmosphere and pacify the situation, making traveling a pleasant experience. The usefulness of their work has also been recognized, since the initial experiment has been tried elsewhere and developed upon. The idea of "protection and surroundings officers" has also been taken up in other contexts in France, for example the Aubry[45] program to combat youth unemployment.

The library outreach workers' main role is to help children discover books. Experts by experience help nurses and very poor and/or immigrant families to better understand one another. This means fewer children are taken into care, making financial savings, but also reducing the human and social cost.

Several people do a job similar to that of a social worker in their coaching and welcome as volunteers, and are often called upon by town and city councils or the health and social services for their skills. They are useful because they work in an area which is not covered by the average social worker.

However, people working in public services do not always appreciate their work:

– librarians do not always welcome the sight of children in their libraries, whom they see as rowdy and ill-disciplined, disturbing the usual silence. And does not the library outreach worker, if they do their work well, threaten the librarian's precarious status as guardian of heritage and learning?

– nurses think that the experts by experience are too cosseted, and one needs more than just to be from a poor background to be effective in eradicating poverty. Is this jealousy from people who would also like to be cosseted from time to time, or are the experts by experience seen as competitors threatening to undermine the nurses' status?

The skills we have just addressed are therefore useful to society in one way or another. But there is a big difference between the usefulness of a skill and its being officially recognized. The current trend towards recognition or even accreditation of these skills may go some way to narrowing the divide, if we want it enough.

At the same time, it seems that for some there is a need to adapt, and everyone needs their skills complemented by a form of education or training if they are to be used in a more focused way.

Notes

1. Interview no.5.
2. Interview no. 3.
3. Interview no. 4.
4. Interview no. 10.
5. Interview no. 2.
6. Interview no. 3.
7. Interview no. 6.
8. Lecture.
9. Interview no. 8.
10. Interview no. 14.
11. Interview no. 3.
12. Interview no. 10.
13. Interview no. 8.
14. Interview no. 5.
15. Interview no. 10.
16. Interview no. 3.
17. Brussels Regional Employment Office.
18. Interview no. 14.
19. Interview no. 7.
20. Free Technical Institute
21. Interview no. 6.
22. Interviews nos. 3, 6 and 10.

23. Interview no. 5.
24. Lecture.
25. Interview no. 14.
26. Interviews nos. 10, 2, 4, 14 and lecture
27. Interviews nos. 8, 3, 1, 5 and 7.
28. Interview no. 4.
29. Interview no. 8.
30. Interview no. 5.
31. Interview no. 7.
32. Interview no. 3.
33. Interview no. 4.
34. Interview no. 18.
35. Interview no. 8.
36. Interview no. 14.
37. Interview no. 3.
38. Interview no. 11.
39. Interview no. 12.
40. Interview no. 17.
41. Interview no. 3.
42. Interview no. 5.
43. Interview no. 16.
44. Mediation, Information and Service Officer.
45. Named after Martine Aubry, Minister of Employment and Solidarity in 1997.

Chapter 3

EDUCATION AND TRAINING

Our society is increasingly undergoing two simultaneous and contradictory phenomena. On the one hand, people's basic requirements, such as help for those in need, accessible health services and improvements to the natural and physical environment, are very often not met. On the other hand, the people who (potentially at least) are in a position to solve these problems are trapped in unemployment, even marginalized and excluded. The poorest represent a large number of such people.

In the interviews, we saw numerous examples of skills which could be put to use as part of meeting demands which remain unanswered. Why are they not?

It seems to us that there are three main reasons for this paradoxical situation.

– Firstly, these needs, though essential objectively speaking, are not yet highly-regarded enough by the general public, who are swayed by various forms of advertising/media into putting needs which are objectively speaking much less important and often artificial first.

– Secondly, the consequences of the overall reduction in the time needed to produce consumer goods and some services are not yet evenly distributed amongst the population as a whole.

– Finally, in order to be usable and officially recognized, the manual and relational skills of the poorest require in most cases additional education or training.

The first two reasons affect society as a whole, while the third specifically affects people living in extreme poverty. We shall explore this in more depth in the course of this chapter.

We shall therefore attempt to answer a series of questions by following a progression leading us to the nub of the problem: is education/training as it stands accessible to the poorest? What forms of education/training are there which develop manual and relational skills? What forms need to be created? Can the poorest themselves become trainers and educators, and under what conditions? Can teachers and pupils enjoy a reciprocal relationship and work as partners?

Before tackling each of these questions, it seems useful to recall the existing legislation in this field. French law, under which professional training has been a legal obligation since 1971 (known as the "Delors Law"), has recently proclaimed the **right to a professional qualification** for any working person or anyone starting a job, as a result of which they *must if they so wish be able to undertake professional training which, whatever their status, will allow them to gain a qualification in line with the needs of society in the short or medium term*, as has the law in other countries. Still more recently, French law has added a **right to professional training** under which *all young people must be offered professional training before leaving the education system, whatever level they have reached until then* In Belgium, the Charter of Jobseekers' Rights in the Flemish Community recognizes that everyone has a **right to education or training**, though without guaranteeing anything specific.

Under European law, Article 128 of the Treaty of Rome, the founding treaty of the European Union, sets out that the European Council, on the Commission's proposal, shall establish *general principles for the implementation of a common professional training policy*. The second of the principles laid down by the Council's decision on April 2, 1963 determines the goals of the common policy, which are to render effective the **right to receive professional training**. And Article 15 of the Community Charter of Fundamental Social Rights of workers proclaims that the latter must *be able to access professional training*, and that governments, businesses and social partners must make the necessary provisions. Following the Treaty of Amsterdam, in 1997 the Employment Council approved an action plan which was to guarantee each young unemployed person an opportunity for professional training within six months, and offer either work or coaching to every unemployed adult within twelve months. The Social Charter of the Council of Europe for its part, in Article 30, describes the commitment of member states to *promoting effective access, particularly to employment, teaching and training.*

Existing forms of training and their relation to skills

Are existing forms of training in Belgium accessible to the poor?

Professional training programs are a very complex issue. Looking at the skills described in Chapter 1, we may ask: do training programs exist which will provide people with these skills with a qualification?

The first problem is finding adequate information sources. In Belgium, each region has its own information office/s. For the Brussels area, these are the ORBEM (Brussels Regional Employment Office) and Bruxelles-Formation. For Wallonia, it is the FOREM (Regional Office of Training and Employment).

For the Flemish region, it is the VDAB (Flemish Employment and Careers Advice Service). Professional training programs by these offices are targeted mainly at the unemployed and jobseekers. Priority is given to long-term unemployed (more than two years).

Another source of information is the SIEP (Information Service for Education and Professions), mainly known to scholars and students.

The ACFI (Coordinated Training and Professional Integration Project) is another source of information on professional training opportunities for the long-term unemployed, people on the minimex and those without resources.

The first stage is to go to the right place to learn about existing training programs. We explored this as part of our research, but in order to understand the complexity of the system we should point out that the three activists in our group, who were responsible for writing this section, were only familiar with the ORBEM at the start of the project.

Their knowledge of training was limited to what they or those around them had done. The only training programs they had heard of were those offered to the long-term unemployed. The FOREM and the ORBEM give priority to those entitled to unemployment benefit. Therefore training is often not accessible to very poor people who are not entitled to these benefits. However, there are training programs which would be accessible to them, but which they know nothing about because no one has ever told them these programs exist. In addition, given their low level of education, if not failure at school, they are afraid of failing again. This is probably one of the reasons, though not the only one, why they do not enquire more about possible training programs.

It would be tempting to display the information we gathered in table format, clear and unambiguous. But that would diminish the significance of the real problems one can have in gaining access to information. Most of the information comes in the form of documents and books which must be read and understood.

Here, as an indication, are the results of our investigations into training programs relating to the skills we described earlier.

Training programs suitable for people with relational skills

In order to train as a librarian, the required level of schooling is a high-school diploma or an equivalent aptitude test. Librarian training is a form of higher education. In Belgium there is no specific course to be an assistant librarian.

The term "socio-cultural mediator" covers several jobs involved: specialist teacher, organizer, development officer in multicultural settings, social mediator etc.

Specialist teachers are active in several sectors: primary education, care for the elderly, street education schemes etc. There are two ways of training as a specialist teacher: either a short course in higher education (requiring a high school diploma), where training lasts three years, college being interspersed with work placements; or through an adult education scheme (requiring secondary education to age 16, a certificate of secondary education in France, or an entrance exam), lessons taking place in the evenings or at weekends. This training program is aimed at those on unemployment benefit or any working person wishing to complete it, over a three- or four-year period.

Some teachers are not specialist. In order to begin training, they must have secondary education to age 16. After one or two years of training, they can work as teachers in care homes, hospitals etc.

Organizers, mainly organizers of children's summer camps, the training and level required depend on the organization.

To train as a multicultural society officer, education to age 16 is required. Training lasts three years of evening classes. The certificate obtained at the end of the course is recognized by the French-speaking Community in Belgium. The officers then work in community and youth centers or on the street. Knowing more than one language does not seem to be a prerequisite for entry to the profession, unlike for training as a social mediator.

In social work, training programs are aimed at future social workers, carers, family helpers, home-helps etc. In order to train as a social worker, candidates must possess a high-school diploma or pass an entrance examination set by the college, which tests general knowledge. Candidates must be at least 18 years old and training lasts three years including work placements and is a short course in higher education.

Training to become a family helper comes in two varieties: one helping the unemployed back to work and the other in a traditional college setting requiring education to age 16. Training lasts one or two years including work placements, or four years as a short professional training program.

To be a home-help, no qualifications are required. Work-based training is provided by companies which exist for this purpose (*Entreprises de Formation par le Travail*), and is aimed at the unemployed, recipients of the minimex and people without resources. Candidates must be at least 18, have left school and not have a certificate of education to age 16, however education to age 16 is required.

Concerning programs for working with young children, training as a child worker takes two years in post-16 secondary education.

To be a child and family helper, candidates must be between 18 and 40, have not studied in higher education and have been unemployed for two or more years. The certificate they receive after five months of training allows them to work in crèches or homework clubs on a self-employed basis.

There are two sorts of child minders: those who work for the ONE and the self-employed. Various organizations train child minders, and for jobseekers, there are two-year on-the-job and college-based courses.

Training programs suitable for people with manual skills

Television and radio maintenance and repairs: the minimum age to start training is 15, having completed two years of secondary education. Training takes three years of day classes.

There is a two-year program of private evening classes requiring an apprentice qualification. The minimum age is 18, and there are tuition fees of between 4,000 and 7,000 BEF a year ($120–$ 210).

There are also training programs lasting between one and two years for students between 15 and 18 (sometimes 18 to 21 with the permission of the Joint Apprenticeship Board). Students receive a guaranteed income from the CPA of between 11,000 and 26,000 BEF a month ($330 - $780). Their contract cannot be terminated during the first six months.

Students on state-sponsored courses must be 16 or over and have completed professional studies. Training lasts three years. There are also programs requiring a secondary school diploma, lasting between two and four years, after which students receive a certificate of secondary technical studies in TV/radio repair.

To be an audiovisual technician, students must have completed secondary education to at least age 15. Training lasts three years.

To train as a domestic appliance repairperson, students must have completed studies in electronics as part of secondary education to age 16. The non-profit organization/cooperative "Les Petits Riens" offers a training program. There are also state-sponsored training programs, requiring a minimum four years of professional studies. The qualification at the end is a certificate of lower secondary technical studies.

Concerning recycling, there is an introductory course in waste treatment provided by the Brussels *Mission locale* (an office helping people find work), aimed at people with few or no qualifications aged between 18 and 55. Entry requirements are good health and literacy. The program lasts two weeks, plus a work placement.

There are no specifically environment-oriented professions, and therefore no training programs for these in secondary education.

In the construction industry, young people may train as builders on a three-year apprenticeship if they are under 18 and have completed secondary education to age 16. For those over 18 and jobseekers, there are several programs lasting from two to 42 weeks offered by the FOREM and the ORBEM. No minimum qualifications or previous experience in the industry are required, merely that candidates pass a basic arithmetic test and a medical examination.

Entreprises de Formation par le Travail offer training programs for builders, electricians, painters/decorators and tilers etc aimed at those having passed no exams in secondary education but who have been jobseekers for more than two years.

Natural world professions cover horticulture, gardening and forestry work. Several *Entreprises de Formation par le Travail* offer training in these sectors. Pruning is taught only as part of arborist training programs. A certificate of higher horticultural studies or post-16 secondary education and two years working in a horticulture-related area is required.

For professions working with animals, such as gamekeeper, dog-groomer etc there are very few training programs and no colleges. Training to be a gamekeeper is on a state-sponsored course open to anyone. To be a dog-groomer, secondary education to age 16 is required, and candidates must pass an entry exam.

Are these training programs accessible to the poorest?

We saw that the *Entreprises de Formation par le Travail* offer programs accessible to people with few or no qualifications. Their objective is clearly stated in their prospectus: *Finding social and professional roles for young people or adults excluded from the labor market because of their lack of qualifications and/or social situation, who have no access to traditional forms of training. The programs offer work placements lasting a maximum of 18 months during which, following a settling-in period, students experience real working situations giving them the opportunity both to identify barriers to their entering the working world and to hone their skills through appropriate training.* The requirements for starting such programs are not financial since there are no fees and students even receive a salary. The prime requirement is to have been a jobseeker for more than two years. There is no leaving certificate, but there are progress checks after the end of the course.

On the other hand, state-sponsored courses are aimed at all adults, whatever their working situation (whether they are working, a jobseeker or a student), as long as their qualifications are at a lower educational level than that they wish to study at. Sometimes there is an admissions test instead of this certificate. Training is by evening or weekend classes and can last from one to three years, culminating in a qualification[1] equivalent to that1 issued by traditional teaching establishments. Students may study a subject such as a language, or a whole "cycle" of studies such as post-16 secondary technical education specializing in electronics, or higher education studies in heating engineering etc. Courses may be given by certain associations recognized by the authorities of the *commune* or area etc.

The poorest have for the most part received primary education followed by special or "professional" schools. The latter provide an entry into a manual profession for those who complete the full six years. Yet often they do not get this far. Following primary school, very few enter technical schools allowing them to enter higher education. Practically none go to general secondary schools which would allow them to go to university. For example, those at technical school may not, even after six years, study to be electricians. Only those at technical school may choose to specialize in electronics after the first two years, during which all students attend the same classes, and learn a little about electronics over two years, but they then require another two years before being awarded the qualification of electrician-electronic engineer.

It is very difficult for the poorest to find a program which leads to a qualification. We have already seen that one reason is their own fear and reluctance to fail again in a system which too closely resembles a school environment. Another reason is that they are unsure whether their program will lead to a job, and thereby a wage. In this context, they prefer to live day-to-day doing odd jobs or looking for a job on which they and their families can live.

It is also important to note that for some jobs, such as maintaining or repairing TVs or radios, jobs involving recycling and the environment, social work etc, there is no training directly linked to the skills revealed in our research in the adult training establishments to which the poorest might have access.

Some experimental training programs

Whether they be school-based (professional colleges) or a combination of work and school[2] (such as apprenticeships), it is evident that very few young people from poor backgrounds have access to traditional training programs especially since the skills we have highlighted thus far are only rarely (if ever) catered for under this system. Some experimental training programs have been carried out in France and Belgium, and seem to us to allow the poor to develop their skills and work at the same time.

Descriptions of the experimental training programs

Experts by experience[3]: initial training program of 12 weeks (252 hours), divided into four parts—the role of an expert by experience; health and preventive care; lack of basic security and assistance; the role of medical-social workers.

This initial program was complemented by ongoing training. The training the experts by experience received gave a general outline of their work, within which their skills could be put to use. In order to be accepted onto the program:

> You have to have lived in poverty in your own life and have (or have had) young children. You also need to be able to work in a team and have basic social skills. It's not enough to know what poverty is like, you also have to want to talk about it[4].

It was therefore on account of their personal backgrounds and their belonging to the world of poverty that these women were taken on. This was taken into account in their training. One of them said:

> We did a lot on our training course. Amongst other things, we looked at health (mandatory vaccinations for children and bedside manner). After, we learned about services. We worked on understanding our own lives, talking about our stories. Doing this was necessary to explain what we do and say on a habitual basis. For example, if you've always lived in an old house you can't keep clean, you're not so used to cleaning, you haven't learned to run a household[5].

The intercultural mediators[6] were chosen from young foreign women with little education who were offered a combined work-school training program. The selection criteria were these:
– have a certificate of education to age 16[7];
– speak at least two languages (French or Dutch and Arabic or Turkish);

– be sufficiently motivated to follow a long combined training program;
– have some knowledge of social or cultural work;
– have an open, unprejudiced attitude towards different cultures.

The program was at upper secondary (post-16)[8] level. Five years of study entitled the mediators to a certificate. The program improves their knowledge of their languages and provides a basic introduction to healthcare or teaching skills and close supervision during their work placement.

The library outreach workers followed a combined school-work placement for two years: three weeks at the library and a week at the training center. Each of them took something away from their training particularly relevant to their daily work:

> – The first two years I spent on work placement showed me what a library was. I mostly learned about children's books. There were so many good books, really well done with brilliantly well-written stories and great illustrations, I just loved reading them, discovering them[9].
> – The writing workshops were good because we could make up our own sentences, things like that. I use that with the children when they want to write a story or adapt a story in a book into a play or something like that[10].

The surroundings and protection officers, the AMIS, the *Messagers*: These mediation jobs on public transport or in cities were created for young people (sometimes by them in the case of the *Messagers*) or adults from deprived backgrounds. There was either an initial training or a combined school-work program (two weeks for the SNCF surroundings officers).

In the case of the *Messagers*, training included:
– a knowledge of social, integration and exclusion issues;
– an understanding of the role and ability to describe it;
– an ability to deal with people alone or in a group;
– an ability to adapt to diverse situations dealing with people and retain self-control;
– a knowledge of the local environment, to be able to act as mediators between public transport users and local authorities;
– an ability to intervene in an emergency (to help people)[11].

For the AMIS, *it is clear that to do our job, time in combined work-school training is required, so we can acquire the necessary knowledge to fulfill our role. It is more about developing the skills governing how we act and think that we already have, using our experiences of situations we have encountered*[12]**.

The pruners are the only example we know of where manual skills are recognized and developed, though there may be others. This trade was experimented with in France in 1984 as a part of the "New Qualifications" scheme. The young students followed a combined work-school program for 24 months and were "under contract", that is, they received a wage. The only academic requirements to follow the program were literacy skills, but no other qualifications.

Common features of these experimental training programs

For the most part these programs were started by associations and often utilize the relational skills of people from poor or very poor backgrounds. We have seen that a person's social background is one of the conditions of their being accepted onto the programs, since this knowledge of real life is an advantage in the jobs these programs lead to. Living (or having lived) in poverty allows people to feel closer and show more sensitivity to poor people. The programs aim to encourage a critical view of one's background in order to improve relations between that background and the rest of society. They complement and exploit the potential of people's skills.

The programs, with the exception of those for the training of surroundings officers and similar roles, are long-term (between two and five years) and combine work and school, sometimes including initial training. It is of vital importance to keep in touch with real life so as not to "over-intellectualize". A combined program allows students to find theoretical solutions to questions which arise during practical sessions. It is also necessary to take the time to let people bring their basic skills up to scratch. The AMIS in Lyon, however, criticized the lack of time spent on training.

These programs all provide their students with financial security in the shape of a wage, which is vital for some of them to complete the program. Thinking about and taking a critical distance vis-à-vis their own backgrounds is disconcerting enough without adding financial burdens, especially for people who have always had to "pull strings".

Some concerns and thoughts concerning these experiments

There is an obvious risk that the AMIS and atmosphere and protection officers use their skills against their own backgrounds. They can very quickly become quasi police officers (though with no weapons) who keep the peace and look after public safety[13]. This would hush up discussion of violence and antisocial behavior which, though they are inexcusable, nevertheless testify to a maladjusted relationship with the rest of society.

There is a high risk of the requisite level of schooling to enter these training programs rising quickly in the name of short-term success and because demand for the programs is high. The second and subsequent generations of library outreach workers have had to possess a high-school diploma, even a university degree. There is therefore little chance that young people will come from poor backgrounds, even if they have had a "nightmare" finding work. In the longer term, there is a risk these skills will be appropriated by other backgrounds. This would not be a disaster, indeed it would even honor the poor—provided they were not thereby excluded from jobs they invented.

These new jobs, far from taking work away from people already active in these sectors, actually create more work since they bring new people to libraries for example, requiring librarians to adapt. The library outreach workers can in their turn teach the librarians: an example of reciprocity in education in action.

Training programs that should be created

What are the training programs that should be created to convert the skills of the poorest into jobs which are useful to society as a whole, with special regard to needs which are currently unmet? Since these would be new programs for partly-new jobs, what is most important is identifying the necessary criteria for their being created and succeeding.

The starting-point is the awareness on the part of the poorest of what we might, if we wanted to be provocative, call their wealth of experience, of life and struggle, and the skills they draw from that. However, not only does society not have this awareness, but the poorest themselves do not have the necessary distance to achieve it either. This is exemplified by Jacqueline Meton[14], who when describing all she does to help the most deprived said *I do nothing.*

Then the task is to pinpoint those needs amongst those our society is currently unable to meet and which the skills of the poorest can remedy.

Here, there are many examples in coaching people in difficulties, looking after them in medical and social services contexts, encouraging them to read, cross-cultural ethnic mediation etc.

At this point, there generally needs to be some tailored program leading to a useful and recognized trade or job. Here are some essential criteria which in our opinion this kind of program must take into account:

– first of all, the awareness on the part of people in difficulties of their potential, though they may not often know it. This therefore means starting with what they have experienced and not from general or abstract ideas;

– the end goal of this training must be to increase people's independence in their work, that is, acquiring the ability to constantly adapt to new and sometimes unpredictable working conditions;

– as we describe in the following paragraph, the training process must be reciprocal, that is, everyone has to be able to take turns teaching and being taught (knowledge-merging). In other words, a partnership must be set up between people or groups of people who share complementary forms of knowledge or skills because of their life experiences or their educational background.

This new form of training should therefore lead to jobs or professions, some of which will be new, some of which will focus on taking care of and dealing with people in difficulties, but which on the whole should be useful to everyone.

In addition to the sectors we have already mentioned, such as coaching, welcome and mediating, we must also take into account teaching (of citizenship and the history of the Fourth World, for example), environmental work such as scrap recovery, waste treatment etc, research (in relevant sectors), health, protection, the law, culture, activities, leisure etc.

Can the poorest become educators?

It seems to us that a reciprocal relationship between teacher and pupil is an important factor in the success of some of the experimental training programs described in the previous chapter. By a reciprocal relationship, we mean here reciprocal teaching between teacher and pupil, but also the sharing of professional skills between social milieus outside a given program. This sharing can respond to a deeply-held ambition of people living in extreme poverty—it symbolizes a social leveling of the playing field, meaning people outside poverty can recognize the wealth of experiences in the lives of the poorest.

We saw in the previous chapter how some skills are passed down the generations amongst the poorest.

Mr. Gérard[15] told us in an interview that he taught his son and *a friend who is having problems and who is living with us for the time being* how to use a measuring device, how to repair faulty parts of a television set, demonstrating patience and a degree of teaching skills:

> The first thing I do, I let him go about it his own way, and if he can't, he comes and asks me for a hand. I advise him as best I can. But if I do it all for him, he'll never learn anything, of course.

Another person from a poor background who is currently a baker, had a group of young people in his shop one day who asked him for a cake. He taught them to make one in return for them cleaning his shop.

However, passing on these skills between themselves seems not to be entirely satisfactory to the poor. Learning is—correctly—considered as having greater prestige if it takes place in a recognized public institution. Is this not a founding precept of all adult education? Anyone teaching in adult training will accept that their lessons are enriched by the experiences—professional or otherwise— of students from different backgrounds. This is also true in professional training courses with people from poor backgrounds, who bring their life experiences, their own skills and values etc. And the learning process is more effective if there is interaction between their contributions and the skills being taught. Rudy De Cock[16], who was in charge of training the experts by experience, said:

> When we took on the first recruits, training was more focused on the way Kind en Gezin worked. In future, though, we will be looking more at students' using their

own life experiences[17] in understanding the lives of the families we visit. That will help us to better understand the needs of these families and meet those needs more effectively.

Sometimes, roles can realistically be reversed. Some experts by experience have taken part in training nurses, and will be involved in training the Kind en Gezin teachers. One of the lessons Rudy De Cock draws from this experiment is that training the experts by experience has to go hand in hand with training the nurses with whom they will work in tandem. The nurses have to learn to see the experts by experience as colleagues who have a different, complementary form of expertise, not as their helpers. In other words, training is not limited to developing the skills of the experts by experience, but serves to promote knowledge-sharing and transform the way work is used within the institution. This can only happen through dialogue between all the parties affected.

Here then we see tangible examples of an emerging reciprocity and partnership which we predicted in a more generalized way in previous sections.

Is it a lack of reciprocity, an absence of combined training for librarians and library outreach workers, which is behind the misunderstandings and conflict between the latter and others they work with?

At the risk of indulging in navel-gazing, we believe we can say that this form of reciprocal training is also applicable to the Fourth World–University project, in which the authors of the memoir (Fourth World volunteer corps members, activists and academics) were involved. Through meeting, researching and writing together, the former learned about the demands of academic criticism, while the latter learned about life experiences (in a context which narrowed the cultural divide between the academic world and extreme poverty) and about the skills developed by a volunteer corps through working with the poorest. Both groups were required to question the language and vocabulary they used, their ways of thinking and their frames of reference, which broadened the horizons of all the participants.

Why should the poorest not be able to become educators in their turn? Of course, it is sometimes a long road, involving learning a good deal about culture, distancing oneself from one's own background in poverty, practicing speaking in public etc. It is not necessarily a matter of educating in a traditional sense but could be, for example, making an active contribution to courses run by third parties. There are other examples of successful projects of this kind. People who have experienced extreme poverty and who have been trained as activists by ATD Fourth World have as a result been able to pass these skills on to others, in professional and other contexts. In Namur, activists took part in a legal experts' colloquium on the relationship between poverty and human rights. They used real-life examples to show that fundamental rights are indivisible—there is, for example, no right to minimum living benefits without a right to housing, no access to work without the right to health, etc. In Brussels, activists and lawyers wrote down and analyzed together descriptions of injustices done to the poorest. In France, groups of lawyers specializing in representing children planned meetings with Fourth World representatives, as part of their ongoing professional training, in order to better understand the situations faced by the children of the poorest. People living in poverty representing various associations, took part in an ongoing training session for French magistrates organized by the National School of Judges and Magistrates.

At the Regional Institute of Social Workers in Rennes (and also in Alsace), activists helped train social workers as part of a course lasting a full academic year. Their contribution went beyond simple testimonies, and involved analyzing how social workers and poor families viewed one another and using this to arrive at skills which are useful to social workers. Reports and feedback lead us to conclude that the student social workers really learned to see their vocation differently—emphasizing the family rather than taking care of individuals; discovering social bonds, however fragile they may be, where others do not see them; strengthening these links and using them to resolve family problems; helping people without imposing one-size-fits-all solutions on them; learning what they want to do in life and acting as their partner in achieving it; understanding their problems in being independent when poverty saps their morale; respecting their intimate relationships above and beyond professional confidentiality; developing positive strategies to protect and encourage people instead of merely intervening in crises; giving emotions their rightful place, etc.

These innovative experiments show that professional training cannot be limited to passing on technical skills, nor a one-way learning process. In many cases, and particularly concerning people skills, reciprocity is vital for professional training to succeed. In other instances, it makes training for other jobs a more rewarding experience.

Lessons for the future

We can draw several conclusions from the first three sections of this chapter concerning training programs needed to create new trades or jobs accessible to the poorest.

The overview given in the first section shows that in the vast majority of cases, there are programs which correspond to the needs and skills of the poorest, but that they are rendered inaccessible by several obstacles: sometimes the level of formal education required is greater than that attained by people from poor backgrounds; sometimes it seems too great a risk to commit to a program with no guarantee of a job afterwards. More suitable programs in alternative sectors such as companies providing mediation services and on-the-job training do exist, but not enough by a long way, and they are generally not officially recognized, especially in terms of issuing certificates. These barriers need to be removed if everyone is to be given the right to training as enshrined in law.

Analyzing a few experimental training programs, albeit quickly, such as library outreach workers, experts by experience, surroundings and protection officers and pruners, showed us some of the most important features of successfully improving the employment prospects of poor people, which might be summarized as follows.

The recognition of abilities acquired through life experiences

We have seen that abilities stemming from life experiences are difficult to quantify, though no less real for that, and are vital for some jobs, especially ones involving mediation. Yet there is a great risk that these skills will not be accepted (because they are hard to measure) in future experimental programs, and that the academic bar will be raised when selecting candidates. This would undermine the very essence of such jobs, however, which require a knowledge of the social group with which one works. In addition, it removes the right of poor people to become involved in improving their own communities.

Various steps are therefore necessary for the very poor to have continued priority access to the new trades they have invented. The first condition for such access to training should be that candidates are living or have lived in poverty or in close proximity to families in poverty, so that skills garnered from experience may be put into practice.

New programs offering real qualifications

These programs must give students real independence, that is, teach them to go from acting automatically on intuition to acting following considered analysis, meaning they can adapt to new, though similar situations to those previously encountered. After all, what would be the point of a program which maintained the person in a position of dependency in their work, or whose status was insecure? Training must enable the person to transfer their skills to changing working situations.

This means there can be no corners cut in terms of the time required to fully understand all the aspects of an ever-evolving profession. It is justifiable, for example, to ask how well-rounded the initial training for surroundings officers on the trains is, given that it lasts only a few weeks and probably does not give the young people straight off the course any real independence. What, then, will happen when their contract runs out? There is a strong possibility these young people will find themselves in a similar hellish situation to the one they were in before, even though they have had a rewarding experience.

This training must alternate with time spent in real-life working situations, for several reasons:

– work provides the necessary financial security for everyone to commit fully to their training program;

– work in itself provides a learning experience and qualifications;
– it increases the chances of finding a job after training is completed.

Reciprocity in training

These new jobs, such as mediators, surroundings officers etc, open new areas of work. They therefore have consequences on how other jobs in overlapping areas are exercised. For example, we saw that the library outreach workers' introducing new users to libraries required librarians to adapt the way they dealt with these users. The librarians should therefore follow a complementary form of training in their turn, essentially to learn about and understand their new users. For it is clear that it is the library which must adapt to its users and not the other way around.

We saw that librarians play an important role in providing library outreach workers with on-the-job training, for example about book classification etc. We can also confirm that the library outreach workers can teach librarians what they know about extreme poverty. This is essentially what has happened in several libraries where library outreach workers work. This reciprocal form of teaching is desirable on several levels: it shows the new mediator and their librarian colleagues that their skills are valuable; and this will probably lead to library staff really working together for the good of library users, especially those living in poverty, in an atmosphere where everyone feels valued.

The example of the library outreach workers can be applied more generally to the relationships between experts by experience and nurses, atmosphere officers and ticket inspectors and train managers, AMIS and bus drivers, *Messagers* and community police officers etc.

Notes

1. The French equivalent certificate is the *Brevet des collèges*.
2. Combined work and school training programs vary academic lessons with periods spent working and encourage students to learn "on the spot".
3. Taken from the *Report on preparatory activities*, Kind en Gezin Research Department, and *Evaluatie-onderzoek naar begeleidingsmethodieken van kansarme gezinnen*, Brussels, VUB, Medisch-sociale Wetenschappen, 1994.
4. Rudy De Cock, experts by experience supervisor, interview no. 17.
5. Interview no. 18.
6. Taken from *Intercultural Mediation: do young immigrants need contact with coordinators or intercultural mediators?*, Leuven, HIVA, 1995.
7. The French equivalent is the *secondaire premier cycle, brevet*.
8. The French equivalent is the *secondaire 2è cycle, baccalauréat*.
9. Interview no. 14.
10. Interview no. 8.
11. Taken from an article by Jean-Marie Petitclerc supporting the founding of the association of *Messagers*.

12. The double asterisk** indicates extracts from group discussions or personal writings.
13. *This experiment* (the Messagers) *is not without its risks, the worst-case scenario being the creation of a militia or mafia! At the same time, if we are to ensure that the scheme does not become just another form of volunteering, and if we want it to open doors to new jobs, a training program needs to be set up*". Taken from an article by J-M Petitclerc.
14. Interview no. 4.
15. Interview no. 3.
16. Interview no. 17.
17. The life experiences of women taken on as experts by experience.

Chapter 4

RECOGNITION

The skills we have described and analyzed above are most often not recognized as learned abilities. Even if in some cases they are tacitly acknowledged in social contexts such as the family, amongst neighbors, in one's local area or even by those running organizations or services, they carry no official weight, yet those who possess them sometimes feel proud of them.

It is now accepted that everyone's personal, professional or even social background contributes to their knowledge and skills which can be officially recognized and used in social bargaining in the same way as academic qualifications. Some even consider a sense of justice, giving and serving others as quantifiable virtues. This recognition has been formalized to coexist with school or university courses, especially where recognition of professional skills is concerned. But for the poorest, their skills have almost always been acquired outside of any company or organization. This means that acknowledging their skills falls outside the general modus operandi and there is a risk of official procedures making it impossible, especially since there is often no box to tick for these skills, nor any actual qualifications, old or new.

Can the poorest have their skills recognized without being consigned to dead-end jobs or remaining second-class citizens, and without having them exploited to benefit those with more qualifications? How can this be achieved? Can they gain a sense of self-worth through tailored training programs leading to real qualifications and real jobs?

De facto recognition

People with these skills generally do not have a degree or professional qualifications. Yet we sometimes have recourse to them and their skills, which is what we mean by de facto recognition.

Personal awareness of one's skills

As we have seen, some people feel they possess a skill. This can give them the personal pride and strength to carry on fighting to escape poverty, or motivate them in different ways, such as to help others or to fight wastage. Mr. Gérard[1], who repairs televisions, said *I proved that we can do things, that we are not useless*. In order for him to categorize his work as a garbage recuperator[2] under the very broad area of environmental improvement as he does, he must be sure of his abilities and skills.

Members of the Fourth World volunteer corps are experienced in showing the poorest they have skills. We shall take two examples, that of Méca-Jeunes and that of street libraries.

– **Méca-Jeunes** is a traveling mechanics workshop. Many young people who have grown up in poverty leave school at 16 (sometimes even earlier) without being able to read and write, without having learned a trade and believing they are good for nothing and never will be. The Fourth World volunteer corps member in charge of youth work in the Val d'Oise *département* set up a small mechanics workshop and a computer in a van—this is Méca-Jeunes. He developed a battery charging system based on those used by people living in caravans. Most of his young pupils and their families made a living from recovering scrap metal. The piles of scrap metal became not only a direct source of income (through separating and selling what is recovered), but also a source of raw materials for the mechanical constructions they put together. The young people who took part in the workshop week after week were proud to see that what they made had originally come from them and people like them. It was after a few months, when trust had been established between them and those running the workshop, that they asked to practice dictation together to improve their French. By making things they discovered that they were not as stupid as they had thought, and that they were able to make useful things, using their own resources. They were able to broaden their knowledge by starting to use a computer. This meant they could work on their reading and writing without shame or embarrassment, using word-processing packages. After several years, when they had regained faith in their own knowledge and skills, several mustered the courage to embark upon Work Placements for Intensive Professional Preparation (SPER), Credit Training, Individual Training Contracts (CFI) and Active Preparation towards Qualifications and Employment (PAQUE)[3].

– **Street libraries.** In the 1960s, Father Joseph Wresinski* suggested to students wanting to help the poorest that they go down into the streets and into poor neighborhoods to share their knowledge with the children, using books. This is how street libraries began. For years, Fourth World volunteer corps members and allies* of ATD Fourth World ran them alone. Then young people living in the areas gradually started to take an interest in running them. Fourth World volunteer corps members, who knew these young people had talents because of their almost daily contact with them, encouraged them to take part in running the libraries. One library outreach worker said[4]:

I started running street libraries on Reunion Island. To tell the truth, I couldn't really see the point to begin with. I did it because in my area there was nothing to do, no road and no electricity. As I didn't have the chance to study, I was working illegally as an agricultural day-laborer in the sugar cane fields. It wasn't exactly stimulating work. But every Saturday afternoon, the children and I ran the library. Passers-by were surprised to see me working with children in the street. They wondered what I could teach them, since I had hardly been to school myself. The other coordinators and I wanted to show the parents that the library wasn't just mucking about. Gradually they realized that it was important to the children, who, because they knew us better, trusted us more. They weren't afraid to talk to us about their problems at school, because they felt that we would not make fun of them and that we would listen to them.

The parents and neighbors were happy and proud to see that their children were also able to organize the library.

It was because they believed the children had these skills that the Fourth World volunteer corps members started negotiations with the Ministry of Culture and a social worker training college[5] to experiment with the new profession of library outreach worker over a two-year period. They were supported in this by the experiences of running street libraries in collaboration with young people from poor backgrounds.

Recognition by other people

There are many aspects to recognition. There are numerous dictionary definitions of the word *recognition*. The activists were most interested by the idea of self-recognition, which to them seemed most relevant to the research: *self-recognition is seeing a similarity between oneself and someone else*.

Would the individual participants and the groups be able to see a similarity between the skills of the poorest and what they did at work, in society or simply as human beings? Does recognizing the skills of the poorest imply recognizing the poor themselves?

We should note that recognition is not a one-way street: one person can want to be recognized by others, and act in such a way as to indicate this, but it is *other people* who accord recognition based on their own criteria. This is why we shall shortly see both how recognition can come about, that is, how similarity can be perceived, as well as what constitutes difference, which often prevents the skills of the poorest being properly recognized.

Similarities

One of the prime similarities between people doing a job is the job itself, the fact of **doing something**, of one's actions being visible to the rest of the world. For example**, one man was nicknamed "the sailor". He had worked on a trawler for several years, but an accident at sea had left him unable to board a boat since. This accident had never been recognized as an accident at work either. Every morning he boarded a bus with his briefcase containing a flask of coffee and sandwiches, like any other office worker. This was his way of showing he was also a worker. The bus driver was used to seeing him spend all day giving people information. One winter's day all the buses were stuck because of black ice. The conductors were snowed under with work and called upon "the sailor" to show the driver which route to take to avoid roads with too much black ice. Equally, when a new driver did not yet know the bus route, "the sailor" took it upon himself to show them, arriving at five am to do so. He slept in a café near the station at that time, so he could catch the first bus. All the bus drivers knew him. *If you don't know, go and ask "the sailor", he'll tell you.*

Another man**, having spent a long time out of work, found a job as a painter. He wore his work overalls every day, even at weekends, to show everyone he had a job.

Similarity between working people is also expressed through the idea of a **job well done**. This is particularly true of manual work, where quality is immediately obvious. For example, one very poor man, who was working repainting a house front, was told by a neighbor, an electronics expert, *what you're doing is great, you work really well*. Recognition of a job well done and one's ability is equally important for Mr. Gérard, who repairs televisions.

Some of the skills we have described form part of what we might call many people's **civic values**. For example, the campaign against the injustices suffered by very poor people led by Jacqueline Meton6 is appreciated not only by those concerned but also by the local authorities. This can be seen when she telephones the mayor's secretary to make an appointment in order to help people sent from one office to another to no avail. For example, her assiduous work has helped the mayor in winning the cases of people with no financial resources or housing.

Another recognized value, probably because it is rarer, is **willingness to serve others**. Referring again to Jacqueline Meton, one of those running a soup kitchen[7] said:

> What she does is more than useful, it is vital. I always see her hurrying to help other people, very considerately I must say. And she is also very effective since she goes straight to the person who can deal with the problem.

Mr. Gérard[8] said:

> If you can serve people who are having a harder time than you, you can't stop yourself. Because you've been there, you understand, you know what it's like.

Another example of this is the aforementioned man admired for his skills as a painter, who offered to clean the house of the neighbor who had paid him the compliment, using the power hose he used in his own work.

Differences

Though the skills of the poorest are appreciated in some ways, it is also important to remember what they are criticized for and what prevents them being recognized as "real" workers. It is not their skills themselves which are criticized but rather that which reveals their poor backgrounds.

Paul Linden[9] comes under fire for **not being qualified** to run the homeless shelter he started with some friends. When he went to his local authority to try and have his association recognized, he was told he could not and the association had to disband.

If a job is **not a salaried position**, it is not recognized as a job. That was Anne's[10] husband's reaction. She is a volunteer at the ONE.

Working illegally is often criticized too, even if it suits some bosses well. For example, one man had been moonlighting for 10 years. He did not work regularly, and the boss came to look for him every time he needed him. For workers and trade unions, it is difficult to see that sometimes working illegally is the only way to feed a family and retain one's dignity because one is working.

Another criticism concerns **how work is organized**. For example, small scrap metal dealers are seen as polluting the environment, because the piles of scrap next to their houses are visible. But previously, batteries, for example, were returned to wholesalers as they were. Now, scrap dealers have to remove the lead, which is the only part they can sell, leaving the acid and bakelite valueless and pollutants.

We also saw in the previous chapter that the **situation is sometimes paradoxical**. A person can be appreciated for their skills with children (as with the library outreach workers) or with adults (as with the experts by experience), but at the same time they can be criticized for having not shaken off *bad habits* linked to their background, such as fragile health, getting too involved etc. *She's very good with the children, but she's immature* said one head librarian, speaking about a young library outreach worker.

Recognition by other people is also demonstrated in a concrete sense by the trust placed in someone, whether this be by parents letting Jean[11] look after their children during Summer Street Festivals, people who ring Marcel[12] because they want to throw out domestic appliances they have no room for, or who give their TV sets to Mr. Gérard[13] to repair, or trust placed in Paul Linden[14] and his friends' non-profit organization by the police, who took homeless people there at night. But this last example shows that this type of recognition is not enough on its own, even if it is indispensable, since the homeless shelter had to close down. Recognition of being close to the people they help justifies the importance of official recognition.

On the other hand, if there were enough natural, de facto recognition, there would no longer be the exclusion from which the poor suffer. What they do to survive would be valued and their skills, both manual and relational, would have been known about and recognized for a long time. The kind of recognition described in the dictionary as seeing a similarity between another person and oneself can lead to exclusion, even racism, if it is taken to its logical conclusion that I only recognize those who resemble me. Is recognition not about appreciating and treasuring other people's differences while focusing on what one has in common with them? In this sense, recognizing the (manual and relational) skills of the poorest is inextricably linked to recognizing the poor themselves, since they learned their skills through their daily lives. Recognizing the skills of the poorest would therefore indicate standing alongside them in fighting extreme poverty and exclusion.

Official or formal recognition

From de facto to formal recognition

There are various ways of having one's abilities recognized if they have not been acquired in a formal context (at school, for example), including compiling a portfolio, as Gaston Pineau[15] explained:

> Skills often take the shape of knowledge gained from experience which has not been learned in a formal educational context. Personal recognition, that is, becoming aware of one's skills or knowledge through experience, is made more difficult by the fact that one often uses them without really realizing it, making identifying what one can do a job in its own right.

Gaston Pineau makes a distinction between the different levels between personal, social and formal/institutional recognition of knowledge gained from experience. With reference to Bertrand Schwartz[16], he spoke about the new jobs which could be (and in some cases have been) recognized by complementing practical experience with more formal study. He continued:

> A comprehensive approach brings together the various tasks one has to complete to gain each of the various types of recognition. It's called a portfolio of your skills. For example, when an architect applies for a job, they don't just send in their CV they have to show examples of their work, which they often keep in large folders—plans for houses they have designed, such and such a piece of work, etc. That's how they prove they can do certain things. The idea of the portfolio is to say "I haven't got a certificate to prove I've officially studied this, but there are other ways of proving it, I still know things". We work a lot using this method to take people's knowledge gained through experience as a starting-point and see how that can lead to a professional qualification.

This means that both existing skills and the future of the job must be considered. Schematically speaking, we can identify five successive stages:

1) **Giving a considered account of one's life thus far**, not in the formal or schematic sense of a CV, but by describing one's life in terms of one's interests, plans and what one has done. This leads to:

2) **Pinpointing significant experiences,** often linked to specific places or people, with moments where one has benefited from discussing or sharing ideas. It is important for this to have taken place in interaction with others, in a group, in order to:

3) **Identify the knowledge drawn from experience** which gives one specific abilities, or which constitutes in itself both personal and social abilities. At this point one must:

4) **Undertake the considerable task of translating** and to some extent formalizing one's knowledge by experience, thus building up a job profile. We are then able to tackle the all-important phase of the process, namely:

5) **Begin negotiating.** This means putting one's case for professional recognition to the social, economic and political authorities.

All these steps put together make up a file or "skills portfolio", very useful in future attempts to gradually gain recognition of one's skills.

Here are a few examples as an illustration of the process of recognition:

– The experts by experience represent a profession which has gone beyond the experimental stage in Belgium, since a new batch of students are currently being trained. We can say that their process of recognition has reached level 4 of the chart above. On the basis of their pay scale (they are still considered as unskilled workers) and on the transferability of their skills to other working contexts (apart from Kind en Gezin, only a few organizations or institutions show any interest in their profession), the final stage, that of official recognition by the authorities and social partners is yet to be achieved.

– The profession of intercultural mediator has existed in Belgium since 1989. It is aimed at young immigrants and currently enjoys better recognition than that of expert by experience. It has already spread to several sectors, such as healthcare, education, childcare and youth services at several levels, from intercultural assistant to intercultural educator. However, we should note that this profession is much less accessible to the poorest than that of expert by experience (see Chapter 3 for the respective conditions of access to training in these professions).

In addition, academic studies were used to draw up the job profile for intercultural mediators, while such studies are still being carried out for experts by experience.

– The library outreach workers achieved a qualification officially recognized at level V by the French Association of Librarians (AB).

– The profession of pruner has also been recognized by a qualification at level V.

Recognition of one's work

This is an essential part of our research question: supposing that the skills of the poorest and the new training programs intended for them are recognized, will this recognition result in their having a dignified status as workers or as being engaged in human activity?

Salaried work

The word "work" invariably implies a *salary*. This is true of only a part of the workers we are dealing with in our study. Though many of them see a salaried position as their ultimate goal, it seems that this goal is only rarely fully achieved. One 49-year-old man who was long-term unemployed, spent years in psychiatric care, then in a homeless shelter. He suffers from a skin condition. Working for a recycling firm under the social workshop scheme[17] is a dream job for him. His manager is amazed by his enthusiasm and commitment to his job after having lived in poverty for so many years: *He still comes to work every day as happy as if it were his first day. He comes even when he's ill, we have to send him home sometimes**.*

Unfortunately, ordinary contracts are the exception rather than the rule. LST receives no subsidies and operates on the commercial market, having to struggle from one day to the next to keep its head above water financially and remain true to its goals. All 12 of the cooperative's employees (the manager, engineer, workers etc) accepted to have their individual salaries adjusted to meet the cost of the other employees' salaries and training. This is the price they pay for their identity *which is the same as any other worker[18]*.

The problem of a lack of basic security and inferior status is evident from the other examples. André[19] is in temporary employment, the experts by experience are on open-ended contracts but still have no promotion prospects, the AMIS complain their status is temporary and they are not fully included in the workforce of the public transport company which employs them.

> We're sort of there but not there. Our experience tells us that our work is useful but to work more effectively we need to be a real partner in all the various departments of the company, we need to be trained to carry out the work we are assigned, and be recognized by other staff. It does no one any good for us to be working in an insecure position, not us, not the company and not the customers. What's the point of investing in us and us committing ourselves if it's all short-term and there are no prospects once the contract expires**?

There is worse: people entitled to the RMI who are put on part-time, temporary state-aided contracts, being paid no more than what they would receive from the RMI; people on the minimex in Belgium being forced to work, sometimes illegally, sometimes as volunteers, to prove they are willing to work; long-term unemployed people doing casual work for 150 BEF an hour ($ 4.49), but without official working status.

Others have had very short or irregular careers as salaried employees, having had to leave because of conflicts or illness. In some cases, we have seen how voluntary work performed by the poorest was taken away from them when it was turned into a salaried position. We need to be constantly on our guard, therefore, not only to guarantee proper contracts allowing peopie to escape poverty, but also to allow the poor to retain their positions when stable jobs aimed at them are created.

Self-employment

There are a whole host of often informal jobs performed in a self-employed capacity, such as scrap metal recovery, repair work, animal breeding etc. Lack of financial security and the complex nature of the social and taxation services constrain the poorest to work in this grey area. Though some work could be made formal by being given salaried status, it is unlikely that this solution would meet the aspirations of those affected, some of whom have worked alone for many years. Is there no other way to facilitate and support those doing these jobs than relaxation of social and tax regulations? For example, the ADIE (Association for the Right to Economic Initiative, inspired by the Grameen Bank in Bangladesh) is aimed mainly at those receiving the RMI and the long-term unemployed wanting to work for themselves. It offers them a loan of up to 30,000 FF ($5,535) at favorable interest rates, as well as advice. Amongst the self-starters financed have been a scrap metal dealer, tile-cleaner, courier, mobile hairdresser, chimney-sweep, button-collector, snail-breeder, etc.

Other work

It's not that there's no work—there is, it's that there's no money in it said Jacqueline Meton. She perhaps underestimates the possibility of turning the coaching and mediation work she does into paid employment. But the fact remains that many poor people, with no job because of unemployment or health problems, demand the right to perform some kind of work, whether it be voluntary work for an organization, on an occasional basis, helping people in one's neighborhood, or for their own personal fulfillment (such as cultural activities or studies etc). Currently these occupations are accepted only reluctantly by the social security system. The unemployed are constantly suspected and carefully monitored—aren't they working illegally? Don't volunteers take paid employment away from other people? *I had to prove to the ONEM what I was doing here, that they wouldn't pay someone else to do it, that I wasn't taking the place of a worker*, explained Anna[20], a volunteer at the ONE. These kinds of checks cause embarrassment, though they are probably indispensable in protecting legal employment from benefits fraudsters. But if this worthwhile contribution is also to be valued, maybe volunteers should be given a more definite social status. There are many possibilities: avoid repeated checks by giving the unemployed or invalided volunteer status for sufficient periods of time; have those concerned insured against accidents at work; reimburse their fees and make these reimbursements tax-free; give them at least an indirect right to social protection (for example, combining periods of volunteer work with paid work for their health and unemployment insurance and/or pension fund). This approach could be broadened and applied to all what we now call "human activity" (including cultural work, studying etc). Some proposals go even further: the Boissonnat Report[21], for example, puts the case for a system of *contracts incorporating periods of paid work, training and leave of social purposes (for example for family purposes). During these various periods, the person would receive the same social benefits, though their means of payment might vary considerably.* This idea is more or less in line with the basic income suggested by one UK economist[22] and adopted by a political party in the Netherlands.

Another innovation concerns bartering, a very old profession in some poor communities. Lucie Ribert[23] told us how her mother went from door to door and was sometimes given potatoes. When she had more than enough she swapped the surplus for tomato sauce from their Italian neighbors, etc. *Exchange networks* (called LETS or SELS—Local Exchange Systems) run free service-for-service schemes in their local communities. These services can range from babysitting to plumbing, but each hour of service is counted as being worth the same amount of a made-up currency (e.g. grains of sand). In Belgium, the unemployed are currently forbidden from taking part in these networks (some have even had their benefits suspended), since rendering such services is considered as working illegally. However, it would make them feel less alone and make life easier for them. Should these networks not be regulated, for example by issuing checks which are exempt from tax and/or social charges for services rendered?

Notes

1. Interview no. 3.
2. A garbage recuperator recovers objects from garbage cans to sell or reuse them. Their job is therefore making something from what others throw away.
3. SPER, CFI and PAQUE are successive French government schemes introduced between 1988-1992 and aiming to give young people with the fewest chances of being accepted onto a professional training program a sufficient level of basic education to enable them to enter into the world of work..
4. Account taken from *Le médiateur du livre* (The Library Outreach Worker), ATD Quart Monde Marseille, 1997.
5. Institut Supérieur d'Intervention Sociale—Regional Center for Problem Children and Teenagers (Training center for social workers)
6. Interview no.4.
7. Interview no. 9.
8. Interview no. 3.
9. Interview no. 2.
10. Interview no. 11.
11. Interview no. 1.
12. Interview no. 5.
13. Interview no. 3.
14. Interview no. 2.

15. Lecture.
16. The instigator of the new qualifications in France.
17. Social workshops in Flanders are businesses aiming to give very poor people an entry into the world of work. Those working in them have an ordinary open-ended contract and are paid the minimum wage. Their wages are entirely subsidized.
18. Interview no. 10.
19. Interview no. 7.
20. Interview no. 11.
21. J. Boissonnat. (Report of the Committee chaired by -), *Work in twenty years' time*, General Commissariat, Editions Odile Jacob/La Documentation Française, 1995, pp30.
22. A. Atkinson., *Public Economics in Action: The Basic Income/Flat Tax Proposal*, Oxford, Clarendon, 1995.
23. Lecture.

Conclusion

Our research has shown how the very poor possess manual and relational skills, some of which are specialized, and which can often be useful to a changing society.

The aforementioned society's essential needs remain largely unmet, though the poorest could make their own useful and creative contribution in traditional industries, through manual work such as recovery or construction as well as (indeed especially) in sectors where relational skills are more important, such as personal support and mediation work etc.

For this to happen, there need to be tailored training programs, which in some flagship areas are beginning to see the light of day (library outreach workers for example). One essential aspect of these programs is that of reciprocity, that is, students taking their turn to act as educators (see for example the experts by experience), thus communicating the wealth of experience and particularly the struggle of the poorest to escape poverty. These programs, based on partnership between people from different backgrounds and willing to listen to one another, could result in the creation of new professions.

For these new occupations to become a reality, tailored procedures of recognition need to be set up. Specific procedures currently exist for skills acquired through work and school, but those for skills acquired through daily life are still at their earliest stages. It is a long and complex process, which we tackled in Chapter 4 with the help of experts in the field.

As well as this, there need to be appropriate guarantees to avoid these new occupations becoming inaccessible to those from the poor backgrounds whence they sprang by unjustifiably demanding traditional qualifications of their students.

Our research does not pretend to have dealt with all the skills the poorest possess. All we have done is open an avenue for research and initiatives by taking a few examples of people—who are close to us in one way or another—using their skills.

There are probably numerous areas in which the poorest use skills from which they can only just scrape a living or which allow them and their families to get by. As we have shown, these skills could probably be acknowledged, developed and deepened to allow those who possess them to play their part in a changing society, thus regaining their dignity as free people and citizens.

Through their individual and collective stories of resistance to poverty, the poor can make a useful and original contribution to the development of a society in which everyone can develop with the support of others, even in the "traditional" working world.

As we have already said, we limited our research to a few skills used in Belgium and France, but in every society people fight poverty by developing skills suited to their environment, thus making the scope for research immense.

Appendix

Interviews and lectures

To research the skills of the poorest, the group agreed that the activists would carry out 14 interviews. Since they were all from poor backgrounds, the interviewees could bear witness to their parents' skills or those of people in similar circumstances. They themselves have put some of these skills to use for many years. Their personal experience means they know whom to interview and how.

Three interviews were conducted by the activists and one academic. The latter carried out one alone, and the Fourth World volunteer corps member conducted three. That makes 18 interviews which underpin the research, of which 12 were conducted with people from poor backgrounds and 6 with people working in such areas. All the interviews were recorded and deciphered by those who conducted them, and then analyzed by the group.

Some members of our group also met Bernard Schwartz, who set up the new qualifications in France, and Gaston Pineau, a Professor in Educational Science, and a member of another thematic group in the Fourth World–University project.

No.	Name	Age	Family situation	Professional background	Current resources/ Status	Skills
1	Jean*	49	Single	Protected workshop	Invalid's pension, unemployment benefit	Coaching
2	Paul Linden*	40	Married, 3 children		Unemployment benefit	Welcome and Coaching
3	Mr. Gérard*	48	Married, 4 children	Construction, Metalwork	Unemployment benefit	Recovery, repair work
4	Jacqueline Meton*	56	Married	Concierge	Pension, husband's invalid's pension	Coaching
5	Marcel*	56	Married, 5 children	Highways, scrap metal firm	Invalid's pension	Scrap metal recovery
6	Maurice*	44	Married, 1 child	Removal man, maintenance	Wife's salary	Scrap metal recovery
7	André*	22	Single, lives with parents	Recycling firm	Temporary work	People skills
8	Claudine*	25	Single	Paid work placements, Library outreach worker	Unemployment benefit	Street libraries

No.	Name	Age	Family situation	Professional background	Current resources/ Status	Skills
9	Christian*	50	Married	Estate agent	Estate agent	Volunteers at a soup kitchen
10	Luc Lefevre	45	Married, 4 children	Electro-mechanic, plumber, Cooperative, workers' social worker	Runs LST	Work in associative sector
11	Anne*	35	Married, 5 children		Husband's salary	Volunteers at ONE
12	Nancy*	40	Married, 3 children	Nurse	Nurse	Professional and relational skills
13	Young people	15-20	Single	Students	Parents	Apprentices
14	Valérie*	34	Single	Office worker, Library outreach worker	Fourth World volunteer corps member	Street libraries
15	Mr. Lieven		Married	Manager, Van der Stock	Recycling firm manager	
16	Mr. Meganck		Married	Trade union employee	Trade union	Set up several back-to-work companies
17	Rudy De Cock		Married	In charge of experts by experience (receives a salary)	Kind en Gezin	
18	G, C and M	20-30		Experts by experience (receive salaries)	Kind en Gezin	Coaching

Bibliography and sources

– One academic gave a presentation on the Boissonnat Report on the future prospects of the working world: J. Boissonnat, *Le travail dans vingt ans (Work in Twenty Years' Time)*, Editions Odile Jacob, 1995.

– Another academic wrote a note referencing several books on work: G Roustang, *Le travail demain (Work Tomorrow)*; J. Boissonnat, *Pour la maîtrise de l'emploi (Controlling Employment)*; J. Dubois, *Le travail expression du mode de société (Work as an Expression of Society)*; G. Aznar, *Travailler tous pour travailler moins (Working Less, but Everyone Working)*.

– Another academic wrote three notes on the experts by experience, on intercultural mediators and on recycling firms, using works written in Dutch: P. Vanhamel, *Project Horizon—Report on preparatory activities, Kind en Gezin, Research Department*, 24 pages; G. Desnerck, G. De Schryver, M. Leys, F. Louckx, *Evaluatie-onderzoek naar begeleidingsmethodieken van kansarme gezinnen*, Brussels, VUB, Medischsociale Wetenschappen, 1994, 126 pages; A. Jennes, *Intercultural mediation*, Leuven, HIVA, 1995,188 pages; G. Bogaert, *De kringloopcentra in het Vlaamse Gewest: stand van zaken* 1995, Leuven, HIVA, 1996, 141 pages.

– One academic gave a mini-presentation of the book *Reconnaissance et validation des acquis (Recognizing and Valuing Skills)*, Que sais-je? PUF, 1994.

– The Fourth World volunteer corps member gave a presentation on the initiatives taken by the Local Exchange Systems (SELs) and the Association for the Right to Economic Initiative (ADIE).

Our other reading was made up of the following newspaper articles brought along by all the members of the group: Extract from the magazine L'entreprise et l'homme, *Innovative initiatives in the Netherlands*; extract from the newspaper Le Soir, *St Giles puts his money on the unemployed*; the General Commissariat, French official records, *Creating new qualifications*; the Parisien newspaper, *SNCF: a change in atmosphere*; a trade union paper, Partage, *For a third sector*; interview with Bernard Schwartz in Projet magazine; *For training leading to qualifications* and *The Messagers of Chanteloup-les-Vignes* by J.-M. Petitclerc; in the magazine Vif Express, *At your service*; in the LST journal, *ALE: Local Employment Agency*; in ES/EA by JM Petitclerc, *The worst violence hides the worst suffering*; in Le Soir, *The last days of Canal 9.*

V

CITIZENSHIP: REPRESENTATION AND EXTREME POVERTY

by Denise Bernia, Jacques Fierens, Joëlle Meurant,
Georges Mus, Patrice Nouvel and Pierre-Yves Verkindt.

With contributions from Daniel Cornerotte and Françoise Ferrand.

CITIZENSHIP: REPRESENTATION AND EXTREME POVERTY

Introduction

All human beings are born free and equal in dignity and rights. Thus begins Article 1 of the Universal Declaration of Human Rights. Yet this proclamation runs up against the reality of poverty across the world. Can our world be one of justice, freedom and well-being for every human being if we do not take this reality on board? Every day, the right to life is threatened for people who endure vagrancy, malnutrition, even famine and wars. In our countries (Belgium and France) poverty endures in spite of aid and assistance.

Human Rights are indivisible. They are economic, social and cultural (concerning resources, housing, work, health and education), but also civil and political (such as the right to vote, to participate and freedom of expression). This means that material aid cannot combat poverty alone. Financial assistance ensures that to some extent economic rights are respected, but those who are helped are not asked for their opinion, still less to make decisions. To have the right to speak is to be recognized as a citizen. Aristotle defined man as both someone who lived in a community and who was able to speak, for there can be no citizenship without speech.

Any human being living in a country, region, city or village is a citizen. They do not live alone but amongst other people in an organized manner we call society. In many countries this society is democratic, that is to say each citizen can make a contribution to the present and future of their society, but to do so requires that person to be recognized as a member of their community. Are people living in extreme poverty recognized as belonging to this human community, that is, are they recognized as citizens?

The aim of our democratic societies is the participation of their citizens. In order for them to carry out their right to participate, we have created democratic representation. Yet today the poor are not full players and partners in the society in which they live. Based on our experiences, we tried to consider the link between democracy and the participation of the poorest in the life of society, to which we all belong. We proceeded on the basis that systems of representation do not take sufficient account of the views of those who live in poverty, and tried to consider the link between citizenship, human rights and democracy in the light of this. This thought led us to formulate the following hypothesis: *Representation is rendering present the issues of those who are absent.*

Our experience over these two years, of which the following is the first fruit, has shown us that although merging and sharing knowledge are sometimes difficult, the attempt we have made to do so also represents a contribution to democracy. This is why the working method we adopted must be considered as much a part of testing our hypothesis as the memoir itself.

After explaining our methodology (Chapter 1), we will try to establish conditions under which representation is possible for everyone. Concepts must be carefully redefined: what do *representation, testifying, participation* and *being a partner* mean? (Chapter 2). Following this, examples will be used to demonstrate how the mechanisms of representation work in practice. Do the very poor in particular have the opportunity to speak and be listened to? (Chapter 3). Finally, what kind of representation needs to be created for exclusion linked to extreme poverty to end? (Chapter 4)

Chapter 1

METHODOLOGY

Our research method developed alongside those of the other groups participating in the Fourth World–University project. We think it necessary to describe this methodology before continuing with the rest of the memoir. We need to describe how the theme of representation was arrived at (I), before presenting the research bases on the one hand (II) and the group's approach on the other (III).

The themes of representation: Why and how?

The first seminar in the Fourth World–University project identified a number of themes groups could tackle, one of which was citizenship. When the group met for the first time, they decided to address this issue, and chose to adopt a "representation-based" approach.

The theme of citizenship

Of the 32 agent-authors* taking part in the project, 24 wrote a text on citizenship. Here are some of the things they wrote:

– allowing the poor to speak is very important, they know something worth listening to, which will change our view of them, and they have the right to be recognized as citizens;

– how can we make the poor real players and partners in the society in which they live?

– how can they be encouraged to participate?

– what is the point of proclaiming rights if there are people who do not benefit from them?

– society does not recognize the poor as worthy and able to be entrusted with responsibilities, and they live in fear of everyone else with no way to protect themselves;

– the poorest must be able to dialogue with the working world in order to create a just world and a society which is open to all;

– let us teach children from the cradle on not to make inequality and exclusion worse;

– At Fourth World People's Universities*, everyone has the chance to speak, they are a place where knowledge and learning are discussed and shared;

– true democracy can only be created if the poorest are included;

– how can it be ensured that the poorest participate in the decision-making process in society?

The theme *Citizenship, Democracy and Human Rights* is more precisely expressed in the questions asked by the mixed groups*:

– how can each person be guaranteed the opportunity to be included as an active citizen in a modern democratic society?

– which values does democracy truly defend?

– how does one participate in democracy?

– what does it mean to say the poorest are emblematic of rights for all?

– how can one make full use of one's rights as a citizen?

– why does society want an elite which simultaneously lauds both competitiveness and solidarity?

– why are human rights not applied in the same way for everyone?

The decision that this would be the Citizenship group seemed not to cause any problems for the two academics, nor the Fourth World volunteer corps member*. The activists* seemed to be uneasy at the idea, however. Let us give the floor to one of our group's activists to clarify:

> When the activists met at the end of the seminar, each of us wrote the theme of our choice on a piece of paper. It was foreseen that activists living in the same region would work on the same theme. One of my colleagues chose History and Citizenship, another Citizenship and I wanted Family and nothing else. Our group was given Citizenship. I left the seminar angry and despairing. I had to relent, and so out of solidarity with my group I said no more about the theme I wanted and on which I had a lot to say. For three weeks, I refused to work. I didn't understand the word "citizenship", and I couldn't see the point of it either; I wondered what I was doing in this project and I felt like giving up. After a few weeks, I tried to get into it, but it was very hard. I was still angry inside, I wanted to know why I had been asked to choose. Now I say to myself that in life, there are times when you have to do things you don't want to. Now I know that I also had things to say about Citizenship even if I didn't know what the word meant. By asking questions, I helped the group progress.

The group's first task was to work together to draw up their own research framework. The researchers had to take full responsibility for their framework.

The theme of representation

At the first group meeting, each member discussed which aspects of the terms *citizenship, democracy* and *human rights* they would like to focus on.

One academic singled out human rights, another democracy. The Fourth World volunteer corps member stressed citizenship, while the Fourth World activists were more concerned with representation. The activists took away everything the other participants had written on the subject, worked on it and arrived at the three key terms participation (personal and political), representation (groups or individuals speaking on behalf of others with their consent) and values (brotherhood, equality, justice, freedom and so on).

The activists suggested researching the representation of the poorest at all levels, since representation covers both participation and values as well. Their questions were: who may speak on behalf of the poorest? To which criteria must representation of the poorest conform?

It was quickly agreed to research representation, but points of view differed as to how to go about it—representation of the poorest or representation in general? At the end of the day, the question had been formulated thus: *The issue of the representation of the poorest and democracy.*

Planning and carrying out the research

Having identified representation as the subject, which was subsequently approved by all the project participants, the group discussed which materials they would need to address their subject.

The research materials

To kick off the research, it was decided that each member of the group would give a personal example of representation, either representing or being represented. One academic said that he would not base his contribution on his own personal experience, but on the thoughts of philosophers.

Everyone looked in encyclopedias and dictionaries to find a definition of the two words relating to our agreed subject *representation* and *democracy*.

One academic suggested working on the law passed by the French Assemblée Nationale on the RMI[1], researching the way the country's elected representatives spoke of the poor[2] in parliamentary debates from the *Journal Officiel*, similar to the Congressional Record.

In order to avoid working only on legal texts, the activists suggested carrying out interviews. They intended to interview poor people and people in authority, and ask them about the representation of the poor. The interviews[3] sparked negative reactions from some quarters. One CPAS Manager[4] initially agreed to take part, but when she learned that the questions would deal with the representation of the poor she quickly changed her tune. She was evidently annoyed and politely asked the interviewer to leave. To analyze this interview, one academic used laws relating to CPAS.

One Social Housing Association Committee Chair reacted similarly. One activist, a tenant of the association, sent them a written questionnaire. Three days later, a committee member said that there was no point conducting an interview, since the housing was not provided exclusively for the poor. The activist had to ask the Fourth World–University project director to intervene and pour oil on troubled waters.

When the activists conducted interviews with poor people, dialogue was difficult, reflecting the difficulty of the question.

Our group also looked at the lectures[5] from the point of view of representation. Finally, one other source of data was the participants in the project themselves. At one seminar, it was proposed that each thematic group ask each of the others a question. Ours was: *Must one have lived in poverty to represent those who do?* The group analyzed the responses.

One academic suggested comparing the findings of the interviews with what philosophers thought about political representation. The group realized that it was important to understand philosophical ideas since they have an influence on democratic societies.

The Fourth World volunteer corps member brought texts on citizenship, partnership and representation[6] used within ATD Fourth World as reference works.

Using the materials to carry out the research

Our overarching question was: what is representation?

We put this question to the other thematic groups to hear their input on the subject. They were surprised that the word *poor* was excluded from the question. Following the seminar, the activists suggested modifying the question to *The issue of the representation of the poor in democracy.* One academic reacted by replacing *in* by *and.* The group thus agreed to formulate the central question of our research as follows: *The issue of the representation of the poor and democracy.* The hypothesis was thus that "representation is rendering present the issues of those who are absent."

The outline for the memoir was drawn up through dialogue between the various groups of participants using individually-prepared work schedules. Decipherings served as a basis for writing the memoir. The activists deconstructed them and catalogued them according to the outline for the memoir. Their classifications were approved by the group.

The group's approach

As in any research team, there were disagreements over the topic when discussing it, and these had to be worked on and resolved.

Dialogue

The role of the pedagogical team

During group work days and seminars, the thematic group was coached by the pedagogical team. Their contribution was very important in helping the group progress with their work together. They acted as mediators, and tried to facilitate discussions between the three groups of participants. For example, while explaining that the group should discuss representation in general and not that of the poor, one academic made a comparison: *Rather than talking about the case of one sick person, we should consider health in general and that will benefit everyone.* To which the activists responded: *No, first of all we need to deal with that sick person, heal them, and that will benefit everyone.* The pedagogical team noted the different viewpoints resulting from differing life experiences.

Or another example: the academics said that if representation were thought through, it would allow the poor to be represented. The activists thought that it was through representing the poor that everyone would be represented.

Examples of knowledge-merging

One academic presented the thoughts of Hannah Arendt[7], which do not directly tackle the issue of representation, but are very interesting due to their indirect links with the subject. She says: *One is left without rights, dignity or respect if one does not belong to a political community.* Can one be a member of a political community if one is not represented? The activists worked on this text several times. Hannah Arendt bases her thoughts on her personal experience. By the same token, the activists' analysis of the text was linked to their own experiences of everyday life in their fight against poverty. *When is one recognized as a citizen? Under what conditions does the community recognize a person as a citizen?* They take the example of a homeless person arrested for vagrancy[8]. Living on the street, this person's rights were clearly not upheld (no housing, no resources). On leaving prison, his/her rights were recognized. The activists said that prison had therefore functioned as a community.

In discussion, the activists thought that the academics did not appreciate their contribution. One member of the pedagogical team pointed out the relevance of the activists' questions: *Are there situations in which one is more or less of a citizen? That is the question they are asking.* The academics did not answer the question, and on that day, the activists, with no training in debating skills, could pursue the issue no further than the example cited.

That day, the group realized that one text could be interpreted very differently according to one's life experience.

Another example arose when attempting collaborative writing[9]. We chose a public statement made by Father Joseph Wresinski*[10] and tried to answer the question: can one say that in making this speech, Father Joseph Wresinski is a representative, and whom does he represent? The group pooled the individual texts written by each member. Writing together proved to be a way of producing a *plurality of knowledge.*

Disagreement—Progress—Agreement

Representation of the poor or representation in general?

From the start of the project, the Fourth World activists wanted to talk about the representation of the poorest, since they equated representation with recognition. The academics wished to talk about representation in general. The Fourth World volunteer corps member suggested studying the conditions for representation.

The Fourth World activists said that including the poorest in the title of the research was accepting that there are people who are not given the chance to speak. One academic said that he was not there for political ends, but to think about the meaning of representation, and that speaking about the poorest was an aim of political activism.

At this point in the discussion, a member of the pedagogical team reminded the group of the book *Democratie et Pauvreté[11]*, which devotes 800 pages to this issue of the representation of the poor and that the academics who wrote it had not deemed it to be an issue of concern only to activists.

Should we speak of the poorest or the poor?

At the beginning of our research, there was no agreement on whether to use the term *the poorest.* One academic asked how one defined who *the poorest* were. The activists, not wishing to leave anyone out, said that keeping *the poorest* in the title would mean recognizing their existence. The Fourth World volunteer corps member thought that using the term *the poorest* risked becoming trapped in a vocabulary specific to ATD Fourth World, which was not the aim of the project. One academic thought that the interests of the poor would be better served if the group did not seem to be thinking solely about them.

The group agreed to use the term *the poor* in the overarching question. The debate, as we shall see later, would develop, and by the end of the memoir would see us define the meaning we attribute to the expression "the poorest".

Should representation be specific or general?

The activists did not want a specific form of representation for the poor. They thought that would risk deepening the rift between the poor and the rest of society. The academics said that if the poor were represented by a poor person, that amounted to a specific form of representation. The activists did not see who else would really be qualified to represent them, for only the poor know the reality of combating poverty on a daily basis. This issue of "exceptionalism" would arise regularly during our discussions. The activists, wishing to be understood by the other two groups, reflected on this issue and drew a diagram[12] of representation at all levels of society. The aim was not to create a union or political party for the poor, but to represent the People of the Fourth World, the poorest and all those who by choice stand alongside them in combating poverty, be they members of political parties, trade unions, associations, churches etc. This is not representation of a category of people—which would be a specific form of a representation—but that of the fight against poverty, which concerns everyone. In their diagram, the activists showed that education must be a part of this representation. The Fourth World volunteer corps member showed that partnership is indispensable as an approach which allows people to be represented.

Notes

1. Revenu Minimum d'Insertion, French benefit created by the law of December 1, 1988, awarded to people of working age without employment or resources who are not entitled to unemployment benefit.
2. c.f. appendix.
3. Interviews, see appendix.
4. Centre Public d'Aide Sociale, Belgian agency providing the unemployed with a job, benefits, or medical, psychological or social assistance such as budgeting skills, legal advice etc.
5. Lectures by Lucie Ribert, Emile Creutz and Emilie Bourtet.
6. c.f. appendix.
7. American political theorist and philosopher of German-Jewish origin, 1906-1975.
8. The example given dates from prior to January 12, 1993, when the Onkelinx Act in Belgium abrogated the law previously in force under which vagrancy was a criminal offence.
9. Collaborative writing, see Outline Introduction.
10. Speech given on November 17, 1977, at the Maison de la Mutualité in Paris, see Chapter 3.
11. ATD Fourth World, *Démocratie et Pauvreté*, Editions Quart Monde/Albin Michel, 1991.
12. c.f. Chapter 4.

Chapter 2

DEFINITIONS OF REPRESENTATION

As the chapter devoted to methodology indicates, the overarching theme of *Citizenship, democracy and human rights* seems too broad to be tackled in full.

It was inspired by questions stressing the importance of speech and words, in the sense of speaking out, taking part in discussions or making statements: *giving the poor a voice, proclaiming rights, dialoguing with the working world, allotted speaking-time etc.*

Other remarks encapsulate the other issue very much under discussion today in connection with citizenship: *being recognized as citizens, agents and partners in society, participation, decision-making etc.*

This is why it seemed important to us to define the terms *representing* and *representation*, to relate them to the idea of *democracy* and distinguish them from related ideas such as *participation, partnership* and *testifying*.

Examining the words "representing" and "representation"

In common parlance the words *representing* and *representation* mean many things:

– for example, a lawyer represents their client; this is individual representation;

– a trade union delegate represents company workers; this is collective representation;

– a play is performed (but in French it is "represented").

What form of representation are we talking about when we speak of *the issue of the representation of the poor*?

Definitions provided by dictionaries, philosophers and the people interviewed can help us reach a more precise definition of the concept of representation, which will be used in our research. The terms we shall develop are: to represent, to represent (to oneself), representation, representative.

Dictionary definitions

To represent: to be delegated as a spokesperson for one or more people; give a presence to a group of people as a group and not a collection of individuals; to have received a mandate to act in the name of a person or group and defend their interests.

To represent (to oneself): in French, a synonym for "to imagine", someone or something which is not physically present but is in one's thoughts.

Also: to give a concrete depiction of something abstract (in painting, the theatre, etc). This definition will not be explored in this research.

Representation: the act of representing an individual or group by the people appointed to do so. There are different kinds of representation:

– *legal representation:* legal procedure in which a representative acts in the name of and on behalf of the represented party. The term representation in the legal sense is derived from the Latin *repraesentare*, a verb meaning *to be present[1]*.

– *political representation:* legislative power (elected representatives).

Representative: someone who speaks on behalf of an individual or group whose interests and values they share.

In his book *Vocabulaire technique et critique de la philosophie[2]*, André Lalande draws the reader's attention to the prefix *re-* in all the words related to representation. The prefix *re-* seems to signify rendering something or someone present where their presence is due and expected. This prefix seems to express the idea of a second presence, an imperfect imitation of the original, real presence.

Some philosophical approaches to representation

The thinkers who have contributed their thoughts on representation are too numerous to list in full here. We shall mention only three of them, who are especially important: Thomas Hobbes, Montesquieu and Jean-Jacques Rousseau.

Thomas Hobbes (1588–1679), English philosopher. Hobbes writes[3] that in the beginning, in a state of nature, humans waged war on one another, killed and stole from one another without any law forbidding it. In order to preserve their own lives, humans created laws, concluded a contract. This is the social contract, which includes an appointed representative. Once the contract is concluded, it must be obeyed (whether one voted for or against it), without one being able to have a say over every decision made. Hobbes calls the representative *the sovereign*, who is supposed to express the will of everyone: *A Multitude of men, are made One Person, when they are by one man, or one Person, Represented.*

Hobbes's value as a thinker is that he was one of the first to state that political power must result from an initial agreement between those on whom it is imposed. But his theories on representation exclude control by those who are represented and can therefore lead to dictatorship.

Montesquieu (1689–1755), French philosopher. Montesquieu writes about representation in *The Spirit of the Laws* (1748). He declares that there are three kinds of power in any state: the legislature (which makes the laws), the executive (which governs) and the judiciary (which judges)[4].

For Montesquieu, the same people should never be allowed to exercise more than one form of power at the same time so that the three groups keep one another in check. He writes that the legislature can only exist via representation: *it is fit the people should transact by their representatives what they cannot transact by themselves. . . . The great advantage of representatives is, their capacity of discussing public affairs. For this the people collectively are extremely unfit, which is one of the chief inconveniences of a democracy.*

He goes further, and adds: *All the inhabitants of the several districts ought to have a right of voting at the election of a representative, except such as are in so mean a situation as to be deemed to have no will of their own.*

Rousseau (1712–1773), French philosopher. Rousseau distinguishes personal interest and the common interest. This is why he opposes representation. In *The Social Contract* (1762) he writes: *each individual, as a man, may have a particular will contrary or dissimilar to the general will which he has as a citizen. His particular interest may speak to him quite differently from the common interest.*

Rousseau does not believe that the people can be represented: *the moment a people allows itself to be represented, it is no longer free: it no longer exists.* He takes as his model the societies of the Ancient World, where, he writes *In Greece, all that the people had to do, it did for itself; it was constantly assembled in the public square.* For Rousseau, *Every law the people has not ratified in person is null and void—it is, in fact, not a law.*

The interviewees' idea of representation

Everyone interviewed understood the word *representation* in the collective sense. Some elected representatives or officials see themselves as representatives by virtue of their role, as representatives of local government, local people or people who benefit from a service. For them, representation has become a job. But as one mayor said, *It is impossible to represent everyone*[5].

The other, non-elected interviewees who sometimes acted on behalf of others had differing views according to their experience/s. For one friend of ATD Fourth World[6], representation meant being a go-between and spokesperson for people. The issue of the mandate arose here: who issues the mandate? What is one mandated to do?

For others, being a representative was about listening to what people have to say and passing their views on. Others said it was about conveying the precise words people used. One person living in poverty did not describe herself as a representative on the committee she sat on, since she had not been mandated as such by the residents. She said: *You speak in your own name but you try and think about the other residents who can't take part in meetings*[7].

A distinction arose between representing an idea, an ideal, and representing people. For example, *speaking about poverty* is different from *speaking on behalf of the poor*. One person, who devotes their life to working with the very poorest, said: *You can represent an ideal, a goal you have in life*[8]. One man, who also works with poor people like himself, said: *To represent, you need a committee*[9]. A young couple who did not initially understand the word "representation", began to associate *representation* with *protecting*[10].

To conclude, let us give the floor to an activist:

> I think that when you start to speak on behalf of others like yourself—to speak on behalf of more people than just your family, to speak on behalf of this people I recognize—if you do it because they want you to, because you speak for them, you can do it. But it took me a while to accept that[11].

Our concept of representation

Our group chose not to address individual representation in the legal sense. The memoir would examine collective representation.

- Do we represent an idea or ideal?
- In doing so, do we speak on behalf of specific people or of a group?
- Does doing so give them a presence as André Lalande defined it?

The group based its research on the second question, though taking due account of the other two as well. If representation is *speaking on behalf of x*, it cannot take place if those represented do not vote or ask for it. This type of representation depends on the conception the representative has of those represented and the views they are to convey in the places they represent them.

> When speaking about the representation of the poor, the question arises of just how representative the representative is. The qualities of the person or group speaking on behalf of another group must be defined in order for them to properly represent that group.

Representation and democracy

Democracy is a form of government under which sovereignty belongs to *the citizens as a whole regardless of birth, personal wealth or abilities*[12]. They exercise this sovereignty either directly[13] or via their representatives[14]. But democracy is not only a form of government. It is also a recognition that anyone can take responsibility for their destiny and the future of the community to which they belong. The activist expressed precisely this when they said that *the poorest are not recognized as responsible within their country, their local community or even their family**[15].

Democracy as a mode of political organization

Direct democracy is when the people (*demos*) are called upon to govern (that is, to take decisions on a collective basis which determine their future) without recourse to intermediaries or representatives. Truth be told, this means of expression is impossible for practical reasons at national or even municipal level. Jean-Jacques Rousseau expressed as much[16], and today there are still *some places we cannot all go together. The ideal is therefore to have ourselves represented, have meetings, speak together**.* Direct democracy is only possible in small groups, assuming that all members of the group have the same right to voice their opinion. For a long time, writers only wrote of democracy in the sense of direct democracy. They preferred the term "representative government" when the people were called to govern via the intermediary of a representative. Today, we use the term representative democracy to describe the current forms of the people's sovereignty. The idea of representation has become inseparable from that of democracy[17]. Representatives can be appointed in different ways, elections remaining the least bad way of appointing politicians. It is generally considered that representative government is based on several principles:

– Rulers are appointed by elections at regular intervals. Elections are an opportunity for the represented to dismiss a representative by refusing to renew their mandate.

– Rulers maintain a degree of independence in decision-making since their mandate is not imperative[18].

– Those represented retain the freedom to express their opinions. They may demonstrate their disagreement with decisions made by the rulers.

– Decisions affecting the public are discussed before being made.

Accurate representation is the condition necessary for democracy. But democracy is not just a form of political organization, it is also a value.

Democracy as a value

This is what allows everyone to take control of their own future and take part in shaping the future of the community to which they belong. The fact that in theory everyone is able to participate in appointing representatives via elections does not suffice—those called upon to vote must be truly considered as belonging to their community, as citizens (c.f. Hannah Arendt).

Poverty does not remove one's legal right to vote, but it prevents one, materially and morally, from exercising one's rights as a citizen. . . . Democracy created suffrage as a means to help people live together. Illiteracy cannot be eradicated without knowledge being shared by both sides, without recognition that the illiterate have their own thoughts and things to say, read and write. Some abstain from voting, revealing a political illiteracy. It is not enough for these people to better understand the democratic system. We must listen to them to learn what makes democracy impossible on the bottom rung of the social ladder[19].

To sum up, the situation of the poor is a constant reminder that democracy is not just limited to the theoretical proclamation of abstract, formalized rights. In short, democracy is not just a mode of political organization, it is an ongoing demand. It is in this sense that we might say that the Fourth World is a touchstone of democracy.

Representation and related ideas

As we have just seen, representation seems closely linked to democracy. However, it must be carefully distinguished from related terms and ideas such as participation, partnership or testifying.

Representation and participation

These ideas are frequently used together and sometimes confused, as some of the interviews show.

To the question *What does representation mean for you?* one mayor answered: *Our commune has participative representation. . . .* [20] When asked about the problems he faced as a representative, he added: *It is difficult to get people to participate in the life of the commune.*

By the same token, the head of a parent-teacher association, when asked if disadvantaged people took part in meetings, answered:

Maybe you have seen Sylvie. She has been very active on the committee for seven years now. We'd like to have more like her. Even though she's on the Minimex[21] and has three children, that doesn't stop her being incredibly resourceful. Most come once or twice in general, and when they run out of things to say, they stop coming[22].

In terms of the main difficulties he faced in encouraging the poorest to participate, he added: *Dialogue, no doubt about it. Information, too.*

Asked the same question, one activist, a member of a village events committee, answered:

You can speak for yourself and give your own opinion, but you do try and think about the other residents, because they don't all go to meetings, because not everyone wants to participate, but you still try so everyone benefits from what we do[23].

Joseph Wresinski, in his role as rapporteur to the French Economic and Social Council[24], wrote of participation as a means of proclaiming one's citizenship:

In a democracy, injustices can be redressed when people have the right to be heard and to bring pressure to bear on appropriate institutions. They can achieve this in two ways: by contesting administrative or judicial decisions; and by participating in civic associations, labor unions and political parties. . . . Being part of an association can provide people with necessary information. It can also be an opportunity for them to take on a civic or political commitment on behalf of fellow citizens in difficult circumstances. . . . The very poor want to participate. The fact that they come together in local and national groups is a proof of this desire. These associations can promote the progressive involvement of those who wish to participate. . . .

Political rights are essential in order to be able to participate in the life of a country. One does not exist if one is not recognized as belonging to a political body. Politicians have decision-making power. Political representation is participating in this power. Representation allows people to participate in taking decisions themselves. If political bodies can be made to see that the poorest are citizens like anyone else, and that they have the right to be represented, then perhaps laws will be able to be created to benefit the deprived.

However, representation and participation are not synonymous. Representation is something more artificial than participation (which means *the act of associating oneself, taking part* according to the Larousse dictionary). Being in dialogue with someone is not enough for representation to occur. There are forms of participation which do not involve representation. For example, organizing a village fête is participating but not representing anyone.

Nevertheless, representation can be a way of participating. The same is true in politics. Representation is necessary to participate in wielding power.

Representation and partnership

According to the Larousse dictionary, partners are people who are involved in carrying out a project. The meaning is very close to that of participation.

A partnership implies that everyone involved is involved in planning, carrying out and evaluating a project. Being a partner is more than just being a participant. The French Economic and Social Council[25] report highlights the importance of partnership as a source of recognition, knowledge, trust and citizenship, allowing projects to be carried out in the future.

(Such a) partnership, which the most disadvantaged people need but have rarely experienced, depends on the support of public officials and civic leaders. They have to take the initiative in informing and consulting with the most disadvantaged people, who will then see themselves as active citizens . . . both public authorities and public interest groups have their respective responsibilities in promoting this partnership.

Are there any connections with representation?

René Martin[26], one of the co-authors of the book *On voudrait connaitre le secret du travail*[27], gave us a few pointers. Throughout his involvement with ATD Fourth World, he has been able to work in partnership with others, whether off his own bat or in a joint effort and with the support of members of the Fourth World volunteer corps. The first stage in this for him was meeting a Fourth World volunteer corps member on his estate, then taking part in meetings organized by a friendly, relaxed group working in the associative sector where he felt free and at ease. It was then a natural progression for him to start participating in the Fourth World People's University and discovering that there were others living like him in poverty, but also people who had not experienced poverty, but who wanted to show solidarity with them. He took the brave step of speaking in front of these people, sharing his experiences and thoughts. He then took part in a work and education/training project, after which he felt he could hold his head up high as a working man, to himself and to his family. A few years later, when telling his story in the book and in discussion with academics, he began to compare his experiences and thoughts to other people's situations. When the book was finished, he agreed to represent Fourth World activists from Lyon at a debate.

We might ask whether partnership with the poorest is indispensable in constructing a positive civic identity for them which will allow them to be represented. Partnership does not necessarily involve representation. The involvement of very poor families in writing the Belgian General Report on Poverty did not make them into representatives. They were partners. Conversely, a representative is not always a partner, to the extent that they do not always act alongside the represented—this is common in political representation.

Representation and testifying

The verb *testify* has two meanings depending on the context in which it is used. Testifying is first and foremost attesting to something one has witnessed or heard. In law, for example, a witness is someone who describes what they saw or heard. Testifying is also to affirm the truth or value of someone or something by one's words, declarations, actions[28] or life in general.

But what connections are there between representation and testifying? In her speech at the Caen Colloquium[29], Alwine de Vos van Steenwijk[30] combined the two ideas, meaning we must distinguish more precisely between them. Under the title *Father Joseph, representative of his people* she recounted that she had never heard Joseph Wresinski describe himself as a representative, and that he preferred the word *testifying* to *representation*. She said, *We cannot say that Father Joseph acted as a representative. His entire life was a form of representation.* Examining this closely, however, Alwine de Vos van Steenwijk means that Joseph Wresinski did not want to be a political representative. We cannot conclude that he was in no way representative.

Through what he said and did, he was the very model of representation. He neither dispossessed nor betrayed those he represented. It seems impossible to systematically oppose *testifying* and *representation*. The two terms are not mutually exclusive and can even be used concurrently. A person can testify in some cases, and represent in others. They can also lend weight to their representation by testifying.

Notes

1. Encyclopédie Universelle II, *Les notions philosophiques*, Paris, PUF, 1980, V.0./ Représentation.
2. *Vocabulaire technique et critique de la philosophie*, Paris, PUF, 1972.
3. Thomas Hobbes, *Leviathan*, 1651.
4. In modern society, we might also add financial power (international financial markets) and the power of the media which are powers in fact if not in name.
5. Interview no. 5.
6. Interview no. 6.
7. Interview no. 7.
8. Interview no. 10.
9. Interview no. 15.
10. Interview no. 9.
11. Lecture by Lucie Ribert.
12. *Vocabulaire technique et critique de la philosophie*, PUF, 14th edition, Chapter V—Démocratie.
13. This is known as direct democracy.
14. This is known as representative democracy; see Dictionnaire Le Robert, Chapter V—Démocratie.
15. A double asterisk ** indicates extracts from group discussions or personal writings.
16. Jean-Jacques Rousseau, *The Social Contract*, Chapter XV. Rousseau recalls that the Greeks were able to practice this form of democracy because of the mild climate, so people could gather out of doors, that there were not many of them and so could hear speeches properly, and particularly because they could spend time doing all this because . . . they had slaves to do all their work!!!
17. Whether this be democracy at national or local level (the *commune* or other local authority) or democracy in other organizations such as trade unions or associations.
18. An imperative mandate is when the representative can only do what those they represent have authorized them to do. The opposite case is called a representative mandate.
19. B. Boureau, *Le droit de vote ne serait-il qu'un privilège? Revue Quart Monde*, 1988/2, p. 59.
20. Interview no. 5.
21. Form of benefit in Belgium, the minimum required to survive on.
22. Interview no. 2.
23. Interview no. 7.
24. *Chronic Poverty and Lack of Basic Security: The Wresinski Report of the Economic and Social Council of France*, Fourth World Publications 1994, p 75-76.
25. *Ibid*, p. 9.
26. Fourth World activist—René Martin is an alias.
27. X. Godinot (editor), *On voudrait connaître le secret du travail*, Editions L'Atelier/Editions Quart Monde, Paris, 1995, 333 pp.
28. Dictionnaire Le Robert, the verb "témoigner".
29. Démocratie et Pauvreté, *op. cit.* p. 658.
30. A. De Vos Van Steenwijk, President of the International Movement ATD Fourth World until 2002

Chapter 3

MEANS OF REPRESENTATION

Examining a few examples of representation from the past or the modern age, especially concerning the representation of the poorest, led us to question the means of representation used. We have examined a diverse range of examples, and drawn some lessons from these which will help us in our search for the reasons why the representation of the poorest is a prickly subject.

An example of the representation of the poorest from history

The French Revolution and the Declaration of the Rights of Man and the Citizen provide an opportunity to examine the representation of the poorest.

When the *Cahiers de doléances*[1] (Notes on Grievances) were written and representatives elected to the Etats Généraux[2], one man, Dufourny de Villiers[3], led a political campaign to raise the issue of the representation of the poorest. Three groups were represented in the Etats Généraux: the clergy, the nobility and the Third Estate, and these were intended to represent the whole of the French population.

In a book entitled *Cahiers du Quatrième Ordre, celui des pauvres, des indigents, etc*[4], Dufourny de Villiers explains his thoughts on what he calls the representation of the Fourth Order.

The rich and powerful cannot decide the fate of the poorest, who are not represented:

It seemed necessary to distinguish between French people on the basis of which Order they belonged to, and the number of these Orders has traditionally been limited to three. But is it necessary to divide the French Nation into Orders? And do these three Orders incorporate the whole Nation? Perhaps this division will be abolished—we have to hope so, and if it is not, a Fourth Order must be created. Whatever happens, that part of the Nation whose inherent right demands that they be represented and yet who are not summoned, must be represented.

The Nation is gathering to discuss and establish rights applicable to all which will be enshrined as constitutional law, and laws of exception and privilege which will be attacked or defended. The Nation is gathering to determine taxation and its distribution. The rich and powerful seem the only ones interested in these debates, yet they will inevitably determine the fate of the weak and the poor. . . . I would ask all the Orders, especially the Third Order, if they do not enjoy great privilege in comparison with the Fourth Order? And, since they must agree that they do, how might they avoid the axiom being applied that the Privileged may represent the non-Privileged?

The Deputies of the Third Estate did not take all their citizens into account, only the wealthy:

No one has shown me any specific mandate drawn up to protect and preserve the weakest in the lowest class. . . . It is therefore not enough, if we are to do good, to send individual Memoirs to the Deputies; we must publish these Memoirs, and channel this love of the common good towards relieving the Fourth Order. This love will steer the nation and her Deputies. . . .[5]

The Declaration of the Rights of Man and of the Citizen, the initiators of which were the three Orders (clergy, nobility and the Third Estate), rendered the poor, the sick and the homeless unable to represent themselves or speak at the Etats Généraux. People like Dufourny de Villiers, however, took up the cause of the poorest and tirelessly recalled that one of the fundamental ideas which ought to have figured in the preamble to the Declaration of the Rights of Man and of the Citizen should have been: *Man is greater than the citizen. The unfortunate is greater than man*[6]. Dufourny de Villiers attempted to win recognition of the political rights of the poorest in publishing the *Cahiers du Quatrième Ordre*, and declared the right of the poorest to be citizens.

During the bicentenary of the French Revolution and the Declaration of the Rights of Man and of the Citizen in 1989, an academic colloquium was held in Caen at the initiative of ATD Fourth World, called: *The poorest in democracy*[7]. At this colloquium, Henri Bossan drew attention to the continuing relevance of Dufourny de Villiers's thinking[8].

Some current examples of representation

People we met through our research shared their experience with us as people who were either representatives or represented.

Examples of being represented

One person spoke freely about the elections she votes in at local, national and European level. She asked: do the people I vote for really represent me? Do elected representatives not follow their own beliefs or their party line?

Others said they had been represented in specific instances, personal situations, such as by a lawyer in court, by a councilor when looking for work, by a former teacher when applying for a job requiring qualifications, etc. The feeling of having been represented, even if it was an act carried out on an individual basis, comes from a shared knowledge and trust.

A young couple had to live on the street for several months with no resources[9]. For around three years, the man has lived in a furnished room. To get it, following several failed applications through various CPAS agencies (see note chapter I), he agreed to the conditions imposed by one agency. These were that the CPAS would take the rent and building charges out of their minimex. In order not to lose his entitlement to the minimex, the man had to prove every month that he had applied for five jobs. The words *represented, representative* or *representation* mean nothing to this couple. They have never felt that someone was speaking on their behalf, or on behalf of deprived people. They said they know nobody and they fend for themselves. However, as we spoke, when they were asked if they knew people who spoke on behalf of the poor, they began talking about a television report on people living on a campsite who were threatened with eviction. Léonce Berton[10] had been involved with the report.

There are several forms of representation on the international stage. For example, as part of the United Nations International Year of the Family in 1994, a delegation from ATD Fourth World met the United Nations Secretary General. In one town, a group wrote a text based on the experiences of very poor families. This text was given to the delegates, who passed it on to the United Nations. Here, the group was represented not by a person but by a text. Many very poor families participated in writing the Belgian General Report on Poverty in 1993. We can say that this report was a way of representing the poor, but the follow-ups to it are questionable since there is no real representation of the poor in these instances. One text is not enough to protect the interests of those represented, there must be a representative, this is vital.

Examples of being a representative

Representatives are not all appointed in the same way. The most official way is by election, but sometimes a group chooses someone to represent them, or someone declares themselves a representative.

– Of those representatives appointed by election, some are political representatives, others are in professional, associative or administrative spheres.

One member of the group gave an example of an elected representative from his workplace. He was elected by his colleagues to represent them on the governing body at their university. This body's role is to define and implement the research policies of the whole university and decide on the financing of the various research teams, including that led by this representative:

I applied to be on the council because I wanted to represent the Law faculty, since we are in the minority there. And also because my colleagues asked me to**.

One is elected according to one's professional position: professors elect other professors, lecturers elect other lecturers, jurists elect other jurists etc. He accepted that he was a representative in the sense that he was a spokesman for his colleagues. He had to report back regularly. His job as a representative was sometimes problematic: *I didn't know what to do when a fellow jurist put forward a motion I didn't think was any good. Should I put the case anyway, given that I was supposed to be representing them? Or should I oppose it? I sometimes found myself having to argue motions I didn't think were very good.* Another problem was that he himself was a director of a research team, and was therefore tempted to use his position to benefit young researchers in his own team.

Sometimes representatives, even elected ones, find themselves faced with conflicts of interests between the groups they represent. This is particularly the case for politicians. For example, the Abbé Pierre said that to be a member of parliament, one has to *dare to be very brave, be sure in one's abilities and not let oneself be influenced*[11]. He was driven by the idea of *giving priority in all circumstances to those who suffer the most.* It was probably because he wanted to be closer to *those who are suffering* that he resigned from the French parliament.

French members of the Assemblée Nationale met in session in 1988 to draft the act bringing in the Revenu Minimum d'Insertion, or RMI (see note Chapter 1). Claude Evin, Minister for Solidarity, Health and Social Protection, met with poor people before submitting his bill. Reading the *Journal Officiel,* the record of parliamentary debate, we can see that several members of parliament were aware that the poor want to be recognized as citizens in their own right, but they are often asked to integrate into society, that is, to *make the necessary effort.* Some members stressed that human rights and the rights of the citizen are inseparable. They do not describe themselves as representing the poor, some attribute Father Joseph Wresinski with this role.

At local level, one mayor said: *I personally represent my commune*[12]. He added that his *commune* uses *participative representation* with numerous committees, but that in spite of this, not everyone is represented, since *people don't all approach local representatives.* He has a surgery for individuals to express their requests, and concludes: *It is impossible for me to represent every individual.* He thinks that the poor in his *commune* are not represented on the local council. For one of the his deputies, called *mayoral deputies,* representation is first and foremost about representing the local administration, i.e. the different committees composing it, more than it is about representing the people themselves. When asked about the representation of the poor, he answered: *The first thing they need to do is look after their children*[13]. He spoke in terms of aid and assistance from the CPAS.

One CPAS Manager explained the composition of the CPAS council. Members are CPAS employees and councilors appointed by political parties. For her, the social workers on the council represent the poor *because they know what their lives are like*[14]. She also said that they could be represented by their lawyer. It is worth noting that social workers may not represent recipients of benefits in court, but can represent the CPAS administration. Concerning the possibility of someone receiving CPAS benefits being a member of the council, she said: *You're talking about revising and changing the law there. That won't work. Are you trying to throw a spanner in the works?*

One person from a housing organization who was elected by the tenants and who also lives in poverty said they were a spokesperson for others on the committee they sit on, and that they were trusted by them[15].

In the associative sector it is often the Chair who is the official representative of their association. The Chair of one Parent-Teacher Association told us how difficult it was to get parents involved, which he thought was because of insufficient dialogue and information[16].

– Other people become representatives through initiatives they take part in.

Sometimes a person does not set out to be a representative, but becomes one through their participation in a group. For example, one woman sits on a committee organizing events in her local area, and alongside others would like to improve the quality of life there. She started sitting on the committee as an individual, but gradually has started to hope that her participation will help other residents. The first stage is to win the trust of the residents, which is why the committee has organized an event to which everyone is invited[17].

On one campsite where people are threatened with eviction, the camp leader Léonce Berton set up a "protection committee". The media were informed and reported from the camp. Léonce found himself acting as a representative. Outside groups confirmed him in this role over the next few days. The local authorities took no account of the media campaign and did not accept Léonce as a spokesman, who said: *They don't want to meet us, and I'm an irritation to them*[18]. The authorities applied pressure to the travelers and threatened them, resulting in their becoming afraid, losing heart and leaving the site.

Sometimes through their work people create a means for the people they work with to be represented. For example, one social worker spoke of a *Community Action Network* which was set up during the European Union's "Poverty 3" project in Charleroi[19]. The Network is composed of people from various backgrounds. Once a month, a problematic issue is chosen for discussion. *It is essential to listen to those who have had problems if we are to change things*[20]. Thus, following a discussion of the problems of being refunded for prescription charges, a letter was sent to the Minister of Social Affairs, who took the comments made within it on board:

If it had been one or two people asking, no one would have listened to them. You need to be in a Network for those in authority to listen to you.

Emile Creutz[21], a Doctor of physics, expanded upon the theme of representation at international level, using his own experience in developing renewable energy sources in Third World countries. He sits on several international committees at the National Center for Cooperation and Development, and constantly calls for real partnership between Europe and Africa in developing new sources of energy. But he always comes up against the financial interests of rich countries and their oil and nuclear energy companies. There is so much money at stake for Northern countries that any real representation of Southern countries is stifled, blocking the necessary research to develop solar energy.

– Some examples of representation in ATD Fourth World deserve a mention.

In 1977, on the 20th anniversary of the founding of ATD Fourth World, Father Joseph Wresinski launched an *Appeal for Solidarity[22]* at the Maison de la Mutualité in Paris. In his speech, he described himself as a representative of ATD Fourth World. It is interesting to note that he spoke by turns of *we* and of *you*, depending on whom he was addressing. When he addressed "recognized" citizens, he used *we*, both to make them feel more involved, but also because he was a recognized citizen. When he addressed Fourth World volunteer corps members, he said *you Fourth World volunteer corps members*. He did not represent members of the Fourth World volunteer corps, for he himself had not followed the same path in life as they had. Instead, he was saying to society: these are Fourth World volunteer corps members. When he addressed Fourth World activists, he said *we*, because he too had lived in poverty.

One activist[23] gave several examples when she had represented others during a meeting at the prefecture, or speaking to journalists. In one instance, she recounted:

> I spoke up because I felt there were people I knew who weren't there. I knew what their lives were like, the problems they had every day with schools, with their children. I wanted to tell people about their struggles and I shouted them out to the whole world.

Sometimes activists act as representatives for the odd event here and there. For example, one activist was sent to an international meeting of the United Nations in Geneva in 1996 as a delegate. *I felt I was on a mission***. She took a great deal of notes throughout the meeting, so that other families could get a sense of what it was like on such a momentous occasion. Another activist spoke at a public lecture in her town on the subject of *The role of ATD Fourth World in society*. She opened the lecture, demonstrating that it is imperative that the poor have a voice[24].

At a colloquium on exclusion, a member of the Fourth World volunteer corps explained his work to young people representing organizations and movements from across Europe. His explanation took many forms, using slides, theatre and speech etc. But he realized that he had not gotten his point across. During the session, he met some young people from poor backgrounds in an area near where the colloquium was taking place. The next day he spoke about this experience to his audience and this time successfully communicated his message**.

Some people involved with ATD Fourth World act as permanent representatives, for example on a housing, health or social integration committee, either at local, national or international level. One of them sits on a housing committee as a representative. She was chosen to do so because she knew other people on the committee.

> Sometimes you just have to let it pass, otherwise you'd spend your whole time harping on and on, and other people would be saying, There she goes again. . . . When you say something, it's got to be worth saying. You often feel very alone. It's like trying to move mountains[25].

A question of representation

The preceding examples of representation show the diverse situations in which representation occurs, from the point of view of the representative and from that of those represented.

The diverse situations in which representation takes place

This diversity is sometimes attributable to the representative's "status in law", sometimes to the relationships existing between them and the person/s represented, sometimes to the specific circumstances of the representation.

In terms of the representative's status in law[26], we see that in some cases this person is elected to represent the People (member of parliament, mayor or deputy) or an elected member of a specific group in society (a university board of governors, Senior Common Room or Junior Common Room). In other instances, they are not elected but appointed according to a specific procedure, which is often the case in the associative sector. In other cases, they "naturally" assume the role of representative by force of circumstance which has prompted them to speak in public, and, to some extent, they have just "gone with the flow" of events. This legal status can be more or less clearly defined and more or less precise. In a democracy, it is generally considered that the means by which representatives are appointed should be defined in advance and agreed upon by those they represent.

The diversity of situations is just as clear if we examine relationships between representatives and the represented. Sometimes the representative is happy to *speak for x* or on *behalf of y*. They testify to a situation they know of or have experienced themselves. In other instances, they act on a mandate given to them by a group. Sometimes, one person is both *representative* and *testifier*. The example above highlights this nicely. In his capacity as a friend of ATD Fourth World, he is called upon to represent the Movement at meetings. On other occasions (in his personal life), he testifies without necessarily claiming to represent the very poor[27].

Sometimes a person finds themselves representing someone without being asked, or without it being planned from the outset. The person then gradually becomes a representative as dialogue progresses. This seems to be what happened to Léonce Berton[28]. As *camp leader*, he was naturally chosen by the committee which was set up in the camp to issue statements, act on the travelers' behalf, etc. He became a representative little by little, through his contact with the committee members and travelers on the one hand, and the media on the other. This might initially not have been an intentional policy or specific strategy, but his experiences and the fact that others saw themselves in him made him into a representative.

We can draw some useful lessons from the way representation in general works today, particularly representation of the poorest.

How representation works

All representation requires time and money. It also assumes that the representative is *subject to the (dis)approval* of the represented.

Representation is first and foremost a long-term affair. Time is required for a representative to emerge, whether they be appointed by a special procedure or no. This means that it is difficult to create representation on the hoof if the groundwork has not previously been laid. Time is also required for representatives to carry out their work. They must meet negotiating partners, attend meetings and prepare for them with those they represent. This is true whether we are talking about Léonce Berton or preparations for the Belgian General Report on Poverty. Time is also required for the representative to report back to those they represent.

To differing degrees, representation means representatives are subject to the (dis)approval of those they represent. This is one of the foundations of democracy. Concerning elected representatives, this (dis)approval can be voiced at elections, such as for members of parliament. This seems simple enough, but the question of scrutiny between elections remains unanswered. Where there is no election but a procedure of appointment or non-elected mandate, (dis)approval can be effected by the withdrawal of the said mandate. Finally, when a representative emerges through force of circumstance, those who are represented, and who by definition did not choose to be so, are in a trickier situation.

A distinction must be made here between temporary or one-off representation and permanent representation. In the first instance, (dis)approval is fairly simple.

When the representative has been issued with a specific task (going to a meeting, speaking at a gathering, being interviewed etc), the represented can make their feelings known if not immediately, then very quickly. And if the representative has abused his position, the represented can react straight away. For example, they can contact the representative and express their disagreement, or refuse to be represented by the person again. However, when representatives are permanent, there is a greater risk of their abusing their position or misrepresenting the views of those they represent. And (dis)approval will come later, sometimes too late[29].

Research into how representation works led us to question the underlying relationship between representation and a person's individual rights. It is widely accepted in democratic societies that being represented gives people rights, or at any rate allows them to exercise them. Thus, the right of parents to give their views on their child's schooling and their expectations of it depends largely on the existence of Parent-Teacher Associations. By the same token, the right of tenants to decent and well-maintained housing would rarely be respected if tenants' associations did not exist to make sure it was. But studying the thoughts of Hannah Arendt also showed us that in order to be represented, one must first of all be recognized as being entitled to rights. This is a necessary prerequisite and probably the defining issue in the representation of the poorest. Recognition of citizenship must be won before there can be any talk of representation.

Leaders and the representation of the very poor

Most of the time, politicians are appointed as representatives of not only those who have chosen or appointed them, but of the population as a whole[30]. It follows that this by necessity includes the poor, who in principle therefore *determine* their representation in the same way as other citizens.

Some positions have particular responsibilities linked to combating poverty. Here again the poor ought to be the specific raison d'être, *the goal* of representation.

The same goes for the mandate of a CPAS Manager[31]. The CPAS in Belgium are responsible for allocating benefits which will allow *everyone to live in human dignity*[32] and, under certain conditions, for providing a minimum to live on[33]. One CPAS Manager was asked for her views on the representation of the poorest on the benefits committee[34]. To the question *Is there a representative of the poorest on the committee?* she replied: *No, I think we've got enough on our plate already without them coming along and adding their two cents.* When asked if she thought it might be a good idea for a benefits recipient be appointed to the committee, she answered: *That won't work. Are you trying to throw a spanner in the works? What is your name?* She also deemed that the poor were represented by their social worker who knows what things are like for them, though this is neither the de facto nor the legal role[35] of a social worker.

We also interviewed a mayor[36], who thought the poor were not represented in his community:

> I personally represent the commune of X. The people I represent are the people of the commune. But I can't represent everyone.

Not everyone is represented, because *not everyone gets involved. It is impossible to represent each individual.* The mayor conflated his role as a representative with his work on behalf of particular individuals. His view is that those represented expect their representatives to *give them time, listen to them and act on their behalf.*

However, there is a lack of poor people as representatives which needs to be filled:

> I would see someone on the verge of escaping poverty or who has escaped it as a representative. Not only have they had a hard life and the resultant knowledge, but they know how to stand up for themselves. They could really push things forward in the way we work with the poorest.

We could read this suggestion as supposing that the person is no longer poor. However, the mayor did not want the poor represented as a specific group.

One mayoral deputy[37], also a representative at local level, saw himself as representing the *local administration* and pointed out that no councilor had probably personally experienced poverty. When asked if it would be a good idea for a poor person to be elected, he dodged the question:

> The first thing they need to do if they have children is to try and look after those children before they start getting involved with things like that.

The *commune* and the CPAS *do as much as they can* for the poor, some of whom *don't take care of their children* and *are alcoholics.*

Studying parliamentary debates concerning the Act passed on December 1, 1988 introducing the RMI showed that representatives at the national level had taken the Fourth World's experiences on board, especially those of Father Joseph Wresinski and ATD Fourth World. Both ATD Fourth World and its founder were mentioned by members of parliament many dozens of times. Some mention was made of meeting the poor and of their experiences. One deputy even quoted word for word the testimony of two poor women:

> *When we visited families yesterday in the town of Herblay in Val d'Oise with members of ATD Fourth World, the Minister of Solidarity, Health and Social Protection heard men and women demand their right to dignity through independence and work, to which the RMI should form an intermediary stage, a "springboard", one woman said. Another added; "We want to bring up our children ourselves. We're not lazy. But if we have no shoes, we can't go to work, and if we don't have any exercise books, we're not going to send our kids to school[38]."*

However, in the drafting of an Act which was aimed at the poor themselves, one cannot help having the impression that they were consistently considered as the subject of discussion, never as represented. Even if the tone was rarely contemptuous, and though there was an evident concern to integrate recipients of the RMI, poverty was treated as a complex problem, but still only ever as a problem.

Throughout the often complex debates, no member of parliament seemed prepared to speak on behalf of the poor, though in principle this should have been part of their job. The feeling was that those who were being spoken about were not there, that their voices were muted and heard only indirectly through Father Wresinski or ATD Fourth World. Never was the issue raised of those who were absent from representation at the national level.

These examples, sometimes almost caricatured, of the way our leaders envisage representation, do not seem exceptional. For representatives at local and national level alike, the poor have no role in legitimizing their power, neither as voters, nor as the reason they are elected in the first place. In addition, only rarely do they say that they represent the poor. Most do not accept that disadvantaged people can act as representatives themselves. The very idea seems alien to them.

Poverty is often the focus of attention of representatives. Thus, the objective of some institutions such as the CPAS in Belgium can be seen as attempting to reduce it, if this is not the goal of political representation itself. But the poor are seen in the most negative cliched fashion (as alcoholics or unhygienic), a kind of social problem that needs solving. They are not seen as citizens.

Some people, however, such as the mayor we interviewed, are aware of the necessity for the whole of society for the poor to represent themselves.

Representation of the poorest is a disturbing issue

Even if representation of the poorest seems to be increasing[39] in some places or on some occasions, on reading the examples above, we must conclude that their representation is disturbing. The interviews (or attempts at interviews in some cases) with the Manager of a housing association and a CPAS Manager are from this point of view typical, as are the problems encountered by French members of parliament in taking into account the realities of life for those living in extreme poverty. Even asking about representation of the poor upsets them, and is met with an aggressive response, even thinly-veiled threats.

We need to consider the reasons behind these reactions, and we can use the work we have done to formulate some hypotheses:

– The first would be related to the fact that the interviews were conducted by an ATD Fourth World activist. The change in the behavior of the housing association Manager (at least his tone of voice) in response to what a member of the Fourth World volunteer corps said would seem to confirm this. If this is indeed the explanation, it clearly shows the difficulty the poorest face in being recognized as real negotiating partners able to ask relevant questions about the way democracy works. It shows how much work still remains for the Fourth World to be properly represented[40].

– The second would be that representatives or those who—rightly or wrongly—see themselves as such end up forgetting (either deliberately or through habit) those, or some of those, whom they are supposed to represent.

– The third would be that representatives have an inkling that they are supposed to be representing the poorest but are not doing so, and that they do not like to be reminded of the fact.

These three hypotheses are not mutually exclusive and should be borne in mind when, in the next chapter, we attempt to investigate ways the poorest can be better represented in democratic societies.

Notes

1. Documents in which the *assemblées* setting up the *États Généraux* wrote the demands and wishes they wanted their representatives to express for them.
2. The *États Généraux* were composed of representatives from all the provinces of France from the three orders: clergy, nobility and the Third Estate.
3. Louis-Pierre Dufourny, born in Villiers-le-Bel (France) December 6, 1738, died in Paris June 12, 1796. Architect by profession. Outraged that in convening the *États Généraux* and sending out the *Cahiers de doléances* the King left out the homeless, those with no fuel, those in hospital and beggars, as well as people who were not registered as taxpayers. Having failed to win recognition for the poorest in the *États Généraux*, he published *Les Cahiers du Quatrième Ordre*, on April 25, 1789, a citizen's statement.
4. *Cahiers du Quatrième Ordre*, EDHIS, Editions d'histoire sociale, rare text, reprinted 1967, p. 7.
5. *Ibid.* p. 18.
6. Dufourny de Villiers, *Adresse aux citoyens sur le meilleur plan de la municipalité, conclu de la Déclaration des Droits de l'Homme et du Citoyen*, April 25, 1790, BN, Lb 39/332.
7. *Démocratie et pauvreté, op. cit.*
8. *Ibid.*, H. Bossan, *Du quatrième ordre au Quart Monde*, pp. 141-155.
9. Interview no. 9.
10. See examples of representation arising from personal involvement on the following pages.
11. B. Chevallier, *Emmaüs ou venger l'homme*, Editions Le Centurion, Paris, 1979.
12. Interview no. 5
13. Interview no. 13.
14. Interview no. 1.
15. Interview no. 4.
16. Interview no. 2.
17. Interview no. 7.
18. Interview no. 15.
19. A European Community pilot project which took place from 1990 to 1994.
20. Interview no. 14.
21. Lecture.
22. *Quand l'histoire se rétablit*, Igloos no. 97, pp. 81-88.
23. Lecture by Lucie Ribert.
24. Interview no. 12.
25. Interview no. 6.
26. A person's status in law is the name given to their legal rights and duties, as well as the role the law gives them in society.
27. Interview no. 6.
28. Interview no. 15.

29. This issue also arises when we try to establish what is necessary for the poor to be properly represented, see Chapter 4.
30. The Belgian Constitution states in Article 42: *The members of the two Chambers represent the nation, not just those who have elected them.*
31. c.f. articles 25 onwards of the incorporating Act passed July 8, 1976 on CPAS centers. The CPAS Council elects its own president whose role is described in Article 28. The members of the CPAS Council are elected by Council of the *commune* (article 11, § 2), itself elected by popular vote.
32. c.f. Article 1 of the Act passed on July 8, 1976.
33. Act passed on August 7, 1974 establishing the right to a minimum income to live on.
34. Interview no. 1.
35. For a legal critique of the positions taken in this interview, see Interview document.
36. Interview no. 5. Of the members of the Council of the *commune*, the mayor is appointed by the King (Article 13 of the new Communes Act passed on June 24, 1988).
37. Interview no. 13. The mayor's deputies and the mayor constitute the executive power of the *commune*. They are elected by and from within the Council of the *commune*. See Articles 15 onwards of the new Communes Act quoted.
38. Intervention by Marie-France Lecuir, *Journal Officiel*, debates, Assemblée Nationale, October 5, 1988.
39. This is attested to by, for example, the recognition accorded to the Fourth World by the Economic and Social Council of France, which in 1987 led to the adoption of *Chronic Poverty and Lack of Basic Security: The Wresinski Report of the Economic and Social Council of France* and then, in 1995, the adoption of the G. de Gaulle Anthonioz-led *Report on the Evaluation of Public Policies on the Fight Against Extreme Poverty*. A similar phenomenon can be observed in Belgium with the General Report on Poverty.
40. The Manager the activist wanted to interview had displayed some aggression towards him, even going as far as thinly-veiled threats. We might ask whether his behavior really changed or whether the intervention of the Fourth World volunteer corps member did not simply result in putting an end to the incident.

Chapter 4

REPRESENTATION AS A PATH
TOWARDS DEMOCRACY

If representation is really the cornerstone of our democratic societies, and if there is only true democracy where the poorest are represented and heard, that is, where they are considered as full citizens, then we must ask ourselves what is necessary for everyone, regardless of origin, background or social status, to be considered a real player in society. This leads us to reexamine the traditional means of representation, using the experiences of those who are denied the right to speak, whether by law or force of circumstance. Since representation is a two-fold relationship between represented and representatives on the one hand, and between representatives and their negotiating partners on the other, we must first examine what is necessary to be represented and to be a representative. On the basis of this, we will be able to develop some proposals allowing all citizens to be properly represented.

What is necessary for representation?

Legal representation and civic representation

One can be represented and know nothing about it. This is the situation for many of those known in law as "incapable"—the mentally ill and children, for example. All that is necessary to be represented, then, is to be recognized as a legal entity, as subject to the law. We shall see that this condition exists for conscious representation as well, and that it is the underlying issue beneath all forms of representation.

However, what we are seeking here is what is necessary for civic representation, where those represented have chosen to be so and by whom, and who stick by it. Being represented obviously involves the ability to participate in the mechanisms of representation, such as elections, cooptation and mandates.

Some basic conditions for representation

In order to be properly represented:

– One must be capable of choosing, which presupposes the ability to judge and have one's own critical opinion[1]. This assumes one has the requisite information, education and knowledge. Inevitably, those who are represented need sufficient general knowledge and culture for the means of representation to function properly. This is both quantitative and qualitative: the better-informed one is, the more valid representation is.

– However representatives are appointed, there is always some recourse to speech. In the electoral system, this is nicely expressed by the phrase "to have a voice"[2].

– There must be mutual trust between representatives and those they represent. This often comes before any speeches etc are made.

– This speech or voice must be heard, and it must have an effect in the process of representation, it must influence decision-making.

– Those represented must be known to the potential representative. This has nothing to do with knowing information, but knowing about the most important aspects of the lives of those who are represented, including being sufficiently close to them. It is observable that the more distant a representative is from those they represent (for example, the President of a country), the more motivated they are to narrow this distance, and the more problematic it is.

– On a deeper level, in order to act via representatives and to participate in choosing them, one must be a member of the community affected: an association, trade union, political entity such as a *commune*, the state or an international authority. This means that the community must recognize a person, their existence, voice and rights in order for them to be represented. This is a condition basic to all forms of representation, which already exists in the case of representing those who are "incapable".

Recognition as a legal matter

The Fourth World and the thinking of Hannah Arendt

The issue of recognition deserves to be addressed in its own right. One of the things the "Citizenship" group analyzed was the writings of Hannah Arendt, who discusses the status of the "right-less", and who has influenced thinking on the issue of the citizenship of the poor.

For example, she writes:

The first thing the "right-less" lost was their home, meaning their whole social fabric, the place where they had been born and had created a special place for themselves in the world. . . . The great tragedy of the right-less is not that they have been robbed of life, liberty and the pursuit of happiness, nor even of equal-

ity before the law and freedom of opinion—mantras intended to solve all a specific community's problems—but that they have ceased to belong to a community at all. Their defect is not that they are not equal before the law, it is that for them there is no law. It is not that they are oppressed, it is that no one even thinks about oppressing them[3].

For Arendt, it is only if one belongs to a nation or People that an individual's fundamental rights can become at all effective. In reality, human rights do not concern "abstract", non-existent humans, but by necessity humans who are part of a political community.

Being deprived of human rights is first and foremost being deprived of a place in the world which gives significance to one's opinions and value to one's actions. Something much deeper than freedom or justice, namely the rights of the citizen, are at stake when it is no longer to be taken for granted that one belongs to the community into which one is born. People deprived of their human rights do not lose the right to freedom, but the right to act. They do not lose the right to think, but the right to have an opinion.

In other words, all human rights are political rights. Or to put it another way, some fundamental rights must be respected for the others to take effect—those allowing one to fully enter into a political community. Being represented is a specific right and is no exception to the rule. There is no representation for anyone who is excluded, who is not listened to, whose opinion is literally insignificant, that is, it has no meaning.

The Fourth World and the thinking of Hegel

We found a similar view expressed in the testimony of one ATD Fourth World activist, whose insights are astonishingly close to those of Hegel. In trying to escape exclusion, Lucie Ribert constantly stresses the need to find similarities with others, because similarities are necessary for mutual recognition. Recognition allows her to feel part of a group, either her family, the traveler community, the Fourth World or sometimes that of the human race as a whole. In Lucie's eyes, part of combating exclusion is always trying to understand oneself, others and the world. What need to be understood are the similarities which transcend the inevitable differences, i.e. what is "the same" between one person and others. Together, recognition, which results from similarities, and trying to understand these similarities, allow one to be represented. They allow us to raise the issue of the absent:

Does one have the right to speak on behalf of others? We spent a long time discussing this. But I think that when you start to speak on behalf of others like yourself—to speak on behalf of more people than just your family, to speak on behalf of this people I recognize—if you do it because they want you to, because you speak for them, you can do it. But it took me a while to accept that. . . . I spoke because I felt there were people *I knew* who were not present, *I knew about* their lives, their everyday problems with school, the problems they had getting their children a proper education. . . . But it was just that, carrying people who simply weren't there[4].

The risk is not opening oneself to the outside world, meaning similarities become a prison.

Hegel also considered, though with a more pessimistic undercurrent, that man is not a full human in isolation, but becomes one in a fight to the death for "recognition". Humans do not exist for themselves. Their self-awareness, that is, their individual freedom, only exists to the extent that it is recognized as awareness or freedom by another awareness or freedom[5].

Hegel's point of view is more individualistic than that of the Fourth World, and especially that of Lucie, who speaks of recognition of a group.

What is necessary to be a representative?

Being a representative is a responsibility which carries risks and constraints for anyone who accepts to do so. As well as having to be motivated, they must be recognized by those they represent and also recognized as a legitimate negotiating partner by those they talk to. A representative must get to know all these people and therefore agree to be educated in a way. Finally, if they are to be effective, it is to be assumed that they will be in it for the long term.

Motivation

One must be motivated to be a representative. Anyone accepting the job of *rendering others present,* either temporarily or permanently, gives their time and energy, and above all takes risks.

One must be brave to speak on behalf of other people, to act as their spokesperson. Being a representative often means taking risks, for negotiating partners are not always willing to listen, or possibly even have ideas which are totally different or opposed to the representative's interests, which must be challenged without forgetting those who are represented. If we look at the way the CPAS Manager[6], the deputy mayor[7] or the Housing Association Manager[8] treated the activists, who just wanted to ask them about representation, the risks representatives take are clear. As we shall see later, this makes it necessary for the representative to be trained for the task, and in particular be able to draw not only on one's own abilities but also on real partnerships with those they represent, especially if one is speaking for the poorest.

Motivation can be entirely personal. Being a representative is about feeling useful to someone. This personal dimension must not be overlooked, but it alone is not enough. There must also be a sense of responsibility to the group or person represented, or even to society as a whole. In a word, they must feel a full citizen. This sense of responsibility often develops gradually as the representative meets people and gains experience. Lucie Ribert's testimony shows how her perception of her own responsibility has evolved since her childhood. She draws particular attention to how, following the death of Joseph Wresinski and her husband saying to her *It's now or never. People like you can't give up now,* she became slightly more involved, though *it was still sporadic, off and on, just when I felt like it.*

In a word, though motivation sometimes results from one's enjoyment at doing one's bit, other conditions must be met as well. One can become a representative because others prompt one to do so. By the same token, an academic agreeing to sit on a committee does so not just for personal satisfaction but also because they have certain views on what would be good for the university, and because their colleagues have asked them to be their representative.

The difficulty of the representative's job is, however, that motivation alone is not enough. One must be recognized by those one represents and as a real negotiating partner by those with whom one must negotiate.

Being recognized by those one represents

However a representative is appointed, whether by election or other means, they must be recognized by those they represent. What does that mean? How is it possible?

First of all, those represented must to some extent recognize themselves in the representative as one recognizes oneself in the mirror. As Lucie says:

I saw plenty of people like me who spoke, who said powerful things and spoke about their lives. I thought: "Their lives are the same as mine". I could recognize the homelessness, the shame, lots of things like that.[9]

But the word *recognition* also contains the word *cognition*, knowledge. Those represented must feel in charted territory, so to speak, that is be sure (as far as is possible) that the person speaking on their behalf will not betray them because fundamentally they understand and share their concerns. This is why there can be no recognition without trust. The word *trust* also captures the idea of *faith* and *faithfulness.* Trusting someone is believing in them. Trusting one's representative is being able to believe that they will speak for those represented without distorting their message. It is believing that they will give a faithful image of those represented (the parallel with the mirror again).

It seems important to us to highlight the idea of reflection, since we can then say that the representation cannot work one-way. A mandate is the task with which the represented entrust the representative. Of course it is important, but it is not sufficient alone. For the represented to be able to recognize themselves in the representative, the latter must reflect the former, which they can only do by taking the time to listen, ask questions and report back. Only then can the represented know if the representative has given a true image of them.

Asked about this by an activist, a Fourth World delegate to the UN in June 1996 explained: *I brought back all these notes so that other families could experi-*

ence what it was like, just as I had[10]. She said *could experience.* There is no better way to express the fact that those represented must be able to identify with the representative and vice versa.

In the same way, preparation for being a delegate or for one's mandate often proves decisive: *Before writing these texts, we spoke about them with other families.*

Being recognized as a legitimate negotiating partner

There are two conditions here. First of all, representatives must be negotiating partners. Secondly, they must be legitimate negotiating partners.

Representatives are called upon to speak or act (which is also a means of self-expression). When one speaks, it is always in relation to someone. One speaks in order to be heard or listened to. One does not speak in(to) a vacuum. For true representation, therefore, representatives must be recognized as negotiating partners by those they speak to or with. The very negative reaction on the part of some people interviewed by ATD Fourth World activists seems to show that they did not view them as real negotiating partners. We can assume the same is true for representation, which cannot work properly if the person one is talking to refuses to consider one as a negotiating partner[11].

Representatives must also be seen as legitimate negotiating partners. What does that mean? Negotiating partners are legitimate if their rights to speak and self-expression are recognized. They must also be recognized by those they address, such as another person, a government department or court, not just as someone with the right to speak, but with the right to speak on behalf of others.

What is necessary for representatives to be considered legitimate? In instances of legal representation, legitimacy depends primarily on the way the representatives are appointed (the issue of their mandate). If they are appointed by election, then checks ensure that no foul play has taken place. In an association or trade union, a representative's legitimacy depends on the statutes being observed.

This legitimacy in law is easy to check, but there is often also a social legitimacy, when the social group, or even the whole of society, recognizes the representative's legitimacy. This form of legitimacy means other negotiating partners will agree to listen to and take account of what the representative says. Other factors may be relevant depending on the circumstances:

– Is the representative *competent?* We need to know who measures this competence and how it is measured.

– Do they use the same language as their negotiating partner? Do they have the same frame(s) of reference?

We realized that these aspects of legitimacy can become debatable and carry significant risks of misconduct. If the representative is not careful, they can end up dancing to their negotiating partner's tune because they are from the same background or because in order to achieve a result, they have to water down their demands[12]. This is a risk allies* of ATD Fourth World and that those they represent may run. As allies, they are fully involved through their jobs, families or associations etc, and as such constantly meet other people who not only are not poor themselves, but who are often also hostile to the poor. They have to take care not to clash with these people, they do not want to rub them up the wrong way and would rather avoid having anything further to do with them, meaning they can often end up playing along with them. There is therefore a considerable risk of their playing down their own beliefs.

Abbé Pierre[13], when interviewed by Bernard Chevallier, showed that he was aware of this last risk as a member of parliament and that he had decided not to continue the experiment. He said in explanation:

Because I was neither good enough nor brave enough. With this kind of responsibility, one has to be terribly brave, and sure of one's own abilities. Because I did not have this confidence in myself, I was easily influenced, at least to begin with, by subtle appeals to my friendship.

There seems to be a moment where it is no longer those represented but the negotiating partner who decides whether the representative is legitimate. At that point, representation is on dangerous ground.

When Abbé Pierre said that the representative must be competent to avoid being influenced, one activist responded by saying that *most of all, you have to be worthy of trust*. In saying so, he revealed something absolutely fundamental about representation in general and the representation of the very poor in particular: It is those represented who must remain in control.

The abilities of the representative are a means to effective representation but if this leads to the aim of representation being forgotten, the means must be reconsidered. Put simply, the negotiating partner must be reminded that it is not up to them to say whether the representative is competent, because they will always define this competence according to their own criteria.

For example, if the representative has certain legal expertise and asks a lawyer about a legal issue (in a government or court setting), the latter will accept the representative's legal abilities and will agree, more or less willingly, to discuss the matter. Yet perhaps the legal dispute is not really what is at stake, and if the discussion is only developed between "jurists", there is a risk that the underlying issue will be forgotten.

In conclusion, though the representative defines him or herself in dialogue with the negotiating partner and in partnership with those represented, as we shall see later, it is not up to the negotiating partner to define the representative's qualities or views.

Knowing those one will represent and those with whom one will negotiate

Representatives must know what those represented have experienced

The interviewees often expressed an opinion on the issue of knowing what people had experienced. When the CPAS Manager said that the social worker was very familiar with the lives of the poor and could therefore represent them[14], what familiarity or knowledge did she mean? When a young couple who are very poor said that the local authorities cannot protect those they do not know[15], are they only talking about knowing "from outside"?

Knowing someone from outside is, for example, seeing the poor in the street or only encountering them through one's profession as a social worker, doctor, lawyer etc. Often this means seeing everything which is going wrong in these people's lives: housing, clothes, children doing badly at school, "unnecessary" costs etc. Can we say that we know these people from what we see of them from the outside? One cannot get to know people by force. We think we know them but do we really know what drives them, their struggles, their hopes, their demons? One representative partly answered this when he said that someone who had escaped poverty could well be a representative for the poor since they knew *what it means to have a difficult life and how to protect themselves*[16].

To represent the poor, we must know them. Knowing the poor is not the same thing as knowing what poverty is. To really know, do we not also have to have had a difficult life, or are there other ways of knowing? If we ourselves have experienced poverty, we know what we have personally gone through, but is that enough to represent others? Whether one is poor or not, one has to walk for a time alongside those one wants to represent. This is a real commitment, it means linking one's own life to the very poor. The knowledge that people who have experienced poverty can bring to the table is uniquely valuable to representation, as long as they have the opportunity to think about what they and those around them experience. This does not exclude other types of knowledge, but these people can never replace what is contributed and expressed by the poor themselves.

Representation is knowing, but for those represented, it is also recognizing themselves in their representative. For example, ATD Fourth World activists say they recognize in Joseph Wresinski a representative of the poor: *He was someone like us, so he could represent us. People can tell straight away if you have gone through the same things as them***. This common experience is not indispensable in all contexts, and can sometimes be replaced by common interests, as one academic pointed out: *I do not need to say "The representative must be like me". One of my colleagues represents us in the Department, who is very different from me***. His personality is different but they have something in common which is fundamental to their representation—their work. For the poor, this is their lives.

Recognizing themselves in the representative is not saying *they are like me*, but rather *they are like us*.

Representatives must know their negotiating partners' interests

For representatives to be listened to, they must know what is at stake for their negotiating partners. The latter must understand that combating poverty is in their own interests. For example, in a school context, representing poor families whose children are often failing at school is also knowing that the school's reputation will improve if all its pupils succeed and go on school trips and excursions. It is also highlighting that the school will be pioneering if it really manages to integrate poor children. Representation is about getting the idea across that everyone stands to gain, not just the poor.

Representatives must know the places where representation takes place

Knowing the institutions, the people inside these institutions, being able to speak their language—all this is part of representation. It is rare for poor people to have this knowledge, a handicap often used to justify why they should not represent themselves.

One cannot but concede that knowing those places where representation takes place is indispensable and a priority in choosing representatives to speak on behalf of the poor, while knowing what they have been through, though necessary, is difficult to check and monitor. In order for disadvantaged people to represent themselves, they need to be trained to do so.

Training to be a representative

People who have not lived in poverty, who have been lucky enough to have an education, need to learn about the experiences of the poorest. This knowledge can only be gained by working alongside them, so that they can bear witness to the poor and their efforts to defeat poverty.

For poor people, one of the first priorities is to take the time to learn. They are so busy with the fight for survival that the risk is that a distinction starts being made between those poor people "who can speak" and the rest. One activist who has been involved with ATD Fourth World for 20 years said:

There is no difference between Fourth World activists and other poor people. It is just that the activists have had time to learn and be educated[17].

Whether one is an activist or not, daily life is still the same fight against humiliation and injustice. Believing that every poor person has abilities and a right to education is very important if a new form of exclusion is not to be created.

The goal of all education is to acquire skills. In the context of representation, these skills are: the ability to communicate what one has to say, and to know how to dialogue.

For poor people, one of the first stages of education is understanding their own lives and realizing that they are not alone in enduring poverty. It means learning to condemn the injustice they have suffered whilst simultaneously discovering what they can be proud of in their lives or those of their parents or peers. The task is really one of research which they cannot undertake alone, the aim of which is that they realize they have nothing to be ashamed of in their pasts. Fourth World People's Universities or national and international gatherings are places where people can realize that they are not alone in living in poverty and that some are even worse off. Sometimes this realization makes them want to get an education so they can be better equipped to fight against poverty.

But to be a representative, it is not enough to know and understand one's background. Poor people need education in order to understand *the world in which they are marginalized*, as Lucie Ribert said. They need to know about institutions and laws, and they also need to become cultured. Poverty traps those who live in it. Leaving the house, the estate or the area to brave joining a choir, a painting class, a library or an association demands considerable effort, and is rarely something people do off their own backs. Yet broadening one's horizons in this way is an essential part of being able to dialogue with people from different social backgrounds.

Dialogue is an integral part of representation and must be learnt. Listening is the cornerstone of dialogue. Lucie Ribert explained that her main priority is listening to the very poor families she meets:

> The families I know have things to say. They want to say them and they don't always have the strength to do so. It is more dangerous for them than for me to do it. I'm not saying I don't have setbacks in my life sometimes, but I can deal with them. But very poor families can't, they're constantly told they're failures.

The representative is called upon to dialogue with people from different backgrounds. Where does one learn to dialogue? Underpinning dialogue is a mutual respect and recognition of one's partner as a fellow citizen beyond that of common humanity.

In order to dialogue, one must understand the other's way of thinking and find the words and sentences to allow one to communicate. *If you're not used to speaking, it isn't easy. You don't want to look stupid*[18]. Having not had the opportunity to learn how to express themselves orally and in writing at school, disadvantaged people *have to play catch-up, they have everything to learn*.

One of the risks of education is that poor people lose their identities, wanting to *change* to be more easily accepted in contexts of representation. They carry within them the awareness of injustice, which drives them to act.

> My life's biggest challenge is basically to do with the school system. Throughout my life I have been really frustrated by all the hoops I have had to jump through and all the procedures, which have shown me the extent to which society rewards you for sitting up and begging[19].

Awareness of injustice can lead to revolt. The aim of education is not to stifle this, but to channel it and work with it for the better. Revolt is often a means of expression for the poor, but though it is sometimes necessary, it is insufficient as a form of representation. Lucie Ribert said that it was as part of ATD Fourth World that she learnt how to use her revolt usefully, by thinking and listening not only to her heart but to her head as well.

Education must allow poor people's ability to represent themselves to be recognized, and that takes time.

A long-term project

No one can say they are a representative until a certain amount of time has passed. They need the time to prepare for their role, carry it out, see the results etc. Representation requires a long period of preparation and fastidious work to meet and get to know those represented, prepare what the representative has to say to their negotiating partners and report back. Whether it be sporadic or permanent, representation is a long-term responsibility which requires time to be set aside for it.

> You realize that things move slowly, but that's OK. It's really good in fact, because you're part of it. I feel I'm really a part of a story which is unfolding. I feel that we poor are really writing our own chapter in history[20].

Proposals for all citizens to be truly represented

How can we ensure that all citizens are really represented and in so doing ensure that our society fulfils the demands of democracy? In other words, how can we avoid being satisfied by a democracy in name only which leaves the poorest on "the sidelines"? The first part of the answer lies in a real partnership, different to merely the token presence of the poor in decision-making instances. Must we therefore put forward specific representation for the poorest as a solution? If by specific representation we mean representation by category, then we think no, and suggest some approaches we might use for a true representation of the poorest in places where decisions are made, not only relating to combating poverty, but affecting society as a whole.

The demands of partnership

When society thinks about partnership today, it thinks about the various interconnected public or private institutions. There is a growing awareness in society of the importance of these connections. But this does not guarantee that the poorest actually have the wherewithal, nor people on their side, to come up with ways of rejecting poverty. Joseph Wresinski said that accepting poverty in our societies was admitting that not every human being had the right to the means and responsibilities necessary to realize their own dignity. In his view, being a partner[21] was wanting to communicate on a deep enough level for one's whole way of acting to be influenced. It meant feeling the reasons the poor have to act in order to give them back the initiative and responsibility when acting, even if they could not succeed alone. It meant learning not to get ahead of them, nor educate them, nor give them a conscience, but walking alongside them to ensure they succeed in what they undertake. In this sense, René Martin, a Fourth World activist, has had experiences which are very revealing of the means and conditions necessary to be a partner. What were the stages necessary to achieve that?

An initial meeting with Fourth World volunteer corps members took place *on his estate*. Speaking about them, René Martin says:

> They helped us get back in touch with the working world by giving us confidence. They listened. You could talk openly. They didn't make us talk about our problems. I felt I was meeting the third type! Meeting them helped me reassert my rights**.

Beyond René Martin's problems, such as power cuts, unemployment and health problems, there is a relationship of trust and mutual respect between him and the Fourth World volunteer corps members, which has been established over time. This relationship allows them to build a real partnership, which is only possible because it is reciprocal. Reciprocity means learning from one another, and thinking and acting together.

They met in 1986, and their relationship has evolved over time, as René and his family and ATD Fourth World have got to know one another. The members of the Fourth World volunteer corps learned that René was born in 1954 and is married with four children. Of gypsy origin on his father's side, he lived in social housing in a Lyon suburb. In 1979, he had a serious road accident and was classified disabled by COTOREP[22], with an incapacity rating of 35%. In 1986 he was unemployed. By becoming involved with the associative sector and taking part in Fourth World People's Universities, René became aware that what he said counted.

> What amazed me was that I listened to people speak and felt like I was listening to another world. I found myself outside what I was experiencing. At the start I was shy, I never used to speak like I do now. . . .

Fourth World People's Universities are partnerships where priority is accorded to those who do not talk, and where people ask for both the thoughts of the poorest and those who have not experienced poverty. It is a place where the poorest can compare what they are going through with other currents of thought.

Having gained a sense of confidence and learned to express himself once more, René could not leave it at that. He asked the Fourth World volunteer corps members to do more than just help him out, and give him prospects for the future so he could find a real job. Without realizing it, René became the spokesperson for thousands of parents who hope for a better future for themselves and their children. ATD Fourth World could not help but become more than just a "brother" to René, and live up to its own ideals. In Lyon, ATD Fourth World tried out a project called *A qualification against exclusion*[23], which set up a twin partnership between workers from poor backgrounds and various institutions who were asked to take part.

In 1994, René helped write some pages in book called *On voudrait connaître le secret du travail*[24], which explains the campaign ATD Fourth World ran for several years in order for every worker to be able to learn a trade and bring up a family by practicing that trade. It was an opportunity for activists like René to meet academics and trade unionists and to dialogue with them on the subjects of work, education/training and finding work. A year later, he spoke representing Fourth World activists in front of representatives of social partners and four hundred others!

Partnership with the very poor is a necessary condition for representation to be accessible to all. To build a long-term partnership with people living in poverty, it is indispensable that three aspects of the person are taken into account: their background (past), their thoughts (present) and their intentions (future). It is necessary beforehand that other people commit on an everyday basis with the very poor to get to know and to recognize the other as a human being and not as a *problem to be solved*. This partnership is a way in which citizens can find new paths towards a more democratic society where no one will be excluded because of poverty.

The issue of specific representation for the poorest

The question of whether *specific* representation is necessary for the poorest is complex and difficult, and raises a number of debates.

On the issue of specific representation

JF: I'm ready to agree that you need to know someone before you can represent them, and yet it seems to me that saying "You must have lived in poverty to represent the poor" is going a bit far.

JM: That's what the poor couple we met thought.

JP: And you?

JM: I do too. You can't explain something you haven't experienced. You can't explain what it means to have no food on the table all day, if you do.

JP: I get where you're coming from. But we're not talking about explaining, we're talking about representing.

JM: When poor people read what Father Joseph wrote or when they listen to what he said, they see themselves in what he went through. When he explained what he was going through, you could say "That's just like my life". Representation is recognizing yourself in your representative. It's seeing yourself. I reckon that someone who hasn't experienced poverty but has had constant dealings with it could represent the poor, but they'd need to be ever so sensitive. They'd need to be able to suffer as much as the others.

PN: If I follow you, if I'm poor, I want someone poor to represent me. If I'm a worker, I want a worker to represent me. If the President of France isn't a worker, then it's got nothing to do with me. He hasn't lived as a worker, so he doesn't know what I have experienced. . . . What would allow someone to represent us both, you who have lived in poverty and I who have not?

DB: I reckon that someone poor would be better prepared to represent another poor person and to stand up for them, because they have the same life experiences.

JP: You said "The representative must know and the person represented must recognize themselves in the representative".

JM: For example, the representative's job is to talk about the situation of the poorest. The poorest, who are there listening to them, must be able to say "Yes, that's exactly what I would have liked to say because it's exactly what I have been through"

Second session *(three months later)*

JM: I'd like to say something. Why is it that every time we speak about representation of the poorest, we do so in terms of specific representation? There are a lot of people who are represented nowadays, and in general, the people who are represented are always looking for people to represent them who live in the same situation as themselves or who do the same job.

PYV: We never talk about representation of employees in terms of "specific representation". Why do we do so when talking about the representation of the poorest? Why do we think we have to talk about specific representation every time we think about the representation of the poorest? . . .

JM; Representation is already categorized. We want to be represented like everybody else.

PYV: So that means that as of now . . . we have to stop using the word "specific".

CP: The word "specific" doesn't describe the representation of the poorest, who are absent.

PYV: Representation itself cannot be specific. But for representation of the poorest to exist, there are a few methodological requirements. The aim is to find the methods and the qualities a representative has to have so that everyone can be represented, including the poor . . .

CF: As soon as one starts thinking about those who are absent, one sees that representation in general is called into question, if not undermined completely. In this instance, it is fitting to say that representation by category is perverse.

DB: I've realized that the poorest must not be assigned their own special category apart.

From the start of research, our group was careful to recognize the poor but refused to see them as a group apart. Our search for a solution led us to ask firstly who may speak on behalf of the poor, then to question the expression *the poorest*, and finally to investigate the idea of specific representation.

Who may speak on behalf of the poor?

This question was asked of the project participants, and received varied answers. Some said that it was not strictly necessary to have lived in poverty to be a representative. *You have to be able to put yourself in poor people's shoes* said one academic. We do not think that is possible. Coming into contact with poverty and trying to understand it is not the same as experiencing it from within. The non-poor can speak of their fight against poverty but they cannot talk about it like the poor themselves can. In one of the previous chapters, we have already seen that one must have been a part of the group one wants to represent (whatever group this may be). One academic said:

> For jurists, the issue is one of representativeness. Who is legitimately allowed to speak on behalf of others? You need to have been . . . you need to have belonged . . . have been a part of the group you represent. But that's not the case historically speaking. Historically, it has always been non-poor who have spoken on behalf of the poor. That may go some way towards explaining the continued existence of poverty**.

In their answers to the question *who may speak on behalf of the poor?* several activists stressed that poverty gives one knowledge, experience and a mindset which provide a solid foundation to representation. Those who have escaped poverty are better equipped to deal with the risks. But with time and education, poor people can also be ready to represent others. The view people have of them is important. If we think them up to the task, they will be able to represent others because we have confidence in them.

Defining the term "the poorest"

The term *the poorest* is misunderstood. To start with, it needs to be distinguished from the category of people living in extreme poverty in the sense used in the Wresinski Report, for whom it is more accurate to speak of *the very poor.*

Lack of basic security is the absence of one or more factors that enable individuals and families to assume basic responsibilities and to enjoy fundamental rights. Such a situation may become more extended and lead to more serious and permanent consequences. Chronic poverty results when the lack of basic security simultaneously affects several aspects of people's lives, when it is prolonged, and when it severely compromises people's chances of regaining their rights and of reassuming their responsibilities in the foreseeable future[25].

Various reports have drawn attention to the fact that a significant number of people, at both national and international levels, endure a severe lack of basic security in many aspects. Besides the Wresinski Report itself, there is the Despouy Report for the United Nations Economic and Social Council[26] and the Belgian General Report on Poverty[27].

The expression *the poorest* does not aim to describe a group of people in extreme poverty. It is more of an intention, an approach, a *quest towards those people who are poorer and more excluded than those already encountered. These concepts serve to evaluate action, which is always faced with the danger overhanging anyone acting alongside the poor: the men and women they meet grow and progress, and those who follow behind or whose paths they did not cross are forgotten. . . . In this sense, the poor are those who have not yet been encountered, towards whom we are still moving[28].*

In other words, the expression *the poorest* can never describe a social group able to be represented. Any attempt to do this would be destined to failure from the outset. It would be impossible to say who is one of the poor*est*. We could even say that *the poorest* is by necessity a single person, and therefore alone.

The expression indicates that an effort has been made to consider our use of language, everyone's attempt to do their bit as a human being, and first and foremost those who voices are barely audible. Referring to the poorest is a way of listening, thinking and acting; straining to pay attention to the weakest voice.

We could put it another way. For ATD Fourth World, *the expression 'the poorest' is to be seen as a question: who are the poorest?[29]* The question allows us both to adopt an approach which takes account of the excluded amongst the excluded, and to make a partnership possible, a form of reciprocal thinking and action.

Who are the poorest among a given population? What is the specific reality of their lives? What are their aspirations? What efforts do they make to resist their situation? How do others support them?[30]

If referring to the poorest is a reference to an approach, we cannot represent "the poorest". Nevertheless, the tactic of approaching the poorest, that is, confronting the issue of those who are absent, must remain in our minds at all times. The presence of *the very poor* in representation will guarantee that of *the poorest.*

Specific representation or common interest?

Dictionaries define *specific* as a property of a species or group, and common to all the members of that species or group. The word can be considered alongside *special* which also means *proper* or *particular* to something or someone.

Specific representation therefore means the rendering present of a particular group who share the same interests. There are plenty of examples of this in civil society, such as tenants' associations, trade unions, Parent-Teacher Associations etc. In this context, it would be inappropriate for the group to be represented by someone with interests alien to those of the group (for example a farm worker representing railway workers or a hairdresser representing the Faculty of Law at a university). This kind of representation in terms of "categories" leads to one section of the population being excluded, since everyone defends their own interests with no regard to the common interest.

There is no point creating an additional category for the poor, since combating poverty is everyone's business. It is the common interest of all citizens. *The common interest* is what is important and what is useful, it is acting in the interest of society (Larousse dictionary). In political representation, elected representatives are called upon to represent all their citizens. If they do not take the common interest into account, this can unleash problems, such as in Belgium over child protection. Following the tragic events in that country, hundreds of thousands of people demonstrated their common interest—child protection—during the *White March* in October 1996. The common interest of parents in children, for example, might stop children (any children) from failing at school. In this case, very poor families would certainly be taken into account and we would have gone beyond specific representation by categories.

Combating poverty requires us to reject representation by category, since categories exclude. Even if a poor person represented the category of the poor, there would be a risk of deepening the divide between them and the non-poor. Associations which combat poverty are often open to all citizens[31]. Those which stand alongside the poor know that what the very poor say is true for all of us because they know about injustice and what needs to be done for there to be more justice and solidarity in society.

To conclude this point, we can say that specific representation of the poor is definitely not what is needed, but that on the contrary, poverty must be combated everywhere (see diagram). Our research shows that the most important thing is that the very poor can participate in representing everyone, both in existing places of representation and those which remain to be created. Until now, it has been the

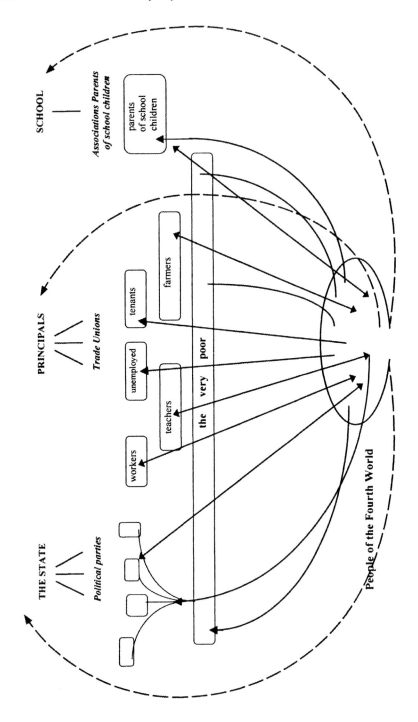

non-poor who have presided over places of representation. Though the demand to give the floor to the poor has been heard, it is often limited to sporadic participation, as if representation were one of the privileges the non-poor do not wish to share.

Notes

1. In Greek, the verb krinein, which is the root of our word "criticism", means "to choose", "to separate", "to decide" and "to distinguish".
2. The Latin verb vocare, from which "voice" is derived, means "to call". This expression is perfectly suited to representation where those represented call upon the representative.
3. c.f. Hannah Arendt, *The Origins of Totalitarianism*, Imperialism, (English translation), published by Harcourt, 1968, pp 6-280. c.f. also internal group documents.
4. Lecture by Lucie Ribert
5. c.f. (in particular) *Elements of the Philosophy of Right.*
6. Interview no.1.
7. Interview no. 13.
8. Interview no. 3.
9. In representation in a strictly political sense, this phenomenon is sometimes less marked to the extent that elected representatives represent ideas more than people.
10. Interview no. 11.
11. To take up the image of the mirror again, if the person the representative is talking to does not see them as a person but as a transparent sheet of glass, there can be no representation.
12. Interview no. 6
13. B. Chevallier, *op. cit.*, pp122-124.
14. Interview no. 1.
15. Interview no. 9.
16. Interview no. 5.
17. Lecture by Lucie Ribert.
18. Lecture by Lucie Ribert.
19. Lecture by Emile Creutz.
20. Lecture by Lucie Ribert.
21. c.f. definition in Chapter 2, Representation and Partnership.
22. French Technical Committee for Life Choices and Careers dealing with the disabled in France.
23. Started by ATD Fourth World and co-directed by the Regional Authority for Work and Employment, the "A qualification against exclusion" project was carried out in and around Lyon between 1989–1992. 75 adults aged 25–40 living in extreme poverty were paid to attend a course part-time, and achieve a qualification at the end at least equivalent to a Certificate of Professional Skills (CAP—holders are normally skilled manual workers practicing a trade).
24. X. Godinot (editor), *op. cit.*
25. *Chronic Poverty and Lack of Basic Security: The Wresinski Report of the Economic and Social Council of France, op. cit*, p. 25.
26. *Human Rights and Extreme Poverty*, June 28, 1996, approved in 1997. Resolution 1997/11 of the UN Commission on Human Rights.
27. General Report on Poverty, commissioned by the Ministry for Social Integration and carried out by the King Baudouin Foundation in collaboration with ATD Fourth World and the

Union of Belgian Cities and Communes in 1994. This report's main originality lies in the fact that people affected by extreme poverty were involved throughout the writing of it.

28. J. Lecuit, *La rencontre avec les plus pauvres provoque la connaissance*, in *La connaissance des pauvres*, Louvain-la-Neuve, Academia-Bruylant, 1996, p214.

29. ATD Fourth World, *Reaching the poorest*, New York/Paris, published by UNICEF & ATD Fourth World, 1996, p4.

30. *Ibid.*, p12.

31. The expression *Fourth World* is sometimes incorrectly used to replace *poverty*. The term *Fourth World* does not denote a social group, lumbering the poor with yet another label. The term *Fourth World* contains the idea of gathering together citizens from all backgrounds and situations, alongside the poor and drawing inspiration from them. This is the meaning of the idea of the People of the *Fourth World*.

Conclusion

The experience of the Fourth World activists, Fourth World volunteer corps member and academics over the two years of this research project demonstrated that merging knowledge raises new issues. Everyone had arrived with their own beliefs and gaps in their knowledge about citizenship and representation.

During the research, both very poor people and well-known intellectuals reminded us that belonging to the community of humanity is a part of being recognized as a citizen. This recognition is a two-way affair, between the person and the community.

However, the examples given in the various chapters of this memoir show how difficult dialogue can be between the very poor and other citizens. Yet dialogue is possible, under certain conditions. Our research brought to light some of these conditions, such as:

– How we view the poor: the view we have of the poor is of prime importance. They are citizens and not people with problems who need assistance. They are actors in their lives as individuals and as members of a community. Their thoughts can contribute to democratic society.

– Awareness of a common interest: for example, child protection, a more just world, combating poverty, etc.

 Meeting through acting: for example, local initiatives in a school or association, or equally in a project like this one between universities and the Fourth World, allow people to work together and get to know one another, discover other people's abilities and trust one another.

We need to rethink representation to include those who are too often excluded if the democratic ideal is to be fulfilled. The various forms of representation, even classing people by social or professional groups, always exclude someone. The challenge is therefore not to add another category, that of the very poor. Our hypothesis was basically that *representation is rendering present the issues of those who are absent* within all bodies where decisions are made, such as political parties, trade unions, associations etc. Our research showed us that this can be achieved with reference to the poorest, not by classing them as a social group in their own right, but by adopting an attitude which constantly seeks out the excluded amongst the excluded.

Who can render *the poorest* present? Throughout history, it has often been the non-poor who have spoken on behalf of the poor. This is not to question their sincerity, for their commitment and bravery in doing so were real. They raised awareness of issues related to extreme poverty and helped determine some of the solutions. But can we really say the very poor were represented by them? Can a very poor person recognize their daily struggle in these representatives? For the *very poor* to be able to say of a representative "he/she is like us", it is vital that some of them act as representatives themselves.

That takes time, education, and most of all partnership between poor and non-poor. This partnership is essential. Without it, this approach to representation is rendered meaningless. Without it, what the very poor have to say goes unheard. Without it, the very poor are even at risk of becoming more excluded.

It is not enough to put an extra chair at the table for the poor, who are too often there only to recount their own experiences. Representation of the poorest is an integral part of combating poverty and affects all citizens since society is the poorer if it chooses to ignore the contributions those who are excluded have to make.

This is why thinking about the representation of *the poorest* is also thinking about the representation of *everyone*.

Appendix

The research materials

Work on parliamentary texts leading to the creation of the RMI

RMI (French Minimum Income Benefit), created by the law of December 1, 1988.

How do those representing France speak about the poor in the texts of parliamentary debates (from the *Journal Officiel*)? We answered this question from four angles:

– How do members of parliament speak about the poor?

– How do members of parliament speak about ATD Fourth World?

– How do members of parliament use what Father Joseph Wresinski wrote in his report for the Economic and Social Council?

– How does discussion treat the rights of the poor?

The interviews and lectures

The activists carried out fifteen interviews between October and December 1996.

No.	Job title	Job description	Familiar with ATD Fourth World?
1	CPAS Manager	Manages the CPAS (Public Center for Social Aid)	Not familiar with work of ATD Fourth World; has heard of the ATD Fourth World.
2	Chair of a Parent-Teacher Association, which aims to improve children's relations with and life at school.	Chairs meetings	No
3	Social Housing Company Manager	Heads a committee dealing with residents' complaints pertaining to building upkeep	No
4	Member of a social housing committee	Listens and makes complaints on behalf of residents	A little
5	Mayor	Mayor of a town of 7,000	No
6	Friend of ATD Fourth World	Father, grandfather, retired.	Yes, Fourth World activist since 1987.
7	Member of a local events committee	Helps organize local events and improve quality of life on her estate	Yes, since 1996
8	Mrs. Y	Widow	No

No.	Job title	Job description	Familiar with ATD Fourth World?
9	Young couple	Receive the minimex	No
10	Food bank organizer	Manages distribution of food parcels	Yes, since 1987
11	ATD Fourth World activist	Mother of 3 children	Yes, since 1989
12	ATD Fourth World activist	Widow, mother of 3 children	Yes, since 1982
13	Deputy Mayor	Adjunct to the mayor. In charge of social housing, culture, youth issues and local events	No
14	Social worker	Organizes projects alongside the poorest	Yes, since 1990
15	Léonce Berton	Camp leader on a travelers' site	No

Bibliography

Philosophy: texts by Thomas Hobbes, Montesquieu, Rousseau, Hannah Arendt, Hegel.

Other texts: extracts from the report *Chronic Poverty and Lack of Basic Security: The Wresinski Report of the Economic and Social Council of France*; *Le Père Joseph représentant de son peuple* (*Démocratie et Pauvreté*, Editions Quart Monde/Albin Michel, 1991, p658) by Mrs. De Vos van Steenwijk; Speech by Father Joseph Wresinski at the Maison de la Mutualité in Paris, November 17, 1977 (Quart Monde IGLOOS, nos. 97-98, 1978, p 81).

VIEWS OF THE ACADEMIC PANEL

The members of the Academic Panel met five times over the course of the two-year Fourth World University project. Some also took part in seminars which brought together all the project agent-authors.

After reading the five memoirs they discussed their views on the methodology and content. Before publishing their views, each member read one memoir in more depth.

The views given here are those expressed in discussion with the participants on April 9, 1998.

OVERALL OPINION OF THE ACADEMIC PANEL
by Louis Join-Lambert

The Academic Panel had the privilege of receiving the memoirs as soon as they were completed. Each of us read them thoroughly. Then, at a day-long meeting with the pedagogical team, we compared our views. My role in this section is to reflect the views of the Academic Panel as a whole on all five of the memoirs.

Each memoir is the considered account of a piece of research. The Academic Panel has tried as far as possible to refer to the memoirs, and only to the memoirs, in assessing the relevance and quality of the research.

The research can also be considered from other angles, which, as the Academic Panel would like to emphasize, do not come within its scope. For example, we do not aim to evaluate the project from a pedagogical point of view. Others are already doing so using the appropriate means and with the help of the participants, who are giving their opinions on this aspect. Neither do we intend to give what from an academic point of view should rightly be called an overview of modern scholarship on the subjects you have tackled in your texts. Neither does the Academic Panel wish to take the place of the bodies of ATD Fourth World in assessing the accuracy of its analyses, still less impose it upon them.

Writing

Writing these memoirs was a gamble. "I've been wondering about this gamble for a year and a half" said René Rémond. "Would we really be able to produce something that could be read? We couldn't expect the work to be identical to our usual academic papers, but it had to be of a similar level. Before reading the memoirs, when each group presented its project to the others in Chantilly, I felt reassured by the progress people had made, the approach they had taken and the work they had done. Upon reading the memoirs, my reservations faded away." These memoirs provide an excellent starting-point for serious discussion.

We would like to say more about the texts. Writing them was a task which required not just reasoning and cognitive abilities, but also a demanding and, I must say, admirable joint effort. At no point does the reader have the impression of reading just one or two people's work, nor something superficial. This writing is the product of considerable cooperation over two years which made room for a panoply of diverse contributions.

The Academic Panel has one other important remark to make before discussing the contributions and limits of these memoirs. The latter were not finished because there was nothing left to research, nor because research reached a particularly important stage in tying up the loose ends, dotting the 'i's and crossing the 't's. The memoirs were finished out of necessity, since it was decided at the start of the project to limit its length in advance. This stage is over. From a researcher's point of view, it would be more interesting for us to be at an interim stage, and for the following remarks to serve as building blocks for future stages. This is the path a thesis usually takes, for example. A student works on it in stages, taking into account the comments of their supervisor/s who read the most important parts of the work as it is written and say: you might usefully explore this direction, this information needs checking, or that assertion needs to be better justified. Looked at like this, the Academic Panel's point of view and that of the participants do not sit comfortably together. The comments of the former will provoke the latter since all are aware that a follow-up to this project is not possible. Yet this is precisely the attitude which produces the most valuable debate.

The memoirs are the starting-blocks on the basis of which the Academic Panel have reached a judgment, which I convey to you here. But what questions did we ask? They can be separated into two main groups:
– Can one say that these memoirs reflect a real merging of knowledge? If so, does this knowledge-merging help our understanding of the subjects addressed?
– How concrete is the academic content of their contribution?

The originality of knowledge-merging

Each memoir has an overriding unity. We perceived no dramatic discrepancies in style or quality when reading them that gave away who had written which part. They are remarkably readable on the whole. This unity might mean that one group of participants imposed their contribution to the detriment of others. Yet this is not what the memoirs show. The panel's view is that knowledge was indeed shared, and that reading the memoirs displays the compromise reached between the different groups in order to do so. This knowledge-merging is visible in the way it displaces the manner in which we might traditionally expect to find debate and research carried out.

The focus of academic procedure was shifted towards education. The memoirs show how the groups of activists seized upon and transformed academic procedure. By working on the recordings of group meetings, they arrived at their own understanding of what happened and explored it more fully. And they returned with written texts expressing their agreement, questions or suggesting ways of refining understanding. But they also returned to express disagreement, or even take a position the other(s) have still not understood. Sometimes they held this position for several months before it was appreciated by the others.

By the same token, the academics also accepted to be taught, though this was difficult for them. One of them wrote in the memoir "It is most striking to find oneself deaf and blind". Beyond the modesty which makes this comment so magnificent, we can say that knowledge-merging requires first and foremost the ability to re-train one's own way of perceiving the world. The texts even show that this was an *a priori* condition for agreeing on how the research was carried out.

The focus of academic procedure also shifted in the research itself by taking into account the activists' experiences. Examples of this abound. In the "Family" memoir, for example, the experience of a prolonged period of time is in opposition to the literature on the subject which tends to see only the burden of immediate difficulties. In "History", the experience of turnaround, the journey from shame to pride, takes center stage.

This debate, this academic procedure, shifted with the taking into account of the academics' resistance towards certain interpretations. This is seen in "Knowledge", about academic learning. The academics said that this knowledge detracts from the understanding of the world that any and every human experience can bring. The activists, for their part, said that one was constantly dependant on others if one lacked this knowledge and that this knowledge liberated people from dependency. This view sparked an intense debate which influenced the research.

Of course, the activists shifted towards a more academic approach as well. They broadened their understanding a great deal, for example by reading Pessin or Hannah Arendt. This goes without saying, indeed it might even be expected.

Beyond the friction caused by their differences, did either side take on board the other's conceptual framework? For example, let us consider the idea of "looped" time, one of the activists' contributions, which showed the limits of the opposition between linear and circular time in doing their experiences justice. There are other examples.

Agreeing to learn from each other shows how the academics were prepared to ask themselves the questions the activists wanted them to, while also addressing the experiences and preconceptions underlying these questions. This was rather unexpected.

What place is there in knowledge-merging for the experience of suffering? This very important and very delicate question clearly emerged in the course of the project as a real hotspot where tensions waxed and group thinking was at its most demanding. Group thinking had to be twice as productive for it to be worth the effort and for people be prepared to run the risk of being hurt.

These memoirs demonstrate the participants' active involvement in a joint adventure they believed in. This belief was certainly a large part of the reason they felt confident to elaborate and express their thoughts more freely, to be heard, to have other people's attention. If one does not agree on another person's interpretation of an injury, this conditions one's relationship to them. Without a shared opinion which is stronger than the circumstances, one reaches the limits of possible discussion. The issue remains unresolved. This requires a renewed effort to share knowledge.

All we have just said, all these "shifts", demonstrate the freshness and originality of the memoirs. These issues arose in carrying out the project. Yet it is they which are often absent from academic research. In this sense, the project represents a real contribution.

Concrete results

The project is finished, as I said earlier, because the allotted time is up. Respect is due to those researchers who forgo other interests and activities for years at a time in order to carry out their research in the fullest depth possible. Research is a kind of asceticism.

Here we were only dealing with a first stage. Yet this has still provided some concrete results, such as:

A better understanding of the participants' experiences and preconceptions. This was one fundamental consequence of what was said above about knowledge-merging. From my own experience, I am not sure I have seen many research groups manage to draw up their research framework based on such diverse social backgrounds. Especially not with such care taken to ensure that every participant's understanding is fully explored and the imperative of it being integrated into the whole.

The limits of this very qualitative approach must be expanded. Generally speaking, the use of life experiences gives greater emphasis to an understanding-based approach. The limit of this method is that for every personal experience backing up one way of understanding, one can probably cite other unique and different experiences in contradiction. Sometimes in the memoirs, generalizations are arrived at too quickly. Inspired by an insight into one person's situation, one tends to think the same is true of everyone.

This can be a rather hasty assertion if it has not first been thoroughly researched and contested, if someone has not played "devil's advocate", both factually and conceptually speaking.

Factual: We tried to think whether we knew anything contradictory to things we remembered because they supported our view, though we did not realize it. Each group's work was largely based on the experiences of that group's members and their understanding of it. For this project, these were the most fertile sources of information. The interviews are in much the same vein, on the whole. But we were demanding readers and asked whether the sample of interviewees provided sufficient opportunity for the hypotheses to be contradicted. This is probably the weakest link in the materials used, which would probably be ironed out in future stages.

Conceptual: Did we attempt to intelligently present and discuss ideas which we did not like?

Here is one example which may have those who worked on the People and Pessin's conception thereof gnashing their teeth. Both implicitly and explicitly, the analysis is written with reference to ATD Fourth World and Father Joseph Wresinski. We might usefully ask what result the diagram would give if it were applied to French extreme right politician, Jean-Marie Le Pen, and what the differences would be. What has been arrived at is a very useful way of understanding turnaround at collective level. Do people who feel humiliated and become involved with the French National Front also experience something comparable to the turnaround described here? By comparing and contrasting in this manner, the hypothesis which assumes the experience to be positive would have had to address an aspect of it perceived as being darker. Perhaps this would have resulted in a more precise definition, or at any rate a fuller one.

The last criticism concerns the *weak comparison and contrast with what we call social structure*. Discussion of the long periods spent as a family, or of the family plan as embodied in children, for example, is interesting and fruitful. But how does it relate to other periods of time these families must spend in other ways, especially given their poverty? How does time spent working, finding resources or earning the rent impinge on this family time? Are we to think that this tension strengthens resistance and the sense of family values in family members' subjective experiences, or that it ends up wearing down and exhausting them prematurely? This direction is barely explored in the memoir, though the pedagogical team tell us that it was discussed within the group.

In conclusion

The constraints we have already mentioned mean we cannot ask more of these memoirs than they are able to give. They reflect an in-depth dialogue which is exceptional because of the different social experiences they incorporate and because of the attempt to be as rigorous as possible in this dialogue. This is what makes the memoirs so fertile.

Asking of them that they sustain the same degree of rigorous examination as a long research project would be to misunderstand their purpose and the reasons for publishing them as they stand. The project's goal was to demonstrate that given time (much longer than the two years for this project) and the means to share their knowledge, those who have experienced extreme poverty and are looked down upon in society can provide an illuminating contribution to our society's collective knowledge.

COMMENT ON THE HISTORY MEMOIR
by Georges Liénard

This memoir aims to address and broaden understanding of several vital issues, five of which I wish to emphasize:

1. How are cultural and identity issues to be seen in the context of the fight for social recognition[1] waged by the poor, whether acting as a movement or as individuals? How are we to understand the rationale behind the ambivalent behavior of the poor in various situations and socially challenging contexts?

2. What can we say about the interaction and social relationship between the academics, activists and Fourth World volunteer corps members in addressing the question of who has the right to determine the interpretation of the behavior of the poor in socially challenging contexts, including in situations described as "poverty which destroys humanity"?

3. The construction of a collective identity of which the People of the Fourth World can be proud is demonstrated by the use of a "positive" version of the myth of the People, but there is no hypothesis of a "negative" version of this myth.

4. Analysis of the rapport with (to give it its full name) the International Movement ATD Fourth World's "guide", its role and founding words, focuses almost exclusively on the "positive" use of charismatic power, but does not examine how this charisma can create (or not create) an open democratic power, and it does not emphasize enough the task of creating social dignity for the poor through the Movement's work as opposed to individuals' innate ability.

5. The necessity of maintaining and reinforcing the theoretical and axiomatic creative tension between several different points of view in order to understand the complex reality of turnaround, is perhaps not stressed enough.

Though each of these five subgroups deserves and requires development in order to do the finished work justice, space constraints mean I can only sketch out the main areas dealt with in debate and encounters.

1. One important first aspect of the memoir is its attempt to explain the rationale behind various types of behavior linked to poverty. These types of behavior might appear irrational or attributable to deficiencies on the part of the individuals concerned, if measured against the criteria applied in measuring legitimate and dominant behavior, or seem senseless to us because they have meanings and motivations that we don't understand (not to mention that this behavior may also have relevance and limits that we don't understand given their challenging social situations) This means we have to observe and interpret how behavior, culture and society have active and constructive effects on positive self-recognition. In short, behavior, culture and society can allow people to surpass themselves, but the tendency is for even this behavior that allows people to surpass themselves to be seen merely as a consequence of domination or alienation, that is, as a reaction to their surroundings, suggesting that the only option for them is what is objectively seen as fate. This is the case, for example, in these extracts from interviews which require analysis in the light of the twofold cultural and symbolic dimension described above for them to be understood .

> – I feel sorry for those we call the "newly poor". I'm not sure they have the same problems as us, because we've been taught how to get by. . . . They don't have the knowledge we have. We have different ways of surviving in society that our parents have taught us.

> – We poor marry among ourselves . . . it is a bond of pure love. It's a real bond of love. It knows no limits. That's why we stay together living amongst ourselves. We have no fear: we bring our love and that's all. We have nothing material to give.

> *Or*: We are very religious too, even if our faith is not always recognized by others. But we don't care because God knows who we are. . . . Some say, "I pray when the church is empty. I feel closer to God and the Saints, I light a candle for them and we commune together". We can't be with people who aren't from our poor background, as it makes us feel misjudged and out of place.

By the same token, the intense feelings of anxiety and insecurity expressed by individuals are explained not by the intrinsic weakness of those individuals but with reference to the systematic pressure (justified or not) exerted on them by institutions such as the social services, school and care orders.

> – I fought that shame but I was never able to get rid of it. It was as if it was stuck to me.

> – If poverty was not seen as totally negative, you wouldn't feel the same shame and you wouldn't be ashamed of what your parents or grand-parents did.

> – When I was a schoolgirl, I wasn't allowed to hang my coat next to the others' in case they caught lice. My peg was the last one. I was ashamed of this, so I was always the very last one to leave the hall. My shame caused me to stay on my own and cut myself off.

– You have to force yourself to go and ask for something, for food or medical care or a free bus pass. It's humiliating for us to be forced to beg for help like this.

Thus, the paradoxical situation arises whereby a social institution created to help the poor is seen by them as a threat. However, there is no contrastive analysis examining in what circumstances and under what conditions the social services' actions are justified and legitimate or not.

2. The memoir addresses another vital issue: who should have the "last word" in interpreting the acts of those in poverty or the acts of others which affect them? This is therefore an issue of who governs the analytical interpretation of the self, a right claimed by the person or group concerned. We are dealing here with a demand made by the people or groups concerned, and control of self-image (including an analytical view of the self, whether this be sociological, historical, psychosocial or philosophical). This demand poses a problem for the imperatives of academic research, because the academic world determines the criteria used for evaluation and acknowledgement, and because individual academics wish to determine the final analytical interpretation (at least in writing) of the actions of the people and groups concerned.

In order to prevent any misunderstandings obscuring the question I have just asked, we should point out that the claim, the demand even, made by one group or another to determine its image in analysis is usual, and is most often made by the superior and dominant groups in society. Indeed, groups with dominant or significant power in society try, in numerous ways and according to their will, to control the symbolic image and the reputation of sociological, economic, social or political analysis concerning them.

As examples we might cite their refusal to allow the release of information about them concerning income, property and investment strategies, their refusal to fund studies directly concerning them; their funding and use of studies concerning other social groups; their attempts to monitor the content of studies concerning them and the way they manage relations with interviewers.

The question and the demand made in this educational process and the production of the memoir are therefore an important social and epistemological issue linked to the social consequences of any analytical discussion centered on one social group.

Let us recall how this discussion is presented in the memoir.

– *Fundamental issues raised by the research.*

Tensions arose on three issues: who is entitled to speak about poverty? Does the way poverty is discussed vary depending on the audience? Who do we mean when we say People?

The activists said that it should be up to them to decide whether they wanted to discuss their lives in the context of the project. They had made a commitment to it, and were thus obliged to talk about their and their families' lives, but they did not feel able to do the same with other people's lives. In the interviews they carried out, they captured what the interviewees wanted to have expressed. One activist reacted to a text that had been written about her family written some time previously and which had offended her. It is up to us to write what we want to, it's our lives, she said.

The discussion was long and painful. Out of respect for the activists' feelings and her own views, [the Fourth World volunteer corps member] decided to withdraw a text she had written.

The question of who is entitled to speak and write about poverty, and how, became a fundamental issue.

This debate, which concerned both knowledge socially acceptable for both groups, and the production of knowledge which was academically relevant (the two of which are always linked to some extent), covers two socio-cognitive issues. The first is to do with the relationship to scientific power and therefore to the expression "scientifically proven". It can be expressed as "Whom can the analyst observe and analyze? What do they have the right to describe? Who judges their academic writing? Can they write only about those from whom they fear nothing?" The second concerns the relationship to orthodox expression, the group's accepted form of communication—what a group allows to be said and written about it, the way it is organized and how it monitors its image. This socio-cognitive debate, conflict even (though a peaceful one), is important in producing "academically relevant" knowledge, according to at least two conditions. Firstly, there is the construction of an interactive process between two extremes[2]. Secondly, social orthodoxy cannot triumph over academic demands, and maintaining orthodoxy within the group cannot hinder the writing of the final analytical interpretation (no material must be suppressed, any information withdrawn must be mentioned, any disagreement on the final interpretation must be noted).

3. Alongside the role of myth in the process of turnaround, it is important to examine that of the relationship to the guide and their founding message and that of the relationship to ATD Fourth World and to the social, political and ideological motivations of those in charge.

All processes of turnaround take place in relation to a guide and a founding message. Cardijn was this guide for the Christian Youth Workers' movement (JOC) and let us not forget that Wresinksi was also a member of the JOC. But movements and associations of all kinds are obliged to use the guide's founding message (or original prophecy) as a reference, and voluntarily treat them with reverence. The process must be understood, but so must its variations.

In this situation, the relationship to the guide and his founding message (or original prophecy for the group and the people concerned) is partially one of charisma (c.f. the story of Noël Jacques and others).

Once more, the issue concerns not so much a charismatic power, but the academic usefulness of expanding hypotheses on the guide, the founding message given by the guide, the movement they start and which (under certain conditions) survives them. The central question then becomes "Under what conditions and according to what social, cultural, political or religious customs can the partially charismatic power of the guide in question and the commitment on the part of various participants (activists, Fourth World volunteer corps members, leaders and allies) to the direction given by and for the Movement produce a form of open, democratic power rather than an autocratic form which closes and excludes?" History shows us that the conditions established to monitor the power exerted by the Movement's leaders, the replacement of those leaders and the Movement's ideological direction with reference to the original mission statement, are essential factors in determining the Movement's socio-political direction.

It also appears that in analyzing the process of turnaround and the construction of the myth of the People, the memoir paradoxically does not sufficiently investigate the significance of all the historical work carried out by ATD Fourth World. ATD Fourth World (c.f. the origins of the International Movement ATD Fourth World's name) represents a central factor in structuring the way turnaround is practiced and the content of the myth, because the relationships between the Movement and individuals (not only those left to their own devices and not part of any movement or institution) are in fact the sole creators of pride in one's social identity. But to accept this would be to state implicitly that charismatic ideology wishes to establish not only a circular relationship between the poor, the guide and their founding message, but also and especially a fundamental and founding dignity of the poor as such[3]. Perhaps this is because there is no in-depth analysis (perhaps a temptation to reject analysis, even) of the conditions which cause some people to remain in the rather negative version of the effects of poverty, which one member of the group described as "the poverty which destroys".

However, tension arose every time the Fourth World volunteer corps member mentioned extreme poverty destroying the humanity of those who suffer it. This notion of extreme poverty that destroys seems to contradict the notion of a People and the activists' pride at belonging to a People. To talk about what poverty destroys in people is to push them further into this poverty. It is a way of speaking that attacks the pride of some activists.

This demand for the poor to be recognized as such (as workers are—Cardijn said that "a worker is worth all the gold in the world") is probably valid politically and in terms of cultural-political interaction. However, scholarship demands that we also consider that "poverty which destroys" does exist, that its processes must be understood, that it must be understood why some people do not escape it, why domination exists in poor families as it does in others, why there are poor (and non-poor) people who vote for Le Pen and the National Front and who also display social and/or political racism (it is important not to confuse the two). This desire on the part of academics to understand "the poverty which destroys" does not intend to plunge people further into poverty, nor to "emphasize their shame" (though I admit it is difficult to avoid it), but to understand the specific features of the process of this "poverty which destroys humanity" and the political, social and cultural conditions which must operate in tandem for action to have a positive effect on what has been created by structural and individual inequalities.

This is also almost certainly linked to the qualitative sample, which perhaps was not contrastive enough in its choices, and therefore did not produce data with a sufficiently high degree of variety. It is probably also linked to the distinction not being clearly enough made between on the one hand poverty or extreme poverty (defined as a social situation or position), which I cannot see as having intrinsic "positive" values, and on the other hand the positive values such as solidarity, love and friendship which the people and their Movement create in order to resist, fight back, survive, in spite of the negative effects of their lives and their poverty which society creates and furthers, and tries to impose on them and assign to them.

Notes

1. The strategy for achieving recognition also includes a strategy for legitimizing the knowledge of the poor, spearheaded by ATD Fourth World and including a process of education and training. However, if this legitimizing strategy is to be analyzed and evaluated as such, it must be distinguished on the one hand from the evaluation of the knowledge the education and training process produces, the memoir, and on the other hand from the critical and constructive discussion of this knowledge. This note attempts to take account of this evaluation and constructive—but critical—discussion. The point of this note is not to analyze and evaluate ATD Fourth World's legitimizing strategy, of which the education and training process is one aspect of several.

2. Social sciences attempt to partially deal with this issue by specifically integrating the interviewee/s' relationship to the words on a social, methodological or epistemological level. For some different sociological approaches to this issue, see: A Touraine, F Dubet, Z Hegedus, L Maheu, M Wieviorka, *La méthode de l'intervention sociologique*, Paris, Atelier d'Intervention Sociologique, Cadis, 99 pp, P Bourdieu, (editor), 1993, *La Misère du monde*, Paris, Seuil, 949 pp. and especially the point of view on this issue given in the chapter " Comprendre ", pp. 903-904 and "L'espace des points de vue" pp. 9-11, and J C Kaufmann, 1996, *L'entretien compréhensif*, Paris Nathan, 128 pp.

3. This belief in the strength of the poor person's fundamental dignity as such is probably necessary as a basic starting-point in constructing identity, but analytically speaking, its ideological and symbolic necessity cannot hide the fact that the production of this fundamental pride is linked to initiatives taken in the relationship between the Movement and the person concerned, and does not result from an innate capacity on the part of the individuals.

COMMENT ON THE FAMILY MEMOIR

by Xavier Godinot

I was given the task of commenting on the memoir entitled *The Family Plan and Time.* My first reaction was one of confusion. Why ask me to comment on this memoir when my academic specialization is more labor economics and political science, not the family? I felt that this subject was not in my field of expertise. Then on reflection it occurred to me that this might be positive, since this was the case for everyone involved in this project.

On the other hand, having been a member of the Fourth World volunteer corps for a long time, I felt well at home with this topic which, as you mention in the memoir, is well-established in ATD Fourth World's work. ATD Fourth World was founded as a family-based Movement, "using the strengths of even the very poor, the determined hope and desire of the parents to give their children a better life than they had had".

Finally, I, like all of you, have experienced being part of a family.

This morning we spoke again about the importance of recognizing everyone's fragility, the part of them which remains mysterious, what they lack, what they fear. Recognizing these deficiencies, not being aloof, knowing that one needs others—all this is an essential condition for merging knowledge. What would be the point of sharing if everyone could get by alone?

This brings me to the first part of the evaluation, concerning the approach taken in writing the memoir.

Reading the memoir, it is evident that dialogue between the group members was not easy, and I even felt that what is written does not fully reflect the extent of tensions within the group. The memoir mentions "heated debates" and raises four main problem areas. At the same time, it is clear that relationships of mutual trust and respect allowed group unity to be maintained and problems to be overcome.

– The first problem was finding a common language. In the memoir, we read that "the academics' language was often a closed book to the rest, the activists were not sufficiently articulate to express their thoughts, the Fourth World volunteer corps member wondered whether some basic terms meant the same thing to everyone". To overcome this problem, the activists spent some time reformulating what the academics had said to make their own sense of it, and the academics tried to be careful to use language understandable to the rest of the group.

– The second problem was to agree on a common research framework. The hypothesis was drawn up that for the poorest, family life was the first and most important starting-point to give their lives meaning. It seemed to us on the Academic Panel, that there was a second hypothesis which was not formulated in the original framework, but which emerged throughout the memoir; that is, that the family is itself a means of long-term self-definition.

– Differences of interpretation between academics and activists represented a further difficulty. They caused very heated discussions notable for the activists' refusing to allow the group to write that poor families have no conception of time.

The most important question we have to ask in evaluating this approach is whether it produced a real merging of knowledge, an original creation. It seems to me that in this memoir, the answer is incontestably "yes". The best illustration of this concerns the discussion on representations of time, where the activists triggered a paradigm shift in the academics' thinking; that is, they caused them to abandon the theoretical model underlying their views. To recap what happened: in their presentations, the academics used two diagrams representing time—linear time marking a progression, and circular time going round and round. For some sociologists, poor families are caught in circular time and unable to see a future for themselves. But the group's activists did not recognize themselves in this depiction, which did not correspond to their own experience. With the pedagogical counselor, they redrew the academics' diagrams, and said they both exist simultaneously. If one combines linear and circular time, the result is loops. Thus emerged the new concept of "looped" time, combining moments of progression with moments of stoppage or return to certain points. This is clearly a result of knowledge-merging.

The most original aspect of this approach was that the Fourth World activists were able to question, contest and discuss the academics' interpretations and be listened to. The activists' and Fourth World volunteer corps member's right to contest the academics' monopoly on interpretations, and acknowledgement of their own interpretative abilities, is a central tenet in the knowledge-merging process. This process was made possible by all the conditions of the project, such as each participant's willing choice, the time spent with the activists, the role of the pedagogical team etc.

The second part of my evaluation concerns the content of the memoir. Having been fortunate enough to listen to the memoir being presented *viva voce* in Chantilly, I had found it to be of a very high standard, with a good balance between each of the six members' contributions and good use of diagrams, drawings and slides which explained the overall progression. One of the group's academics concluded the oral presentation by saying "After two years of work, we are only just beginning to get a handle on the subject". This shows that working together opened up new avenues to explore beyond previous certainties, which for me was another sign of knowledge having been successfully shared.

The memoir shows how precious the family is to the poorest. It is their only defense, all they have left when all else has gone. Some of the turns of phrase are felicitous, and capture the existential aspect of the family nicely, for example "Children bring the warmth back into living", "I drew my strength from my relationship with my partner and from my children. I tore down walls of anguish for them". I was impressed by the thoughts on childbearing and its significance as a potentiality of being, as a gift, as a beginning or a hope. These thoughts spark a kind of deep meditation on creation, giving and continuity. The language used sometimes departs from academic parlance and becomes poetic, which is enriching. For the reality of family life is a lot of going toe to toe with anguish, tensions, confrontations, but also tenderness, contemplation and poetry. On the other hand, the terms creation, giving and continuance do not fall outside the remit of sociology, but are concepts constructed in a different branch of the discipline, one with a less utilitarian view of social relationships. They open onto a different dimension of reality, a different perception of the individual and of social relationships, concepts other than those of maximizing profits or power.

I found the analyses of different sorts of time illuminating—long-term, desired, chosen time; short-term, suffered or disrupted; time as a problem or as a resource. This subtle analysis of the various perceptions of time, the movement between them, the oppositions between time spent in the family and time spent in institutions, is one of the great statements this memoir has to offer. Is not every reader able to identify with time as a problem or as a resource? As well as this, the initiative and dynamism of poor families and the obstacles they encounter are very much in evidence in the idea of the project. But is this vision of the individual and the family from a poor background not rather too optimistic? Is it not biased for lack of sufficiently diverse research materials? The Academic Panel wondered whether the group members had met families completely trapped in poverty who have never been able to create a plan of their own and who would contradict their hypotheses. The table of qualitative interviews shows that of the 16 interviewees aged from 20 to 64, 11 were not aware of ATD Fourth World. Analysis of the interviews shows that a good few of those 11 people had experienced chronic, rock-bottom poverty, and shows the circumstances in which plans can be created—or not. Finally, the memoir displays the deep rift between the impression one often has of poor families and the reality. These families have plans, which often go unseen or are denied by the institutions which are supposed to help them.

I was struck by some of the testimonies which made me want to shout out loud, such was the unacceptable injustice they revealed, especially that of the child who provided for his entire family, and the mother who was refused housing for 20 years and had to live in one room with her five children. I liked the lesson drawn from action "The ability to wait before becoming a parent is crucial to succeeding" and the discussion of partnership.

My criticisms are mainly that work carried out on the subject prior to the project was not sufficiently taken into account. I was disappointed at the paucity of references to the studies on the family carried out by the Atd Fourth World Research and Training Institute, of which there have been many since 1960. I am thinking here of Jean Labbens's and Christian Debuyst's studies on the family in the underclass in the early 1960s, Paul Vercauteren's work on how the underclass structures private and public life from 1970, Alwine de Vos's evaluation of 15 years of the community development program from a child's perspective, Marie-Catherine Ribeaud's study on motherhood in the underclass etc.

In conclusion, I would like to express a wish. It seems to me that the last chapter, "Is the family plan a stepping-stone to entering society?" needs to be continued by sociologists and historians. The policies systematically destroying very poor families must be condemned. This condemnation must be recorded in the history of organized violations of human rights and find its way onto university syllabuses. Under the cloak of combating poverty and preserving racial purity, Switzerland destroyed the Yeniche culture for 50 years by taking children away from their families, and Australia did the same to the Aborigines for 100. Great Britain deported more than 100,000 poor and orphaned children to her colonies between 1850 and 1960. Germany, the Scandinavian countries, Australia and the United States have passed eugenicist laws under which hundreds of thousands of women, amongst them society's poorest, were forcibly sterilized. For several decades, France and Belgium continued to systematically place children in care and to forcibly sterilize some of their societies' poorest women. Sterilization policies continue today in the poorer Eastern European, Asian and Latin American countries.

The Family memoir clearly shows and analyzes from within the vitality of the family plan for the poor and its immense liberating potential linked to the primal urge to create, to engender one's own, to love, give and surpass oneself. It thus proves itself to be a means of condemnation, a weapon in the fight against deathly ideologies, exploding the blindness and the inhumanity of policies and practices which confuse combating poverty with attacking the poor.

COMMENT ON THE KNOWLEDGE MEMOIR
by Michel Serres

I read the "Freeing Knowledge" memoir very carefully. I found it very interesting for reasons associated with my personal reminiscences, since it dealt with the experiences of those whose parents—like mine—had no education or books, and especially the experiences of those who were excluded and who gained self-confidence through knowledge. It also dealt with the experiences of academics, of which I am one. As a result, I understand this memoir very well.

The memoir is well written, clear, and in terms of its outline and shape it is put together in a disciplined way. It has a real intellectual progression: it sets out its *a priori*, describes its methods and carries them out, and shows all the marks of a solid and well-executed piece of research.

The memoir is divided into three clearly-demarcated sections: the first deals with school and academic learning; the second with knowledge gained from experience within the family, on the street, and from life in general; and the third with knowledge garnered from action, involvement in general, for example activism. The various groups take turns to make their point in each section—participants, interviewees, activists, Fourth World volunteer corps members, academics.

From the first section concerning methodology, I was able to see an opposition between the activists' and the academics' points of view. The activists expressed their desire for knowledge because they were deprived. They said that knowledge would bring them something very important for which they hungered and thirsted, which they desired; they did not want a form of knowledge specific to the poor. Conversely,

the academics bridled at playing the schoolteacher. They wished to discuss the specific nature of the knowledge of the poor and give pride of place to knowledge gained from the lives and experiences of the poorest. The former, it seems, thought themselves under-, the latter over-resourced. The activists had no suspicions concerning knowledge which they saw as liberating, while the academics expressed only suspicion, since for them no knowledge is in itself liberating.

This opposition between the desire to acquire knowledge on the one hand, and a measure of reticence to provide it on the other comes through very strongly and it seems to me that the issue remains unresolved, though the memoir tends towards the second attitude on the whole.

I wish to examine three points:
– what I learnt from the memoir
– how it could be further developed
– what overall verdict can be reached on the memoir's validity as research.

The memoir has shown me something very important, namely that whether knowledge be academic, drawn from life experience or one's personal commitment, what cuts across all three groups and crops up time and again is a word which, in my view, becomes the real subject of the memoir. A word which you have analyzed most and which has taught me most, i.e. *recognition.*

What do you—and we—mean by knowledge? We mean recognized knowledge. Someone who has knowledge is someone who is recognized. A teacher possesses a recognized form of knowledge. Research, when properly carried out, has a recognized value. Knowledge only exists if it is recognized, as do people. This issue is present from the start of the memoir, arises at regular intervals throughout, and concludes it as well.

When we go to school, we ask to be recognized by our peers, our fellow pupils, the teachers. The core, underlying form of suffering is this lack of recognition, being prejudged to lack intelligence and culture. The real question is always "Do I exist in the eyes of others? Do I, in the views and opinions of others, exist in the same way as they do? Do I stand out, am I excluded?"

Your research does not deal with knowledge content, but with knowledge recognition. Nothing is more important, nothing is more true. This corresponds with my own experience, as it does with that of all those who have had contact, at whatever level, with educated society. The request is made "Can we have the knowledge of the poorest recognized?" Exclusion is a lack of recognition. Knowledge allows one to be recognized. As a consequence, it is true that knowledge is part of combating poverty, since knowledge allows us to be part of a community. This memoir deals perhaps less with knowledge than with knowledge communities. The three sections all deal with communities. There is a school community because school allows everyone to be recognized; life, family and street experience are a community in which there is reciprocal recognition with respect to experience. And by taking part in any group, a group of activists or a group project, everyone is together and recognizes one another as participants in the same activity.

The memoir addresses the question of how merging knowledge—knowledge gained at school, on the street and in personal involvement—can feed into the process of recognition.

Where do we go from here? One of the functions of knowledge is to enable recognition, but is it the only one? Knowledge is not only something we talk about or enter into. So, what type of knowledge? Why? Under what conditions? Which is worth knowing more—arithmetic, geography, history? Knowledge content and usefulness need to be examined.

Suddenly, I had stumbled upon the real focus of your memoir. Reading it, the analysis of recognition visibly grows, deepens and opens out into a truly dazzling insight. At one point, you describe Daniel, who is a member of a group, of whom you write that *he had a secret.* You seek to discover Daniel's secret, as I did, and it seems to me this: that all of us, men and women, young and old, all need recognition. We all want recognition, but that is impossible. You cannot give it to me, you need it for yourself; neither can he, and so on. We all hunger and thirst for it in the same way, whether rich or poor, learned or ignorant. Why are we afraid? Because we have this need. Recognition cannot be awarded. And Daniel's secret is that he has realized that one must take the initiative, give before one can receive. This is the great moment when the teacher says "Everyone is good at something. Most people are intelligent." He gives others recognition, though he needs it as much as anyone else.

This recognition must be given before it can be received. And that is the definition of knowledge—nourishment we can receive as long as we give it as well. This is a definition of extraordinary knowledge. Knowledge is like recognition—if I give it, I keep it, and instead of it being divided, it is increased. That is Daniel's secret.

Does knowledge allow us to do without recognition? According to one person, *I don't see things the same way any more, I've changed my viewpoint and now my life is so worthwhile.* She has discovered Daniel's secret, which allows us to change our way of seeing things, to enter a community where everyone shares out recognition.

The memoir's academic value is therefore quite clear. To begin with, I thought "They're not talking about knowledge, they're talking about the condition of knowing. They're talking about school, family, the street, but that is not knowledge itself, it is the society of knowledge." And then little by little, you won me over. The memoir examines the fundamental question of the relationship of knowledge function to knowledge content. Its primary merit is that it puts forward a process, constructing a staircase towards knowledge, passing several floors on the way—escaping exclusion, sharing and merging knowledge, achieving recognition and, perhaps, forgetting we need it. You have successfully shown that this process exists at school—I am excluded, so I climb a step on the staircase, and this step means belonging to a community which will give me recognition. I notice that this step will not suffice alone, since you will not give it to me, you need it like I do, so I must proceed to the second step. This is a contradictory process, for I must give before receiving. Climbing the third step is saying that he who explains knowledge to another gains a clearer and better understanding of that knowledge. This is captured well in the proverb "If you do not understand something, explain it to a friend, and then you will understand it."

There is something mysterious at work in this process which you have almost discovered, you are on the point of doing so. As a result, that is the best one can say of a memoir, that it takes you right to the door and says "Daniel has a secret, just give the door a little push and you will enter into the secret too". This is what gives your memoir its depth. It asks the vital questions: If knowledge is essentially social in nature, how is it that institutions and the powerful have such a stranglehold on it? If knowledge allows us to resist this oppression, is this not because it contains something non-social? And therefore something very precious to those crushed by society?

COMMENT ON THE WORK AND HUMAN ACTIVITY MEMOIR

by Matéo Alaluf

The reports which make up the memoir identify the relevance of work from the outset. Work is by turns "fulfilling" or "bitty", often "unstable", and appears to be " linked to production levels which vary with the economic climate or subject to company relocations, all of which goes hand in hand with ever-faster changes in jobs and qualifications".

If the memoir only examined these immediate features characterized by relocation, redundancy and unemployment, that is, being deprived of work, it would be tempting to conclude that work has lost its relevance to the lives of individuals, for the very reason that it is so hard to come by. Yet the memoir invites us to listen to those who have no work to appreciate the importance of work in all aspects of living in a society.

Though work is not easy to pin down, and comes across as precarious in these instances, it remains a part of our lives. It gives direction to education and training for both children and adults, influences migration and settlement, which are factors in everyone's lives, and those of their children. It gives structure to our lives and subordinates them to its own demands. Basically, work is so present in our lives that eventually we no longer notice it.

What is the role of the poor in a society founded on work, when they have none? In former times, says the memoir, they made up the "underclass". Today they are "destined to unemployment, on the fringes of society". So much so that the salaries they should receive are allegedly even higher than they are worth because they lack so many useful skills. Basically, they are worth less than nothing and deserve the same.

In opposition to this cynical synopsis of the prevailing ideology, the writers of the memoir set out a dual approach, initially understanding the patterns of work and unemployment and proceeding to the research subject, namely the discovery of "new professions, new markets based around the skills the poor already possess". Essentially this means exploring the possibilities for transforming the work potential of each individual's talents into jobs beneficial to society.

At the same time, the writers of the memoir look at matters unrelated to employment policy. Indeed to some extent it is not work but employment which is lacking. Offering employment supposes a pre-existing correspondence with a product or market and a defined position. Yet it is this which is rare. Asking for employment is therefore not quite the same as offering one's labor. Offering labor also suggests new possibilities, projects, a product, a potential service or innovation for the worker. Taking offers of labor seriously is the way to create employment. The memoir explores the work and talents the poorest have to offer. It is both a matter of aiming policies at companies in a position to expand their business and introducing conditions to allow the associative sector to grow as it needs to. This could, in my view, enable workers in personal services industries to escape the relationship of personal dependence which render them servile. Their work could become real employment, and they could gain both a decent wage and some small measure of dignity.

In other words, this research suggests a way forward which aims to assimilate unemployment-reduction measures into the direction pursued in employment policies, that is, policies based on individuals' working capacities, able to create employment which in turn provides those who are outside the world of work with access to jobs.

Having carefully identified these manual and interpersonal skills, the authors then describe the risk of their being used against people from their own background. Do not the new professions suggested often smack of social monitoring or simply control of the people (*they can very quickly become quasi police officers, though with no weapons*), and do not the forms of training which can quickly aid in getting a job often lead from socialization to exclusion? In this respect, the memoir again provides an innovative answer: instead of an educational system based on discipline, the group explores a "reciprocal form of education" in its research.

The issue of how best to develop the potential of those born without a silver spoon in a profoundly unequal society is far from resolved, of course. Sometimes, life experiences and the authors' beliefs are indistinguishable. How can life experience be taken to a more abstract level? Fortunately, the questions this research asks remain open. But this memoir succeeds in overturning traditional disciplines, and by letting those who are usually kept out of the spotlight speak and write, raises vital questions about critical distance and committed participation.

COMMENT ON THE CITIZENSHIP MEMOIR

by René Rémond

Representation, citizenship, extreme poverty. Of the five topics, this one is probably the most political, and as such is the one that raises the most general issues.

I read and reread it carefully and with interest, and hope I have understood it properly. It is well put together on the whole, the approach taken both consistent and progressive. I shall pass over the first chapter, which is very similar to those of the other memoirs, reiterating as it does the approach and process followed and the rules observed.

There then follows a discussion of terms, particularly whether it is best to talk of the poor, the poorest, the very poor or extreme poverty. It is the last and most abstract term which was finally decided upon, denoting the phenomenon rather than the individuals involved and sitting most easily alongside the other two terms: representation and citizenship. The memoir elucidates the three ideas. To start with, the group was dealing with a vague host of interacting notions, such as democracy, citizenship, human rights and representation. It is the last idea which is at the heart of the matter, but it is part of a larger whole which seeks to answer the question "How can we make the poorest fully-active citizens of a democratic society?" A democratic society without them as citizens would be incomplete, were they rejected, excluded or marginalized. It is therefore citizenship which is at stake here, equality of rights for all, especially political rights.

In this respect, I found the fact that political rights were approached from the opposite angle to normal particularly interesting. To quote the memoir, *Human Rights are indivisible. They are economic, social and cultural (concerning resources, housing, work, health and education), but also civil and political.* It is the word also which is significant. Normally, the argument is the other way round: when talking of rights, the first group is political rights. Then it was discovered that if rights were merely political, something would be missing, and economic and social rights were added. Now, after two centuries of experimentation, it is so widely accepted that economic and social rights are part of democratic society that we need to come full circle and reaffirm political rights. Frankly, there is not a lot of difference between the three. We know how debatable and even dangerous it can be to oppose allegedly real freedoms with those we assume to be a formality, since by doing so we compromise freedom itself. I found it very interesting that you have rediscovered the necessity, the price and the legitimacy of political rights by examining economic and social rights.

There are degrees of citizenship. There is participation, to which the memoir pays relatively little attention in order to spend more time on probably the most delicate issue: representation. The memoir proceeds on the basis that the poor are neither present nor represented, which does not mean that their views are necessarily absent from political debate, but it is one thing for them to be spoken of, and quite another for them to be doing the talking. More often than not, debate revolves around their lot in life and how to improve it, but without them, outside of them, and they are neither players nor partners. For example, when a law is being drafted which deals with the poor, one has the impression that they are considered as objects in debate and are never represented. It is commendable to look after them, but they remain excluded all the same. This is the problem of participation, and, without participation, of adequate representation.

Based on this observation, the memoir raises two related issues. The first has already arisen in the other memoirs—who is qualified to talk about extreme poverty? Does one have to have experienced it personally in order to talk about it credibly? It is a unique and incomparable experience—no-one who has not gone through it personally may talk about it authentically. Here we encounter a major problem—if we apply this principal rigidly, if we take it to its logical conclusion, there can be no communication between experiences which are simply too difficult. Humanity is fragmented, it is impossible to open oneself up to other people. No generation, no people can understand any other. There is therefore no unity to humanity. The writers of the memoir have well understood the seriousness of the consequences of this, and therefore stop short of being over-categorical in applying this principle.

The second is more precise—does extreme poverty need its own spokespeople in public life? This is not to suggest that this public representation would take the form of a pressure group; it would merely be a mouthpiece for a group with a different experience of life. Here, we encounter another fundamental issue, namely that of the relationship between the individual and the universal, the part and the whole. This is an especially burning issue confronting today's political society. It is the same as the current debate in France on gender equality. It comes down to the major fundamental innovation in breaking with previous tradition, that on which democracy is founded: the invention of the citizen and the people, the painstaking creation of a new kind of reality. The people is a creature of reason, composed of what all citizens have in common, an abstraction of all that is different between them—gender, age, living conditions. This invention was liberating, and emancipated people from the constraints of their individual communities. It was an important step towards universality. As experience shows us, however, declaring all citizens equal does not eradicate inequalities, and even risks increasing the gap. Hence the criticism of this notion from two different sources: on the one hand, the organicist political right for whom society is necessarily unequal, and on the other, the socialist-inspired left-wing which takes issue with social divisions. Hence the claim for recognition of the diverse groups composing this society. Opposite the political reality that is the people, we have civil society, with which the French Government now operates in partnership. But if the principal of equality between men and women is enshrined in the French Constitution, why are other categories of person not also included? The memoir's authors have perceived this problem, and therefore dispense with the idea that specific representation of the poor could be anything but socially divisive in the end. But how can these two opposing demands be reconciled? I can think of no better way than to quote the authors when they write *Who may speak on behalf of the poor? . . . "You have to be able to put yourself in poor people's shoes"* said one academic. We do not think that is possible. Coming into contact with poverty and trying to understand it is not the same as experiencing it from within. The non-poor can speak of their fight against poverty but they cannot talk about it like the poor themselves can . Do the poor need their own representation? The memoir adds, pertinently, *There is no point creating an additional category for the poor. . . . In political representation, elected representatives are called upon to represent all their citizens. . . . Combating poverty requires us to reject representation by category, since categories exclude. Even if a poor person represented the category of the poor, there would be a risk of deepening the divide between them and the non-poor.* There is a deeper idea at work here—combating poverty concerns more than just the poor. It is in the common interest of all citizens and involves the whole of society. Tolerating or accepting poverty degrades society. Here again we find the demand for universality. The debate remains open and continues to divide society and political thought.

INITIAL EVALUATION
OF THE PROJECT

by Patrick Brun

The evaluation of the Fourth World – University project by its participants: what did they learn?

At a first glance, the aim of the Fourth World – University project could be seen as being to broaden and deepen knowledge of the realities of life lived in extreme poverty, and that this knowledge was arrived at via the contributions of academics, members of the Fourth World volunteer corps and agents who had themselves experienced poverty.

However, listening to and reading the feedback given by the project participants, one realizes that it was first and foremost a shared fundamental human experience. This experience, shared over two years by 37 participants (the 32 agent-authors and the five members of the pedagogical team) from different backgrounds, reveals itself as a source of personal change.

In particular, their comments display a certain "displacement" on the part of each participant, brought about by their (at least temporarily) "letting go" of certainties, or at least their unqualified approval, of ways of thinking or frames of reference, of preconceptions about research methods. "All our boats were rocked," said one of the academics.

It was through this self-questioning, founded on gradually-achieved mutual trust, this entrusting oneself to others' hands, that thinking and writing together was possible. "We learned humility," said another academic.

The testimonies collected over the two years tell the story of this experience, a trial even, initially individual but which slowly became collective as participants became aware of belonging to a group linked by strong bonds of shared trust and respect. Similarly, the collaborative research project also produced more personal forms of awareness or change. The participants described this as "becoming aware", "discoveries" or "rediscoveries", "identification", "remembering", a "new way of understanding" amongst others.

To quote one of the participants, it was an experience within which "words could open up to another person's view". Not only words, but the different types of knowledge that each participant wanted to convey or produce. That knowledge (*connaissance*) thus became a source of recognition/re-cognition (*reconnaissance*). This last word is perhaps the key term to the entire project, if examined in all its connotations. It was one of the most frequently-used terms, and one that conveys most succinctly both the aim of the project and the basic issue between the participants.

Can it not be seen as a leitmotif linking the three aspects of collective experience which enable us to understand the participants' feedback?

– a common experience shared by each participant
– an experience that brought about socio-existential changes
– an experience that helped open each participant to other people's knowledge and bring these different types of knowledge together in a collective piece of work.

A common experience but one with its own difficulties

It was not easy to bring the three groups of participants together, and many obstacles had to be overcome:

– **Fears:** fear of the others, more specifically of the academics, who were seen by some as "holy cows"; fear on the part of the activists of "being had" during discussions; fear of not being intelligent enough, of being "judged", and of not being able to last the course.

– **Misunderstandings:** Misunderstandings arose as a consequence of the different types of language and expression used by the academics on the one hand, and the Fourth World volunteer corps members and activists on the other. These differences were a sign of each group's imperfect knowledge of the others. At the start, each participant remained within their own world, their own frame of reference. As a result of this, misunderstandings, and sometimes even mutual antagonism, arose.

– **Resistance and dead ends:** The claims and convictions of the Fourth World volunteer corps members and activists were often seen as questionable by the academics. The questions and doubts of the academics with regard to the voicing of personal experience were often seen as "attacks" or, in the eyes of the activists, as questioning the authenticity of what they said.

– **Deviations and differences:** These arose between each group of participants. The activists also had to establish some kind of agreement between different thematic groups in the places they met to work.

Nevertheless, it was agreed upon by all that these confrontations, although they were sometimes unpleasant, were the result of straightforward and honest intentions. The activists were keenly aware of representing "their people". Many of the academics admitted they wanted to retain their academic viewpoints.

Paradoxically, it was the members of the Fourth World volunteer corps that had the most difficulty finding a role in the debate: they were not there as spokespeople, nor representing ATD Fourth World, but rather to contribute their own knowledge born of action and drawn from their experience as mediators between the poorest and society.

According to the participants, these obstacles were only overcome through establishing good relations, especially within each thematic group, but also between all the participants during the conferences at Chantilly, during the meals and free time. Everyone participated in the joys and sorrows of the other participants. Births and birthdays were celebrated together. Family life provided common ground. They sang together and sometimes even suffered together. They comforted one another during difficult times.

It was in this way that the participants got to know one another, relationships improved, and they began to communicate on a deeper level. They acquired greater subtlety in their views of one another and tried to think and speak on the same wavelength. Many activists would come to recognize themselves in the words one activist had used to characterize the academics: "They came down a level so we could be equal to them."

The participants often emphasized that the procedure and assistance provided by the pedagogical team played a large role in bringing the participants together. The pedagogical team acted both as a safeguard and a communication and research facilitator. It also ensured equality between the three groups of agents. the constant presence of the pedagogical counselor gave the activists confidence in their abilities, and allowed them to put these capabilities into practice throughout the project.

This common experience was a source of personal change throughout the project

The words used by the participants to describe the experience are an indication of this change: "pleasure," "pride," "confidence," "enthusiasm," "energy," "renewed desire to fight," "moments of happiness and sadness", "very moving experience," "turned my world upside down", and many others.

These existential "impacts" can be placed in three categories.

– Awareness
– Learning processes
– Validation of the project's underlying hypotheses (given certain conditions).

Awareness

This came about with regard to the other participants in the project and what they represented.

The academics discovered the resources the activists had to offer, the richness of their experience, and their cognitive and expressive abilities. More importantly, they discovered the capacity of the very poor to take the initiative and act and the force of a family project.

The activists became aware of how human the academics actually were. They also realized that the thoughts of philosophers and scholars were applicable in their own lives.

An even stronger awareness arose concerning identity. One discovers oneself by contrast and comparison. This can come about as a discovery of what makes one what one is: "I found my identity as an activist"; "I recognized myself in the people I questioned"; or through examination of one's family roots: "It made me remember painful events from my past". One participant even spoke of "cleaning out the skeletons from my familial and social closet".

It was this that became a trial for some. Some felt deeply, probingly questioned with regard to their motivation for becoming members of the Fourth World volunteer corps or academics. Many felt lonely. These remarks display the psycho-emotional consequences linked to a new level of awareness.

The activists in particular said that their relationship to society and institutions in society had changed. The project gave many the "power to assert themselves", gave them "strength", "greater self-confidence", made them feel "more self-assured". Some no longer feared arguments with school principals, and in the case of one participant, with a judge and a social worker. This represented a complete turnaround from prior to the project: "anxiety", a feeling of estrangement, "powerlessness".

In addition, everyone gained a new insight into people and things: a new attitude towards one's work (activist, academic, or Fourth World volunteer corps member), a new view of the very poor or academics, or of oneself as an academic or member of the Fourth World volunteer corps.

The academics placed most emphasis on acquiring a new critical awareness with regard to language and frames of reference. For some, a link had to be created between social and/or socio-political involvement and academic life.

Once trust had been established between participants, fears allayed and personal relationships struck up, they were finally willing to open their knowledge and understanding (drawn from life experience, study, or active involvement) to other agents, and to have their own conceptions questioned.

Summing up, one activist said of an academic: "He has changed and so have we."

It was thus possible for the participants to learn from one another, to acquire more specialized knowledge from others (knowledge that justified their being part of the project), and to integrate this knowledge into their own for further development.

Knowledge gained and developed
In addition to what has been recorded in the memoirs, the academics learned

the following from the activists:
- the realities and circumstances of their everyday lives;
- the mental capacity needed to face poverty and the means of resisting it;
- their capacity for reflection and expression;
- their power to determine their own lives.

To summarize, some academics claimed to have discovered a new approach to poverty-related issues and a new way of perceiving the researcher-agent relationship in social sciences research.

From the members of the Fourth World volunteer corps, the academics received a better understanding of ATD Fourth World and the specific role of Fourth World volunteer corps members within ATD Fourth World.

From the academics, the Fourth World volunteer corps members learned specifically:
- to analyze their experiences of action and mediation in the light of contemporary currents of thought;
- to learn to enjoy reading and formulating questions, specifically in philosophy and sociology;
- to identify the knowledge they possess through experience.

From the academics, the activists learned specifically:
- an introduction to textual analysis, specialist vocabulary such as "hypothesis", "conclusion", and research procedures;
- to be more rigorous and organized in the way they spoke and thought;
- not to make claims without some attempt at justification or proof;
- to distance themselves from their emotions, to be more "calm" and composed, to be willing to let their beliefs be questioned.

With regard to the project as a whole, many activists said that it had improved their spelling, reading and writing skills. Some said they were now more interested in televised news reports and newspapers and felt more involved in society.

Some participants also drew attention to the contributions made by the various resource people who worked in the various sites helping the activists to express themselves.

The overall validity of the project is recognized by all

"It was possible," commented the participants (meaning meeting, combining different types of knowledge, getting along, researching together, writing the memoirs, "sticking it out" for two years etc).

To summarize, we can state the common features of some of the participants' comments:
- A new approach to knowledge can be created to produce new, original learning by identifying the three different types of knowledge and creating a dialogue between them.
- Two conditions are necessary for this:

– Positive relationships must be established between participants before and during the process of research and contemplation.

– "Similarities" between participants must be identified before attempting to work on "differences".

– It seems fair to say that, even if certain elements of knowledge exist from the outset, knowledge becomes more properly defined through mutual interaction, to the extent that it allows the participants merging knowledge and points of view to become aware of each others' contributions, to understand themselves in their relationship to one another, to appreciate different forms of knowledge differently expressed as part of their own knowledge and to present it as part of a structured argument.

– The writing of a collaborative text in which each participant is involved without losing their individuality is only made possible by a process of reciprocal deconstruction and reconstruction. This text must further be the object of much discussion which weaves the contributions of each participant into a coherent whole without losing sight of essential points of difference.

To conclude, let us reiterate the comparison made by one of the academics concluding his group evaluation: When thread is woven into a cloth, the individual threads still remain distinct. However, to make a grey thread, it is necessary to use a white thread and a black thread. In much the same manner, the different types of knowledge were woven together to produce a new type of learning. What this image leaves out is the definitive alteration in the nature of the threads, brought about by their rubbing against each other. (Here *"alter*ation" in the sense of other, alterity, and of change. It is not to be taken in the more pejorative sense of degradation.) The participants' comments show that each participant changed to varying degrees, and it was these changes that allowed the different types of knowledge to be successfully shared.

Appendix

THE THINKING OF THE POOR
IN A KNOWLEDGE
THAT LEADS TO COMBAT

Joseph Wresinski
(Founder of the International Movement ATD Fourth World)

Very early in the history of the International Movement ATD Fourth World, its founder declared that "knowledge [must not be] simply secondary to charity." He constantly called on scientific researchers to contribute to a body of knowledge useful for the liberation of the poorest of the poor. In December 1980 Joseph Wresinski brought together an international committee of specialists at the UNESCO headquarters in Paris. The text that follows is a translation of his opening address.

1. Introduction

As I greet you this morning within the walls of UNESCO, I realize that for nearly twenty-five years you, scholars, researchers, and the scientific communities you represent, have responded generously to calls from ATD Fourth World with faithfulness, concern, and shared hopes. . . . I want to remind you this morning of the role, even the duty, of all those dedicated to scientific research on poverty to make a place for the knowledge which the poor and the excluded themselves have of their condition. Beyond that, to give it pride of place because it is unique and indispensable, as well as autonomous and complementary to all other knowledge about poverty. Finally, you should help this knowledge to develop.

To this function, you will guess, one needs to add another: that of making room for the knowledge of poverty and social exclusion which is available to those practitioners who live with the very poor and carry out projects with them, giving it the importance it deserves, and helping its development.

We have spoken to you before about these two components of global knowledge of poverty, of which yours, that of the outside observer, is the third. But in view of the work to be carried out during this three-day session and the months to follow, I take the liberty of once more clarifying some ideas our Movement has on this topic. . . .

2. Academic Knowledge and Mobilization for Action

From the beginning, our Movement has held that in order to fight effectively against poverty and exclusion the following questions must be posed:
– What kind of knowledge do the poorest people need?
– What kind of knowledge do practitioners and action teams need?
– What kind of knowledge do our national societies and our international communities need?

It is fair to say that we have lived and struggled in a historical period when the answer to the question What knowledge? has for the most part been, Properly scientific knowledge.

Many expected that the knowledge best suited to the struggle, and thus to the promotion of social policies and legislative measures, would be of the same kind as that created in universities and other standard research institutions. In other words, one expected much, if not everything, from that part of knowledge available only to academics and specialists who are observers from outside the reality of poverty. This latter knowledge has been highly regarded because of its methodology, its rigor, and what was thought to be its objectivity or neutrality. These characteristics were reassuring to those who, faced with immensely complex problems which politicians construed subjectively, wished to find an objective truth, capable of guiding a clear plan of action, rooted in truth and effective for the poor.

The university came to be regarded as a guarantor of security in face of problems so difficult to understand. It was a refuge for those who did not want to be frustrated or led into error by ideologies, whether of the dominant or the dominated. You, as well as we, have at certain times wanted to use the university in this way. And, no doubt, we weren't wrong, but we weren't totally right either.

However, contrary to what some seem to think, it is not the general discovery of the non-neutrality, the non-objectivity, of science, and particularly the human and social sciences, that proves us wrong today. Neither is it the knowledge that all science and scientific methodology are tainted with ideology that convinces us that we were not right. These are interesting problems, but, in our opinion, they are of secondary importance.

The basic problem, which we did not recognize and still haven't mastered, is that academic knowledge of poverty and social exclusion—as of all other human reality—is only a partial knowledge. We ourselves haven't said, or even sufficiently understood, that it can be only indirect and purely informative, that it lacks, by definition, a direct grasp of reality and, consequently, is not a knowledge that can mobilize people and prompt them to action.

Many of us have had the experience of being keenly disappointed when one or another of our studies had no effect. Perhaps we did not pay enough attention to the fact that academic research in the strict sense must necessarily produce an abstraction, an image of reality seen from the outside and translated into general terms that no longer include the feelings, colors, and other things that move people to take action for others.

Of comprehensive knowledge about poverty and social exclusion, knowledge meant to inform, to explain, and to lead people to action, academic research will never be more than one component among others, namely, the information component, partially explanatory, and thus lifeless. It will remain lifeless as long as two other components of knowledge are missing. These two autonomous and complementary components, which will add life and meaning, are:

– the knowledge which the poor and excluded have, from their first-hand experience, of the twin realities of poverty and the surrounding world which imposes it on them; and

– the knowledge of those who work among and with these victims in places of poverty and social exclusion.

Caught in the trap of a society that believes in the supremacy of academic knowledge, our universities believed this themselves. . . . And when the costliest and most thorough studies and research disappeared into the drawers of politicians and administrators, we said that it was for political reasons. . . . This was correct, but did not allow for the possibility that the problem was not with the politicians but rather with our studies that were not the kind to prompt politicians to take action.

However, I believe that at no time did the universities admit that the political ineffectiveness of their research could be attributed to the fact that knowledge thus constructed was instructive but not convincing; nor acknowledge, moreover, that the supplements needed to convince could not come from the university researcher but solely from the poor and those who work with them.

3. Without Freedom of Thought, No Communication

Certainly, not all researchers ignored the two components of knowledge represented by the poor and those who work with them. However, and this is the crux of the matter, they did not regard them as autonomous components to be pursued by and for the authors themselves. Scholars quickly turned them into the object of their own research; they regarded these components as sources of information to be used for their own purposes, rather than as equally valid research projects, as supporting subjects and not objects of exploitation. They have, to some extent, subordinated these components to their own exploration as outside observers of the life of the poor and the actions undertaken with them. Thus, they have deflected a knowledge, which did not belong to them, from its own goal. More seriously, these researchers have often, unintentionally and unwittingly, upset or even paralyzed the thinking of their interlocutors. This happened essentially because they did not recognize that they were dealing with a thinking and an autonomous inquiry that followed their own path and goals. Consequently, they have not respected these goals. They have treated their research subjects as sources of information rather than as independent thinkers. This is why we have always doubted the value of the information obtained by academics.

As for communicating with the very poor, many years of observation have convinced us that even the so-called participatory observation practiced by anthropologists and ethnologists runs the danger of misusing, tampering with, and paralyzing the thinking of the poor. This is so because it is an observation for a goal external to their life situation, one that they did not choose and which they would never have defined in the same way as the investigators. Consequently, the observation is not truly participatory since the thinking of the investigators and that of the population which is the object of their observation do not pursue the same goals.

It is not a problem of method, but a question of life situation, one that cannot be resolved by adopting other methods but only by change in situation. Moreover, participant observation, which certainly will not disturb the thinking of a group in full possession of its powers of reflection and culture, runs the serious risk of disturbing the thinking of the very poor who do not master them nearly as well.

It goes without saying that a similar problem arises for the cooperation between investigators and men and women of action. These difficulties have often been analyzed. For example, it has been said that action teams have difficulty collaborating in research because they don't see the point of the project and because they are suspicious of the scrutinizing look of the researchers and of their inability to understand the human reality and chaos of everyday life. It has even been said that collaboration does not work because practitioners lack logical skills and base their action on intuitions and impressions rather than rational reflection.

There may be some truth in these explanations, but it seems to us that they do not go to the heart of the matter. The basic problem is that if practitioners are to make a valuable contribution they must be seen from the outset not as mere providers of information, but as thinkers having to pursue to the very end their own quest for knowledge, according to their own goals.

Here again we are convinced, thanks to what we have learned from many years of experience, that even social scientists who have been brought in to analyze an action and evaluate its results often run the risk of going astray. In fact, don't they often arrive when the die has already been cast and try to understand, after the fact, a situation which is totally foreign to them? They face a situation different from any they know, one fraught with unimaginable insecurity and for which they have very little feeling.

One will not be able to grasp such a situation and perceive its dynamics unless one experiences the insecurity and shifting sands of conducting an action within a population living in extreme poverty. One can understand such an action only to the degree in which one has participated in the development of the thinking of the action team and by adopting the objectives of that thinking.

Having said this, our purpose was not to draw attention to the weakness of academic studies resulting from problems of communication. We wanted above all to make the point that these studies all together, whatever their quality, would not be able to provide the totality of the required knowledge.

Let us turn again for a moment to the two other sources of this knowledge. In principle, they are complementary to that of the university, but they can only take shape and be fully complementary when they are autonomous and allowed to reach their final goals on their own.

4. The Secret Garden of the Poorest of the Poor

Let us consider for a moment the knowledge and way of thinking of the people of the Fourth World. They deal not only with their life situation but also with the environing world which traps them in poverty and with the contrast between what is and what ought to be if the weakest are no longer to be excluded.

Thinking and knowing are acts which all human beings perform, and they do them with whatever means, sophisticated or not, that life has provided. Each person thinks, knows, and strives to understand in order to achieve his or her own goal. Since their thinking is oriented to that goal, every act of thinking can become an act of personal liberation. The Fourth World Movement, on the basis of its experience in diverse areas of poverty throughout the world, can attest that every person and every group attempts to perform this act, however meager their means of thinking and analysis. All human beings and groups are researchers, seeking independence through understanding themselves and their situation so that they control their destiny rather than submitting and being afraid.

Those who think that human beings reduced to total poverty are apathetic and consequently don't think, that they retreat into dependency or the simple struggle to survive day to day, make a serious mistake. They ignore the strategies of self defense that the poor create to escape the influence of those on whom they are dependent.

They protect their own existence, which they carefully hide behind the "life" that they spread out like a curtain and "play" to create an illusion for the external observer. Finally, they ignore the desperate effort to reflect and explain of those who constantly ask themselves, *"Just who am I, after all?"* or who say, *"They treat me like a dog, like a spineless coward, an idiot, a non-entity. . . . Am I really a spineless coward?"* And there are those who through a painful effort of thinking constantly rise up from under their own personalities and those accusations which are so many monstrous identities heaped upon them by repeating to themselves, *"But I am not a dog. I am not the idiot I am made out to be. I know things, but they will never understand."*

And they are absolutely right to come to this conclusion that always emerges once the doubts have been dispelled, even though they are left totally exhausted in body and mind.

Surely they "know things" that others are unlikely ever to understand or even imagine. This knowledge, not well structured to be sure, is about being condemned for life to contempt and social exclusion. It covers everything that that signifies: facts, suffering, but also the resilience and hope called forth by those facts. It also includes knowledge of the surrounding world, including certain attitudes toward the very poor that only they would know.

Even the best researchers find it difficult to imagine these things; consequently, they have a hard time formulating suitable hypotheses and questions. They find themselves facing something that they do not have the tools to master. It is so to speak the secret garden of the very poor. Entry is open only to those who change their life situation and become partners with the poor in a project which is no longer one of mere research but of liberation. Otherwise, it is hard to imagine how those coming from another world and whose thinking is shaped by that world could gain entrance to the secret garden. And there is more. Besides not being able to enter, they would not have the right to do so.

In fact, no one has the right, even in the name of science, to hinder another's effort, perhaps clumsy but nonetheless relentless, to develop a liberating outlook. No researcher has the right to exploit the efforts of the poorest to liberate themselves in order to put them back into servitude. For it cannot be said too often that to hinder the poorest by using them as informants rather than encouraging them to develop their own thinking as a genuinely autonomous act is to enslave them. All the more so because their thinking is almost always a search for their history and identity, and they alone have direct access to an essential part of the answers. They ask themselves questions about their history and identity, much more than about their needs or even their rights, because they know, perhaps confusedly but profoundly, that it is through these questions that they will find the path to freedom.

We do not mean to say that it is always a mistake to speak to them about their rights or to question them about their needs. However, such an approach can be liberating for them only the extent that these exchanges take place within the perspective of their understanding of their historical identity, the only knowledge that can help them to be subjects and master of their rights and needs.

This has rarely been the case so far. Throughout the entire period of what was called "the war on poverty" in the United States, we did not see a single truly historical piece of research on the lives of those who in those days were called the "hard-core" poor. Nor, even less, was there research carried out in close collaboration with the "hard-core" poor themselves.

In the European Community at last some interest is being shown in what is called persistent poverty, that is to say, poverty having an historical dimension from which would logically follow the historical identity of a "lumpen-proletar-iat." But this dimension or this historical identity is rarely brought out and can be developed only through an ongoing dialogue with the families of the Fourth World. We are concerned because we do not see any bridges being built between the University and the Fourth World. We do see a search for ways of collecting information without having to go through a process of creating a lasting collaboration with the families concerned.

This also holds true for Great Britain, a country which we regard as exemplary because it steadfastly continued research on poverty even during the great prosperity of the 1960's. But even there, historical research does not exist. The only identity the poor have is through what they need, what they lack. This is partially attributable to the respect researchers have for the poor and their concern not to put them in a category of their own, thereby contributing to their segregation. However, is this right when we consider that their historical identity is one of immeasurable resilience and inalienable dignity? When we consider furthermore that it is an identity that carries an essential message to the whole society?

It is not our intention to criticize, much less to denigrate in any way, the sincere and intelligent efforts made by our friends from the United States, Great Britain, and Europe. Our role is simply to remind everyone what the very poor families gathered in the Fourth World Movement have taught us. To talk to them only of their needs, or of those "social indicators" which characterize them, without helping them to better understand their own history or the common traits of their lives is just another way of trapping them. It is the families themselves who call on the Movement; and their request is not, *"Explain to us,"* but rather, *"Help us to think."* Some families, and they are growing in number, say, *We must think, because others will never be able to understand."*

5. Restoring Thinking, Supporting the Effort of the Fourth World to Know

We count on you academic researchers for a careful study and interpretation of what the Fourth World has taught us about its right to have its thinking and autonomous knowledge recognized. It is up to you and to us to discover how to support its effort of reflection. For, if the people of the Fourth World have shown clearly that they want to carry out their own thinking to the end, they have never said that they need no help in this undertaking. On the contrary, wherever our teams are established we hear, like a leitmotiv this request: *"You, who have learned to think, teach us how to."* Whether it be in Guatemala, Switzerland, New York, Bangkok, or the run-down areas of London, the poorest are calling for the presence not of "thought masters" (they see too many of them), but of competent and intelligent men and women who can teach them how to think without insinuating themselves into the thinking itself.

However, do we know enough about the tools, the methodology, and the pedagogy needed for this endeavor? I am not so sure. It is not that there are no pioneers in this area. But, a careful look at the experiments carried out in several countries leaves us with our doubts. Perhaps it is because the projects carried out in the name of one or the other of the pedagogies of "conscientization" in Latin America, India, or even Europe seemed almost without exception to leave out the poor. Whether in Indian villages of Colombia, hamlets of untouchables of India, slums of Calcutta, or a poor area of Portugal, the most impoverished inhabitants find themselves marginalized even from these projects.

Perhaps these projects raise questions for us because they transport curiously Western language and concepts all the way to the Far East and to the perched villages on the high plateaus of Bolivia far from modern civilization. Did these people invent this vocabulary strangely familiar to our Western ears: "power relations," "exploitation of man by man," "class warfare"? Would they not have chosen to speak in the words of their own civilization?

I believe that those of us here could have something to say about this question: we could bring to light the conditions required for authentic support of the thinking of the poorest; we could recognize those projects favorable to the development of an independent knowledge proper to the Fourth World. Without the knowledge that the poor possess and ought to be able to develop, university studies risk being knowledge which is much too partial and which lacks precisely what would make it life-giving and precipitate action and struggle.

Without getting into philosophy or social psychology, let us simply state the two reasons which, in the experience of the Movement, explain why only the voice of the poor is conducive to action and why all other knowledge is only supportive.

First, in a world full of good causes, appeals of less than far-reaching importance, despite what we might expect, are not going to convince our fellow citizens to make a serious commitment to sustainable action. Partial knowledge which does not go to the heart of the problem, namely [Here, the French text resumes.] the suffering and the hopes of the totally excluded, will not challenge people and call forth indispensable major commitments. It is because it never compromised its presentation of the extreme consequences of poverty that our Movement of ordinary citizens managed to take on dimensions that its modest resources could not explain. Yet, only the very poor know these extreme consequences. They alone know all the injustice, all the denial of human rights, all the suffering due to exclusion. They alone know what must be changed in hearts and minds and in the structures and functioning of our democracies. But of all that, the conclusions of the past twenty-five years of academic studies are only a weak reflection, an abbreviated message.

Second, when we look at the totality of the message communicated by the families of the Fourth World, we can see that it is not marginal but central and essential because it tells us everything we need to know about society as it is and as it ought to be. Some of you will recall the attempts made to get that message across in the 1960's at the International Association of Sociology Forum. These efforts were repeated in the 1970's in the pilot program, "European Program of Research and Action Against Poverty." Our Movement proposed a study of the tools and conditions which would be required to enable the poorest of the poor of the European Community to speak for themselves rather than having to wait for social scientists to do it for them. Even though the proposal came at the time of the election of the European Parliament by universal franchise, governmental experts did not find the project of immediate interest.

Experience shows us that the Movement gains new members around the world only when it gives Fourth World families the floor and lets them express their own truths. We are only a non-governmental organization; yet, if we have been able to endure and expand, is it not because the message from the poorest can convince, is irrefutable because of its integrity?

Let me repeat, what matters to a Movement that is confronted every day with the harsh reality of a struggle is that our fellow-citizens hear the voices of the poor themselves, in their very own words, rather than a translation by some university study. Should we not be modest enough to admit this? [I don't understand the previous sentence.] Political support has been gained because people realize that our Movement makes the voices of the poor heard so that everyone can listen.

Our Committee should spend at least part of its time strengthening both the thinking of the poor, which is essential in gaining an understanding of exclusion, and their way of expressing themselves, which is essential in securing the commitment of our fellow citizens to the struggle. The issue will be brought up as early as today during our debate about the Seminar, "The Fourth World in Africa." It will come up again tomorrow during our debate on the significance of European policies on poverty in the member states of the European Union. And the issue will come up for a third time in its most crucial dimensions when the subject of alliances and partnerships in the struggle against exclusions will be broached by our friend, Professor Jona Rosenfeld.

The question is therefore relevant to all the discussions planned for this session of the Committee, but more importantly, in our opinion, it seems to be part both of the raison d'être of this Committee and of its long-term goals. This is the reason why we felt it appropriate to bring it up right at the start of this conference.

6. An Action that Thinks and Communicates Itself

Is it necessary to expand on our previous comments about the necessary independence of the knowledge gained by people of action? What we have just said about the rights of the Fourth World in this regard obviously applies to them as well. A necessarily unique way of thinking must be built on the action, the uncertainties, the stalemates, the reactions and changes, as well as the new ideas and actions that are called forth. This thinking needs to be supported by competent outsiders while remaining autonomous and free to pursue its own objectives.

Those responsible for action need this thinking in order to be able to fulfill their commitments. Equally obvious is that Fourth World families need to have alongside them teams that are free and able to think independently.

Of course, as is the case for the poorest of the poor, practitioners and their activities can become a topic of academic research. One can even attempt, as we have mentioned, to evaluate the results of their efforts. While admitting that there exist very interesting studies in this area, we have reservations. Our first concern is that these academic studies attempt to capture the action from the outside and cannot replace the knowledge that the action can and should have of itself, for itself. This is an area that remains virtually inaccessible to social scientists for the same reasons which put the reality experienced by the poorest of the poor beyond their reach.

The knowledge of practitioners, the third kind of knowledge mentioned earlier, is an essential component of the comprehensive and stimulating knowledge that we need. The wider world needs it to be able to take action. It needs examples of citizens who are committed to action. It needs to listen to them as much as it needs to listen to scholars teaching.

Besides listening to the very poor, is it not the stories of actions told by the actors that prompt people to action? These stories can instill in others the desire and the courage, in their turn, to undertake new actions.

Here again, academic researchers could render an invaluable service by committing themselves to value and support this knowledge rather than appropriating it for their own purposes.

7. A Committee Ready for Action

We believe that the very poor point to a key role for university researchers. They can bring together academics, people from the Fourth World, and teams of practitioners for a successful collaboration in which each partner remains free. Together the three groups can value, support, and assist in developing new approaches to knowledge of poverty. This Committee is in position to contribute to this effort.

Whereas academics can do other valuable things, at this time this work appears to be the most necessary and innovative. That is the case, provided that we all agree that this Committee, into which we have put our energy and hope, should be not be just a wise and intelligent reminder of the extreme poverty in this world, but rather a leader calling our fellow-citizens to action.

GLOSSARY OF TERMS

Activists (Fourth World activists): people who deal with poverty on a daily basis, whether it affects their own lives or the lives of those close to them, who have decided to commit to ATD Fourth World on a long-term basis by working with poor people in their area.

Agent-authors: The name given to participants in the Fourth World – University project who agreed to share their respective forms of knowledge (15 activists, one of whom had to leave the project halfway through for family reasons, 12 academics and 5 Fourth World volunteer corps members).

Allies: People from all backgrounds who spread awareness of the realities of life for those in extreme poverty and ATD Fourth World's contribution to eradicating it, whether at work, in their free time, as part of a trade union, political or religious organization, etc. Some of them work in poor areas alongside children, young people and adults.

Fourth World volunteer corps members: Men and women both single and married from very varied social and professional backgrounds and many different nationalities who join ATD Fourth World, receiving a small salary and living and working together. There are more than 350 in 23 countries across the world.

International Movement ATD Fourth World: Founded in 1957 by Father Joseph Wresinski and a few very poor families in the Noisy-le-Grand homeless camp. An international movement whose initiatives mainly aim to provide access to the necessary finances to support family life, access to learning and culture, to education and training and to a say in public debates.

> In the US: Fourth World Movement/USA, 7600 Willow Hill Dr., Landover, MD 20785
>
> In the UK: Fourth World Movement/UK, 48 Addington Sq., London SE5 7LB
>
> In Canada: Fourth World Movement/ATD Quart Monde, 6747 rue Drolet, Montréal, Qc H2S 2T1
>
> International Headquarters: International Movement ATD Fourth World, Hameau de Vaux, 95540 Méry-sur-Oise, France

Coats of arms: We have experimented with coats of arms in research and education work to allow everyone to present the personal and intellectual information about themselves they deem relevant to the experimental project. Each coat of arms is drawn on a large sheet of paper with a motto, a symbolic image, shaping experiences in that person's life and some questions that the agent-author would like to have addressed during the project.

Cultural center: an integral part of family and social development, the cultural center is aimed at school-age children and provides book-based artistic and cultural activities.

Deciphering/s: Recordings of meetings and discussions were transcribed in such a way that the transcription became a tool the participants could use in their work. The transcription is therefore not always word-for-word, for easier reading, but preserves nevertheless the course of group discussion as faithfully as possible.

Father Joseph Wresinski (1917–1988): He was born in a poor neighborhood of Angers to immigrant parents (a Polish father and Spanish mother). Between the ages of 13 and 19, he worked as a baker and cake-maker, during which time he encountered the Christian Youth Workers' movement. He entered the seminary in 1936 and was ordained as a priest in 1946. He was appointed vicar in Tergnier, then curate in

Dhuizel (Oise). In 1956, his bishop suggested he go and meet the families living in the homeless camp at Noisy-le-Grand outside Paris. He went and remained there, founding what would become the International Movement ATD Fourth World. He is buried in Méry-sur-Oise (Val d'Oise) at ATD Fourth World's international center.

Fourth World House: a place where ATD Fourth World members can come and meet each other or receive training.

Fourth World People's Universities: meeting-places where adults living in poverty and the citizens working alongside them can learn from one another. Participants discuss a prepared topic, giving their views and suggestions and asking questions. Guests are regularly invited, contributing to discussion and learning by listening to what is said.

Live-in family development camp in Noisy-le-Grand: In 1970, a live-in family development camp was built on the site of the former homeless camp at Noisy-le-Grand. Families were given individual housing there for a period of two or three years. The camp's aims were to preserve the family unit, assert the families' right to housing and allow each family to take control of their lives. A team of Fourth World volunteer corps members helped each family to carry out their plans and ran community projects, such as a family drop-in center, pre-school, cultural activities etc.

Mixed groups: A method of working suggested by the pedagogical team during the seminars, whereby the agent-authors were not split into thematic groups, but into mixed groups of academics, activists and Fourth World volunteer corps members from different thematic groups.

October 17: World Day to Overcome Extreme Poverty, recognized by the United Nations General Assembly of December 22, 1992.

Pierrelaye: Site of ATD Fourth World's international center and also of the ATD Fourth World Research and Training Institute.

Summer Street Festivals: Working people, tradesmen and women, artists etc are invited to share their practical and artistic skills with people living in poor areas. Enjoyable and friendly sessions are held for children and their parents.

BIBLIOGRAPHY

Books and documents about the Fourth World Movement

Caillaux, M., *Germaine*, 2002, 32 pp, Fourth World Publications, $5

Despouy, L., *The Realization of Economic, Social, and Cultural Rights*, 1996, Geneva: Commission on Human Rights, United Nations, E/CN.4/Sub.2/1996/13

De Vos van Steen Wijk, A., *Father Joseph Wresinski: Voice of the Poorest*, 1996, Queenship Publishing Company

Fanelli, V., *The Human Face of Poverty: A chronicle of Urban America*, 1990, 144 pp., New York: Bootstrap Press, $ 12.50

Fanelli, V. and Tardieu, B., *Passport to the New World of Technology . . . Computers*, 1987, Fourth World Publications

Fourth World Movement, *The Wresinski Approach: The Poorest—Partners in Democraty*, 1991,Fourth World Publications

———, *Family Album*, 1994, 160 pp., Fourth World Movement, $ 19.00

———, *This is How We Live, Listening to the Poorest Families*, 1995, 170 pp., Fourth World Publications, $ 12.00

———, *Talking Us, Not at Us*, 1996, Fourth World Publications

———, *Reaching the Poorest*, 1999, 124 pp., ATD Quart Monde and UNICEF, Fourth World Publications

———, *Education: Opportunities Lost*, 2000, 58 pages, Fourth World Publications, $ 9.00

———, *How Poverty Separates Parents and Children*, 2004, 155 pp., Fourth World Publications

———, *Valuing Children, Valuing Parents*, 2004, 176 pp. www.atdfourthworld.org/europe/valuingchildren/index_vcvp.htm

Rosenfeld, J., *Emergence from Extreme Poverty*, 1989, Fourth World Publications

Rosenfeld, J., Tardieu B., *Artisans of Democracy*, 2000, 304 pp., University of Press of America, $ 24.50

Wresinski, J., *Blessed Are You The Poor!* 1992, 288 pp., Fourth World Publications, $14.00

———, *The Very Poor, living Proof of the Indivisibility of Human Rights*, 1994, Fourth World Publications

———, *The Poor are The Church*, 2002, 208 pp., Twenty Third Publications, $ 16.95

Subject Index

Name Index